1989

IRELAND

Patricia Tunison Preston
& John Preston

A WORLD OF TRAVEL PUBLICATION

AUTHOR'S CHOICE

PROBABLE COSTS
PER DAY FOR
FOOD & HOTEL

Careful $50
Moderate 80
Elegant 145

PER PERSON

Author's Acknowledgments

With special thanks to our families, the Prestons and Sabalises in New York and the Tunisons of Florida, and to all of our friends in the U.S. and in Ireland—for all their encouragement to us in the writing of this book.

We would also like to acknowledge the help, guidance, and enthusiasm we received from the following: Pat Hanrahan of Aer Lingus in New York; Simon O'Hanlon, Orla MacCurtain, and Brian Nolan of the Irish Tourist Board in New York; Paddy Derivan and James Larkin of Bord Failte in Dublin; and Frank Hamilton of the Shannon Development Company at Shannon Airport.

Special thanks also go to the four outstanding writers who have contributed articles to enhance the pages of this book:

Ray Brady, Business Correspondent of CBS-TV and Radio, New York
Hon. Desmond FitzGerald, The Knight of Glin, author and art historian, Glin Castle, Co. Limerick
Bernard Share, Editor of "Cara"—the Inflight Magazine of Aer Lingus, the Irish national airline, Dublin
Brenda Weir, Editor of "Inside Ireland," an Information Service and Quarterly Review, Dublin

The World of Travel series is published by Fisher's World, Inc.
1988-89 Publications:

Australia & New Zealand	Hawaii	New York City
Bahamas	Italy	Pacific Northwest
Bermuda	Ireland	Paris/Northern France
Canada/East	London/England	San Francisco & North
Caribbean East	Los Angeles & South	Texas & Oklahoma
Europe/Major Cities	Mexico/Resorts	USA/Major Cities
Miami/Gold Coast	New England/Fall & Winter	

with more to come....

Map graphics by Marit Jaeger-Kanney
Cover design by Salie Clemente

ISSN 0894-2102
© 1988 by Fisher's World, Inc.   **ISBN 1-55707-022-9**

Contents

* Town-by-Town lists and ratings for Hotels, Restaurants, Pubs, Entertainment, Shopping, Festivals, Tours, Perks, Sports, Getting Around, Directory.

THE HARD FACTS

LIST OF MAPS

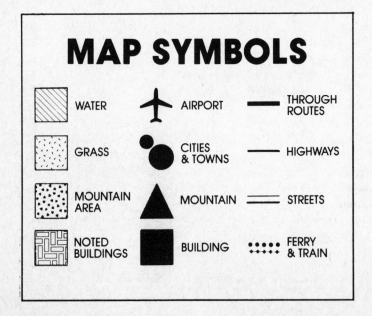

MAP SYMBOLS

WATER   AIRPORT   THROUGH ROUTES

GRASS   CITIES & TOWNS   HIGHWAYS

MOUNTAIN AREA   MOUNTAIN   STREETS

NOTED BUILDINGS   BUILDING   FERRY & TRAIN

"Ireland" and its Authors

Pat and John Preston have given us a lyrical, promise-filled story of Ireland, enough to fill this book and more. To it we have added countless maps and some charming articles by Brenda Weir, Ray Brady, The Knight of Glin and Bernard Share.

To all of *this*, we have added, in the back of the book, a wonderfully useful *TRAVEL PLANNER*, created for the reader who wants only the basic facts with no embellishments, in a package small enough to fit a pocket or a purse. Within this removable 64-page section, we have included two-color copies of all 37 maps, along with detailed information about places to go, where to eat, how to make special arrangements, and a great deal more—a first class abstract of the book, the ultimate in convenient, functional carry-alongs.

If you don't love Ireland, it means you haven't been there. All the "blarney" you may have heard about the spell the country casts upon you has to be taken at face value, for the land and its people will entrance you. Ireland isn't known for its mythical qualities just by chance. Who wouldn't fall in love with the most personable folks on earth? Or with clean air, lovely countryside and a marvelously relaxing pace?

It's obvious the authors of our Irish book are in the very middle of a long-standing love affair with the country, too. Residents of New York City, Patricia Tunison Preston and John J. Preston, a husband-wife writing duo, are frequent visitors to Ireland.

A graduate of St. John's University, Pat first traveled to the Emerald Isle as a tourist in 1966. She was so enchanted by the country that she talked the Irish Tourist Board into hiring her; she was the Board's public relations manager until late 1984. Since that time she has been working full-time as a freelance journalist, and is an active member of the Society of American Travel Writers.

John is practically a full-fledged Irishman—both his parents were born in County Mayo, and he can bake some of the best traditional Irish raisin cakes on this side of the Atlantic.

A Bit of Background

Inside Today's Ireland

Ireland is a gem. Steeped in history, this is a land that dates back over 5,000 years, and yet it is one of the world's youngest republics. Ireland has no symbolic attractions like Big Ben, the Eiffel Tower, or the Coliseum, but still it attracts over two million tourists a year. Though an integral part of Europe, Ireland can also be described as an outpost—an island situated west of the continental mainland, and still farther west of the British Isles.

What draws visitors to this little patch of green in the Atlantic? Most of all, it is her people—exuberant and enthusiastic folk who are known far and wide for their hospitality. "There are no strangers in Ireland," the old Gaelic saying goes, "only friends we have yet to meet."

Within a few seconds of your arrival, you'll see that a smile comes as naturally to the Irish as taking a breath. And when the people of Ireland want to express their welcome for you, they do it in a grand and heartfelt way. "Cead mile failte" ("one hundred thousand welcomes") is the customary greeting. Not one or two welcomes, or even a few dozen—only a hundred thousand will do. And after you settle in, the Irish will beguile you with their intangible assets, from quick wit and ready conversation to lilting music and song. You'll sit by the hearthsides and make new friends, savor the lifestyle in the pubs, wander the open countryside, and breathe the sweet air. But save time for the creature comforts, too, because Ireland's world-class hotels, smartly refurbished castles and country manors, gourmet restaurants, and treasure-trove of shopping can rival the rest of Europe's.

Ireland is also known for its storied scenery. Your first sight of the land will probably be the patchwork quilt of verdant fields seen from

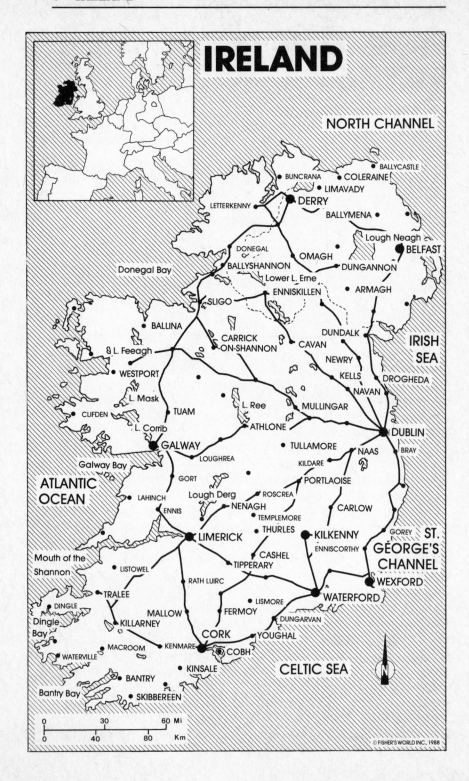

IRELAND

NORTH CHANNEL

IRISH SEA

ATLANTIC OCEAN

ST. GEORGE'S CHANNEL

CELTIC SEA

BALLYCASTLE
BUNCRANA   COLERAINE
LIMAVADY
LETTERKENNY   DERRY
BALLYMENA
Lough Neagh   BELFAST
DONEGAL   OMAGH
BALLYSHANNON   DUNGANNON
Donegal Bay   Lower L. Erne   ARMAGH
ENNISKILLEN
SLIGO
BALLINA   DUNDALK
L. Feeagh   CARRICK-ON-SHANNON   CAVAN   NEWRY
WESTPORT   KELLS   DROGHEDA
L. Mask   NAVAN
L. Ree   MULLINGAR
CLIFDEN   TUAM
L. Corrib   ATHLONE   DUBLIN
GALWAY   TULLAMORE   NAAS   BRAY
LOUGHREA   KILDARE
Galway Bay   GORT   PORTLAOISE
Lough Derg   ROSCREA
LAHINCH   NENAGH   CARLOW
ENNIS   TEMPLEMORE
THURLES   KILKENNY   GOREY
LIMERICK   CASHEL   ENNISCORTHY
Mouth of the   TIPPERARY   WEXFORD
Shannon   LISTOWEL   RATH LUIRC   WATERFORD
TRALEE   LISMORE   DUNGARVAN
DINGLE   MALLOW   FERMOY
Dingle Bay   KILLARNEY   YOUGHAL
MACROOM   KENMARE   CORK
WATERVILLE   COBH
KINSALE
BANTRY
Bantry Bay   SKIBBEREEN

N

| 0 | 30 | 60 Mi |
| 0 | 40 | 80 | Km |

© FISHER'S WORLD INC., 1988

the air. Neat little white-washed cottages, sturdy stone fences, and mighty medieval castles dot the countryside, with hundreds of lakes and rivers adding to the tableau. The rounded stacks of hay look like gum drops on the hillsides and what appear to be tiny lanes curve through the open countryside. You can almost see the shamrocks and count the "forty shades of green," as your plane swoops down over the nonchalant sheep and grazing cows to come in for a landing at Shannon or Dublin. No wonder they call it the "Emerald Isle!"

Where else but in Ireland can you stroll the broad and narrow streets of Dublin's Fair City, see the sun go down on Galway Bay, kiss the Blarney Stone, hike the hills of Donegal, find the Rose of Tralee, or discover that it's not such a long way to Tipperary. Only in this Emerald Isle can you experience "Beauty's Home," otherwise known as Killarney, dream your fondest dreams on the Lake Isle of Innisfree, and see Irish eyes smiling everywhere.

ONE ISLAND AND TWO IRELANDS

Ireland is totally surrounded by water. The Irish Sea flows between Ireland and England, Scotland, and Wales, and the Atlantic Ocean rims the remainder of the island.

The topography of the land is saucer like; a broad limestone plain in the center is rimmed almost completely by coastal mountains and highlands. The central plain, largely bog and farmland, is broken in places by low hills. It is also dotted by hundreds of lakes and rivers, including the Shannon, which is the longest river in Ireland or Britain.

The total area of the island is 32,524 square miles, or about the size of the state of Maine. At its widest, the country is 189 miles across, and 302 miles in length. The 3,000-mile coastline follows a path of various natural indentations, with the result that no part of Ireland is more than 70 miles from the sea. The population is approximately five million.

The island of Ireland is divided into 32 counties, and into two distinct political parts, the "Republic of Ireland" and "Northern Ireland." The Republic, which is also known by the Gaelic word of "Eire" (pronounced: "air-ah"), takes up four-fifths of the land and is comprised of 26 counties; the capital city is Dublin.

The Republic of Ireland is a parliamentary democracy, with a duly elected President (a largely ceremonial role) and a Prime Minister, called the "Taoiseach" (pronounced: "tee-shock") who is the head of the government. The Irish Parliament has two houses, a House of Representatives, called the "Dail" (pronounced "dawl"), and a Senate.

The remaining six counties, designated as Northern Ireland, are part of the United Kingdom, and their capital city is Belfast. This

COUNTIES & PROVINCES

© FISHER'S WORLD INC., 1988

northeastern section of the island is tied to Britain for its government, currency, postal system, and many aspects of its economy. Although most of the North is peaceful and prosperous like the Republic of Ireland, parts of Northern Ireland have been the focus of world headlines since 1969 because of internal violence and sectarian unrest. The situation is not an easy one to solve, but it is hoped that the New Ireland Forum, established in 1983, and the subsequent Anglo-Irish agreement, will create a framework for a more peaceful future.

Geographically, the island of Ireland is also divided into four provinces, dating back to medieval kingdoms: Leinster in the east, Munster in the south, Connacht in the west, and Ulster in the north. Although you will often see reference to the provinces, the division is largely historical and has no administrative significance. The exact breakdown is as follows:

Leinster (twelve counties)—Dublin, Carlow, Kildare, Kilkenny, Laois, Longford, Louth, Meath, Offaly, Westmeath, Wexford, and Wicklow.

Munster (six counties)—Clare, Cork, Kerry, Limerick, Tipperary, and Waterford.

Connacht (five counties)—Sligo, Mayo, Galway, Roscommon, and Leitrim.

Ulster (nine counties)—Antrim, Armagh, Derry, Down, Fermanagh, Tyrone, Cavan, Donegal, and Monaghan. This province takes in both political parts of today's Ireland—the first six of these counties comprise the area known as "Northern Ireland"; the final three counties are part of the Republic of Ireland.

As you travel around the island, you will find that there is little distinction among the provinces; at most, there is only a small sign to alert you that you have traversed from one county to the next. There is, however, a patroled border between the Irish Republic and Northern Ireland, and you will have to pass through a customs post at most border crossings.

Although it is difficult to separate one part of such a small country from another, this book focuses on the Republic of Ireland, the 26 counties which are usually referred to simply, in travel destination terms, as "Ireland."

A FEW FACTS ABOUT THE REPUBLIC OF IRELAND

With a total of 3.5 million people, the Republic of Ireland is the least densely populated country of Europe. The statistics also reveal that more than one-half of the population is under the age of 25. Although a young and vibrant citizenry is one of Ireland's attributes, it has also presented a problem in recent years. Disproportionate numbers of youth are suddenly seeking to enter the work force. Sadly, the number of jobs has just not kept pace, and consequently emigration has been on the rise. It is estimated that nearly 100,000 young Irish people, most of whom are college-educated and well-trained, have left Ireland since 1981 in search of jobs abroad. Needless to say, the current Irish government is making a concerted effort to attract foreign investment, create new jobs, and keep the talented young people at home.

The economy of Ireland is largely agrarian, with farming and livestock the chief source of income. Light manufacturing takes second place, thanks to a large number of high-tech companies. In many respects, Ireland prides itself on maintaining its industry on a small scale over preserving a pollution-free environment.

Ireland's third largest income-producer is tourism, one of the country's oldest established industries. Records show that organized touring in Ireland began in the mid-19th century when Charles Bianconi established a transport network of horse-drawn coaches; this development encouraged travel, particularly by the British, to many remote towns which could not readily be reached by boat.

By the 1850's, tourism had extended to scenic counties like Kerry and Galway, thanks to the advent of railroads and Queen Victoria's much heralded visit to Killarney. The enthusiastic accounts of writers like W.M. Thackeray ("Irish Sketch Book") further motivated more travel to all parts of the Emerald Isle. In 1895 the first U.S. group on a package tour cruised into Bantry Bay and visited Glengariff.

Although Ireland had its first tourist office by the 1920's, the real growth in the industry has been concentrated over the past 30 years. Today tourism is a billion dollar business for Ireland, providing employment for over 75,000 people. It also plays an important role in bringing prosperity to isolated and underdeveloped parts of the country where the rocky soil makes farming difficult and other industries do not exist.

The greatest numbers of visitors to Ireland come from Britain, North America, and continental Europe, in that order.

HISTORICAL HIGHLIGHTS

To understand Ireland today, it helps to look back over the centuries. Although there is evidence of human settlement as early as 6,000 B.C., most accounts focus on the period around 3,000 B.C. when Neolithic farmers and colonists arrived. Those people have left their mark—and traces of their civilization—on places like Newgrange, north of Dublin, and Lough Gur, near Limerick.

The Celts are thought to have arrived in 350 B.C., imposing their language and customs on the inhabitants. Celtic Ireland was divided into 150 local kingdoms, with a handful of provincial high kings. A simple agrarian economy prevailed. There were no towns, people lived on individual farms, and the unit of currency was the cow.

The next major influence was Christianity, which arrived in the 5th century A.D. with the preachings of St. Patrick. Ireland's first written documents date from this period, as great monasteries and centers of learning sprang up at places like Glendalough and Clonmacnois.

From 500 to 800 A.D. Ireland enjoyed a "Golden Age," because it sent missionaries to all parts of Europe. To this day, the names of Irish monks are associated with religious sites in all parts of the continent, including St. Virgil (Salzburg), St. Colman (Melk), St. Kilian (Wurzburg), St. Martin (Tours), and St. Columban (Bobbio). This was the era when Ireland earned the title of "Isle of Saints and Scholars."

The days of glory were to be short-lived, however, as the Middle Ages also marked the beginning of an 1,100-year period when Ireland was to be raided and conquered by outsiders. The Vikings arrived first, plundering monasteries and building forts at Dublin, Wexford, and Waterford, among other places.

By the 12th century, it was the Normans who ruled, erecting medieval walled cities and castles. Although the Normans inter-married with the native population and gradually became "more Irish than the Irish," England would continue to dominate Irish history for many more years.

Henry VIII declared himself King of Ireland in 1541, the first English monarch to do so. He not only introduced a new religion, but he also sent over English settlers who were loyal to him, rewarding them with choice lands and pushing aside the native residents. When the Irish began to rebel, a warrior named Oliver Cromwell was sent to crush all opposition. And crush he did; Cromwell and his army became notorious for wholesale massacres of entire villages and towns. He ruthlessly desecrated churches, chopped down trees, confiscated lands, and banished former owners to poorer areas.

When King James II came to power in 1685 it looked like Ireland was to see better days, but all hope was dashed five years later when James was defeated by William of Orange at the Battle of the Boyne. As a result, more and more people loyal to the British crown and the new religion were "planted" in the choicest Irish lands, particularly the northeastern counties.

To make sure that the native Irish were kept in their places, oppressive measures, called "Penal Laws," were enacted. These laws had the effect of keeping the native population without land or influence. Eventually, thanks to Kerry-born Daniel O'Connell, in 1829 the Gaelic Irish won the right to vote and to enter Parliament.

By the mid-19th century, however, yet another force—that of nature—took a toll against Ireland. Long a staple of the Irish diet, the potato, was afflicted with a serious blight and massive crop failure followed. Millions of people died of starvation or were forced to emigrate. That is why you'll see so many abandoned cottages in remote parts of the Irish countryside.

Although the famine years put a hold on political activity for a while, the Irish yearning for independence re-surfaced with the turn of the century. Finally, in 1916, the fledgling Irish Volunteer Movement seized the General Post Office in Dublin and proclaimed the Irish Republic. The rebellion was quickly suppressed and its leaders were executed. Only one, Eamon De Valera, escaped the death penalty because he had been born in New York and could claim U.S. citizenship.

The killing of so many brave leaders did not put an end to the unrest but rather fueled a new determination to win freedom for all of Ireland. An outright Anglo-Irish War began in 1919 and lasted for two years until a partial victory was achieved by the Irish and a truce was declared in 1921. A treaty was signed conceding dominion status within the British Commonwealth to 26 counties of Ireland, designated as the "Irish Free State." The remaining six counties, in the northeast, became a separate entity linked to Britain.

In 1937, the 26 counties abandoned membership in the British Commonwealth and adopted a new constitution, officially becoming the Republic of Ireland. In 1972, Ireland became a member of the European Economic Community (EEC).

The Cultural
Scene

LANGUAGE

The Irish constitution designates Irish (or Gaelic) as the official language of Ireland, and, as such, it is one of the recognized languages of the EEC. However, everyone in Ireland speaks English, so you needn't worry about having to learn a new language. To gain a better understanding of the Emerald Isle, however, it is useful to know something about this ancient vernacular.

Irish is basically a Celtic language, related to Scottish Gaelic, Welsh Breton, and ancient Gaulish. The earliest known written form of Irish is "Ogham," a script dating mainly from the 5th and 6th centuries. Many examples of this script can still be seen on ancient stones throughout the countryside. Ogham-based crafts are also for sale in many shops.

Ireland was an Irish-speaking nation well into the 17th century, but with the establishment of the English system of land tenure, an English-language upper class emerged. In many cases, the native Irish people learned English to improve their socio-economic positions.

Today Irish is still taught in the schools and is required for some government positions. You'll hear Irish used on national radio and television at certain times of the day; articles written in Irish also appear in the daily newspapers, although communications are (overwhelmingly) in English. The survival of the language is a major cultural priority because it is intrinsically linked to the music and folklore of the land.

There are certain rural parts of Ireland, classified as "Gaeltacht" regions, where Irish is still the everyday language. If you visit one of these areas, primarily located in Donegal, Mayo, Galway, Kerry, and Cork, you will not only hear the local folk conversing in Irish, but you will also see Irish written on street signs and used in other forms of public communication. The Gaeltacht population is approximately 80,000 people, about half of whom are farmers; the remainder make a living from fishing or native crafts like weaving.

In addition, the Irish language is featured in certain forms of traditional entertainment throughout the country. Among the most well known venues are the "Siamsa Tire" program in Tralee and Killarney; the "Taibhdhearc" theater in Galway; the "Cois na hAbhna" center at Ennis; and "Culturlann na hEireann" near Dublin. Visitors are welcome at all of these events. (Details are given in the "Inside Information" section.)

LITERATURE

With a literary tradition dating from the 6th century, the Irish are known the world over for their contributions to literature. Ireland's earliest writings, of course, were in the Irish language. The same monks who produced religious manuscripts like the *Book of Kells* also composed some lyric poetry of a high quality. Most of Ireland's literature remained in the vernacular through the 17th century.

It is actually Anglo-Irish literature (Irish literature written in English), however, that has made the greatest impact on the world, starting with Jonathan Swift in the early 1700's. Other great names of the late 18th century include Oliver Goldsmith, Richard Brinsley Sheridan, and the poet Thomas Moore.

The late 19th and early 20th centuries produced such writers as Oscar Wilde, James Stephens, George Russell (AE), and George Moore. Ireland's three Nobel prize winners, George Bernard Shaw, William Butler Yeats, and Samuel Beckett, all belong primarily to the 20th century.

No list of Irish writers is complete without mention of a man who pioneered a style all his own, James Joyce, whose "Ulysses" challenges students of literature to this day. Other distinguished modern Irish writers include Flann O'Brien, Frank O'Connor, Patrick Kavanagh, Mary Lavin, and Thomas Kinsella.

As the home of the Abbey, the Gate, and dozens of other theaters, Ireland is also known for its great dramatic traditions, including works by John Millington Synge, Sean O'Casey, Brendan Behan, Brian Friel, and Hugh Leonard, who recently dazzled Broadway and won a "Tony" for his play "Da."

ART AND ARCHITECTURE

The earliest specimens of Irish art range from the geometric and three-dimensional figures etched onto pre-historic granite slabs and burial tombs to the delicate enamel work and manuscript illumination of the 6th century.

The Tara Brooch, the Ardagh Chalice, and the Cross of Cong are just a few of Ireland's early artistic gems. They constitute part of "The Treasures of Early Irish Art, 1500 B.C. to 1500 A.D.," a collection of masterfully-crafted gold, silver, and bronze pieces which toured the U.S. ten years ago, and which is now housed in Ireland's National Museum.

Ireland is also known for its decorative arts, particularly the silverware, plasterwork, cut glass, hand-carved furniture, and tapestry creations which flourished in the 17th and 18th centuries. All of these items were used to fill the interiors of the great Georgian and Palladian-style houses, built for the landed gentry who settled in Ireland at that time. Today many of these stately homes and mansions, described in detail within our text, are open to the public. (For a true appreciation of these landmark structures, see the article by the Knight of Glin elsewhere in this book.)

The lush Irish countryside, with its varied colors and ever-changing skies, lends itself to landscape painting. Among Ireland's great artists of this genre were James Arthur O'Connor and Paul Henry, the latter of whom studied at Whistler's studio in Paris before settling down in Connemara.

Ireland's leading Impressionist painters were Nathaniel Hone and John Butler Yeats, father of the poet William Butler Yeats. The foremost Irish painter of the 20th century was Jack B. Yeats, the poet's brother, whose works focus on key moments and actions in the lives of individuals.

The architecture of Ireland comes in many sizes and styles, from the sturdy round towers and ancient fortresses of earliest days to grandiose castles of medieval origin, as well as the simple thatched-roof farmers' cottages of more recent vintage. Much of Ireland's most distinguished architecture dates back to the Georgian period of the 18th and 19th centuries. Dublin, in particular, is known for its wide Georgian streets and squares, palatial public buildings, and tidy townhouses with colorful doorways and brass fixtures.

MUSIC

It may come as a shock to some folks, but "Mother Macree," "When Irish Eyes Are Smiling," and "I'll Take You Home Again, Kathleen" are not really examples of Irish music, but rather of Irish-American origin. When you come to Ireland you'll find an entirely different repertoire, ranging from haunting patriotic melodies to spirited foot-tapping tunes.

Like most of Europe, music in Ireland can trace its beginnings back to the bards of medieval times who traveled the countryside singing songs and telling tales, usually to the accompaniment of a harp. So important was such music that the harp was adopted as part of the coat of arms of Ireland in the 17th century and remains the chief symbol of the country to this day.

Although this bardic music was seldom written down, the works of one such poet, harpist, and composer, Turlough O'Carolan, have survived and provide the basis for many modern-day airs. What is said to be his harp is on display at Clonalis House, in County Roscommon.

In many ways, music is second nature to the Irish. Wherever the Irish gather—be it by a hearthside, in a pub, or at a cross-road—music is bound to result. As a people often conquered and oppressed, the Irish have always found music to be a source of joy and self-expression.

In addition to the harp, other instruments have come into use over the centuries. One of the most popular is a form of bagpipe named the "uilleann pipe" (pronounced: "ill-un"), often referred to as the "Irish organ." First used almost 300 years ago, it is pumped with the elbow in a sitting position and produces a softer and more resonant sound than its Scottish counterpart. Other instruments used in producing the distinctive sounds of Irish music are the accordion (sometimes called the "concertina"), fiddle, flute, tin whistle, and the "bodhran" (pronounced: "bow-rawn"), a hand-held drum which can best be described as a goat-skin tambourine. The Irish have also been known to improvise, using anything from a wash board to a set of spoons to make music.

To preserve and promote the best of traditional Irish music, an organization called Comhaltas Ceoltoiri Eireann (known as "CCE," for short) was formed in 1951. Today there are more than 15,000 members, not only in Ireland but also in the U.S., Canada, Britain, and Australia. Musical groups, like The Chieftains, have likewise brought the sounds of Irish traditional music to all parts of the world.

CCE sponsors sessions of Irish music, song, and dance at venues throughout Ireland on a year-round basis. Often called a "ceili" (pronounced: "kay-lee"), these events are open to visitors as well as members. In addition, you might like to attend one of the many festivals designed to foster Irish music, usually known by the Irish word "fleadh" (pronounced: "flaah") which literally means "a feast of music." The major fleadhs take place in late May and late August.

No matter when you visit, however, scheduled and spontaneous music sessions are sure to be on tap most evenings in hundreds of pubs throughout the land (see the "Inside Information" section for some tips on pubs that are known for their music). Irish music is also featured at hotel cabarets, such as Jury's and Doyle's in Dublin, and at organized dinner-shows like the Abbey Tavern at Howth, north of Dublin, and the Shannon Ceili in Bunratty Folk Park, Co. Clare.

One lesser known form of music in Ireland is mumming, particularly associated with Wexford, a county that has at least six groups of mummers. It is said that mumming started in this area as a result of early trade between Wexford and Cornwall. Irish mummers dress in white shirts, green and gold sashes, dark pants, and tall hats, similar to a bishop's mitre. Each member of a group represents an Irish patriot such as Kelly from Killanne, Wolfe Tone, or Patrick Sarsfield. They dance to traditional music, using wooden sticks or "swords" as props.

In the scope of modern music, the Irish have made a considerable contribution. For starters, Ireland is the only three-time country winner of the Eurovision Song Contest (the 1988 event is scheduled to be held in Dublin). Pop music concert organizer Bob Geldorf is Irish, as are the members of the universally acclaimed rock group U2. In addition, Ireland has several award-winning resident orchestras including the New Ireland Chamber Orchestra and the RTE-Irish Television Symphony Orchestra, both of which play regularly at the National Concert Hall in Dublin.

Each year Ireland is also the setting for a variety of festivals showcasing different genres of music, from the Waterford Festival of Light Opera and the Wexford Opera Festival, to the Letterkenny International Folk Music Festival, the Festival of Classical Music in Great Irish Houses in and around Dublin, the Cork Choral and Folk Dance Festival, and the Cork Jazz Festival (see "Inside Information" for complete details on each event).

FOLKLORE AND STORYTELLING

In Ireland, all kinds of legends, tales, and superstitions abound. So intrinsic are these beliefs to the essence of Irish heritage that a special Department of Folklore is a part of the national university.

Over the centuries, much of this lore has been passed by word of mouth from one generation to the next. As a result, storytelling has always been considered an Irish art. In the days before books, newspapers, and television, storytelling was a genuine and highly respected profession. A man who would travel from area to area bringing news and telling tales was officially called a "seanachie" (pronounced: "shan-ah-key"). He would have a large repertoire, often up to 400 separate tales.

There are still some seanachies in Ireland today, including a few who appear as part of a traditional Irish cabaret or local festival. Favorite tales often feature the heroics of Cuchulainn, legendary hurler and strong man, and the saga of the Children of Lir, four youngsters whose stepmother changed them into white swans.

By far the most popular folk tradition focuses on the early inhabitants of Ireland, known variously as fairies, "Little People," or leprechauns. Legend has it that leprechauns are no more than 24 inches tall, wear bright green tunics, and live in round fairy forts hidden deep in the woods. These little people are skilled shoemakers by day. Late in the evening, when it is fully dark, they can sometimes be seen dancing to the music of the wind in the trees.

It is said that each leprechaun possesses a crock of gold. If you are lucky enough to see one of these little people, you may be able to win his treasure by fixing him with a steely stare. If you blink, however, he'll disappear and so will his pot of gold. Now if you believe all of this, you know what Irish storytelling is all about.

CRAFTS

The crafts of Ireland are an expression of traditional lifestyles. The very items that tourists consider to be irresistible buys started out as basic necessities for the Irish people. One of the most famous is the thick bainin handknit sweater which originated on the Aran Islands as protective wear for the local fishermen. These oatmeal-colored garments are still knitted in cottages on the islands and in homes all over the west of Ireland.

With all the sheep that graze on the Irish hillsides, it is not surprising that wool is also a source for another major craft, hand-weaving. Weaving is done in the homes and in local factories which are usually open to visitors, particularly in areas like Donegal and Connemara. Ireland's oldest hand-weaving mill, dating back to 1723, is in a cluster of stone buildings at Avoca in Co. Wicklow. The Avoca tweeds are a reflection of the landscape's predominantly mauve, heather, and teal tones, blended and fashioned into capes, coats, ponchos, suits, jackets, bedspreads, and rugs.

One of Ireland's most famous craft trademarks is Waterford. For anyone coming within striking distance of Ireland's southeast coast, a tour of the Waterford Crystal Company is almost impossible to resist. Every step of production in this revered craft is open to view, from the glass-blowing and shaping, hand-cutting and engraving, to polishing and packaging. More than 3,000 observers pass through the Waterford factory every workday, and this is only one of several Irish glass-making centers which welcome visitors. Others are located at Galway, Cavan, Sligo, Killarney, and Dublin.

A craft that is newer to Ireland but equally artful is Irish Dresden, a line of porcelain figurines produced at Drumcollogher, Co. Limerick. These delicate pieces are fashioned in the tradition of a business originally founded in Volkstedt, Germany, and brought to Ireland 25 years ago. Four hundred-year-old German master molds are used by a team of 50 potters, artists, and designers to turn out new patterns inspired by life in rural Ireland.

Irish pottery and porcelain crafts are practiced in all parts of the Emerald Isle; some of the leading names include Royal Tara China in Galway, Donegal Parian China in Ballyshannon, and the most famous of all—Belleek in Fermanagh, Northern Ireland.

Other leading Irish crafts include basketry, heraldry, batik and patchwork, wood-carving, doll-making, enamel-painting, lace-making, pewter-casting, book-binding, candle-making, gold and silver jewelry design, graphics, and stained glass and beaten copper art, to name only a few. One of the bonuses of shopping in Ireland is to be able to watch and talk with the craftworkers as they practice their trades. The "Inside Information" section of this book will give you details on the many different craft complexes, workshops, and stores where visitors can shop for unique Irish crafts.

In Dublin's Fair City: 988–1988

by
Bernard Share

To celebrate anything that happened a thousand years ago requires, first of all, a major leap of the imagination. Dubliners have never lacked that quality. James Joyce, in exile in Paris, recreated his city in minute detail, peopling it not only with the larger-than-life citizens of the year 1904 but with the substantial shadows of generations of Dubliners before them. But one book, even a book as multi-layered as Joyce's *Ulysses*, cannot encompass a millennium. Dublin's long and convoluted history becomes apprehensible only in the place itself, in the faces of its people—richly expressive of their Celtic-Norse-Norman-Saxon-Huguenot-Jewish-Italian ancestry—and in the tangible echoes of its past. When the city celebrates its tenth century in 1988, it will be inviting its visitors to share in a common experience of rediscovery.

It all began so long ago that even where to establish a foundation remains uncertain. There is no clear evidence as to when the first settlement began to coalesce on the banks of the Liffey. The name in Irish gives some clue: *Baile Atha Cliath Dubh Linn:* the Town of the Ford of Hurdles by the Dark Pool. Modern-day Irish retains the first part of the name, *Baile Atha Cliath*—you'll see it, for instance, on the airport terminal building—whilst the latter description, the dark or black pool, passed into English as Dubhlinn, and so Dublin. To be more precise it passed first into Norse, the language of the first colonizers, as Dyflinn, and it was under this name that the city took on its "modern" shape. It was thus a city in embryo at least some years before the Irish king Mael Sechnaill II invested it after a twenty-day siege and imposed an annual tax on the inhabitants. This, the first patently municipal event in the fragmented early history of the settlement, provides an appropriate point from which to count the years of Dublin's development.

The Dyflinn of the Vikings, beginning as a fortified outpost in a hostile land, quickly developed into a centre of trading rather than raiding. By the tenth century there were already communities of mixed Viking and Irish blood, and the Norsemen were beginning to speak broken Irish and to embrace Christianity. Thus was established a pattern that was to be constantly repeated in the course of the history of Dublin and of Ireland: that of the invader being absorbed into the society he set out to dominate and frequently becoming in the process "more Irish than the Irish themselves." Recent excavations in Dublin have greatly increased our knowledge and appreciation of these first Viking Dubliners, and one of the major set-pieces of the Millennium celebrations will be the re-creation, in the crypt of the 13th century St Audeon's Church, of a complete Dyflinn street of the year 988. Specially-trained actors will portray the citizens of the period against a background of authentic buildings and artifacts, inviting the audience to immerse themselves in the urban preoccupations of a thousand years ago.

After the Vikings there followed, in the 12th century, the Normans—in reality Anglo-Norman military adventurers from Wales—and in their wake "Henry II, King of England, Duke of Normandy and Acquitaine and Earl of Anjoy," as a contemporary charter describes him. British involvement with Dublin and Ireland was to continue for more than 700 years—from 1170 until 1922—but its beginnings were piecemeal, spasmodic and uncertain. Dublin remained, for some time, in many ways a Viking-Irish town, whilst absorbing waves of new and largely peaceable immigrants, tradesmen and artisans from the neighbouring island. The citizens, of whatever origin, lived in a state of intermittent friction with the "wild Irish" living beyond the Pale—the Pale being the effective area of Norman hegemony centred on the city. Against this background of embattled existence, Mediaeval Dublin took shape: "This City, as it is not in antiquitie inferiour to anie citie in Ireland," wrote Richard Stanyhurst in 1577, "so in pleasant situation, in gorgious buildings, in the multitude of people, in martial chivalrie . . . it is superior to all other cities and towns in that realme." He was equally enthusiastic about the environs: "If you would traverse the hills they are not far off. If champion ground, it lieth in all parts. If you be delighted with fresh water, the famous river Liffey runneth fast by."

Though Dublin is today a city of a million people, it retains to a large measure those qualities praised by Stanyhurst. The green and purple hills still seem to rise immediately behind the long prospect of leafy thoroughfares, the Liffey still lies at the core of the community, a capricious stream that rises a bare 15 miles from the city centre but requires 92 miles to reach the sea. And from the tower of Christ Church Cathedral, a foundation pre-dating both Stanyhurst and the earliest Normans, the bells will ring out on New Year's Eve, 1987, to inaugurate the millenary celebrations, a peal that will be echoed by countless other bells in this richly campaniled city.

Before midnight strikes, however, the Millennium will have been perhaps more melodiously ushered in with a gala concert at which will be performed a Millennium Suite specially commissioned from a leading Irish composer. Dublin is, and has been, a musical city. "For the relief of the prisoners in the several gaols and for the support of Mercer's hospital in Stephens Street and of the Charitable Infirmary in Inn's Quay," wrote *Faulkner's Dublin Journal* in 1742, "on Monday 12th of April will be performed at the Musick Hall in Fishamble Street, Mr Handel's new grand sacred oratorio called *Messiah*." That world premiere will be re-enacted in 1988 with a special performance in the old city, which will resound in the course of the year to every kind and condition of music, from brass bands to street ballads, and from grand opera to traditional jigs and slow airs. The first grand piano arrived in Dublin in the hot summer of 1798, and 190 years later the city will launch a prestigious International Piano Competition, to be held over a nine-day period in May. The same month will see another international musical invasion; for Dublin will host the 34th Eurovision Song Contest, following an historic third win for Ireland in the 1987 event in Brussels.

The earliest "first citizens" of Dublin had been known as Provosts; but in the 1229 the English king Henry III introduced the annual election of "a loyal and discreet Mayor," with power to try "felonies, trespass, misprisons, contempts and concealments within the city." The office was dignified with the title of "Lord Mayor" in 1641, though it was not actually adopted until 1665. Every year the Mayor had led a procession round the city in a ceremony known as Riding the Fringes, or Franchises—in 1488, for example, he is recorded as having proceeded "well horsed, armed and in good array . . . . " The ceremony lapsed sometime in the 18th century but will be revived with the election of the new Lord Mayor for 1988-89, who will lead a colourful procession round the boundaries of the old city. The new first citizen will on that occasion be taking over from only the third lady Lord Mayor (the title retains its masculine form) in the city's history. The Millennium will be officially inaugurated by Carmencita Hederman, whose name, Spanish-German, offers appropriate evidence of Dublin's racial richness.

The civic power will, as might be expected, play a central role in the city's celebrations throughout the year. In February, for example, the Lord Mayor will host a gala concert to be followed by a dinner in the magnificent setting of the Royal Hospital, Kilmainham, recently restored and one of Dublin's showpieces. Opened in 1680, and built on the model of Les Invalides in Paris, it was described by a contemporary as "a most stately and beautiful piece of building perhaps as Christendom affords." Its construction, under the Viceregency of the cultured and discerning Duke of Ormonde, heralded the golden age of urban development in Dublin. The next hundred years were to witness the erection of all the great buildings which still distinguish the city today and which will play a central role in the celebrations. The elegant streets and squares, the work of the far-seeing Wide Streets Commission of 1757, will themselves witness the more spontaneous and demotic demonstrations of the city's first thousand years: the St. Patrick's Day Millennium Parade, mile races, marathons, street parties, open-air art exhibitions, bicycle races . . . and a June Carnival that will explode colourfully all over the city, as will the spectacular fireworks display that will be one of its main attractions.

There can be few cities anywhere which have expressed themselves—or seen themselves expressed—so comprehensively in literature. The contribution of Dubliners to creative writing in English has, by any standards, been remarkable. The names of Swift, Shaw, Yeats, Joyce, Wilde, Synge, O'Casey, Beckett have created an image of Ireland's capital in the minds of many who know it otherwise as no more than a name on a map. If not all these literary Dubliners wrote explicitly about their city, the atmosphere of Dublin, its many-stranded heritage, its reputation for mordant wit, its history of civilised polity side by side with the starkest poverty, its Byzantine religious and political preoccupations, all have served to inform the writing of even such an unrooted writer as Samuel Beckett. Over the centuries the literary life of the capital has assumed many forms, moving from the coffee house to the salon, to the street, the university and the pub but characterised always by its vigour and, many would say, its venom. In recent times the public acknowledgment of literary Dublin has crystallized in Bloomsday, the anniversary, on June 16, of that overloaded 24 hours in 1904 into which James Joyce packed the events chronicled in *Ulysses*. The habit of the Joycean pilgrimage on this mythic anniversary has developed beyond the strict limits of the peregrination itself; and in 1988 it will expand dramatically into a two-week literary festival embracing book exhibitions, lectures and readings . . . and, no doubt, a good measure of concomitant tribute to another of the city's outstanding luminaries, Arthur Guinness, whose brewery has occupied a significant locus in the consciousness of Dubliners since it first opened in 1745.

If much of Irish literary pub-talk is discovered to be theatrical in its manifestation, it is probably because theatre has constituted an integral expression of the city's ethos since the first professional playhouse, the New Theatre in Werburg Street, opened its doors in 1637. There had already been evidence of dramatic fever at Trinity College, founded in 1591, its Provost, Robert Ussher, "no friend to the levities of theatrical gaieties and representations," having banned all undergraduate productions in 1629. In the public domain, however, the theatre, although enjoying a chequered career, became firmly embedded in the fabric of Dublin life, associated in the 18th century with names like Sheridan, Peg Woofington, Congreve, Goldsmith and Farquhar, and in the 19th and 20th with the Irish Literary Theatre, the Abbey, Lady Gregory, Yeats, Synge and O'Casey—the modern Irish dramatic movement which has contributed so much to contemporary drama. The Dublin Theatre Festival has served in the last number of years as a focus for this achievement and its aftermath, and in 1988 it will present a range of plays, new and old, on Dublin themes.

There is more, there will be more. Dubliners are a resilient, resourceful people, and once they have taken in and absorbed the thousand-year perspective of their city they will find ways to write in on the margins of the official programmes their own individual scenarios of celebration. Half the fun of being in Dublin in Millennium year will be in seeing it reflected in the reactions and attitudes of those whom it most intimately concerns. Do not expect undue reverence or unabridged solemnity—or even overt approval. The Dubliner, bred of a long line of citizens who often had to take life as they found it, is highly adept at withholding enthusiasm until he is convinced that the game is worth the candle. Do, however, expect sharp and prescient comment on what is going on—and a few things that are not. These views will be delivered in a subtle variety of accents deriving from an ancestry as thoroughly cosmopolitan as any in Christendom. As the Ulster poet Louis MacNeice put it:

> Fort of the Dane,
> Garrison of the Saxon,
> Augustan capital
> Of a Gaelic nation,
> Appropriating all
> The alien brought . . . .

BERNARD SHARE is editor of CARA, the inflight magazine of Aer Lingus, the Irish national airline, and of the literary journal BOOKS IRELAND. He is co-editor, with Kathleen Jo Ryan, of *Irish Traditions* (Abrams, New York) and his published work includes books on travel and history and two novels.

Irish Food and Drink

Although recognized as one of the world's best-fed nations, Ireland has long been branded with a reputation for overcooked meats, water-logged vegetables, piles of potatoes, and cream-on-cream desserts. But, as the saying goes: the times, they are a changin'. If you are worried that Irish food is all stew and starch, you're in for a very pleasant— and delicious—surprise.

While it can't be denied that Ireland always had some all-too-rich traditional meals, the country's overall cuisine has undergone a healthy metamorphosis in the last 20 years. Imaginative preparation and appealing presentation of fresh natural ingredients are now the norm.

The transformation from stewed dishes to tender and flavorful entrees of star quality has not come about by chance. It's true that the basic assets were always there—beef and lamb nurtured on Irish pastures, an abundance of freshwater fish and ocean seafood, a bounty of agrarian produce, and dairy goods straight from the local creamery. But it took the broadening influence of travel to inspire this Irish culinary revolution.

Irish chefs went abroad to continental Europe and the U.S. and learned the arts of French "nouvelle cuisine" and California "au courant." At the same time, visitors came to Ireland in greater numbers and made demands for rarer meat, crisper vegetables, and more seafood on the menus.

Sparked by these dual factors, the Irish were quick to appreciate their own natural raw materials and non-frozen ingredients—and to adapt creative ideas from abroad. In kitchens from Kerry to Killaloe and Dublin to Donegal, a new day has dawned, and to prove it, Irish chefs now bring home dozens of gold medals from the International Food Olympics.

What then, you ask, makes "Irish food" any different from other parts of the world?

Well, first of all, because Ireland is such a small country, food does not have to travel very far and is not subject to chemical preservatives. Fruits and vegetables are picked as they ripen from local gardens; fish finds its way from unpolluted waters to your plate in a matter of hours; and the livestock feeds on the lush green grass of the country-side. You'll not only savor an abundance of fresh tasting and natural foods, but you'll also experience modes of preparation unique to the Emerald Isle.

SEAFOOD AND MEATS

Seafood, which was formerly considered penitential fare, now heads most menus. In particular, it is hard to equal wild Irish salmon which is caught daily from local rivers. Served steamed or broiled with a wedge of lemon, it's pink, delicate, and sweet. As an appetizer, salmon is slowly oak-smoked and thinly sliced with capers and lemon. Most visitors become so addicted that they take home at least a side of smoked salmon, vacuum-packaged specially for travel.

One of Ireland's most popular seafoods is the Dublin Bay prawn, a more tender version of one shrimp but a cousin to the Norway lobster in flavor. Plump and succulent, they are equally tempting served hot with melted butter or cold with a light sauce. Other Irish shellfish varieties which have their own unique briny flavors include Galway Bay oysters, Kinsale and Wexford mussels, Kerry scallops, Dingle Bay lobster, and Donegal crab.

Irish beef, which is exported to all parts of the world, has always been a favorite with the natives as well as visitors. Today's menus, however, are a lot more varied than they used to be. You'll not only get your choice of steaks, but you can also order filet of beef en croute, stir-fry beef, beef stuffed with oysters, beef flambeed in Irish whiskey, or beef sauteed in Guinness, and other creative combinations.

All the sheep that graze on the Irish hillsides produce a lot more than wool. Their offspring are the source of the lean racks and legs of lamb that are the pride of Ireland's chefs. Taste this tender meat and you'll find a dramatic improvement over the mutton stew of two decades ago.

Pork products come in many forms, from the famous Limerick ham to thick country bacon or zesty homemade sausages, all of which are featured in hefty portions as part of the standard Irish breakfast.

If you order traditional roast chicken, it will usually be the tasty free-range variety, accompanied by lean Irish bacon or ham and a herby bread stuffing. Breast of chicken wrapped around local mushrooms or smoked salmon mousse are also popular choices.

IRISH BROWN BREAD

One of Ireland's most humble foods is also one of its greatest culinary treasures—brown bread. Made of stoneground whole meal flour, buttermilk, and other "secret" ingredients, Irish brown bread is served on the tables of every restaurant, hotel, country inn, and home in the country. The amazing thing is that no two recipes are exactly the same; brown bread can be light or dark, firm or crumbly, sweet or nutty, but it is always delicious, especially when the crust is crispy. For sheer ambrosia, add a rich creamery butter or homemade raspberry jam.

Like the sourdough of San Francisco, the bagels of New York, or the baguettes of France, brown bread is "de rigueur" in Ireland for breakfast, lunch, and dinner. To add a little variety, some of the classier restaurants also fashion the basic ingredients into scones, biscuits, and rolls. No matter what shape it takes, however, it is still brown bread and a very healthy alternative to its floury white cousin. We guarantee you'll think of stuffing a few loaves into your suitcase when packing your bags.

As you travel deeper into the countryside you may encounter a few regional Irish dishes, although they are usually found more in the homes than in the restaurants. These include tripe and onions (tripe is the stomach lining of a sheep); drisheens (a wide sausage of sheep's blood with cream and breadcrumbs); black and white puddings (sausages made of pig's blood); crubeens (pig's feet); colcannon (potatoes mashed with scallions and cabbage); coddle (boiled bacon, sausages, onions, and potatoes); and boiled bacon and cabbage, which is actually a precurser to the Irish-American St. Patrick's Day favorite, corned beef and cabbage.

DESSERTS

A typically Irish dessert dish that you'll find on the menus of some restaurants near the water, particularly in the Cork area, is carrageen moss pudding. Carrageen moss is an edible seaweed that is picked from the rocks by the shore. After it is laid out in the sun to dry, it is washed, soaked in water, boiled, and strained into a vanilla or cocoa pudding. They say the secret of this dish is to use just enough moss so that you gain all of the seaweed benefits but none of the aftertaste!

Irish desserts are tilting more and more toward fresh strawberries and other local garden fruit combinations, although you can still find some traditional dishes like "trifle," a fruit salad combined with custard and sherry-soaked cake and then topped with rich cream. Other native desserts include barm brack, a light and yeasty fruitcake; raisin-filled soda cake; and plum pudding, a rich whiskey-based soft fruitcake usually reserved for Christmas and special occasions.

For those without a sweet tooth, Irish farmhouse cheeses offer a piquant alternative. More than 60 cheeses are now produced throughout the land, and many restaurants pride themselves on the quantity and quality of their all-domestic cheeseboards. (For a complete rundown on Irish cheeses and the trends of Irish cuisine in general, don't miss the article by Brenda Weir elsewhere in this book.)

DRINK

Fine whiskey and beer are synonymous with the Emerald Isle. In fact, the Irish are credited with inventing whiskey distilling; the story goes that Irish monks concocted the first brew for medicinal purposes in the 6th century. These same monks carried the recipe to Scotland. They called their invention "uisce beathe" (pronounced: "ish-ka ba-ha") which in Gaelic means "the water of life"; shortly afterward, it was Anglicized to "whiskey." In 1608, a license to distill alcohol was granted to Old Bushmills, making it the world's oldest distillery still in operation.

Irish whiskey differs from Scotch or English whiskey in the method of distillation. The Irish use a combination of local malt and unmalted barley, which is allowed to dry naturally without the aid of heat and smoke, while the Scottish/English mode of distilling requires the use of smoke-dried malted barley. The result gives Irish whiskey a clear, smooth, and smokeless taste.

Most Irish whiskey today is brewed at a central distilling plant located at Midleton, Co. Cork; it has the largest pot still in the world, with a capacity of 33,000 gallons. Among the leading brands are John Jamison, Powers, Paddy, Tullamore Dew, Murphy, and Dunphy.

The Irish like to drink their whiskey "neat," which means without ice, water, or other mixers. It is also used as the "sine qua non" for Irish Coffee, a drink that was invented in 1947 at the bar of Shannon International Airport. Irish Coffee is made by adding whiskey to a goblet of hot coffee mixed with sugar, and topping it off with a dollop of fresh cream. It's a favorite with visitors from all parts of the world.

In recent years, Irish Coffee has found some competition in sweet Irish whiskey-based drinks like Bailey's Irish Cream and Irish Mist. These mostly after-dinner libations have also given rise to inventive desserts like Irish Mist souffle and Bailey's Irish ice cream.

The most largely consumed national drink is Guinness stout, a black, yeasty ale with a foamy head. The Irish like to drink it on draft in a large tumbler glass called "a pint." Sipping a pint of Guinness is the favorite pastime in the pubs. First produced by Arthur Guinness in 1759, this dark brew is considered to be a healthful drink and the advertising boldly proclaims "Guinness is good for you." The Guinness Company also makes a light lager beer called "Harp" and a non-alcoholic beer known as "Kaliber." Other local beers include Smith-wicks, brewed in Kilkenny, and Beamish and Murphys, both from Cork.

If you think that Ireland has no wine, you'll be surprised. As a member of the E.E.C., Ireland imports a great variety of French, German, Spanish, Italian and other wines from the continent. California labels can be found on better wine lists, but the six thousand mile journey makes them rather costly. Some enterprising Irishmen are even experimenting with native wines; the most successful is a pleasant dry white vintage called "Longueville Fion Cois Moire." Irish-made from grape to bottle, it is produced at Longueville House, Mallow, Co. Cork, and geared primarily for consumption by guests who overnight and dine at this charming country inn. This success, however, will surely encourage more Irish wineries in the future.

As a country surrounded by the sea and with hundreds of lakes and rivers, Ireland has a water supply that is both pure and plentiful. Several sparkling bottled waters, such as Ballygowan and Glenpatrick, are readily available, rivaling Perrier and other international brands. Not surprisingly, Irish tea, strong and flavorful, is a drink that has no equal in the Emerald Isle.

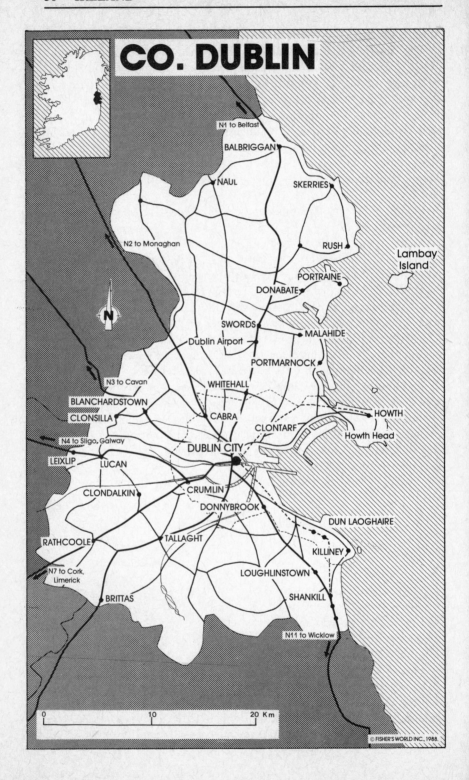

CO. DUBLIN

N1 to Belfast

BALBRIGGAN

NAUL

SKERRIES

N2 to Monaghan

RUSH

Lambay
Island

PORTRAINE

DONABATE

SWORDS

Dublin Airport

MALAHIDE

PORTMARNOCK

N3 to Cavan

WHITEHALL

BLANCHARDSTOWN

CLONSILLA

CABRA

HOWTH

CLONTARF

Howth Head

N4 to Sligo, Galway

LEIXLIP

DUBLIN CITY

LUCAN

CLONDALKIN

CRUMLIN

DONNYBROOK

DUN LAOGHAIRE

RATHCOOLE

TALLAGHT

KILLINEY

N7 to Cork,
Limerick

LOUGHLINSTOWN

BRITTAS

SHANKILL

N11 to Wicklow

0   10   20 Km

© FISHER'S WORLD INC., 1988.

Dublin's Fair City

THE CAPITAL AND ITS ENVIRONS

Like many capitals, Dublin is the political, historical, and business heart of the nation. It is also the soul of Irish literary, architectural, and cultural achievement.

Long overshadowed by London, Dublin has its own unique identity. It is not a mecca for pomp and pageantry, royal palaces and crown jewels, nor does it have superhighways and skyscrapers. Rather, Dublin is a city where over a millennium of history blends harmoniously with wide avenues and narrow laneways, grassy squares and cobblestone quays, designer boutiques and clusters of craftshops, more than 30 golf courses and a thousand pubs.

Where else but in Dublin would you find a core of landmarks ranging from two medieval cathedrals to the Abbey Theatre, and from the colorful open-air street markets of the Molly Malone genre to the largest urban park in the world?

Dublin has been home to a roster of citizens as diverse as its own urbane charms—from literary figures like Jonathan Swift, Oscar Wilde, George Bernard Shaw, William Butler Yeats, Sean O'Casey, James Joyce, and Brendan Behan, to actress Maureen O'Hara, runner Eamonn Coghlan, and fund raiser/rock concert organizer Bob Geldorf.

One of Europe's most picturesque capitals, Dublin sits on Ireland's east coast overlooking the Irish Sea. It is bi-sected from west to east by the River Liffey, and sheltered on three sides by a crescent of gentle mountains. More than a million people reside in the Dublin metropolitan area, and that is a quarter of the entire Irish population.

A BIT OF BACKGROUND

The earliest accounts of Dublin go back to 140 A.D. when the geographer Ptolemy, using the word "Eblana," pinpointed it on a map as a place of note. The present name is derived from the Irish or Gaelic word "Dubhlinn," meaning "Dark Pool." The official Irish name, however, which you'll see on some contemporary signs, is "Baile Atha Cliath," which means "The Town of the Hurdle Ford."

Like a lot of places in Ireland, St. Patrick is believed to have visited Dublin in 448 A.D. and converted many of the inhabitants to Christianity. During the next four centuries a Christian community grew around the site of the primitive ford on the River Liffey.

The city owes much of its development to the Norse, who built a seafort on the banks of the river in 841 A.D., and the Danes who took possession of the town 12 years later. During the 10th century, Irish kings laid claim to the settlement, and in 988 A.D. Dublin was officially recognized as an Irish city, hence the current celebrations of Dublin's Millennium throughout 1988. The Danish power was not fully thrown off, however, until 1014, when Irish chieftain Brian Boru was victorious at the Battle of Clontarf.

The Irish were not to enjoy Dublin as their own for long. In 1171 the English Earl of Pembroke, otherwise known as "Strongbow," took the city by storm. Shortly afterward, Henry II came to Dublin to survey his newly acquired domain. After receiving allegiance from the Irish chieftains, he granted Dublin its first charter in 1172.

History tells us that sporadic warfare continued through the next few centuries, with England never wholly victorious, nor Ireland thoroughly subdued. This eventually led to the occupation of Dublin in 1649 by Oliver Cromwell and his dreaded forces.

With the dawning of the 18th century, however, Dublin enjoyed one of its most colorful periods. Architecture and other arts were readily encouraged, new streets and squares were opened, and the nobility built palatial town houses. This was during the reigns of four English kings, George I, II, III, and IV, and so the architecture is referred to as "Georgian."

It was during this Georgian era that the Irish Protestant ruling classes achieved legislative independence and a separate Dublin-based Parliament House was built on College Green. Even though this independence was relatively short-lived (1783-1800), it spurred many other grand new buildings, such as the Customs House, Four Courts, Leinster House, the Rotunda Hospital, City Hall, the General Post Office, and parts of Trinity College. Most of this work was designed by a quartet of brilliant architects, James Gandon, Edward Lovett Pearce, Thomas Johnston, and Richard Cassels (a/k/a Castle). In a short time, Dublin grew into the second largest city of the British Isles and one of the great cities of the world.

Politically, however, Dublin still had much to achieve. By 1800, the Act of Union was passed, which once again melded the British and Irish legislatures. The great Irish Parliament building was converted into a bank, and political unrest began to swell. By 1803 the repressive policies of the British led to a brilliant but quickly quelled insurrection on the streets of Dublin by Robert Emmet.

All of the turbulence culminated more than a century later, when the Irish Rising took place in Dublin during Easter weekend of 1916, followed by a week of fighting during which much of the main thoroughfare, O'Connell Street, was demolished. After the Declaration of Independence was adopted in 1919, Dublin became a storm center in the Anglo-Irish War (1919-21) and a brief civil war (1923). Although many of her buildings were shattered during these years, Dublin finally emerged as the capital of a new and independent nation.

Much restoration followed and gradually the streets of Dublin returned to their former grandeur. As a result, the Irish capital today is a largely intact example of an 18th-century European city. The landmark public buildings, sweeping avenues, and graceful squares are surrounded by rows of brick-fronted Georgian town houses, each with its own unique door. Often referred to as "The Doors of Dublin," these portals are prized for their variety of style and structure. Some doors have fanlights, arches, columns, or sidelights; many have decorative brass bells or knockers; and each is painted a different color, a rainbow of classic individuality.

DUBLIN HIGHLIGHTS

A compact capital, with lots of pedestrian areas, Dublin is a very walkable city. In fact, during rush hours and other busy times, getting around on foot is the easiest way, as well as the fastest.

The River Liffey divides Dublin into a north side and a south side, with a dozen pedestrian and vehicular bridges linking both sections. On the next few pages, we'll give you suggested sightseeing routes which take in both banks of the river plus some highlights of the suburban areas.

To savor the ambience of Ireland's number one city, you should walk up Grafton Street, sip a coffee at Bewley's, stroll through St. Stephen's Green, browse along the quays, step into a few pubs, and, above all, chat with the Dubliners. And that's just for starters. . . . You could devote a week, a month, or a lifetime to Dublin and still not see all the sights and breathe in all the experiences. If you only have a day, however, here are a few priorities to give you an overview of the city.

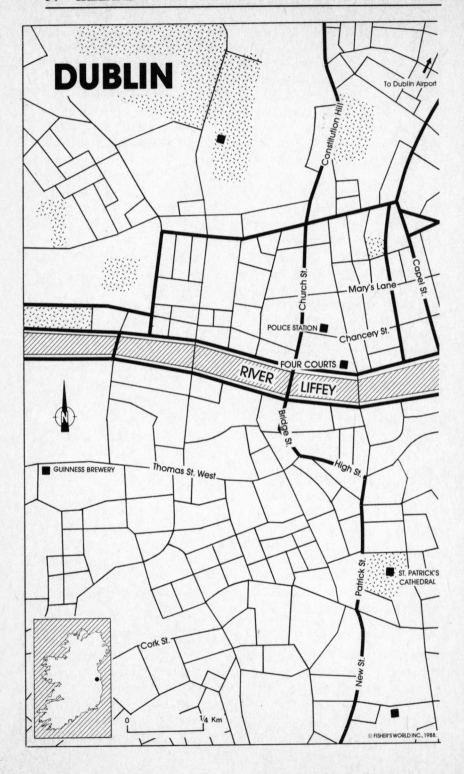

DUBLIN

To Dublin Airport

Constitution Hill

Church St.

Mary's Lane

Capel St.

POLICE STATION

Chancery St.

FOUR COURTS

RIVER LIFFEY

Bridge St.

High St.

N

GUINNESS BREWERY

Thomas St. West

Patrick St.

ST. PATRICK'S CATHEDRAL

Cork St.

New St.

0 1/4 Km

© FISHER'S WORLD INC., 1988.

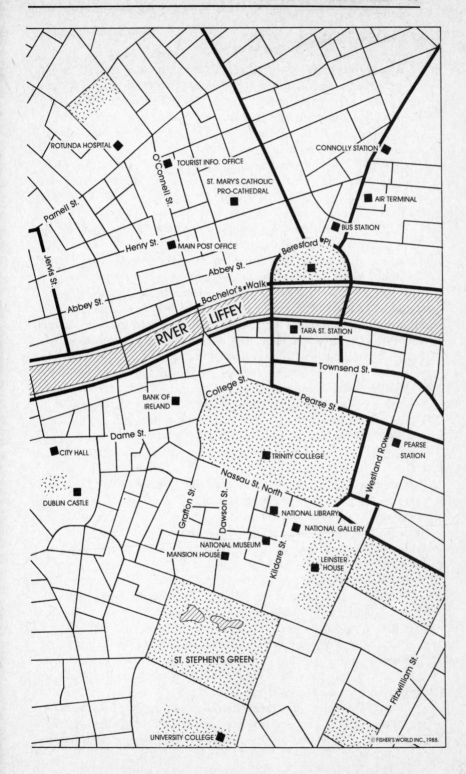

IF YOU ONLY HAVE A DAY

Start your tour on O'Connell Street, Dublin's main avenue. If you are registered at the Gresham, just step outside the front door; if elsewhere, take a taxi. (You could walk, but you'll need the time to amble later.) The Dublin Tourism Office is also in the middle of O'Connell Street, just a few doors from the Gresham, so do stop here to pick up some sightseeing folders and maps.

Originally an elongated residential square known as Gardiner's Mall, this thoroughfare was extended and called Sackville Street in its early days. By the mid-19th century, it was re-named in honor of Daniel O'Connell, former Lord Mayor of Dublin and the champion of Catholic Emancipation in Ireland. The adjoining bridge spanning the River Liffey was also re-christened in tribute to O'Connell.

Now ranked among the grand ceremonial boulevards of Europe, O'Connell Street is one of the few broad two-way arteries in the city, with a center strip dotted by a series of monuments, ranging from a statue of Daniel O'Connell at the southern tip of the street near the bridge, to remembrances of Charles Stewart Parnell, a 19th-century advocate of Irish Home Rule, Jim Larkin, an early labor leader, and Fr. Theobald Matthew, an exponent of temperance.

Up until 20 years ago, O'Connell Street was considered the center of Dublin, "the place" to go and to be seen. In recent years, however, the emphasis has shifted to the opposite side of the River Liffey, to Grafton Street and St. Stephen's Green, spilling into the city's southern sector and the suburb of Ballsbridge. That is why you'll observe most of the finer hotels and restaurants are clustered in the area south of the Liffey.

You'll still find grand old stores like Clery's and Eason's on O'Connell Street, but, for the most part, today's shopfronts primarily beckon you to fast food cafes or cinemas. The main sightseeing attraction here is the large granite building known as the General Post Office (GPO), and not just for buying stamps for your postcards, but for a look at a pivotal scene of Irish history.

The Republic of Ireland was proclaimed here in 1916 when the Irish Volunteers commandeered the GPO as their headquarters. The was shelled building by a British gunboat anchored in the River Liffey and completely gutted by fire. Now fully restored to its original 1818 grandeur, the GPO commemorates the Irish Rising in its main hall with a huge bronze statue of the dying "Cuchulainn," a legendary Irish folk hero. Words from the "Proclamation of the Irish Republic" are also cut in stone on the building's front facade.

From O'Connell Street, cross the Liffey and walk down Westmoreland Street to College Green. Here you will see the Old Parliament House, regarded as one of Dublin's finest specimens of 18th-century architecture. Begun in 1729 from the designs of Sir Edward Lovett Pearce, the Surveyor-General of Ireland, in 1785 the building was enhanced by James Gandon. It is unique because it has a windowless facade.

Even though it is now the home of the Bank of Ireland, you can still ask to see the original House of Lords room, with its elaborate coffered ceiling, heirloom tapestries, and a Waterford Glass chandelier dating back to 1765. (Open only during banking hours.)

Across the street from the Parliament House is one of Dublin's best-known landmarks, Trinity College, founded in 1591, although the earliest surviving portions of buildings date from 1722. As you enter the main gates, note the great 300-foot Palladian facade, erected from 1752 to 1759; statues at the entrance commemorate two distinguished 18th-century alumni, Oliver Goldsmith, the poet and dramatist, and Edmund Burke, political philosopher and orator. Inside this 7,000-student enclave you will find a cobbled walkway and a series of buildings which include the chapel (1798), public theater or examination hall (1791), dining hall (1761), the old library (1732) and the new library (1967).

★★★ The piece de resistence of the old library is its Long Room, 210 feet long, 41 feet wide, and 40 feet high, which houses a large collection of medieval manuscripts and early printed books. The most famous item on display is the hand-illustrated manuscript of the four gospels known as the *Book of Kells*, dating back to the 9th century or earlier. Each day a new page is turned for visitor viewing. Other ancient items on permanent exhibit include the *Books of Armagh and Durrow*, and the elaborately carved ancient musical instrument considered to be the 11th-century harp of Irish chieftain Brian Boru. The complete Trinity College Library contains over a half-million volumes, a figure which is constantly growing, thanks to the copyright law of 1801 which specifies that a copy of every book published in Britain or Ireland must be sent here.

The next segment of this little tour will take you back to Dublin's earliest days. It would be wise to take a taxi (there is a taxi rank right across from Trinity on College Green), or you can walk eight blocks directly westward via Dame Street and Lord Edward Street to Christ
★★★ Church Cathedral.

Standing on high ground in the oldest part of the city, this cathedral is one of Dublin's finest historic buildings. It dates back to 1038 A.D. when Sitric, the then-Danish King of Dublin, built the first wooden Christ Church here. The original city of Dublin was then located in the two-block area between the church and the River Liffey. Likewise, from this ridge the Anglo-Norman city was built.

The original simple foundation of Christ Church was extended into a cruciform design and rebuilt in stone by Strongbow in 1171, although the present structure dates mostly from 1871-78 when a huge restoration was undertaken. Only the transepts, the crypt, and a few other portions date from medieval times. Highlights of the interior include magnificent stone work and graceful pointed arches, with delicately chiseled supporting columns. Strongbow himself is among the historic figures buried in the church, as is Archbishop Browne, the first Protestant to occupy the see of Dublin, during the reign of Henry VIII.

As you leave the cathedral, you may wish to explore the neighborhood where "old Dublin" flourished. On the adjacent High Street, you can see a portion of the old city walls. If you walk toward the river along Wood Quay, you will find modern civic offices, but this was the site of the original Viking city. Before the modern offices were built, recent archeological digs revealed the layout, houses, walls, and quays of Dublin as they existed in the 9th-11th centuries.

From beside Christ Church, follow Winetavern Street southward as it becomes Nicholas Street and then Patrick Street. Now you have arrived at Dublin's second medieval cathedral, St. Patrick's, founded ★★ on this site in 1190 A.D..

Because of a fire and a re-building in the 14th century, not much remains from the cathedral's foundation days. It is mainly early English in style, with a square medieval tower, a spire which was added in the 18th century, and a 300-foot-long interior, which makes it the longest church in Ireland.

The building's history is as colorful as Dublin itself. In 1320 it was the headquarters for a great university which flourished for over 100 years until it was suppressed by Henry VIII. During the 17th century, Cromwellian troopers stabled their horses in the aisles, leaving the building in a forelorn state. Fortunately, a complete restoration followed in the 1860's.

St. Patrick's is closely associated with Jonathan Swift, who was dean here from 1713-45. You can not only see his tomb in the south aisle, but also the pulpit from which he preached, and the epitaph he wrote for himself: "He lies where furious indignation can no longer rend his heart." Nearby is the grave of Esther Johnson, otherwise ★★ known as "Stella," one of his two great loves.

From Patrick Street, return to Lord Edward Street and your next stop will be Dublin Castle, built between 1208 and 1220. Representing some of the oldest surviving architecture in the city, this was the center of British power in Ireland for seven centuries until it was taken over by the new Irish government in 1922. The most important section is the State Apartments, once the residence of the English viceroys and now the focal point for government ceremonial functions, such as the inauguration of Ireland's presidents. The castle complex also includes the Church of the Holy Trinity, formerly the Chapel Royal, built between 1807-14.

Adjoining the Castle is Dublin's City Hall, erected between 1769
★ and 1779, and formerly the Royal Exchange. It is a square building in
Corinthian style, with three fronts of Portland Stone. The interior is
designed as a circle within a square, with fluted columns supporting a
dome-shaped roof over the central hall. The building contains many
items of interest including 102 royal charters and the mace and sword
of the city.

Now stroll eastward along the wide corridor of Dame Street,
another of Dublin's rare two-way streets. As you return to College
Green, turn right onto Grafton Street. Now mostly a pedestrian area,
this is Dublin's equivalent of New York's Fifth Avenue or London's
Bond Street, a continuous row of fashionable department stores,
boutiques, and specialty shops. Like a tree with many branches,
Grafton street offers several interesting digressions, such as Duke
Street (for good shops and pubs) and Powerscourt Town House
Centre, also a shopping complex, but worth looking at even if you
have no interest in its myriad craft and antique vendors. Formerly the
★★ town residence of Lord Powerscourt, built in 1771, this grand building
contains some of the finest rococo plasterwork and woodcarving in
Ireland.

When you reach the south end of Grafton Street, you will be at the
★★ edge of St. Stephen's Green, a delightful pedestrian park covering 22
acres in an almost perfectly square layout. A verdant haven in mid-
city, it is called "Stephen's Green" or simply "The Green" by Dubliners
who flock to enjoy the flowers, trees, ponds, and free lunchtime
concerts. The grounds also include a garden for the blind, with the
names of plants written in braille on tags.

Start walking around the north side of The Green, and your first
turn left will be Dawson Street. It's worth a slight detour here to see
★★ the Mansion House, a fanciful Queen Anne-style building erected by
Joshua Dawson in 1710, and the home of the Lord Mayors of Dublin
since 1715. Many important events have taken place here, including
the adoption of the Irish Declaration of Independence in 1919 and the
signing of the truce that ended the Anglo-Irish hostilities in 1921. The
current Lord Mayor (until June, 1988) is Carmencita Hederman, the
third woman Mayor in Irish history.

If your timing is right, you may also get a glimpse of the Lord
Mayor's coach, a richly decorated horse-drawn carriage built by
Dublin craftsmen in 1789 and restored in 1976. The body of the coach
is carved and gilded, and the panels are painted with allegorical scenes
relevant to the history of the city.

At this point, return to walking around St. Stephen's Green,
passing the stately Shelbourne Hotel, a grand hostelry dating back to
1824 (see "Inside Information"), as you complete the north side of the
square.

Along the east side you will see a variety of well-maintained Georgian town houses, and as you reach the corner linking the east and south sides you can make a short diversion to Earlsfort Terrace to see Ireland's National Concert Hall, a turn-of-the-century building which was originally part of the University College of Dublin. (For further details, see "Inside Information.") Here you will also encounter the beginning of Leeson Street, a strip known for its after-hours activity of all kinds, including an ever-changing parade of disco/night-clubs in the basements of restored Georgian town houses. (See "Inside Information.")

At the point where the south side of The Green meets the west, you will come to Harcourt Street, a curving Georgian thoroughfare laid out in 1775 and named after the then-Viceroy, Lord Harcourt. Take a look at No. 61, a fine brick building where George Bernard Shaw lived for a time, and No. 16, once the residence of Bram Stoker, author of "Dracula" (now a restaurant; see "Inside Information.")

Stroll up the west side of The Green now, and you will find yourself back at Grafton Street, and at the completion of a one-day tour of Dublin's Fair City.

IF YOU HAVE TWO DAYS

The ideal two-day tour of Dublin would combine (1) the sights described in the previous section, for your first day, and (2) the activities listed below for your second day.

Trinity College, start this day's walk at Dublin's Grand Canal, at Baggot Street, just south of The Green. Here you will find the world headquarters of the Irish Tourist Board (Bord Failte), in case you wish to stop in for some information on other parts of Ireland.

Stroll northward on Baggot Street, the site of Baggotrath Castle until the early 19th century. If you'd like to see some perfect specimens of colorful Georgian doorways and homes, turn left at Fitzwilliam Street and wander along. Most of these buildings now belong to doctors, dentists, and creative professionals (such as advertising and public relations people) who use them for offices. Return to Baggot, which also has its share of fine Dublin town houses, and make your first turn right onto fashionable Merrion Street.   ★★

Merrion Street not only rivals Fitzwilliam's exquisite Georgian houses, but it also has a lovely public park, called Merrion Square, at its center. Around the square you'll find well-tended houses, many of which were the residences of famous Dubliners, such as Daniel O'Connell (no. 58), William Butler Yeats (nos. 52 and 82), George Russell, otherwise known as "A.E." (no. 84), and Oscar Wilde and his parents, Sir William and Lady "Speranza" Wilde (no. 1).

One of the most important buildings on Merrion Street, however, is not a home but a public edifice. Directly opposite the north side of the ★★ square you will find the National Gallery of Ireland. First opened in 1864, it contains a premier collection of paintings by Irish artists as well as works by such international masters as Fra Angelico, Rembrandt, Gainsborough, Manet, Degas, El Greco, Goya, Monet, Rubens, and van Dyck. There are over 2,500 oil paintings, almost 3,500 drawings and watercolors, and 240 pieces of sculpture, plus an important display of icons and a room devoted totally to American painting. Benefactors over the years have included George Bernard Shaw, who left one-third of his estate to the perpetuation of the gallery. You may wish to spend some time here, or return later at your leisure.

At the corner of Merrion Street and Nassau Street, turn left and go for one block until you come to Kildare Street, and turn left again. Kildare Street is the back end of Merrion Street, or the front end, depending on which way you approach it. In any event, here you have ★ the legislative hub of the Irish government, Leinster House, a splendid Georgian mansion dating back to 1745. Standing in the center of a quadrangle, it is the meeting place of the "Oireachtas" (Irish Parliament), consisting of Dail Eireann (House of Representatives) and Seanad Eireann (The Senate). It is normally not open to visitors, unless you have a special introduction. If the lines of the building look a little familiar, that is because Leinster House was used as a model by James Hoban, the Irish architect who designed the White House in Washington, D.C.

On the right of Leinster House is Ireland's National Museum, a ★★★ building well worth visiting to gain an appreciation of Ireland's progress through the centuries. The museum is divided into three divisions, Irish antiquities, art and industry, and natural history. Of the three, the antiquities section is the most interesting for visitors. Here you'll see art work from the first known appearance of man in Ireland in the form of decorated stones from the megalithic tombs of 6,000 B.C., and items from the early-Christian, Viking, and Romanesque periods, as well as a comprehensive display of Irish silver, glass, ceramics, furniture, musical instruments, coins, medals, costumes, and lace.

In addition, there is a suite of rooms aptly called "The Treasury," which contains such one-of-a-kind pieces as the Ardagh Chalice, Tara Brooch, Cross of Cong, and the Shrine of St. Patrick's Bell. Most of these items, along with the *Book of Kells* (housed in Trinity College Library), toured the United States in 1977-78 as part of the "Treasures of Early Irish Art Exhibit."

To the left of Leinster House is the National Library, the largest public library in Ireland. Founded in 1877, it is the repository for a half million books, prints, and manuscripts. It also has an unrivalled collection of maps of Ireland, plus an extensive accumulation of Irish newspapers. If you are trying to track down your ancestry, this is a good place to start. You might also want to look into the Irish Genealogical Office while you are here. (See "Inside Information.")   ★★

From Kildare Street, return to Nassau Street, with its row of fine souvenir, book, and clothing shops opposite the grounds of Trinity College. You may wish to take some time out for shopping. Next, we suggest you go to College Green and get a taxi to the city's far west ★★★ side, an area called Kilmainham.

Start by visiting the Royal Hospital, otherwise known as Ireland's Centre for Culture and the Arts. It is the oldest surviving fully classical building in Ireland, and is the largest Irish structure, other than a monastery or castle, existing from before 1700. It was founded in 1680 by James Butler, the Duke of Ormonde, who obtained a charter from King Charles II to create a hospice for retired soldiers similar in style to "Les Invalides" in Paris. It is designed in the form of a quadrangle, with two stories and dormer windows.

Fully restored throughout, the building includes a Great Hall with an extensive portrait collection and a magnificent chapel with a baroque ceiling, stained glass, and intricate wood carvings. Many of the rooms are now used for international exhibits and also for public concerts, recitals, and theatrical productions. (See "Inside Information" under Dublin Entertainment.) On weekends you can also enjoy a buffet brunch in the former cellars of the building, followed by guided tours, open-air concerts, and other outdoor events. Many Dublin families will spend an afternoon or a day here, as the grounds also encompass a sculpture park and an 18th-century formal garden.

The entrance to the Royal Hospital is across the street from Heuston Station, one of Dublin's three main rail depots. While in the ★ neighborhood, you may also wish to visit the Kilmainham Jail, opposite the west entrance of the Royal Hospital. Inmates have included such figures as Robert Emmet, Henry Joy McCracken, William Smith O'Brien, Charles Stewart Parnell, and Patrick Pearse. Built in 1789, it operated as a prison until 1924, when it was abandoned. Now fully restored, it stands as a memorial to the successive Irish independence movements and to the patriots. Items on display include personal effects of the former prisoners, death masks, firearms, uniforms, and documents relating to the Easter Rising of 1916.

This southwestern corridor of the city is also the home of the Guinness Brewery, founded in 1759, the largest brewery in Europe and ★★ the biggest exporter of stout. Although the public is no longer allowed to tour the brewery itself, there is an excellent visitor center within the Guinness compound, on Crane Street, off Thomas Street. It's housed in a former hop store, and you can still smell the aromas in the air as you watch an audio-visual about the making of the famous brew, complete with free samples. Other things to see are the Guinness Museum, the Cooper's Museum, and an ever-changing exhibit of traveling arts and science shows.

IF YOU HAVE THREE DAYS

If you have seen the sights already outlined, we suggest that you spend your third day exploring the north side of Dublin City.

You will have already experienced some of O'Connell Street on your first day, but now we suggest that you go to its northernmost end, otherwise known as Parnell Square. This block-long landmark is named after Charles Stewart Parnell, a 19th-century Irish Protestant leader who is fondly referred to as "the uncrowned king of Ireland." Here you will also find the Garden of Remembrance, a peaceful small park dedicated to all those who died in the cause of Irish freedom.

Other buildings in the Parnell Square complex include the Rotunda Hospital (built in 1751-55), the second oldest maternity hospital in the world, and the Gate Theatre, founded in 1928 by Hilton Edwards and Michael MacLiammoir, pioneers in contemporary Irish theater.

★★ This corner of Dublin is also the home of the Municipal Gallery of Modern Art, at Charlemont House on Parnell Square. The building itself was erected between 1762 and 1765, but the museum was founded in 1908 by art collector Sir Hugh Lane, who subsequently died in the sinking of the "Luisitania" in 1915. With the Lane collection as its nucleus, this museum also includes paintings from the impressionist and post-impressionist traditions, sculptures by Rodin, stained glass, and a small collection of works by Irish artist Jack B. Yeats.

★ If you walk west on Parnell Street for two blocks, a considerable contrast awaits you at a lively pedestrian area known as Moore Street, the city's largest alfresco market for fish, fruit, vegetables, and flowers. It is the home of Dublin's famous street barrow vendors, who peddle their wares in the tradition of Molly Malone. You'll be charmed by their persuasive salesmanship, sharp wit and sing-song voices, rich in the unique Dublin dialect.

★★★★ From Moore Street, you can return to O'Connell Street and walk one block past the General Post Office to Middle Abbey Street. Cross over O'Connell to the other side (which now becomes Lower Abbey Street). The main building of note here is the Abbey Theatre, the country's premier stage. Originally founded in 1904 by William Butler Yeats and Lady Augusta Gregory, the Abbey has given the world such classics as "The Playboy of the Western World" by John M. Synge, "Juno and the Paycock" by Sean O'Casey, "Philadelphia, Here I

Come" by Brian Friel, and "Da" by Hugh Leonard. The present theater is quite modern (1966), having replaced the original which ★★ burned down in 1951.

A turn northward from the middle of Lower Abbey Street will bring you to Marlborough Street, site of St. Mary's Pro-Cathedral, the main Catholic church of Dublin. Dating back to 1825, it is a Doric-style edifice which combines a portico modeled after the Temple of Theseus in Athens, and an interior patterned after the Church of St. Phillippe du Roule in Paris.

Head southward toward the Liffey, via Lower Gardiner Street. This will bring you to a crescent-shaped street called Beresford Place, and a building known as Liberty Hall, a 1960's addition to the Dublin scene and the closest thing you'll get to a skyscraper (16 stories) in this city. It's the headquarters of the Irish Transport and General Workers Union. Adjacent is another modern structure, Busaras, the main ★★ Dublin City bus depot.

Continue now to the north bank of the River Liffey and to one of Dublin's foremost public buildings, The Customs House. Designed by ★★ James Gandon and completed in 1791, it is beautifully proportioned, with a long classical facade of graceful pavilions, arcades, columns, and a central dome topped by a 16-foot statue of Hope. Although the Customs House was burned to a shell in 1921, it has been masterfully restored.

From the Customs House, walk along the northern quays of the River Liffey. You'll pass a variety of second-hand shops, used book dealers, and auction rooms. When you reach Ormond Quay, you'll arrive at yet another 18th-century James Gandon masterpiece, The Four Courts. The headquarters of the Irish justice system, this building ★★ has a distinctive vast lantern dome which makes it stand out on the Dublin skyline. It was also shelled during the warfare of the 1920's and was later restored.

One block further west you will come to Church Street and St. Michan's Church, a 17th-century structure on the site of an 11th- ★★ century Danish chapel. It has some very fine woodwork, and an organ (dated 1724) on which Handel is said to have played his "Messiah." The most unique (and, in some ways, macabre) feature of this church, however, is the underground vaults. Because of the dry atmosphere, bodies have laid for centuries without showing signs of decomposition. If you touch the skin of these corpses, you'll find it to be soft, even though it is brown and leather-like in appearance. If you "shake hands" with the figure known as "The Crusader," it is said you will always have good luck. Good luck!

At this point, you may want to call it a day for the sightseeing and do some shopping, or perhaps return to O'Connell Street to get yourself a taxi. If so, you can head for the most northwesternly corner of the Liffey quays—the Phoenix Park, opened to the public in 1747. With a circumference of seven miles and covering an area of 1,760 acres, this is certainly Dublin's premier park, and it is also said to be the largest enclosed urban park in the world. Situated just two miles ★★ from the city center, Phoenix Park is traversed by a network of roads and quiet pedestrian walkways. It is informally landscaped with ornamental gardens, nature trails, and broad expanses of grassland, separated by avenues of trees, including oak, beech, pine, chestnut, and lime. Livestock graze peacefully on pasturelands, deer roam the forested areas, and horses romp on the polo fields or gallop on the on-premises racetrack.

Monuments in the park range from the Wellington Testimonial, a 205-foot obelisk, reputed to be the tallest of its kind in the world, to a giant white cross commemorating the papal visit of 1979. Among the several historic buildings in the park are the permanent residence of the U.S. ambassador, and "Aras an Uachtarain," the traditional home of Ireland's presidents. The park is also the setting for the Dublin Zoological Gardens, a 30-acre animal habitat dating back to 1830 and the third oldest zoo in the world (after those of London and Paris). More than 235 species of animals and birds from all parts of the world can be seen. The zoo has also been recognized for over 125 years as an international leader in lion breeding.

IF YOU HAVE MORE TIME . . . THE DUBLIN SUBURBS

If you are spending more than three days in this fascinating capital, you owe it to yourself to see some of the suburbs—the towns just south and north of the city where Dublin executives and professionals reside. Situated within a ten-mile radius of downtown, these suburban enclaves are literally at the doorstep of the big city, yet offer a distinctive change of pace, ranging from country village charm or fishing port ambience to seabreeze refreshment.

Thanks to Dublin's efficient new rapid transit network, DART, you don't even need to rent a car or invest in a taxi ride to reach most of these destinations. Just board a DART train in mid-town, or near one of the major hotels (such as the Berkeley Court or Jurys), and you'll be whisked along a scenic seaside route to resorts like Dun Laoghaire or Howth in less than a half hour.

You can easily visit both the south side and the north side suburbs of Dublin in a day, thanks to DART, but, if you have the time, the ideal plan is to spend a day or more in each direction.

SOUTHERN SUBURBS

The best place to start is in the southside suburb of Ballsbridge, which you can actually walk to from St. Stephen's Green (about four long blocks away). In many ways, this fashionable residential area is considered a part of the downtown milieu, especially since so many major hotels and restaurants are now located here. The focal point of the Ballsbridge area is the U.S. Embassy, located on Pembroke Road. ★★★ Patterned after an ancient Irish round tower, it is a cylindrical building of fairly recent vintage (1964). You may wish to stop in, pay your respects, and sign the guestbook.

Just south of the embassy is one of Dublin's landmarks, the Royal Dublin Society (RDS), on Merrion Road. Founded in 1731 by a group of 14 benevolent Dublin citizens, it was established to foster the development of the arts and sciences in the area.

Some of the projects initiated over the years by the RDS include the Botanic Gardens, the National Library and the National Museum, but since 1877 the organization has been primarily concerned with encouragement of scientific agriculture and stock breeding. This is currently reflected in two annual shows which take place on the RDS grounds, the Spring Show and Industries Fair (early May), and the Dublin Horse Show (early August). At other times of the year, the extensive RDS halls and grounds are used for concerts and public gatherings.

Just a block west of the RDS grounds is Herbert Park, a pleasant outdoor area, ideal for strolling, people-watching, relaxing, or perhaps a game of tennis.

Nearby you will find one of Dublin's most prized international attractions, the Chester Beatty Library and Gallery of Oriental Art at ★★★ 20 Shrewsbury Road. Twenty years ago this collection was bequeathed to the Irish nation by Sir Alfred Chester Beatty, an American-born mining tycoon (1875-1968) who made Dublin his home. The bulk of the exhibits are Islamic, but there are also large numbers of manuscripts, paintings, and objets d'art from China, Japan, India, and Western countries. Highlights include authentic second-century New Testament texts (the oldest known in the world), an 8th-century Buddhist print, a Koran (Qur'an) collection, and the world's largest assortment of Chinese jade books.

At this point, you may wish to walk over to the DART station on Lansdowne Road, about a block east of the Berkeley Court Hotel (or get into your rental car, if you are driving around). Head southward, aiming for Dun Laoghaire. En route, you'll pass two charming, mostly-residential, towns, Blackrock and Monkstown. If time allows, you may wish to disembark and pass some time in one or both of these places. The next stop on the DART route will be the harbor of Dun

Laoghaire, at Marine Road, well worth a stop or a few hours. If you are driving, just follow the "seafront" or "coast" road and you will arrive at the same point along the marina. This is also the terminus for the mailboat and car ferry services to/from Holyhead, Wales.

Dun Laoghaire (pronounced: "Dunn-Leery") is named after a 5th-century Irish king, and literally means "Leary's Fort." It is one of the largest boroughs of Dublin, with a population of 100,000 (including the surrounding suburbs of Blackrock, Dalkey, Killiney, and Glenageary).

For Dubliners and visitors alike, this town offers a cluster of outstanding seafront restaurants plus a two-mile-long paved beach walk; it is also the chief yachting center of Ireland. In addition, the nearby villages of Dalkey and Killiney provide expansive views of Dublin Bay from cliffside heights; the stretch known as "the Vico road" is often likened to the panoramas of the Bay of Naples. Killiney is also the home of Fitzpatrick's Castle, the only deluxe castle hotel in the Dublin area. (See "Inside Information.")

A little over a mile south of Dun Laoghaire along the bay is a spot called Sandycove, site of one of the area's most famous attractions, the James Joyce Martello Tower Museum. This circular stone fort, visible for miles along the coast, is one of a series of towers built in 1804 to protect the British Isles from a threatened Napoleanic invasion. Used by poet and novelist James Joyce as a home for a brief period in 1904, this tower also served as the setting for the opening scenes of his most famous work, "Ulysses." Today it is a mecca for lovers of Joyceana, with displays of the author's assorted personal belongings, original manuscripts, and rare book editions.

NORTHERN SUBURBS

Dublin Airport, located near Swords about six miles from downtown, is the focal point of the city's northern suburbs. As in most major capitals, there is regular bus and taxi transport linking the airport with the main business district. (See "Inside Information.") In addition to the airport, however, quite a few other attractions beckon Dublin's visitors in a northerly direction.

If you are traveling on the DART's northward tracks, the end of the line is at Howth (pronounced: "Ho-th"), an ancient seaport town ★★ nine miles from the city center. Howth draws outdoor-lovers to its sheltered beach and pier, lined with fishing and pleasure boats, and the town itself is very walkable and compact, with a couple of outstanding seafood restaurants. (See "Inside Information.")

In addition, you can climb the Hill of Howth, a 560-foot rocky promontory encircled with pathways, or stroll around the Howth Castle Gardens, a 30-acre natural expanse rimmed with thousands of rhododendron plants. Howth also looks onto an island in the Irish Sea known as "Ireland's Eye." Remnants of an old stone church on the island indicate that early Christians founded a monastery here in the 6th century. In the summer months, boat trips to "Ireland's Eye" are operated from the Howth pier according to demand.

Not all of the attractions in Dublin's northern suburbs are on the DART path, so you'll need a car to reach the remaining destinations.

★★ As you drive northward from the city center, follow the main airport road, otherwise known as N 1. After a series of name changes, it becomes Drumcondra Road; when you come to Botanic Avenue, turn left and this road will bring you to the National Botanic Gardens at Glasnevin. Founded in 1795, this is one of Ireland's most extensive displays of flowers and plants and a delight for horticultural buffs. The complex includes two huge century-old glasshouses, a herbarium, vegetable garden, and a lily pond.

★★★ Return to the main airport road (N 1), and continue in a northerly direction; you'll soon see signs for Malahide Castle, about ten miles northeast of the city center. The castle is well sign-posted and you should have no difficulties finding it.

Malahide is one of Ireland's most historic castles, founded in the 12th century by Richard Talbot and occupied by his descendants until 1976. Fully restored, the interior of the building is the setting for a very comprehensive collection of Irish furniture, dating from the 17th through the 19th centuries, and the walls are lined with one-of-a-kind Irish historical portraits and tableaux on loan from the National Gallery. The furnishings and the art reflect life in and near the house over the past eight centuries. After touring the castle you can also explore the 270-acre estate, which includes 20 acres of prized gardens with more than 5,000 species of plants and flowers. (Note: as we go to press, plans call for the opening of an extensive model railway exhibition on the Malahide grounds by mid-1988).

★★ About two miles north of Malahide, you will come to Newbridge House, at Donabate, the residence of the Cobbe family and a relatively new addition (since 1986) to the ever-growing list of Ireland's stately homes that are opened to the public. A well-kept country mansion dating back to 1740, it is a showcase of family memorabilia including original hand-carved furniture, portraits, daybooks, a museum of world travels, and an extensive doll collection. The great drawing room, in its original state, is reputed to be one of the finest Georgian interiors in Ireland. Downstairs, in the quarters originally occupied by the servants and staff, visitors can view a mid-18th century kitchen and laundry room complete with utensils and implements of long ago. In the adjacent courtyard, you can also visit the coach house and various workshops belonging to the estate. There are 365 acres of grounds, (one for every day of the year), laid out with picnic areas and walking trails.

DUBLIN CITY, Co. Dublin

Hotels

★★★★★ BERKELEY COURT

Lansdowne Road. Tel. (01) 601711. 262 rooms and suites. Dublin's most elegant modern hotel, the Berkeley Court (pronounced "Barkley" Court) is the flagship of the Doyle Hotel Group, and was the first Irish member of Leading Hotels of the World.

Located in the posh suburb of Ballsbridge, near the major embassies, it is decorated with fine antiques and the best of Irish-made carpets and furnishings. Guest facilities include a gourmet restaurant, "The Berkeley Room," plus a verdant conservatory grill room, shopping arcade, a health center with indoor swimming pool, and ample parking. It's a favorite with diplomats and international business leaders. *Very expensive.*

★★★★★ JURYS

Pembroke Road. Tel. (01) 605000. 300 rooms and suites. Opposite the American Embassy in the Ballsbridge section of the city, this large hotel has just undergone a major ($3 million) renovation and boasts a new three-story skylit atrium lobby and a refurbished decor of marble and teak. There are two top class restaurants, "The Embassy" and "The Kish," a seafood specialty room, plus a 23-hour coffee shop. This is also the home of Jury's Cabaret Show, Ireland's longest running evening entertainment (over 25 years).

Amenities include a heated indoor/outdoor pool, therapeutic hot whirlpool, hairdressing salons, a lively turn-of-the-century themed pub, "The Dubliner," an extensive craft/clothes shop, and plenty of parking. *Expensive.*

★★★★★ THE SHELBOURNE

27 St. Stephen's Green. Tel. (01) 766471. 172 rooms and suites. Built in 1824, the Shelbourne was named after the Earl of Shelbourne by its original owner, Richard Burke. Now a Trusthouse Forte Exclusive hotel, this grand hostelry is significant in Irish history (the new nation's constitution was signed here in room 107 in 1921), and it has often played host to international leaders, stars of stage and screen, and literary giants.

Always striving to keep up with the times, this luxurious landmark has recently undergone a $6 million restoration and refurbishment. The up-to-date guest rooms now have mini-bars as well as antique furnishings; and the front units overlook St. Stephen's Green. This hotel is a favorite rendezvous for Dubliners, either for afternoon tea in the "Lord Mayor's Lounge," or a convivial drink in the vintage "Horseshoe Bar." Other facilities include a fine restaurant, "The Aisling," and a private enclosed car park. *Very expensive.*

★★★★★ WESTBURY

Grafton Street. Tel. (01) 791122. 150 rooms and suites. Another Doyle Group property, this is Dublin's newest hotel, and the first of the deluxe caliber to be built downtown in over 50 years. Situated in the heart of the city's fashionable shopping district and near St. Stephen's Green, Trinity College, and all the major sights, it is also a member of the Leading Hotels of the World.

A tasteful hybrid of modern and traditional design, the Westbury blends a sleekly contemporary facade with a serene interior of soft pastel tones and antique furnishings. There is a top class restaurant, "The Russell Room," plus a seafood pub, hairdressing salon, underground parking, an arcade of 20 boutiques, and a chic "Terrace Lounge" which is a favorite with discerning Dubliners for afternoon tea or a quiet drink. *Very expensive.*

★★★★ THE BURLINGTON

Upper Leeson Street. Tel. (01) 605222. 472 rooms and suites. A favorite venue for international meetings and conferences, this is the largest hotel in Ireland and also a member of the Doyle chain. It's a modern, smartly furnished seven-story property, located two blocks south of St. Stephen's Green, with two restaurants, a trendy conservatory-style pub, and all-star cabaret featuring Irish music and song. Facilities include underground and outdoor parking, an arcade of shops, and hairdressing salons. The best after-hours night spot in town, Annabel's, is also located here. *Expensive.*

★★★★ THE GRESHAM

O'Connell Street. Tel. (01) 746881. 179 rooms. Centrally located on the city's main business thoroughfare, this is one of Ireland's oldest (1817) and best known hotels, now a member of the Ryan Hotel group. With high ceilings and individual decors, the guest rooms vary in size and style, and include a selection of one-of-a-kind luxury terrace suites. The public areas are a panorama of marble floors, moulded plasterwork, and crystal chandeliers. Although much of the Dublin City visitor emphasis has shifted south of the River Liffey in recent years, the Gresham is still an ideal location if you want to be near the Abbey and Gate Theatres, General Post Office, or Eason's and other landmark shops. Facilities include an all-day grill, lounge, theatre desk, a private parking garage, and an adjacent nightclub. *Moderate to expensive.*

★★★★ BLOOMS HOTEL—QUALITY INN

Anglesea Street. Tel. (01) 715622. 86 rooms and suites. Lovers of Irish literature will feel at home at Blooms. Named after Leopold Bloom, a character in James Joyce's "Ulysses," this hotel is in the heart of Dublin, near to Trinity College and Dublin Castle. The bedrooms are modern and functional, with little extras like garment presses and hair dryers, as well as electric shoe shiners and ice machines on all floors. There is as grill room and a unique pub called "Bogie's," designed to reflect a touch of Hollywood with photos of Bogart, Bacall, Hepburn, and other stars of yesteryear. An added plus for this mid-city lodging is an enclosed private car park which is free to overnight guests. *Moderate to expensive.*

★★★ BUSWELL'S

25 Molesworth Street. Tel. (01) 764013. 67 rooms. Centrally located close to Trinity College and Leinster House (the Irish seat of government), this old-timer (dating back to 1736) is a favorite with literary folk and politicians. Recently refurbished, all the bedrooms have been up-dated with a modern decor and standard facilities, plus added amenities of tea/coffee makers and hair dryers. Public facilities include an old-world style restaurant, "The Leinster Room," and the "Georgian Bar," a real charmer with a decor of Wedgwood trim. *Moderate.*

★★★ TARA TOWER

Merrion Road. Tel. (01) 694666. 84 rooms. A member of the Doyle Group, this modern seven-story wide-windowed hotel offers the best views of Dublin Bay, just ten minutes from the city center in a residential area. Known for its good-value policy, it's an ideal place to stay if you are renting a car, as there is ample parking space; if you prefer to use public transport, this hotel is within easy walking distance of major bus routes and a DART (Dublin Area Rapid Transit) station. The guest rooms offer very modern convenience and there is a restaurant/grill room, lounge bar, and shop on the premises. *Inexpensive.*

★★★ MONTROSE

Stillorgan Road. Tel. (01) 693311. 190 rooms. The largest of Dublin's modern hotels on the outskirts of the city, this dependable good-value lodging offers ample parking for car-renters. Located on a major bus route into the city, it is nestled on its own palm tree-lined grounds in a residential neighborhood, across the road from the Belfield campus of Dublin University and close to the Irish National TV Studios. Guest rooms are modern and functional, and the public facilities include a restaurant, grill room, lively lounge bar, health centre, hairdressing salon, souvenir shop, and a full-service bank on the premises. *Inexpensive.*

★★★ SKYLON

Upper Drumcondra Road. Tel. (01) 379121. 88 rooms. This is one of the few hotels of merit on the city's north side, situated mid-way between the city center and the airport. It's a modern five-story building, recently refurbished, and set on its own grounds in a residential neighborhood next to a prominent teacher-training college. The guest rooms have all the latest amenities, and the public areas include an all-day grill room, lounge bar, and shop. If you have a rented car, the Skylon has plenty of parking space; it is also located on a major bus route which will bring you into the heart of Dublin within ten minutes. *Inexpensive.*

Guesthouses and Private Homes

★★★ ARIEL HOUSE

52 Lansdowne Road. Tel. (01) 685512. 15 rooms. A Victorian-era townhouse converted and expanded into a guesthouse by San Francisco-trained Michael O'Brien. Located close to a DART (Dublin Area Rapid Transit) station and across the street from the Berkeley Court Hotel in the Ballsbridge section of thee city, it has a very homey atmosphere, with all the modern conveniences including private bath, telephone, and color TV in each guest room. There is also a full-service garden-side restaurant on the premises, plus a private car park. *Inexpensive.*

★★★ MOUNT HERBERT

7 Herbert Road. Tel. (01) 684321. 88 rooms. Although technically classified as a guesthouse, this three-story much-expanded property is more like a small hotel. Originally the family home of Lord Robinson, it is a gracious residence set in its own grounds and gardens in the same residential neighborhood as Ariel House. All rooms have private bath and direct-dial phones. Guest facilities include saunas, indoor solarium, a TV lounge, sun balcony, badminton court, miniature putting green, gift shop, and a restaurant with a wine license. *Inexpensive.*

★★★ GEORGIAN HOUSE

20 Lower Baggot Street. Tel. (01) 604300. 10 rooms. Newly opened as a guest lodging, this four-story 200-year-old brick townhouse is centrally located less than two blocks south of St. Stephen's Green in the heart of Georgian Dublin. The bedrooms are smallish, but they have all the essentials including private bath/showers. The only drawback is that no guest rooms are on the ground floor and there is no elevator. On the plus side, there is a full-service restaurant on the premises and a private enclosed car parking area which is free to overnight guests. *Inexpensive.*

★★★ ANGLESEA TOWN HOUSE

63 Anglesea Road. Tel. (01) 683877. 7 rooms. A true "bed and breakfast" experience is the keynote of this 1903 Edwardian-style home of Sean and Helen Kirrane. Located in the Ballsbridge section of the city, close to the Royal Dublin Showgrounds, the Chester Beatty Library, and the American Embassy, it is furnished with guest comfort in mind—rocking chairs, settees, a sun deck, and lots of flowering

plants, as well as all the modern conveniences of private bathroom and direct-dial phone in every guest room. You can count on a warm welcome and a breakfast of home-made goodies. *Inexpensive.*

Restaurants

★★★★★ **ERNIE'S**
Mulberry Gardens, Donnybrook. Tel. (01) 693300. One of Ireland's premier chefs, Ernie Evans, gained a far-reaching reputation 20 years ago for great seafood at his original restaurant on the Ring of Kerry. Today he carries on the tradition on the south side of the Irish capital at this chic 48-seat dining room in a courtyard-mews. A must for lovers of impeccably prepared salmon, scallops, prawns, and other seafoods. Open for dinner only, Tuesday through Saturday. *Very expensive.*

★★★★★ **LE COQ HARDI**
35 Pembroke Road. Tel. (01) 684130. A Georgian townhouse in the Ballsbridge section of the city, close to Jurys and the Berkeley Court hotels, is the setting for this award-winning 50-seat restaurant of chef John Howard. Specialties include Dover sole stuffed with prawns, turbot with beef marrow, pot au feu, caneton a l'orange, and steaks flamed in Irish whiskey. The 600-bin wine cellar boasts a complete collection of Chateau Mouton Rothschild, dating from 1945 to the present. Open for lunch on weekdays and dinner on Monday through Saturday. *Very expensive.*

★★★★★ **PATRICK GUILBAUD**
46 James Place, off Lower Baggot Street. Tel. (01) 764192. In the heart of the city, this is a modern skylight restaurant featuring French nouvelle cuisine and artful service. John Dory sole, mignon of lamb, and breast of duck are some of the featured entrees, often accompanied by delicate mousse trimmings, sublime sauces, and exotic fruits. Guilbaud's is a favorite lunch and dinner venue for Dublin's top executives. *Very expensive.*

★★★★★ **WHITE'S ON THE GREEN**
119 St. Stephen's Green. Tel. (01) 751975. Dublin's newest "in" dining spot in the downtown area, White's blends a Georgian country garden decor with a French nouvelle cuisine menu prepared by Michael Clifford, a chef whose culinary expertise reflects his years at some of France's top ranked restaurants. Lunch and dinner choices include terrine of lobster, veal sweetbreads, grilled quail, sea bass with leeks, and chicken in lemon sauce. *Very expensive.*

★★★★ CELTIC MEWS

109-A Lower Baggot Street, at the corner of Lad Lane. Tel. (01) 760796. As its name implies, this is a cozy Georgian-style mews in the heart of the city, not far from the Shelbourne Hotel. It was converted into a restaurant by the Gray family almost 20 years ago. The atmosphere here is warm and welcoming, and the menu ranges from Celtic steak flambe, rack of lamb or giant prawns, to a gourmet Irish stew. Dinner only. *Expensive.*

★★★★ DOBBINS

15 Stephen's Lane, off Upper Mount Street. Tel. (01) 764679. Just a block from fashionable Merrion Square, this friendly enclave is a haven for inventive Irish/international cuisine. The menu changes often, but usually includes such items as avocado and crab salad with pink grapefruit; laces of sole and salmon with prawn tails and spinach souffle; teriyaki beef; or breast of chicken in garlic and vodka butter. You'll have a choice of sitting in the main bistro-style restaurant with sawdust on the floor or in the leafy tropical patio area with an all-weather sliding glass roof. The wine list is particularly varied in origin and price. *Moderate to expensive.*

★★★★ THE GREY DOOR

23 Upper Pembroke Street. Tel. (01) 763286. Scandinavian and Tsarist Russian delicacies top the menu at this 35-seat restaurant, located one block south of St. Stephen's Green in a fine old Georgian townhouse with a grey front door. Specialties include seafood Zakuski (in puff pastry) and a chicken Kiev stuffed with cream cheese, spinach, and wild rice. to add to the ambience, there is live guitar music each evening. *Expensive.*

★★★★ LOCKS

1 Windsor Terrace, Portobello. Tel. (01) 752025. Located along the banks of the city's Grand Canal, Locks is French Provincial in decor and style of cuisine. The menu features daily "fish market" selections, as well as warm salads, stir-fry vegetables, and entrees ranging from filet mignon to breast of pigeon or roast duck. The service is especially obliging. Open for lunch on weekdays and dinner on Monday through Saturday. *Moderate to expensive.*

★★★★ RAJDOOT TANDOORI

26/28 Clarendon Street. Tel. (01) 794274. Chefs from India and Nepal combine their talents to produce meals of impeccable quality at this elegant outpost of Eastern cuisine, located next to the Westbury Hotel. Northern Indian tandoori cooking with charcoal clay is featured here; other entrees include spicy quail, pheasant, and lobster dishes, as well as chicken and prawn curries and lamb shish kebab. *Expensive.*

★★★★ STOKERS

16 Harcourt Street. Tel. (01) 782441. A block from St. Stephen's Green and close to the National Concert Hall, this restaurant is located in the renovated cellars of a building first known as Clonmell House, dating back to 1778 and then the home of Ireland's Lord Chief Justice. In the late 19th century it became the residence of Abraham (Bram) Stoker, an author most remembered for writing "Dracula" and hence the name for the present restaurant.

The decor is modern, light, and airy, with art deco tones, while incorporating the original hearth and stove; the former coal bin is now a wine cellar. The menu, which is basically French with Austrian and Bavarian influences, features such dishes as chicken filled with crab and spinach mousse; brill baked in cider; and filet of beef with blue cheese sauce. Interesting and tasty diet items are also always available. Open for lunch on weekdays and dinner Tuesday through Saturday. *Moderate to expensive.*

★★★ BENTLEY'S

46 Upper Baggot Street. Tel. (01) 682760. Owner Maureen Malkinson has succeeded in providing a country inn charm in the middle of Dublin. Cane chairs and floral prints dominate the old world decor of this 45-seat restaurant, and the menu ranges from hot spinach tartlets to stuffed chicken with apples and almonds, or lamb kidneys with red currant tarragon sauce. The desserts and breads are homemade. Open for lunch on weekdays and dinner Tuesday through Saturday. *Moderate.*

★★★ GALLERY 22

22 St. Stephen's Green. Tel. (01) 686169. Just a few doors from the Shelbourne Hotel, this 50-seat basement restaurant is a convenient in-town dining venue. You'll find a garden-like setting and a French/Irish menu, specializing in rack of lamb, country pate, seafood brochettes, turkey with fresh peaches in bourbon sauce, and breast of chicken with fresh strawberries in champagne. Open for lunch Monday through Saturday, but dinner only Tuesday through Saturday. *Moderate.*

★★★ LA GRENOUILLE

64 South William Street. Tel. (01) 779157. This restaurant is unique for Dublin City—open for dinner every night (including Sunday); also open for lunch on weekdays. Small and intimate, like a Parisian bistro, this is just the spot for steak au poivre, carre of lamb, duck a l'orange, or chicken au fromage. Situated within a block of the Westbury Hotel and the Powerscourt Town House complex. *Moderate.*

★★★ THE LOBSTER POT

9 Ballsbridge Terrace. Tel. (01) 680025. Positioned between the Ameri-

can Embassy and the Royal Dublin Society Showgrounds, almost opposite Jurys Hotel, this upstairs restaurant is known for its lobster dishes, as its name implies. Other entrees on the menu range from plaice on the bone and coquilles St. Jacques, to lamb kidneys, coq au vin, or steak tartare prepared at tableside. *Moderate to expensive.*

★★★ THE TAIN
59 South William Street. Tel. (01) 791517. If you crave good beef, this is an Irish steakhouse of great charm. Part of the Powerscourt Townhouse complex, it has a modern light wood decor with a traditional Irish ambience including background music by a harpist each evening. It's the best choice for sirloin steaks and filets of beef; veal steaks and Dover sole are also often on the menu. *Inexpensive to moderate.*

★★★ UNICORN
12-B Merrion Court, off Merrion Row. Tel. (01) 688552 or 762182. Ever since 1939, this has been the place to go in Dublin for Italian food. Renato and Nina Sidoli combine the freshest of Irish ingredients with old family recipes from their homeland. Pastas, pizzas, veal, and seafood are featured. Situated close to St. Stephen's Green, this 76-seat Irish trattorria is a favorite with local TV personalities, university professors, and politicians. No credit cards. *Inexpensive to moderate.*

Suggestions for Light Lunches or Quick Meals

★★★★ BEWLEY'S CAFE
78/79 Grafton Street. Tel. (01) 776761. You haven't experienced the real flavor of old Dublin until you have sipped a cup of coffee or tea at Bewley's. Founded in 1840 by a Quaker named Joshua Bewley, this is a Dublin tradition par excellence. It's a three-story 344-seat coffee shop-cum-restaurant which serves full breakfast, light meals, home-baked scones, and "sticky buns." Although there are five Bewley branches in the greater Dublin area, this is the flagship location, with high ceilings, stained glass windows, and a dark wood decor. There's a choice of self-service or waitress/waiter service at this branch; otherwise Bewley's Cafes are mainly self-service establishments. Open continuously from 8:15 A.M. until 6 P.M. *Bargain.*

★★★★ MITCHELL'S CELLARS
21 Kildare Street. Tel. (01) 680367. Originally a wine cellar, this trendy 60-seat luncheon spot has lots of atmosphere, with barrel-shaped tables, tiled floors, a beamed ceiling, and red and white lights. A favorite with Dubliners, it's located close to Grafton Street, Trinity College, St. Stephen's Green, and the Irish government buildings. The ever-changing menu often includes seafood salads, country pates, vegetable quiches, sweet and sour pork, beef braised in Guinness, or chicken a la Suisse. Open for lunch only and closed on Saturday during July and August. *Bargain to inexpensive.*

★★★ SHRIMPS
1 Anne's Lane, off South Anne Street. Tel. (01) 713143. This is a small and stylish wine bar/restaurant with a continental ambience located near Grafton and Dawson Streets. It's an ideal spot for lunch or a light dinner, with a menu that includes salads, vegetarian platters, seafood brochettes, couscous, oak-smoked salmon, mussels marinere, and croquettes of codfish. *Inexpensive to moderate.*

★★★ TIMMERMAN'S
Powerscourt Townhouse Center, South William Street. Tel. (01) 794186. Located in the original kitchens of a restored 1774 mansion, this popular eatery is known for its hefty salads, fish pies, quiches, pastas, fondues, and cheese/fruit/vegetable platters. The old world decor includes recycled choir stalls, church pews, wine casks, and old barrels. Open continuously from noon to midnight; and there's music nightly including jazz, blue grass, folk, and ballads. *Inexpensive.*

★★★ BEEFEATERS
100 Lower Baggot Street. Tel. (01) 760784. For lunch or dinner, the big attraction here is steak, steak, and more steak, prepared 16 different ways. You can have sirloins, T-bones, filets, kebabs, or Chateaubriand, not to mention teriyaki, tartare, and beef fondue. This basement bistro near Fitzwilliam Street is also known for its prime ribs, sole, and prawns. *Inexpensive to moderate.*

★★★ FORTUNE COOKIE
6 St. Stephen's Green. Tel. (01) 719371. If you are in the mood for authentic Cantonese cuisine, this is one of Dublin's best restaurants with an Oriental theme. It's located in the lower level of an old Georgian building, adjacent to the Grafton Street shopping district and near the Shelbourne Hotel. Open from noon to midnight Monday through Saturday and from 1 P.M. to 11:30 P.M. on Sunday. *Bargain to inexpensive.*

★★★ THE GASWORKS
21 Bachelor's Walk. Tel. (01) 731420. On the north side of the Liffey, you'll find this lively spot just a block from O'Connell Street. Housed in a restored 300-year-old warehouse with original gas lamps and fittings, it is a good choice for fast food—a quick burger, chili, taco, hot dog, pizza, or ribs. Open continuously for lunch, dinner, and snacks, from noon to midnight. *Bargain.*

Pubs

★★★★★ THE BRAZEN HEAD
20 Lower Bridge Street. Tel. (01) 779549. Dating from 1198 and licensed in 1661, this is the city's oldest pub. It is located on the south

bank of the River Liffey at the end of a cobble stone courtyard. Once the meeting place of Irish freedom fighters such as Robert Emmet and Wolfe Tone, this brass lantern-lit pub has been recently restored and rejuvenated by a new owner. Hours vary slightly from the norm (it opens at 4 P.M., Monday through Saturday, with regular Sunday hours). There is live music (from traditional to blues) on Wednesday through Sunday nights.

★★★★★ W. RYAN

28 Parkgate Street. Tel. (01) 776097. Three generations of the Ryan family have contributed to the success of this gem of a public house, located beside the River Liffey and near the Phoenix Park. Some of Dublin's best traditional pub features are a part of the scene here, from a metal ceiling and a domed skylight, to beveled mirrors, etched glass, brass lamp holders, a mahogany bar, and four old-style snugs.

★★★★ KITTY O'SHEA'S

23/25 Upper Grand Canal Street. Tel. (01) 609965. Fairly new to the Dublin scene, Kitty's is called after the sweetheart of 19th century statesman Charles Stewart Parnell. Like its namesake, this pub abounds with a warm and friendly charm, attracting a mixed clientele of executives, journalists, sports fans, and visitors-in-the-know. The decor reflects the Parnell era, with ornate oak paneling, stained-glass windows, old political posters, cozy alcoves, and brass railings. Full meals are served including Sunday Brunch (complete with zesty Bloody Marys). Traditional Irish entertainment is on tap Monday, Tuesday, and Sunday evenings. This pub is so good that it has spawned a branch of the same name in Paris.

★★★★ THE STAG'S HEAD

1 Dame Court. Tel. (01) 779307. Mounted stags heads dominate the decor here, as its name implies, but there are also wrought iron chandeliers, old barrels, stained glass sky-lights, and ceiling-high mirrors. More than 200 years old, this pub is a favorite with lawyers. Hearty pub lunches are a trademark, with such dishes as bacon and cabbage, leg of pork, or rib of beef usually on the menu.

★★★★ DAVY BARNES

21 Duke Street. Tel. (01) 775217. Referred to as a "moral pub" by James Joyce in "Ulysses," this imbibers' landmark has drawn poets, writers, and lovers of literature ever since. Located just off Grafton Street, it actually dates back to 1873 when Davy Byrnes first opened the doors. He presided here for more than 50 years and visitors today can still see his likeness on one of the turn-of-the-century murals hanging over the bar. The pub menu offers such delights as fresh salmon, wedges of brie, or meat pies.

★★★★ DOHENY AND NESBITT
5 Lower Baggot Street. Tel. (01) 762945. The locals call this Victorian-style pub simply "Nesbitts." It's frequented by government officials and a sprinkling of lawyers, doctors, and architects. There are two fine specimens of "snugs" (a small room with a trap door where women were served a drink in days of old). Sandwiches and snacks are served.

★★★ O'DONOGHUE'S
15 Merrion Row. Tel. (01) 607194. This pub is widely heralded for its spontaneous traditional music sessions at all times of the day or night. It's often very crowded, with different musical groups vying for attention in this stand-up, smoke-filled, and casual atmosphere. Snacks and sandwiches are served.

★★★ FOLEY'S
1 Merrion Row. Tel. (01) 606316. Just off St. Stephen's Green, this is a good pub for traditional music every night. Mixed cocktails are also a specialty here, from tequila sunrises to blue lagoons or pina coladas, but the biggest draw is the food menu which includes an extensive salad bar, hefty meat platters, and sandwiches at lunchtime, and restaurant-style dinners each evening including Sunday.

★★★ NEARY'S
1 Chatham Street. Tel. (01) 778596. Near to the Gaiety Theatre, this classy enclave is a favorite with stage folk including Peter O'Toole. Trademarks here are the pink and gray marble bar and the brass hands which support the globe lanterns at the entrance. You'll find "upper crust pub grub" including fresh and smoked salmon, oysters in season, and salads.

★★★ THE OLD STAND
37 Exchequer Street. Tel. (01) 777220. A sporting atmosphere is the "sine qua non" here. It's a favorite meeting place for participants and followers of rugby, horse racing, and Gaelic games. Besides good drinking and camraderie, this pub is known for its steaks, chops, and straight-forward pub grub.

★★★ THE BAILEY
2 Duke Street. Tel. (01) 773760. One of Dublin's most well known pubs, the classy Edwardian atmosphere makes it a favorite with artists, writers, musicians, and the young and successful singles set. A good conversation-starter on display here is the door marked #7 Eccles Street, referred to in James Joyce's "Ulysses."

★★★ BRUXELLES
7 Harry Street, off Grafton Street. Tel. (01) 775362. Located next to the Westbury Hotel, this is a well-preserved Victorian pub with a

touch of European ambience. It's worth a visit here just to see the owner's collection of old tankards and historic hats from around the world. Catering to a largely singles clientele, this pub swings on Sundays with morning and afternoon jazz sessions. Good soup-and-sandwich pub lunches are also an attraction.

★★★ THE PALACE
Fleet Street. Tel. (01) 779290. A favorite with the staff of the "Irish Times" and other literati, this old charmer is decorated with local memorabilia, cartoons, and paintings which tell the story of Dublin through the years. It has a convenient midtown location off Westmoreland Street, near the River Liffey and Trinity College. Snacks are served.

★★★ MULLIGAN'S
8 Poolberg Street. Tel. (01) 775582. Established in 1782, this is a typical man's pub known for its superb pints, dark wood decor, and smoky old Dublin atmosphere. It's a favorite with dockworkers, students from Trinity College, and the staff of the nearby "Irish Press" office.

Entertainment

Theaters

ABBEY THEATRE
Lower Abbey Street. Tel. (01) 787222. Founded in 1904, the Abbey is the National Theatre of Ireland. The current modern (1966) building is the second home of the Abbey Players—the original theatre was destroyed in a 1951 fire. Names like Yeats, Synge, O'Casey, Beckett, Behan, and most recently, Hugh Leonard, are but a few of whose works have been staged here. The seating capacity is 638; curtain time is usually 8 P.M., and ticket prices average between $7 and $10.

PEACOCK THEATRE
Lower Abbey Street. Tel. (01) 787222. In the same building as the Abbey, this small (157-seat) theater features contemporary plays and experimental works including poetry readings and one-person shows. In the month of June, the Irish National Ballet also performs here. There are occasional lunchtime or late-night performances. Curtain is normally at 8:15 P.M. and ticket prices range from $6 to $10.

GATE THEATRE
Cavendish Row, off Parnell Square. Tel. (01) 744045. This recently restored theater was founded in 1928 by Hilton Edwards and Michael MacLiammoir to provide a showing for a broad range of plays. This

policy prevails today, with a program that includes a blend of modern works, as well as some classics of sophisticated comedy written by Irish greats like Goldsmith, Wilde, Sheridan, and Shaw. Curtain is 8 P.M. and ticket prices range from $7 to $12.

GAIETY THEATRE
South King Street. Tel. (01) 771717. The Dublin Grand Opera Society performs its spring (April) and winter (December) seasons here. During the rest of the year, this very fine 19th-century theater stages musical comedy, ballet, revue, pantomime, and drama, all with Irish and international talent. Curtain is normally at 8 P.M. and tickets average around $8 to $12.

OLYMPIA THEATRE
Dame Street. Tel. (01) 778962. Dating back to the 1800's, this Victorian music hall-style theater was recently refurbished. It presents an eclectic schedule of variety shows, musicals, operettas, concerts, ballets, comedy, and drama. Tickets average $8 to $10, and the curtain is normally at 8 P.M.

PROJECT ARTS CENTRE
39 East Essex Street. Tel. (01) 712321. One of Dublin's "pocket" theaters, this contemporary establishment is located off Dame Street, and specializes in experimental and new works. Curtain is usually at 8:15 P.M. Tickets range from $5 to $8.

Concert Halls

NATIONAL CONCERT HALL
Earlsfort Terrace. Tel. (01) 711888. Just off St. Stephen's Green, this magnificent 1,200-seat hall, restored in 1981, is the home of the Symphony Orchestra of Irish Television, and also features the New Ireland Chamber Orchestra. The programs are mostly classical, but there are also evenings of Gilbert and Sullivan, jazz, and recitals. In the summer months, lunchtime concerts are also scheduled. Evening performances start at 7:30 P.M. or 8 P.M., and tickets range from $6 to $12. Lunchtime prices average $3.

THE ROYAL HOSPITAL
Military Road, Kilmainham, across from Houston Station. Tel. (01) 718666. This beautifully restored 17th century building is the setting for frequent concerts by well-known international performers and Irish artists. The program includes classical, chamber, and modern music. On summer weekends, daytime open-air concerts and performances of Shakespearean works are often staged. Ticket prices range from $4 to $30, depending on the event, and the starting time is usually 8 P.M.

A NOTE ON DUBLIN THEATER/CONCERT TICKETS:
In addition to visiting box offices, you can also obtain tickets at the theater desks at Brown-Thomas and Switzers Department Stores, both on Grafton Street, and from another single and centrally located source: THE TICKET BUREAU, 4 Westbury Mall, next to the Westbury Hotel, off Grafton Street. Tel. (01) 794455. Major credit cards are accepted by this bureau and by the individual theaters.

In advance of your visit, for an additional fee, you can also reserve tickets at Dublin theaters and concert halls through Edwards and Edwards, Suite 1200, One Times Square, New York, N.Y. 10036. Tel. (212) 944–0290 and (800) 223–6108.

Cabarets/Shows

Irish cabarets are unique. They are not the usual mix of Las Vegas-style chorus lines, neon lights, or raunchy jokes. Instead you will experience a delightful program of family-style entertainment, with traditional song, dance, and clean humor.

Although you may hear a few renditions of "When Irish Eyes Are Smiling" or "Danny Boy," these shows primarily present genuine Irish music and folklore. Attending one of these cabarets is a great way to start or finish a stay in Dublin—you'll be refreshed by the Irish zest for laughter and foot-tapping tunes.

DOYLE'S IRISH CABARET
Burlington Hotel, Upper Leeson Street. Tel. (01) 605222, ext. 1162. Featuring some of Ireland's top performers such as singer/harpist Deirdre O'Callaghan and comedian Noel Ginty, this is a two-hour program of music, song, dance, and innocent wit. The evening starts at 7 P.M., with a traditional dinner of Irish potato soup, salmon steak, colcannon, and Irish Mist souffle. At 8 P.M. the show begins and lasts for two hours. Dinner and cabaret cost approximately $33; show and two drinks alone are $18. Scheduled May to October, except Sundays.

JURY'S IRISH CABARET
Jurys Hotel, Pembroke Road. Tel. (01) 605000. Now more than 25 years old, this is the longest-running show in Ireland, enjoyed by more than two million people. Stars include the international comedian Hal Roach and suave singer Tony Kenny. The five-course dinner commences at 7:30 P.M., with a choice of dishes including corned beef and cabbage, seafood, and steak. The two-and-a-half hour cabaret begins at 8:15 P.M. and blends Irish singing, comedy, step-dancing, and harp music. The price for dinner and show is approximately $36; two drinks and show only, $19. Runs from May to October, except Mondays.

Discos/Nightclubs

Although Dublin is not known as an oasis for night owls, there are a number of clubs featuring disco-type music that come to life after 11 P.M. Usually licensed to sell wine only, most of these night spots are open at least five days a week and often charge an entrance fee, of approximately $10 which includes a light supper or buffet.

Two of the city's most popular clubs are:

ANNABEL'S
Burlington Hotel, Upper Leeson Street. Tel. (01) 605222. A special entrance at the back of the hotel leads to this club which is the most long-standing and reliable spot in town. Presided over by personable host Aidan Doyle, it is also one of the few with a full bar. Open Tuesday through Saturday.

CLUB NASSAU
Nassau Street. Tel. (01) 605244. Located in the center of town, opposite Trinity College, this club is open Wednesday through Sunday, and has a full bar license.

Most of the city's other nightclubs are located in a row along both sides of Lower Leeson Street, just south of St. Stephen's Green. The names and themes of these clubs tend to change periodically, so it is best to inspect a few for yourself, or to inquire at your hotel. None would be comparable to what you might be used to in major cities like New York or San Francisco. As a guideline, here are a few of the current favorites, in alphabetical order:

BOJANGLES, 26 Lower Leeson Street. Tel. (01) 789428.

BUCKS, 67 Lower Leeson Street. Tel. (01) 761755.

CLUB TROPICANA, 68 Lower Leeson Street. Tel. (01) 616154.

FANNY HILLS, 70 Lower Leeson Street. Tel. (01) 614943.

SAMANTHA'S, 33 Lower Leeson Street. Tel. (01) 765252.

STRINGS, 24 Lower Leeson Street. Tel. (01) 613664.

STYX, 65 Lower Leeson Street. Tel. (01) 682896.

SUESEY STREET, 25 Lower Leeson Street. Tel. (01) 604928.

For other entertainment suggestions, see also the Abbey Tavern in the Dublin Suburbs (North) "Restaurants" listings; and Culturlann na hEireann in the Dublin Suburbs (South) "Entertainment" section.

Shopping

Clothing and Knitwear

CLEO
18 Kildare Street. Tel. (01) 761421. For more than 50 years, the Joyce family has been creating designer clothing in a rainbow of vibrant tweed colors. Elegant ponchos, capes, peasant skirts, coat-sweaters, decorative crios belts, and brimmed hats, are just a few of the unique high fashion items which bear the Cleo label.

KEVIN AND HOWLIN
31 Nassau Street. Tel. (01) 7770257. Men's tailoring has been an art here, for over five decades, with tweed suits and jackets custom-made for all sizes. There is also a wide selection of men's ready-to-wear tweed jackets, overcoats, "Gatsby" caps, and hats, as well as something relatively new for this shop—jackets for women.

IRISH COTTAGE INDUSTRIES
44 Dawson Street. Tel. (01) 713039. A Dublin tradition for over 60 years. The best of woolens and crafts are on sale here—from Aran knitwear to colorful Donegal tweed jackets (for men and women), skirt lengths, ties, caps, and hats, plus mohair scarves, shawls, and berets.

MONAGHAN'S
15/17 Grafton Street. Tel. (01) 770823. Sweaters for men and women—both cardigans and pull-overs—are the feature here. You'll find the best selection of colors, sizes, and styles of anywhere in Ireland for cashmeres, both Irish and Scottish. Other items include Aran knits, lambswool, crochet, and Shetland wool products.

SHEEPSKIN SHOP
20 Wicklow Street. Tel. (01) 719585. As its name indicates, this is the place for sheepskin jackets, hats, and moccasins, as well as suede coats and lambskin wear.

DUBLIN WOOLLEN CO. LTD.
41 Lower Ormond Quay. Tel. (01) 770301. Since 1888, this Roche family enterprise has been a leading source of Aran handknit sweaters, vests, hats, jackets, and scarves. Other goods include cashmere and lambswool sweaters, kilts, ponchos, and tweeds. Situated on the north side of the River Liffey, it is next to the city's famous Ha'penny Bridge.

TARA MILL SHOP
North Wall Quay. Tel. (01) 787279. Opened in the summer of 1986, this former warehouse along the north side of the River Liffey is a major source of fine Irish and Scottish woolens, tartans, plaids, mohair, and cashmere. You'll also find Irish designer fashions at reduced rates.

There is ample parking and a garden-theme restaurant/snackery on the premises. Open seven days a week, year-round.

Crafts

FERGUS O'FARRELL
62 Dawson Street. Tel. (01) 770862. Ireland's design work from the 5th to 15th centuries has been the inspiration for much of the craft work at this unique shop. These conversation-piece souvenirs range from hand-carved fish boards to beaten copper wall hangings, metallic jewelry, brass door knockers, carved wood sculptures, and miniature wooly Irish sheep.

KILKENNY DESIGN SHOP
Nassau Street. Tel. (01) 777066. A major outlet for the national design workshops of Kilkenny, this modern multi-level shop is a showplace for original Irish designs and quality products including pottery, glass, candles, woolens, pipes, knitwear, jewelry, books, and prints. There is also a first-rate cafe on the premises, ideal for coffee and pastries or a light lunch.

WEST WICKLOW CRAFTS
Duke Lane. Tel. (01) 776488. Leprechauns (of the hand-crafted kind) are on sale in this shop, as well as unusual dolls, clowns, quilt items, pottery, basketry, and wood carvings.

Glassware and Other Gift Items

HOUSE OF IRELAND
37/38 Nassau Street and 64/65 Dawson Street. Tel. (01) 714543. Two adjacent stores on one corner, offering the best of European and Irish products, from Waterford and Belleek to Lladro and Hummels, as well as tweeds, linens, knitwear, Celtic jewelry, mohair capes, shawls, kilts, blankets, and Molly Malone dolls. Located opposite Trinity College.

BEST OF IRISH
Harry Street, off Grafton Street. Tel. (01) 791233. Located next to the entrance of the fashionable Westbury Hotel, this shop has a wide range of Irish-made products, from handknits, linens, lace, pewter, family crests and shillelaghs, to Royal Tara china, Belleek, and Waterford Crystal. Open Monday through Saturday from 9 A.M. to 9 P.M. and on Sunday from 11 A.M. to 6 P.M.

CHINA SHOWROOMS
32/33 Lower Abbey Street. Tel. (01) 786211. Established in 1939, this is not just a source of fine china (like Belleek, Royal Doulton, and Rosenthal), but it also offers one of the city's finest selections of Waterford Crystal.

H. JOHNSTON

11 Wicklow Street. Tel. (01) 771249. If you are looking for an Irish blackthorn stick, otherwise known as a shillelagh, this shop has been specializing in them for more than 105 years. Just in case it rains, they are also known for durable umbrellas.

KNOBS AND KNOCKERS

19 Nassau Street. Tel. (01) 710288. If you find yourself enamoured by the polished brass door knockers on the Georgian entranceways of Fitzwilliam Street or Merrion Square, this shop makes it possible to buy your own to take home. You can also purchase brassy door knobs, decorative door handles and Victorian cupboard knobs, as well as the popular Claddagh-ring door knocker.

Books, Music, and Heraldry

EASON AND SON

40-42 Lower O'Connell Street. Tel. (01) 733811. For more than 100 years, this has been a leading source for all types of books, maps, and guides about Dublin and the rest of Ireland.

FRED HANNA

27/29 Nassau Street. Tel. (01) 771255. Located across from Trinity College, this is a good bookshop for new, used, and antiquarian volumes on all topics; there is also a special "Irish Interest" section.

HERALDIC ARTISTS

3 Nassau Street. Tel. (01) 762391. If you have Irish roots, this shop will help you locate your family crest; it also stocks flags, scrolls, and books on researching ancestry. Located across the street from Trinity College.

MULLINS OF DUBLIN

36 Upper O'Connell Street. Tel. (01) 741133. On the city's north side near the Gresham Hotel, this is the best source for heraldic crests and family name coats of arms. It also stocks a wide range of crystal, china, jewelry, and souvenirs. In addition to normal hours, it's open Sunday from 11 A.M. to 3 P.M.

WALTON'S MUSICAL INSTRUMENT GALLERIES

2/5 N. Frederick Street. Tel. (01) 747805. If you hanker for a harp or want to buy some bagpipes, this is the place. Also a good source for records, tapes, and sheet music of your favorite Irish tunes.

Enclosed Shopping and Craft Complexes

POWERSCOURT TOWN HOUSE CENTRE

Clarendon Street and South William Street. Tel. (01) 794144. As soon as you enter this restored 1774 town house, you'll probably feel like you are in Dublin's version of Ghirardelli Square or South Street Seaport. It consists of four floors and a skylit central courtyard of 65 boutiques, craftshops, art galleries, snackeries, wine bars, and restaurants. The wares include antiques, oil paintings, old prints, ceramics, graphics, leatherwork, silver and gold jewelry, clothing, perfume, hand-dipped chocolates, and farmhouse cheeses.

TOWER DESIGN CRAFT CENTRE
Pearse Street. Tel. (01) 775655. Located along the banks of the Grand Canal, this 1862 sugar refinery has been beautifully restored into a nest of craft workshops. Watch the artisans at work and then purchase a special souvenir—from art metal, hand-cut crystal, hand-painted silks, oak carvings, pewter, pottery, stained glass, tapestries, woodcarving, wooden toys, and tin whistles, to silver and gold Celtic jewelry (including rings hand-engraved with heraldic crests).

Department Stores

BROWN-THOMAS
Grafton, Duke, and Dawson Streets. Tel. (01) 776861. One of Dublin's most versatile and fashionable department stores, with a wide selection of men's and women's fashions, as well as crystal, china, and souvenirs. Specialties include a Food Hall and Wine Shop, an equestrian and saddlery boutique, and hairdressing salons for men and women.

SWITZERS
Grafton Street. Tel. (01) 710824. A glittering Waterford Crystal Palace is a major attraction at this fashionable Dublin emporium, with four floors and over 100 departments. Other wares include china, fashions, knitwear, heraldry, cashmeres, and a Man's Shop for sporting and tailored clothes.

CLERY'S
O'Connell Street. Tel. (01) 786000. This is Ireland's largest store, featuring Irish-made leather shoes as well as Aran sweaters, shawls, gloves, and tweed jackets, caps, and hats, with large stocks of crystal, china, and shillelaghs.

Designer Boutiques for One-of-a-Kind Fashions for Women:

SYBIL CONNOLLY
71 Merrion Square. Tel. (01) 767281.

PAT CROWLEY
14 Duke Street. Tel. (01) 710219.

MARY O'DONNELL
43 Dawson Street. Tel. (01) 778708.

IB JORGENSON
53 Dawson Street. Tel. (01) 718111.

THOMAS WOLFANGEL
99 Lower Baggot Street. Tel. (01) 766547.

Master Tailors for Men:

MICHAEL WALSH
60 Lower Baggot Street. Tel. (01) 760605.

JOSEPH MONAGHAN
98 St. Stephen's Green. Tel. (01) 753598.

Additional Museums and Libraries

★ **DUBLIN CIVIC MUSEUM**
58 South William Street. Tel. (01) 771642. Located in the old City Assembly House, next to Powerscourt Town House Centre, this museum focuses on the history of the Dublin area from medieval to modern times. In addition to old street signs, maps, and prints, you can see Viking artifacts, wooden watermains, coal covers, and even the head from the statue of Lord Nelson, which stood in O'Connell Street until it was blown up in 1965. Closed Monday.

★ **NATIONAL WAX MUSEUM**
Granby Row, off Parnell Square. Tel. (01) 746416. Relatively new on the Irish scene (opened in 1983), this museum presents life-size wax figures of Irish people of historical, political, literary, theatrical, and sporting fame. A push-button narration will give you the background on each character as you walk from section to section. In addition to the Irish men and women of note, there is also a wide range of international tableaux featuring everything from the Last Supper and Pope John Paul II, to world leaders such as President Reagan and Margaret Thatcher, as well as music stars like Michael Jackson. Open daily.

★★ **MARSH'S LIBRARY**
St. Patrick's Close, Upper Kevin Street. Tel. (01) 753917. In a building adjoining St. Patrick's Cathedral, this is Ireland's oldest public library, founded in 1702 by Narcisus Marsh, Archbishop of Dublin. It is a repository for over 25,000 scholarly volumes, chiefly on theology, medicine, ancient history, maps, Hebrew, Syriac, Greek, Latin, and French literature. If you are a fan of Jonathan Swift, you can see a copy of Clarendon's "History of the Great Rebellion," with Swift's pencilled notes still on the page edges. Also on view are the library's original carved bookcases and the cages into which readers were locked to prevent stealing. Open Monday afternoons, Saturday mornings, and Wednesday through Friday, from 10:30 A.M. to 12:30 P.M. and 2 P.M. to 4 P.M.

Special Interest Museums (not rated)

THE MUSEUM OF CHILDHOOD
The Palms, 20 Palmerstown Park, Rathmines. Tel. (01) 973223. Part of a large suburban house on the south side of Dublin, this museum specializes in dolls and doll houses of all nationalities, from 1730 to 1940. Among the unique items on display are doll houses which belonged to the Empress Elizabeth of Austria and Daphne du Maurier. In addition, there are some antique toys, rocking horses, and doll carriages. Open Tuesday through Sunday in July and August, 2 P.M. to 5:30 P.M., and on Sunday afternoons only in September and from November through June.

IRISH THEATRE ARCHIVE
City Hall, Dame Street. Tel. (01) 776811, ext. 113. This is an exhibit of material relating to the Irish theatre and its personalities of the last 200 years. Items on view include posters, programs, manuscripts, costumes, scrapbooks, and set designs, as well as original drawings by Michael MacLiammoir of the Gate Theatre and letters from Lady Gregory of the Abbey Theatre. Open weekdays only.

IRISH JEWISH MUSEUM
3/4 Walworth Road, off Victoria Street, South Circular Road. Tel. (01) 693873 or 534754. Housed in the former Beth Hamedrash Hagodel Synagogue, this is a museum of Irish/Jewish documents, photographs, and memorabilia, tracing the history of Jews in Ireland over the last 500 years. Open Sunday, Monday and Wednesday, from 11 A.M. to 3:30 P.M. during the spring through fall months, and on Sunday only in the winter.

Additional Historic Churches

★★ ST. AUDEON'S CHURCH
High Street. Tel. (01) 791855. Dedicated to St. Ouen of Rouen, this is Dublin's earliest surviving parish church, founded by the Normans in the 12th century. At that time, High Street was Dublin's main medieval thoroughfare. Although the building is now partly in ruins, it is still in use and open to the public daily. The tower contains a peal of six bells, three of which (cast in 1423) are thought to be the oldest in Ireland. Beside the church is St. Audeon's Arch, the only surviving gate of the old city walls, circa 1215.

★ OUR LADY OF MT. CARMEL CHURCH
Whitefriar Street. Tel. (01) 758821. One of the city's largest churches, it is built on the site of an earlier (13th century) Carmelite church, and is the only church in Dublin to return to its pre-Reformation site. This is a favorite place of pilgrimage on February 14th because the body of

St. Valentine is enshrined here, presented to the church by Pope
Gregory XVI in 1836.

Tracing Your Roots

Whether your name is Kelly or Klein, you may have some ancestral
ties with Ireland—about 40 million Americans do, and that's ten
times as many people as there are in all of Ireland today! From
medieval times, the Irish have spread their influence (and their genes)
all over the world—from Montreal to Melbourne, and from Africa to
Argentina.

If you are planning to visit Ireland to trace your roots, you'll enjoy
the greatest success if you do some planning in advance. The more
information you can gather about your family before your visit, the
easier it will be to find your ancestral home or even a distant cousin
once you arrive.

When in Ireland, you can do the research and foot-work yourself or
you can use the services of a commercial agency. One of the best is
Hibernian Research Co., Windsor House, 22 Windsor Road, Rathmines, Dublin 6, Ireland. Tel. (01) 966522. These researchers, all
trained by the Chief Herald of Ireland, have a combined total of 90
years of professional experience in working on all aspects of family
histories, no matter how complicated or compact. An average five-
hour search and full report will cost approximately $150.

Among the cases that Hibernian Research has handled are U.S.
President Ronald Reagan, Canadian Prime Minister Brian Mul-
rooney, tennis player John McEnroe, and television star Patrick
Duffy.

If you prefer to do the digging yourself, here are some of the major
sources of ancestral information:

GENEALOGICAL OFFICE AND HERALDIC MUSEUM
2 Kildare Street. Tel. (01) 608670. This is the ideal place to come for
guidance and advice on how to go about researching your own roots.
The museum includes a display on the various forms and symbols of
heraldry. The office of the Chief Herald of Ireland is also here. Open
weekdays.

THE NATIONAL LIBRARY
Kildare Street. Tel. (01) 765521. For a fund of genealogical data, the
National Library is a prime starting point. The resources include an
extensive collection of pre-1880 Catholic records of baptisms, births,
and marriages, plus other genealogical material, including trade direc-
tories, journals of historical and archaeological societies, local histories,

and most newspapers. In addition, the Library has a comprehensive indexing system which will enable you to identify the material you need to consult. Open weekdays and Saturday mornings.

THE PUBLIC RECORD OFFICE

Four Courts, Ormond Quay. Tel. (01) 733833. This office was severely damaged by a fire in the early 1920's and many valuable source documents pre-dating that event were lost. However, numerous records rich in genealogical interest are still available here. These include Griffith's Primary Valuation of Ireland, 1848-1863, which records the names of all those owning or occupying land or property in Ireland at the time; the complete national census of 1901 to 1911; tithe listings, indexes to wills, administrations, licenses, and marriage bonds. In addition, there is also an ever-expanding collection of Church of Ireland Parish Registers on microfilm and partial surviving census returns for the 19th century. Open weekdays only.

REGISTRAR GENERAL

Joyce House, 8/11 Lombard Street East. Tel. (01) 711000. Here you will find the records for non-Catholic marriages dating from 1845, and of births, deaths, and marriages from 1864 onwards. Open weekdays only

THE STATE PAPER OFFICE

Dublin Castle, Lord Edward Street. Tel. (01) 792777, ext. 2518. This is the repository of records from the former Chief Secretary's Office. Among the relevant data are rebellion reports and records relating to the period of the 1798 rebellion; crime and convict records, and details of those sentenced to transportation to Australia. Open weekdays only.

Sightseeing Tours

BUS EIREANN

59 Upper O'Connell Street. Tel. (01) 787777. A branch of Ireland's national transport company (CIE), this service operates escorted three- to four-hour sightseeing bus tours around Dublin City and its scenic suburbs, from about $8. Extended 10 to 12-hour itineraries are also available to destinations such as Kilkenny, Waterford, and the Boyne Valley. On weekends, there are trips to places as far away as Sligo, Galway, Limerick/Bunratty, Knock Shrine, and the Mountains of Mourne. These all-day excursions range from about $15 to $30. In all, Bus Eireann offers a choice of 27 different day trips from Dublin.

OLD DUBLIN WALKING TOURS

Tel. (01) 556970 or 532407. See Dublin as it used to be, by walking around one of its oldest sections called "The Liberties." Guided walks assemble and depart from historic Christ Church Cathedral, on Monday through Saturday, at 10:30 A.M. and at 2 P.M., and on Sunday at 2 P.M.

The tours last approximately two hours and cost around $5 which includes admissions to Christ Church and St. Patrick's Cathedral.

MEDIEVAL, GEORGIAN, AND MODERN DUBLIN WALKING TOURS
Tel. (01) 794291 or 794386. The main archway entrance to St. Stephen's Green is the assembly point for all of these tours. Time of departure depends on your interests: Georgian and Modern Dublin tours depart at 10:30 A.M.; the Medieval Dublin walk leaves at 3 P.M. All tours operate daily and last approximately two hours. The cost for each is around $5. In addition, by advance arrangement, you can have a tour tailored to more specific interests, such as Joyce, Kavanagh, O'Casey, Pubs, or tours conducted in other languages (French, German, Spanish, Dutch, and Scandinavian).

Sports

Golf

PORTMARNOCK GOLF CLUB
Portmarnock. Tel. (01) 323082. Located ten miles from the city center on Dublin's north side, Portmarnock sits on a spit of land between the Irish Sea and a tidal inlet. First opened in 1894, this 18-hole championship links has been the scene of leading tournaments during the years—from the Dunlop Masters (1959, 1965), Canada Cup (1960), Alcan (1970), and St. Andrews Trophy (1968), to many an "Irish Open." Of the more than two dozen golf courses in the Dublin vicinity, this is the benchmark.

In addition to the 18-hole course, there is also a nine-hole seaside layout. Both courses welcome visiting golfers, particularly on weekdays. Greens fees range from $30 during the week to $38 on weekends. Golf clubs can be hired, if reserved in advance, for $7.50 per round; caddie pull-carts cost $1.50. to arrange a game, call the club manager, Walter Bornemann.

ROYAL DUBLIN GOLF CLUB
Bull Island, Dollymount. Tel. (01) 337153. Often compared to St. Andrews in layout, this century-old 18-hole seaside links is situated on an island in Dublin Bay, three and a half miles north of the city center. Like Portmarnock, it has been rated among the top courses of the world and has also hosted several "Irish Open" tournaments.

The home base of Ireland's legendary champion, Christy O'Connor, the Royal Dublin is well known for its fine bunkers, close lies, and subtle trappings. Visitors are welcome, particularly during the week (except Wednesday). Greens fees are $27 on weekdays and $30 on weekends. Clubs can be hired for $12 per round and caddie pull-carts are free. Phone club manager John A. Lambe to reserve a starting time (direct line: 336346).

ELM PARK GOLF CLUB
Nutley Lane. Tel. (01) 693014. On the south side of Dublin this 18-hole inland course is very popular with visitors because it is located within three-and-a-half miles of the city center and close to Jurys, Berkeley Court, and Burlington Hotels. Visitors are welcome any day (except Thursday); and greens fees are $19 on weekdays and $27 on weekends. Clubs can be hired for $7.50 a round, and caddie pull-carts are free. To arrange a game, call club manager Mr. H. Montag (direct line: 693014).

Note: With over 20 other 18-hole courses and a dozen nine-hole courses, Dublin has more than enough golf courses to give you a new choice for every day of the month. For a detailed booklet listing all the courses and their particulars, contact the Irish Tourist Board before or during your visit.

Horseback Riding

THE KELLETT RIDING SCHOOL
Mespil Hall, Kill, Co. Kildare. Tel. (045) 77208. You'll find this internationally famous riding center twenty miles west of Dublin. an hour's ride averages about $10-$15. Accredited instruction is also available for riding, dressage, eventing, and showjumping to an international standard. In the winter months, hunting can also be arranged.

MALAHIDE RIDING SCHOOL
Ivy Grange, Broomfield, Malahide. Tel. (01) 450211. Located ten miles north of the city center, this riding facility is also known for its instruction, ranging from dressage and showjumping to side-saddle riding. An hour's riding averages about $10. Closed Mondays.

ASHTON EQUESTRIAN CENTRE
Ashton Manor, Castleknock. Tel (01) 307611. Located on the western side of the city near the Phoenix Park, this establishment has indoor and outdoor training facilities. An hour's ride or tuition averages $10.

Tennis

HERBERT PARK
Herbert Park Road, Ballsbridge. Tel. (01) 684364. Located near the American Embassy and the Royal Dublin Society Show Grounds, this tennis facility welcomes visitors. Just phone in advance. The fee for hourly games is usually less than $2. In addition, there are about a dozen other courts in suburban parts of the city; ask for assistance at your hotel or you can obtain a list from the Dublin tourist office.

Perks

Horse Racing

PHOENIX PARK RACECOURSE
Navan Road, Castleknock. Tel. (01) 381411. This is just one of seven racetracks in the Dublin area where you can enjoy the favorite sport of Ireland. Located on the northwestern end of the city's most famous park just three miles from downtown, this track has an old-world ambience and layout. Races occur March through October, two or three times a month, primarily on weekends and Wednesdays. Check at the tourist office or with a local newspaper. You can easily take a taxi to this track or board a bus from midtown (numbers 38, 39, and 39A all stop here).

LEOPARDSTOWN RACE COURSE
Off the Stillorgan Road (N 11), Foxrock. Tel. (01) 893607. Located six miles south of the city center, this is a modern facility with all-weather glass-enclosed spectator stands. Races are scheduled throughout the year, two or three times a month, on weekdays or weekends. You can take a taxi or bus numbered 84 or 86.

THE CURRAGH
Dublin/Limerick Road (N 7), Co. Kildare. Tel. (045) 41205. Often referred to as "the Churchill Downs of Ireland," this is the country's best know racetrack, located 30 miles west of Dublin in neighboring County Kildare. Majestically sitting on the edge of Ireland's central plain, it is the home of the Irish Derby, held each year on the last Saturday of June. Racing at the Curragh also normally occurs on at least one Saturday a month during April through October.

Polo

ALL IRELAND POLO CLUB
Phoenix Park. Tel. (01) 689711. With the Dublin Mountains as a backdrop, polo is played during the May to mid-September period on the green fields of Phoenix Park, on Dublin's west side. Matches take place on Wednesday evenings, and on Saturday and Sunday afternoons. Any of these games can be attended free of charge; for full details, inquire at the tourist office or watch the sports pages of the newspapers.

Greyhound Racing

SHELBOURNE PARK STADIUM
Bridge Town Road, Ringsend. Tel. (01) 683502. Watching these lean and swift canines is one of the leading spectator sports in the Dublin area. Racing is held here at 8 P.M., Monday, Wednesday, and Saturday,

from February to early December, and on Monday and Saturday only during the rest of the year. The stadium is located within two blocks of the Lansdowne Road station of the DART (Dublin Area Rapid Transit) system.

Getting Around the City

Public Transport

For general information about all trains, buses, and rapid transit services within Dublin and throughout Ireland, contact:

CIE—Main Office, 59 Upper O'Connell Street. Tel. (01) 731211; for telephone inquiries only: Tel. (01) 787777. Additional ticket/info office: 14 Upper O'Connell Street.

City Bus Service: Dublin's double-decker buses operate throughout the city and its suburbs, following at least 120 different routes. Most buses originate on or near O'Connell Bridge, O'Connell Street near the General Post Office, College Street, or Fleet Street. Bus stops are located every two or three blocks, with appropriate signposts.

Bus service is daily throughout the city, starting at 7 A.M. (on Sundays, at 10 a.M.), with last bus runs of the night at 11:30 P.M.

Fares are calculated on distances to be traveled; you don't need to know what your fare will be to board—just name your destination and the driver/conductor will tell you the required amount and make the necessary change for you. Minimum fare is about 70 cents.

Destinations are normally posted over the front window; if you intend to do a lot of traveling by bus, it is wise to obtain a copy of CIE's Bus and Train timetable, on sale for about 50 cents at CIE offices and most newsstands.

Destinations are sometimes posted in the Irish or Gaelic language; the chief one you should know is "An Lar." It means "Center" and, if you are outside the city center, any bus with this marking will bring you back to midtown.

Airport Buses: CIE, using its subsidiary name of "Bus Eireann," operates daily services between Dublin Airport and the city center (Busaras Station, Store Street). The schedule from the airport operates every forty minutes, from 7:20 a.M. to 11:05 P.M. To the airport from downtown, it is every 40 minutes, starting at 6:40 A.M. and finishing at 10:25 P.M. The one-way fare is approximately $4.

Out-of-Town or "Provincial" Bus Services: CIE, under the name of Bus Eireann, also operates daily bus service to all other major Irish cities and many small towns. Check with the CIE main office (listed above) for complete schedules and fares. All of these buses arrive and depart from Busarus Station, Store Street.

Trains: Irish Rail, another subsidiary of CIE, operates daily train services linking Dublin with all major Irish cities and large towns. On the principal inter-city routes, express trains are operated at an average speed of 60 m.p.h.

Long-distance trains usually have catering facilities, ranging from bar service and light refreshments to full meals; and first class and standard class seating is available on most routes. Irish Rail also operates many special trains, such as summertime day trips to scenic areas, and excursions to major races and sporting fixtures.

The three main rail passenger terminals in Dublin City are:

Heuston Station, Kingsbridge, off St. John's Road. Tel. (01) 771871; for trains to Cork, Limerick, Galway, Waterford, Killarney, Tralee, and other stations in the west, south, and southwest.

Connolly Station, Amiens Street. Tel. (01) 742941; for trains to the Wexford, Sligo, and points north including service to the Northern Ireland cities of Belfast and Derry.

Pearse Station, Westland Row, Tara Street. Tel. (01) 7776581; trains for the southeast and suburban Dublin points.

Rapid Transit: Although Dublin has no subway in the strict sense, there is a new electrified train rapid transit system. It travels mostly at ground level or on elevated tracks, to link the city center with seaside communities like Howth on the north side and Dalkey and Dun Laoghaire, to the south.

Known as DART (Dublin Area Rapid Transit), this system also connects many of the city hotels located in residential areas (like the Berkeley Court and Jurys) to the midtown shopping district and to the scenic suburbs. Service is swift and clean, operating from approximately 7 A.M. to midnight, Monday through Saturday, and from 9:30 A.M. to 11 P.M. on Sunday. Minimum fare is approximately $1.

If you are planning to be in the city for a few days, you might like to buy a "Dublin Explorer" pass, valid for unlimited travel in off-peak periods on all Dublin bus and DART services. The pass, which costs approximately $10, comes with a handy booklet listing Dublin's major buildings, parks, and places of interest, along with specific recommendations as to which bus to take or which DART Station is nearest.

Well-posted DART boarding points are located throughout the city and its suburbs. For further information, visit a centrally located station (such as Lansdowne Road or Tara Street), or phone (01) 746301.

Taxis: It is the custom in Dublin to get a taxi by going to one of several centrally located "ranks"—taxi depots where available taxis line up (or "queue"), as they wait for passengers. You'll find these taxi ranks outside all of the leading hotels, at bus and train stations, and on prime thoroughfares. You can also phone and request a taxi from a specific rank nearby, such as Upper O'Connell Street, tel. (01) 744599;

Lower O'Connell Street, tel. (01) 786150; College Green, tel. (01) 777440; St. Stephen's Green North, tel. (01) 767381; Aston's Quay, tel. (01) 778053; and Eden Quay, tel. (01) 777054.

Dublin taxis use meters to calculate fares. The minimum fare is approximately $2.75, plus 15 cents for each additional 2/15 of a mile or 1.2 minutes. There are also supplementary charges for extra passengers (60 cents); luggage (60 cents per item); "unsocial hours" (between 8 A.M. and 8 P.M. and all day on Sunday), 60 cents extra for each hiring; public holidays, 90 cents extra; and hiring at the airport, $1.20 extra to the fare. Waiting time is $7.50 per hour. These fares are valid within a ten mile radius of the city center; fares outside of this area are "by negotiation" with the driver. All rates are subject to change in 1988.

Taxis do not normally cruise looking for fares, although you certainly can hail an empty taxi if you see one driving by.

If you need a cab very early or very late, some companies also operate a 24-hour radio-call service, with very easy-to-remember phone numbers. These include Ryan's Cabs, tel. (01) 772222; Blue Cabs, tel. (01) 761111; and Irish Taxi Co-op, tel. (01) 766666. There is usually an additional charge (maximums: $1.75) for a radio-dispatched cab.

Car Rental

All major international car rental firms maintain desks at Dublin International Airport. In addition, there are many Irish-based firms represented at the airport and downtown.

Centrally located downtown car rental offices with international affiliations include:

Avis, 1 Hanover Street East. Tel. (01) 776971.

Budget/Flynn Bros., 151 Lower Drumcondra Road. Tel. (01) 379611.

Hertz, Leeson Street Bridge. Tel. (01) 602255.

Inter-Rent/Boland's, 38 Pearse Street. Tel. (01) 770704.

National/Murrays Europcar, Baggot Street Bridge. Tel. (01) 681777.

Among the Irish-based firms, the most reliable and best-equipped company is Dan Dooley Rent-a-Car, 5 Lyon House, Cathal Brugha Street. Tel. (01) 720777.

Parking

During normal business hours, parking on Dublin streets is very limited. Our best advice is to leave your car at your hotel and take public transport or walk during the time that you are exploring the downtown area.

If you must drive, you can normally find some metered parking in midtown areas such as St. Stephen's Green and Baggot Street; rates range from 30 cents to 50 cents per hour. There are also a number of of car parking lots and multi-story garages within the city, normally charging from $1 to $3 per hour; 24-hour maximum charge is $5 to $12, depending on location. Fines for parking illegally go from approximately $15 to $25.

Festivals

January-December: All of Dublin seems like a festival in 1988, as the city celebrates its 1,000th birthday (see the special feature article on Dublin's Millennium by Bernard Shane elsewhere in this book).

May 1-6: Spring Show and Industries Fair. A festive week of events ranging from horse-jumping and sheepdog trials, to fashion shows and culinary demonstrations, all with much social merriment, at the Royal Dublin Society Showgrounds in Ballsbridge.

June 2-11: Festival of Music in Great Irish Houses. A series of classical and chamber music recitals, performed by Irish and international artists in some of the Dublin area's finest 18th century mansions and public buildings.

June 16: Bloomsday. Literary fans gather at the James Joyce Tower in Sandycove, Dublin, to celebrate this day in memory of Leopold Bloom (a character in Joyce's "Ulysses"). The program includes guided walks of Joycean sights.

June 25-27: Dublin Street Carnival. This annual event promises to be the best ever in 1988, to coincide with the Millennium festivities.

June 25: The Irish Derby. Although this race takes place at the Curragh racetrack in nearby Co. Kildare (30 miles away), it is considered to be a Dubliners' celebration. Carloads and busloads of capital city folk head for this day-long fashionable event; if you're in or anywhere near Dublin, don't miss it.

August 2-7: The Dublin Horse Show. The principal sporting and social event on the Irish calendar, attracting visitors from all parts of the world to the Royal Dublin Society Showgrounds, Ballsbridge. More than 2,000 horses, the cream of Ireland's bloodstock, are entered for this show, with jumping competitions each day, dressage, and the like. Highlights include the fashionable "ladies day," formal hunt balls each evening, and the awarding of the Aga Kahn Trophy and the Nation's Cup by the President of Ireland.

September 26-October 2: Dublin Theatre Festival. Heralded as the major English-language theatrical event of its kind, this festival is a showcase for new plays by Irish authors and quality productions from abroad.

October 31: Dublin Marathon. Thousands of runners from both sides of the Atlantic and the Irish Sea participate in this popular run.

Directory

Tourist Services

Bord Failte, Baggot Street Bridge. Tel. (01) 765871. This is the world-wide headquarters of the Irish Tourist Board. Although this five-story building primarily houses administrative, creative, and marketing personnel, there is also a full-service tourist information office on the ground floor. It's a good single source for information and advice about all of Ireland.

For specifics on the Dublin area, you should visit one of the offices of Dublin Tourism, a branch of Bord Failte. These information centers are located at Dublin Airport Arrivals Hall, tel. (01) 376387/8; and at 14 Upper O'Connell Street, tel. (01) 747733. In addition, in Dublin's southern suburbs, there is an information office at St. Michael's Wharf, Dun Laoghaire. Tel. (01) 806984.

American Express, 116 Grafton Street. Tel. (01) 772874.
Thomas Cook, 118 Grafton Street. Tel. (01) 771721.

Dublin International Airport

From New York, Aer Lingus is the only carrier to offer daily scheduled service via 747 jumbo jets in and out of Dublin Airport. Limited service is also offered on some days by Delta Airlines. All other transatlantic carriers terminate at Shannon Airport.

From Britain and continental Europe, Dublin Airport is served by Aer Lingus, British Airways, Air France, Dan Air, Iberia, Lufthansa, RyanAir, Sabena, and Scandinavian Airlines.

Airport facilities include a full-service bank, open 7 A.M. to 9 P.M. in the winter, and from 7 A.M. to 11:30 P.M. in the summer. There is also a selection of car rental desks, restaurants and snack bars, a post office, women's and men's hairdressing salons, duty free shops, newsstands, a tourist information office, and a church.

The airport is located approximately six miles north of downtown Dublin. For general information, phone (01) 370191.

Flight Information and Downtown Airline Ticket Offices

Aer Lingus, Head Office, Dublin Airport. Tel. (01) 377777 (for flight information within Ireland or to the United Kingdom); or (01) 377747 (for flights to North America and Europe). Ticket desks are located at 40 Upper O'Connell Street; 42 Grafton Street; and 12 Upper George's Street, Dun Laoghaire.
Delta Airlines, 18/19 Grafton Street. Tel. (01) 794830.
Northwest Airlines, 15 Dawson Street. Tel. (01) 717766.

Pan American, 39 Pearse Street. Tel. (01) 798800.
British Airways, 112 Grafton Street. Tel. (01) 686666.
Trans World Airlines, Fitzpatrick Castle, Killiney. Tel. (01) 859900.

Sea Carriers (Services between
Ireland and Britain/Continental Europe)

B & I Line, 16 Westmoreland Street. Tel. (01) 778271; and 12 North
Wall. Tel. (01) 788266.
Sealink, 15 Westmoreland Street. Tel. (01) 808844; and Adelaide
House, Haddington Terrace, Dun Laoghaire. Tel. (01) 807777.
Irish Continental Line, 19 Aston Quay. Tel. (01) 775693.

Religious Services

Roman Catholic
St. Mary's Pro-Cathedral, Marlborough Street. Tel. (01) 745441.
St. Teresa's Carmelite Church, Clarendon Street. Tel. (01) 718466.
(Next to Westbury Hotel.)
University Church, 87 St. Stephen's Green. Tel. (01) 751618.

Protestant

Church of Ireland
St. Patrick's Cathedral, Patrick Street. Tel. (01) 754817.
Christ Church Cathedral, Lord Edward Street. Tel. (01) 778099.

Baptist
Grace Baptist Church, 28A Pearse Street (near Trinity College). Tel.
(01) 345213.

Christian Science
First Church of Christ Scientist, 21 Herbert Park. Tel. (01) 683695.

Lutheran
St. Finian's, 23 Adelaide Road. Tel. (01) 766548.

Methodist
Abbey Street Church, Lower Abbey Street. Tel. (01) 742123.

Presbyterian
Ormond Quay and Scots Church, Lower Abbey Street. Tel. (01) 332588.

Synagogues

Orthodox Synagogue
Dublin Hebrew Congregation, 37 Adelaide Road. Tel. (01) 761734.

Progressive Synagogue
The Progressive Congregation, 7 Leicester Avenue. Tel. (01) 973955.

Diplomatic and Consular Offices

U.S.A./American Embassy and American Consulate, 42 Elgin Road, Ballsbridge. Tel. (01) 688777.
Canadian Embassy, 65/68 St. Stephen's Green. Tel. (01) 781988.
British Embassy, 33 Merrion Road. Tel. (01) 695211.
Australian Embassy, Fitzwilton House, Wilton Terrace. Tel. (01) 761517.

Doctors

Irish Medical Association, 10 Fitzwilliam Place. Tel. (01) 762550.

Dentists

Irish Dental Association, 29 Kenilworth Square. Tel. (01) 978435.

Late Night Pharmacy

O'Connell Pharmacy, 310 Harold's Cross Road. Tel. (01) 973977. Open daily until 10 P.M.

Hair Stylists

Peter Mark, 74 Grafton Street. Tel. (01) 714399.
Chambers, 31 South Anne Street. Tel. (01) 719755.
Aida Grey, Westbury Hotel, off Grafton Street. Tel. (01) 791261.

DUBLIN CITY SUBURBS—South

Hotels

★★★★★ FITZPATRICK'S CASTLE
Killiney Hill Road, Killiney. Tel. (01) 851533. 94 rooms and 8 suites. If you want to live like royalty for a few days, this restored 1741 gem is Dublin's only deluxe castle hotel. A 15-minute drive from the center of the city, it is situated between the villages of Dalkey and Killiney, on nine acres of gardens and hilltop grounds, with romantic vistas of Dublin Bay.

Two generations of the Fitzpatrick family pamper guests with 20th century comforts in a regal setting which includes medieval suits of armor, Louis XIV-style furnishings, Irish antiques, original oil paintings, and specially-woven shamrock-patterned green carpet. Most of the guest rooms have four-poster or canopy beds, and many have balconies with sweeping views of Dublin and the surrounding countryside.

Facilities include a gourmet restaurant known as "Truffles," a grill room, dungeon-style pub, and a complete health center with indoor pool, gym, saunas, squash and tennis courts, and a hairdressing salon. If you prefer not to drive into the city, there is a courtesy mini-bus service to downtown and to the airport. *Expensive.*

★★★ THE COURT HOTEL
Killiney Bay Road, Killiney. Tel. (01) 851622. 32 rooms. Situated on four acres of gardens and lawns overlooking Dublin Bay, this restored multi-gabled Victorian residence is an ideal hotel if you want to enjoy a relaxing country inn atmosphere, yet be within twenty minutes of the excitement of Dublin city. You don't even need a car because there is a DART station (Dublin Area Rapid Transit) adjacent to the grounds. The Court is known for its French-Irish cuisine and friendly service; most of the guest rooms have lovely views of the bay. *Moderate.*

★★★ ROYAL MARINE
Marine Road, Dun Laoghaire. Tel. (01) 801911. 90 rooms. A tradition along the seafront, the Royal Marine sits on a hill overlooking the harbor, seven miles south of Dublin City. A favorite with British visitors, it's a good place to stay for ready access to the Holyhead/Dun Laoghaire ferry which travels across the Irish Sea to/from Wales.

Basically a Georgian building, with a wing of modern bedrooms, the Royal Marine was recently refurbished and renovated by the Ryan group. The public areas, restaurants, and lounges have been beautifully restored, with intricate plasterwork, crystal chandeliers, and antique furnishings. The grounds include a two-acre flower garden and a gazebo, yet the entrance to the hotel is just a half-block from Dun Laoghaire's main thoroughfare. *Expensive.*

Restaurants

★★★★ THE PARK
26 Main Street, Blackrock. Tel. (01) 886177. A modern decor of soft pastel tones prevails at this 50-seat restaurant in the heart of a residential village five miles south of Dublin City. Innovative and light cuisine is the keynote of the menu, with entrees such as quail, pigeon, free-range duck, and assorted fish from river, lake, and sea.

The desserts, which include creme de menthe souffle, strawberries in meringue cups, and pastries with praline cream, are light as a feather; and, if they all seem too tempting to resist, there's always a "sampler plate" with small "guilt-free" portions of every sweet on the menu. If you want to pass on your compliments to the chef, Colin O'Daly, it's easily done—he hangs up his apron at the end of each evening and moves informally from table to table to chat with his satisfied customers. Open for lunch and dinner, Tuesday through Friday, and for dinner only on Saturday. *Expensive.*

★★★★ GUINEA PIG

17 Railway Road, Dalkey. Tel. (01) 859055. Don't worry about the name of this restaurant; there is absolutely nothing experimental about the way guests are treated here. Emphasizing whatever is freshest and in season, the menu often includes a signature dish called "symphony de la mer" (a potpourri of fish and crustaceans), lobster newburg, crab au gratin, steak au poivre, roast stuffed pork, and rack of lamb. The culinary domain of chef-owner Merwyn Stewart, former Dalkey mayor, it is decorated in a stylish Irish country motif with Victorian touches. Open for dinner only. *Moderate to expensive.*

★★★★ DIGBY'S

5 Windsor Terrace, Dun Laoghaire. Tel. (01) 804600. Game entrees like teal, quail, wild duck, venison, and pigeon are often on the menu at this seafront Georgian house, with a bar on the ground floor and a batik-decorated dining room upstairs. Other dishes include seatrout with sorrel sauce, paupiettes of sole stuffed with prawns, rack of lamb, and a variety of pastas. It's one of few top notch Dublin area eateries that serves dinner on Sunday, so bear it in mind if you're in town over a weekend. Also open for lunch and dinner weekdays and dinner on Saturday; sometimes closed on Tuesday. *Expensive.*

★★★ MIRABEAU

Marine Parade, Sandycove. Tel. (01) 809873. Started over 20 years ago by flamboyant chef Sean Kinsella, the Mirabeau used to be touted as the most expensive and exclusive restaurant in Ireland, serving extravagant portions of superb food. But, in the last five years, it has changed ownership and simmered down; it is now no more pricey or histrionic than other restaurants of the same caliber, but, alas, it has lost much of the panache which made it unique.

If you never knew the old Mirabeau, however, you'll probably be quite satisfied. The intimate 40-seat setting remains the same—a lovely old townhouse along the seafront. The food is based on the French "cuisine moderne" influence, with such dishes as smoked salmon in pastry, chicken mousse with asparagus, medallions of beef in walnut sauce, and pan-fried veal kidneys. There is also a "tasting menu" of eight courses which gives you a sampling of many dishes. Open for lunch and dinner Tuesday through Friday and dinner only on Saturday. *Expensive.*

★★★ RESTAURANT NA MARA

1 Harbour Road, Dun Laoghaire. Tel. (01) 806767 or 800509. Housed in a former Victorian railway station, this elegant eatery is located next to the ferry dock overlooking Dublin Bay and the Irish Sea. As its name (which means "restaurant of the sea") implies, it has a mostly seafood menu, with such dishes as lobster thermidor, oysters mornay, sole bonne femme, salmon steak, prawns flamed in Pernod, or a

hearty fisherman's platter. For those who prefer meat, there is always prime filet of beef or steaks. Open for lunch and dinner, Tuesday through Saturday. *Moderate to expensive.*

★★★ SOUTH BANK

1 Martello Terrace, Sandycove. Tel. (01) 808788. One of the newest restaurants along the seafront, this spot has the best views of the water and of the nearby James Joyce Tower. It also has a free parking lot across the street, which is a distinct advantage, and a personable and hard-working owner, David Byrne. The eclectic menu changes often, but usually includes a variety of meat and seafood dishes, such as fresh salmon, baked hake, veal marsala, pepper steak, and lamb kidneys with bacon. You'll also find some very inventive starters like duck and spinach soup, or fresh asparagus in pastry with vermouth cream sauce. On a clear summer's evening, this place is hard to beat. Open Tuesday through Saturday for dinner only. *Moderate.*

★★★ BEAUFIELD MEWS

Woodlands Avenue, Stillorgan. Tel. (01) 880375. Located four miles south of the city (off the Stillorgan Road) in a residential neighborhood, this is one of Dublin's oldest family restaurants. The setting is a converted 18th century coach house, with white-washed walls, beamed ceilings, and an equestrian decor ranging from saddles and harnesses, to stirrups and feed bags, and an antique shop in the loft. The menu includes crab mousse, duck a l'orange, filet of black sole, and roast venison. Open for dinner only, Tuesday through Saturday. *Moderate.*

★★★ THE BRASSERIE

Monkstown Crescent, Monkstown. Tel. (01) 805174. Billed as Ireland's first brasserie, this modern skylit restaurant is about six miles south of Dublin City in a residential area just outside of Dun Laoghaire. Owner Alexis Fitzgerald studied at Cornell University and gained restaurant experience from the Catskills to Switzerland. What makes this place unique is that you can order to suit your mood and appetite, from snacks to four-course meals, throughout the day, in the main dining room or in the stylish wine bar area. The menu ranges from quiches, crepes, burgers, salads, and smoked fish, to beef stroganoff, rack of lamb, coquilles of seafood, pastas, and the sometimes hard-to-find corned beef and cabbage. Open from 10 A.M. to 11 P.M., Monday through Saturday. *Inexpensive to moderate.*

Pubs

★★★★ P. McCORMACK AND SONS

67 Lower Mounttown, Dun Laoghaire. Tel. (01) 805519. You'll find at least three different atmospheres at this trendy pub. The main section has an old world feeling, with globe lamps, stained glass windows, old

books and jugs on the shelves, and lots of nooks and alcoves for a quiet drink. For a change of pace, there is a skylit and plant-filled conservatory area where classical music fills the air, and outdoors you'll find a festive courtyard beer garden. The pub grub here is top notch, with a varied buffet table of lunchtime salads and meats.

★★★★ THE QUEEN'S
12/13 Castle Street, Dalkey. Tel. (01) 859450. On the main street of a harbor town, this historic old pub (dating back to 1787) has a decidedly nautical atmosphere. It's housed in a three-story Georgian building of great character. The pub grub ranges from steak and kidney pie and shepherd's pie to beefburgers.

★★★ HEROES
66A Upper George's Street, Dun Laoghaire. Tel. (01) 800875. A preppy atmosphere prevails at this new wine bar on the main thorough-fare. The walls are lined with old movie posters and the background music focuses on the last three decades. It's a good spot for lunch, with a fare ranging from salads and sandwiches to casseroles.

Entertainment

CULTURLANN NA hEIREANN
32 Belgrave Square, Monkstown. Tel. (01) 800295. This is the home of Irish traditional music, and an informal gathering place for those who want to enjoy the authentic music, song, dance, and language of the land. No meals are served, but there is a bar here. The program includes an old-fashioned ceili dance on Fridays, and spontaneous music on Saturday and Sunday evenings. Admission averages $2 to $6, depending on the event. If you are having dinner at the Brasserie or one of the nearby Dun Laoghaire restaurants, listening to the music here makes a nice finale to an evening.

Shopping

DUBLIN CRYSTAL GLASS COMPANY
Avondale, Carysfort Avenue, Blackrock. Tel. (01) 887932. Dublin's own distinctive hand-cut crystal business, founded in 1764 and revived in 1968. Visitors are welcome to tour the factory and see the glass-making and engraving processes. From the city center, you can take the DART or buses 6 or 6A to the factory.

DUBLIN CITY SUBURBS—North

Restaurants

★★★★ JOHNNY'S
9 James Terrace, Malahide. Tel. (01) 450314. Located north of the city

in an 1832 residence, this old-world 50-seat restaurant specializes in local seafoods, pasture-grazed lamb, and aged Irish beef, imaginatively prepared in an open kitchen by chef-owner John Oppermann. Open for dinner only, Tuesday through Saturday. Closed September to mid-October and Christmas. *Expensive.*

★★★★ KING SITRIC

East Pier, Howth. Tel. (01) 325235. Situated right on the bay ten miles north of Dublin, this long established 70-seat restaurant is housed in a 150-year-old building, once the harbor master's house. The menu features lobster, crab, and seatrout, as well as more unusual seafoods such as squid, John Dory, black sole, and red gurnard (often called sea robin). Steaks and game dishes are also first rate. Open for lunch and dinner, Monday through Saturday. *Expensive.*

Restaurant with Entertainment

★★★★ ABBEY TAVERN

Abbey Street, Howth. Tel. (01) 390307. Irish ballad music, with its blend of fiddles, pipes, tin whistles, and spoons, is on tap at this authentic old-world tavern, with open turf fireplaces, stone walls, flagged floors, and gas lights. A night at the Abbey Tavern includes a complete traditional meal of corned beef and cabbage or river salmon, plus a two-hour musical show (cost for dinner/show is approximately $30).

If you prefer a more leisurely dinner on your own, the Abbey Tavern provides another option. There is also a small gourmet restaurant upstairs, offering a top class seafood menu in romantic candlelit surroundings. You can dine at your leisure, and, if you wish, join in the ballad session later in the evening. *Expensive.*

For other dining suggestions north of Dublin, in Co. Meath, see also Navan and Slane.

The Horsey Sets of Ireland

by
Ray Brady

Here's the scene: in a huge bowl of a field, thousands of people mill about, talking, arguing, bargaining, most of them clustered around individual horses—hundreds of horses—right in the field with the people.

"Can he joomp?" cries one man.

"Joomp?" cries the other, incredulous that the question would even be asked. Quickly two men hold up a pole, horizontal, about three feet off the ground. The horse runs at the pole, and then, in the middle of all those people, over he jumps—and a deal is about to be struck at one of Ireland's most colorful events, one that also rates as the oldest horse fair in the world.

Held in the tiny farming town of Ballinasloe, the fair attracts Irish farmers, selling horses they have bred at home; tinkers, those Irish gypsies whose bargaining habits gave rise to the term "not worth a tinker's dam"; Ireland's newly rising middle class; and the Anglo-Irish gentry—all of them there to buy or sell a horse.

If the Ballinasloe fair attracts Irish by the thousands, there is good reason for it. The Irish have been carrying on a love affair with the horse for centuries, and the traveler who is fortunate enough to get a look at this side of Irish life will see a highly revealing one, a unique glimpse into a side of the Irish character that is hidden from most tourists.

The horse racing news is carried on page two of one of the leading Irish newspapers. When Arkle, the great steeplechaser retired, businessmen used him as a draw at supermarket openings to bring out the crowd. The lovely young lady you see playing the harp, wearing a medieval gown at Bunratty Castle, the big tourist aw, drmay well flash past you at the local fox hunt the next day. She'll ride as hard as any man, and if there's a fox to be caught, she of the angelic voice and face will be right in at the end.

The special bond between the Irish and their horses goes back to the dawn of time. The original Irish had small, swift ponies, and when the invading Celts came to call around 200 B.C., they rode fast, hot-blooded mounts. From that combination over the years came today's Irish horse, one that combines the intelligence and spirit of the thoroughbred horse with the calm good sense of Ireland's heavy draught horse.

The calcium in the soil, aided by copious rain and green grass, builds strong bones in the animal. As for the good sense, an

American, climbing abroad an Irish horse for the first time, is told: "Don't tell him what to do—let the horse do the thinking."

Nearly every Irish farmer has one of those horses, bred in the backyard, so let's return to Ballinasloe, as the start of a horse tour of Ireland. Watch buyer and seller dicker, often for an hour or more. See the man standing between them. He's the "tangler," a volunteer from the crowd, who will try to get both sides together. "Now, gents," he'll cry out, "there's only a hundred pounds stands between the two of yez. Split the difference—fifty pounds more to the seller—and we'll call it a day."

Sure enough, buyer and seller spit on their palms, shake hands, and a dab of mud is slapped on the horse's rump. That's the signal: the deal's done, the horse has been sold. It is a ritual that has been followed for hundreds of years. In the days of the cavalries, buyers from all over Europe came to Ireland to purchase chargers for their armies. Those two great antagonists at the battle of Waterloo, Napoleon and Wellington, both rode Irish horses into their battles.

Now that you've seen the horse fair, you'll want to see the Irish horse in action. For one phase of that, look for the nearest race-track. They are all over Ireland, and at various times of the year, "Race Week" will come to some small Irish town. Then, everybody will turn out, and that means *everybody*. I once heard a story that when "Race Week" came to one town, the Irish factories in the area simply closed up tight. The one German-owned factory stayed open—and not one worker showed up. After all, it was race week!

Don't confuse Irish racing with the highly organized, mechanistic tracks of the U.S. Like everything else about Ireland, racing is highly personal. Tracks are small, and casual. So are the crowds. A woman in a mink coat will be sitting next to a farmer in gumboots, both of them assiduously trying to figure out the winner of the next race.

There's no problem at all picking yourself a winner: at an Irish track, you can walk right up to the horses, and inspect the fellow you're thinking of wagering your Irish pounds on. If you listen carefully, you can hear the trainer, or the owner, giving the jockey his final instructions (an old saying has it that, before you bet on an Irish race, you want to know what three individuals have in mind about the outcome of the race: the owner, the jockey and the horse).

Once you've picked your mount, don't go looking for one of those tote windows at American tracks. Once again, it's highly personal. At every track, there are rows of beefy, red-faced fellows, in caps or bowlers and rough tweed suits, all holding up suitcases emblazoned with Irish names: Donohue, O'Malley, O'Rourke.

Those are bookies, "turf accountants," to use their grand Irish title. They are licensed, and if you're fortunate enough to win, you'll soon learn the reason for the suitcase. To pay off your winning bet, the turf accountant will simply reach into the suitcase, and pull out a wad of Irish pounds.

For the pageantry of the Irish horse, the place to be is in the stands of the Dublin Horse Show, which is held in early August. While the show has slipped a bit in recent years, it is still a colorful spectacle, even for those (like my golfer wife) who have no particular interest in horses. The show runs for several days, but the high spot always is the jumping for the Aga Khan cup (if you wonder why an Eastern religious leader is giving a cup in an Irish event, he has raced Irish horses for years, and has a horse farm in the country).

Once you're seated in the stands of the Royal Dublin Society's charming old world showgrounds at Ballsbridge, in Dublin, look around. That one section—with the ladies in colorful hats, the men in formal or semi-formal attire—those are the ambassadors to Ireland from the other nations of the world. Naturally, Ireland's president is sitting with them.

Their color pales, though, compared with the assemblage marching into the stadium now. They are the massed pipes and drums of the Irish army, the bagpipes skirling, the soldiers in their colorful green jackets and orange kilts marching in precision step. Behind them come the teams, usually about four of them, consisting of four riders each. Those in the red coats are from England, Germany and the U.S. That big white horse is "Abdullah," America's pride. The men in uniform are from the Irish army's jumping team.

All in all, it's a spectacle that is hard to beat.

But what if, after watching horses being sold and being ridden, you want to ride one yourself? One good place to start, especially for those with very little experience in the saddle, is to go up to County Galway, where you can do what's called "trekking."

These are trips on horseback that usually last about six days. One of the better known treks may begin at the Great Southern Hotel in the city of Galway. In a typical group, you may find yourself alongside riders from France, Germany, Switzerland, almost anywhere. "Socially?" says Jane Bradford, the assistant to Andy Rooney, the resident curmudgeon of CBS' "Sixty Minutes." "It was tops! They were all good people, and we were all able to speak English as a kind of international language." Adds Bradford: "I had never gone trekking, and I liked the idea of riding out in the country—not going round and round in a corral."

These particular tours are run by an Irishman named Willie Leahy, who has such a following in this country that, on one memorable St. Patrick's Day, he was invited to (and did) ride up Fifth Avenue on a horse. Once you've met Willie and the other riders at the Great Southern, an autobus may take you to the little town of Barna. There, riders are outfitted with horses—"Grab anyone you want," cries Willie—along with saddles and other tack. Some of the riders may be immaculately dressed in boots and black velvet riding caps. Others will be in blue jeans.

The riders than start trekking—walking, trotting, perhaps cantering if they're up to it—across the gorgeous Irish countryside. There is no way to really describe the austere beauty of Galway: cottony puffs of white cloud seem to hang so low in the sky you can almost touch them; the countryside itself is threaded with low stone walls that stand out in bold relief against the thick, green grass.

The trek moves through the countryside with sops for meals in country pubs. At nightfall, the stop may be at the Corrib Hotel, in Oughtergard, a hotel which combines old world charm with modern amenities and warm Irish hospitality.

The inns are charming," observes Jane Bradford, "not Holiday Inns. At one place, we were assigned Room Eight. I asked for a key. The owner said: 'Key? We've never had keys.'"

"And they hadn't," Bradford goes on. "We left passports, money, everything, in our rooms. Nothing was ever touched."

The consensus of the trekkers: there is probably no better way to see the Irish countryside than trekking, an easy-to-do sport that takes you into areas where a rental car could never make it.

Or, you could go foxhunting. For a small country, Ireland has an incredible number of foxhunts—at least 85 of them, perhaps more. For this, however, you should be able to ride fairly well, and be able to jump a horse. You'll also have to be properly attired: black coat and boots, yellow vest and buff britches, hunt cap and white stock.

But if you've got the skills—and the clothes—Irish foxhunting, at least to this observer, is the finest in the world. There are certain hotels—such as the Dunraven Arms in Adare, or the Cashel Palace, in Cashel—along with people like Willie Leahy, who can line up hunts for visitors. The charge is no longer cheap, however; due to the drop in the dollar, visitors might end up paying as much as $150 for the rental of a horse and the capping fee charged to visitors by all hunts.

But once you're up on an Irish horse, and the hounds are on a scent, chasing a fox, all thoughts of the cost will go flying from your mind. As you gallop along, the soft Irish air brushes past your cheek. There's the smell of peat from the nearby farmhouses. The tinny toot-toot-toot of the huntsman's horn stirs horses, hounds, riders—and, perhaps, even the fox.

If you're in Galway, you'll be jumping those stone walls. In the southern part of the country—if you're out with, say, the famed Scarteen Hunt, with its black and tan hounds—you'll jump over ditches and banks. If you're down near Cork, go out with the West Carberry, which hunts the "Irish RM country," known for that because of the books by Somerville and Ross and the TV series that was based on these works. Incidentally, don't worry if it's raining. Chances are, the hunt is going out anyway. As one Irish rider puts it: "What else would you do on a wet day—except hunt?"

And what else would you do in Ireland, except spend at least a few days looking into that centuries-old love affair with the horse? After all, if you jingle the Irish coins in your pocket, you may find one with a horse on it—a symbol of just how important the animal is to the land that is usually connected with a shamrock.

Ray Brady is Business Correspondent of CBS-TV and Radio in New York City. He has written many articles on Ireland which have appeared most recently in newspapers such as the *New York Times*.

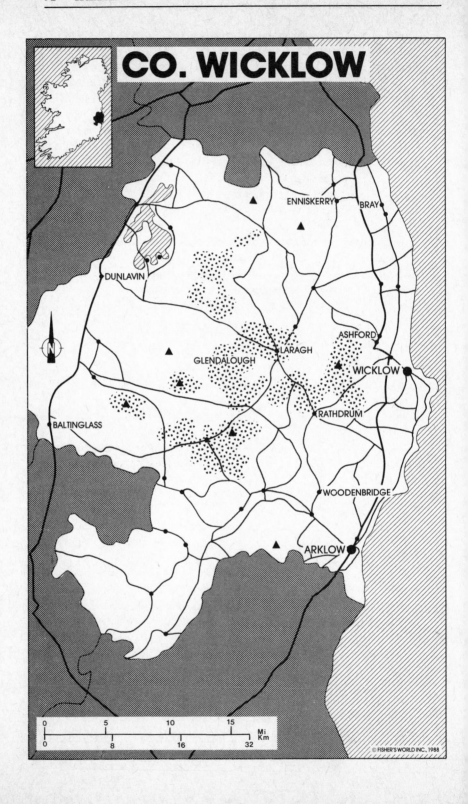

CO. WICKLOW

ENNISKERRY
BRAY
DUNLAVIN
ASHFORD
GLENDALOUGH
LARAGH
WICKLOW
BALTINGLASS
RATHDRUM
WOODENBRIDGE
ARKLOW

N

0	5	10	15	Mi
0	8	16	32	Km

© FISHER'S WORLD INC., 1988

County Wicklow

THE GARDEN OF IRELAND

Less than 15 miles from the Irish capital, County Wicklow is the playground of Dubliners and offers visitors a chance to see some of Ireland's best countryside scenery without going very far. In fact, you can easily spend a day or afternoon in Wicklow and still return to Dublin in time for dinner and the theater. If your visit to Ireland stretches over a week or two, you can savor Wicklow more fully by planning an overnight stay, perhaps at the Tinakilly House, an outstanding country inn at Rathnew (see "Inside Information"), or you can spend a leisurely day driving through Wicklow on your way to Wexford, Kilkenny, or Waterford.

County Wicklow is a refreshing change from the busy pace of Dublin. Aptly described as the "Garden of Ireland," Wicklow is a collage of tree-lined country lanes and nature trails, sloping hills and domed granite mountains, gentle glens and wooded valleys, endless lakes and rivers, and sandy seascapes. At every turn, there are craft centers, elegant estates and gardens, historic landmarks, and welcoming villages with fanciful names like Annamoe, Laragh, Ballinalea, Glencree, Woodenbridge, and even Hollywood.

There are two ways to see Wicklow, either by following the wide main road (N 11) which runs parallel to the Irish Sea coast, or by turning inland and traversing the scenic and twisting roads over wooded mountains. If you are in a hurry or happen to be a beach-lover, then take the main road, and turn off, as time allows, to explore such resorts as Bray, Greystones, Wicklow, Arklow, and Brittas Bay.

If you have more time and want to see the best of Wicklow, then head for Enniskerry and follow the interior roads all the way down to Avoca, where you can rejoin the main road for Wexford.

Either way, as you head south from Dublin into the Wicklow countryside, you'll be greeted by changing views of the Great Sugar Loaf Mountain (1,654 feet) as it gently slopes to meet the Irish Sea.

If you select the coastal route, you'll encounter a particularly noteworthy attraction just south of the seaside resort of Bray, the Kilruddery House and Gardens, onetime seat of the Earl of Meath. The gardens comprise the only surviving 17th-century layout in Ireland, featuring beech hedge "angles," twin canals, a sylvan theater, and a maze of ponds and fountains, with a variety of interesting shrubs. The house, which dates mainly from 1820, features a statue gallery which was built along the lines of the Crystal Palace in London.

About 13 miles south, at Ashford, you will come to another prized garden setting. At Mount Usher, set out along the banks of the River ★★ Vartry, you'll see over 4,000 different species of trees, shrubs, and plants collected from many parts of the world, including many of the sub-tropical variety.

From Ashford, you'll find the rest of the coastal road (N 11) to be pretty straightforward, so we'll now concentrate on the sights of the inner route, which basically starts at Enniskerry. This pretty little village is set in a wooded hollow among the hills, just 12 miles outside of Dublin City. Once you reach Enniskerry, follow the signs for the Powerscourt Demesne, one mile further south.

Nestled beside the River Dargle, this is a 14,000-acre estate which★★★ has been open to the public for over 50 years. It is a magnificent example of an aristocratic garden with Italian and Japanese themes, plus ornamental lakes, splendid statuary, decorative iron work, and a park with herds of deer. Nearby is a waterfall, the highest in Ireland, which tumbles downward from a 400-foot-high cliff. If you visited here fifteen years ago or more, you might remember the splendid 18th-century manor house, tragically gutted by a fire in 1974. The gardens are open in the fall through spring months, and the waterfall is accessible year-round.

After Powerscourt, the road winds through a scenic pass known as The Glen of the Downs through some splendid mountain scenery softened by two much-photographed lakes, Lough Luggala (also called Lough Tay) and Lough Dan. One of the highlights of this area is the 17th-century village of Roundwood, situated deep in the mountains beside the River Vartry. At about 710 feet above sea level, it is said to be the highest village in Ireland.

Continue southward on this winding mountain road for nine miles and you will arrive at one of Ireland's most historic sites, Glendalough. Derived from the Irish or Gaelic phrase, "Gleann Da Locha" meaning

★★ "The Glen of the Two Lakes," this secluded, shady setting was chosen for a monastery in the 6th century by St. Kevin. Over the centuries, it became a leading center of learning, with thousands of students enrolling from Ireland, Britain, and all over Europe. In the 12th century, St. Lawrence O'Toole was among the many abbots to follow Kevin and spread the influence of Glendalough. But, like so many early Irish religious sites, the glories of Glendalough came to an end by the 15th century, thanks to the plundering by the Danes and frequent invasions by the Anglo-Normans.

Today you can stroll from the upper to the lower lake and quietly contemplate what it must have been like in St. Kevin's day. You'll enter through the only surviving monastery gateway in Ireland, and then are free to wander around the grounds. The ruins range from a nearly perfect round tower, 103 feet high and 52 feet around the base, to hundreds of time-worn Celtic crosses, plus a variety of churches. St. Kevin's chapel, often called "St. Kevin's Kitchen," is a fine specimen of an early-Irish barrel-vaulted oratory, with its own miniature round tower belfry rising from a stone roof.

The next village after Glendalough is Laragh (pronounced "Lara"), which borders on a scenic wooded valley known as the Vale of Clara—you're not alone if you begin to feel a bit poetic by this point. For a change of pace, look to the west for expansive views of Lugnaquilla Mountain (3,039 feet, the third highest mountain in Ireland and the tallest outside of County Kerry).

★ At Rathdrum, you will find Avondale Forest Park, the former home of Charles Stewart Parnell, one of Ireland's great political leaders. The house, built in 1777, is filled with Parnell memorabilia and furnishings, but the center of attraction is the surrounding 532-acre estate, which has been developed into a training school for the Irish Forest and Wildlife Service. Visitors can enjoy flowers, shrubs, trees and sign-posted nature trails along the Avondale River.

★★ The final site on this scenic run is the Vale of Avoca, immortalized in the writings of Ireland's 19th-century poet, Thomas Moore. Here you will see the famous "Meeting of the Waters," the spot where the Avonmore and Avonbeg rivers join to form the Avoca River, about three miles north of Avoca village. Although it is basically a peaceful riverbank, there are a few tourist-oriented attractions here, including "Tom Moore's Tree," under which the poet is supposed to have sat looking for inspiration. It's a sorry sight now, however, as it has been picked almost bare by souvenir hunters. There is also an adjacent pub with Moore memorabilia on display (See "Inside Information"). One of the most worthwhile diversions in this area is the nearby craft center operated by the Avoca Handweavers (see "Inside Information").

After Avoca, you can re-join the main (N 11) road and continue on in the County Wexford direction, or return to Dublin, via the coast.

There is one detour you may wish to make, however, if you have ever wondered about the origin of the blackthorn walking stick known commonly as a "shillelagh" (pronounced "shi-lay-lee"). If you travel about 15 miles southwest of Avoca, you will come to the village of Shillelagh, where these sticks got their start. Local legend says that the bushes of the Shillelagh Woods were cut down in the 13th century for use as weapons in a local battle. At the time, it seemed appropriate to call these sturdy cudgels "Shillelagh sticks," and eventually just the word "shillelagh" remained. In more recent times, they have come to be symbols of authority and have been used for hunting and games; not least, they make a great souvenir. Incidentally, the trees from this part of Co. Wicklow were not all made into sticks—the oak roofing in St. Patrick's Cathedral in Dublin is also made of lumber from the Shillelagh Woods.

AVOCA, Co. Wicklow

Shopping

AVOCA HANDWEAVERS

Tel. (0402) 5105. This cluster of stone buildings dates back to 1723, and is the oldest handweaving company in Ireland. With dominant mauve, aqua, teal, and heather tones, Avoca tweeds are a reflection of the landscape and the surrounding countryside. Tradition is naturally a "tour de force" here, and visitors are welcome to view all stages of wool preparation and weaving. Although about 75% of these colorful tweeds are earmarked for export, the mill shop is well stocked with travel rugs, blankets, bedspreads, cushion covers, stoles, suits, coats, ponchos, and hats.

It's open daily, year-round; located 40 miles south of Dublin, just west of the main road (N 11). If you can't get to this original Avoca landmark, you can also buy the tweeds at Avoca Shop branches at Kilmacanogue, Co. Wicklow, 14 miles south of Dublin; Bunratty, Co. Clare, and Letterfrack, Co. Galway, as well as at other quality craft stores throughout Ireland.

Pub

★★★ THE MEETINGS

The Vale of Avoca. Tel. (0402) 5226 or 5291. This pub, idyllically located where the Avonmore and Avonberg Rivers meet to form the Avoca River, stands on a site associated with Ireland's famous poet, Thomas Moore. The pub reflects the Moore influence, with an 1889 copy of his book of poems on display, including the lines that made this area famous: "There is not in the wide world a valley so sweet; as that vale in whose bosom the bright waters meet. . . ."

RATHNEW, Co. Wicklow

Hotels

★★★★ **TINAKILLY HOUSE**
Off the Dublin/Wexford Road, on R 750. Tel. (0404) 69274. 20
rooms. Dating from the 1870's, this was the home of Capt. Robert
Charles Halpin, commander of the "Great Eastern," who laid the first
successful cable connecting Europe with America. With a sweeping
central staircase said to be the twin of the one built on the ship,
Tinakilly is full of seafaring memorabilia and paintings, heirloom
silver, and antique Victorian furnishings.

Completely refurbished as a hotel by the Power family in 1983, it is
adjacent to the Broadlough Bird Sanctuary and surrounded by views
of the Irish Sea, tennis courts, and seven-acre garden of beech,
evergreen, eucalyptus, palm, and American redwood trees. The restaurant, known for fresh fish and local game, blends country house
cooking with a nouvelle cuisine influence. It's close enough to visit
Dublin City (25 miles), but is still an oasis of Co. Wicklow country
life. Open February through mid-December. *Moderate.*

ROUNDWOOD, Co. Wicklow

Pub

★★★ **THE ROUNDWOOD INN**
Glendalough Road. Tel. (01) 818107. If you are exploring the mountain
roads of County Wicklow, it's good to know about this 17th century
inn, located in a village that is said to be the highest in Ireland (over
700 feet). With a typically rustic atmosphere and open fireplaces in
every room, it is known for its good pub grub, from homemade soups
to hearty stews.

CO. WEXFORD

To Dublin

COOLGREANY

INCH

CRAANFORD

GOREY

To Carlow

BUNCLODY

CLOHARNON

COURTOWN

CAMOLIN

BALLYCANEW

STRABART

KILLENAGH

FERNS

BALLYGARRET

KILNAMENAGH

FORD

KILLANN

MILEHOUSE

ENNISCORTHY

KILMUCKRIDGE

RATHNURE

BALLAGHKEEN

CASTLEELLIS

CLONROCHE

BLACKWATER

BALLYWILLIAM

To Kilkenney

PALACE

CURRACLOE

NEW ROSS

ADAMSTOWN

KILLURIN

CASTLEBRIDGE

To Waterford
and Tramore

BALLYNABOLA

WEXFORD

Rosslare Pt.

NEWBAWN

TAGHMON

BALLYCULLANL

ROSSLARE

Dunbrody Abbey

KILLINICK

WELLINGTON BRIDGE

KILRANE

DUNCANNON

CARRICK

BROADWAY

BRIDGETOWN

BANNOW

KILMORE

Waterford
Harbour

FETHARD

TEMPLETOWN

KILMORE QUAY

St. George's Channel

CHURCH TOWN

Saltee Is.

Hook Head

N

0   2   4   6   8   10   12 Mi

© FISHER'S WORLD INC., 1988

The Southeast

COUNTIES WEXFORD, WATERFORD, AND KILKENNY

Wexford, Waterford, and Kilkenny are often referred to as Ireland's "sunny southeast" because these counties usually enjoy more hours of sunshine than the rest of the country. No matter what the weather, however, they also provide a varied touring experience—from the world-famous Waterford Crystal Factory, to the Viking streets of Wexford and the medieval buildings of Kilkenny. Whether you are departing Dublin and heading south or heading for Dublin from Cork/Kerry, this southeastern corner of the country is a convenient and congenial place to stop for a few hours or overnight.

COUNTY WEXFORD

★★★★★ When it comes to scenery, Wexford is one of Ireland's most versatile counties. It is rich in fertile farm and pasture lands, yet rimmed by the Irish Sea and the Celtic Sea. On the north, Wexford is bounded by the hills of County Wicklow and on the west by the River Barrow and the Blackstairs Mountains. All the best elements of the Irish countryside are tied up in one neat little package in County Wexford, yet it is often missed by those dashing between Dublin and Waterford, or others who bypass the entire southeast coast in their rush to get from Dublin to Cork or vice versa. Hopefully, you'll have enough time to discover Wexford.

Wexford is a hotbed of history. The county's most shining hours occurred in 1798 when Wexford men rallied to lead a full-scale rebellion to protest the oppressive penal laws of the 18th century and the cruel treatment of the local people by English landlords. Led by two priests, Fr. John Murphy of Boolavogue and Fr. Michael Murphy of Ballycanew, the insurgents were basically poorly trained and ill-equipped farmers who came with their enthusiasm and their pikes in hand. Eventually called "the pikemen," these brave rebels too Enniscorthy and Wexford town and defeated several detachments of the militia sent to disperse them. After securing control of most of the county, they tried to drive west and north, but were halted at New Ross and Arklow.

Ultimately the militia columns converged on Vinegar Hill, where the pikemen had pitched their main camp, and after a fiercely fough battle, the insurgents were crushed and their leaders captured and executed. But their glory lives on, as evidenced by memorials and statues throughout the county, and by haunting ballads which tell the tales of the heroic rebellion of 1798.

If driving to Wexford from Dublin on the main road (N 11), as soon as you cross the border into Wexford and the lovely town of Gorey, you will be approaching Enniscorthy, the focal point of the 1798 events. Today it is a quiet and peaceful little town, picturesquely set on both sides of the River Slaney. The main attraction is Enniscorthy Castle, a square-towered keep dating back to 1586 and once owned briefly by the poet Edmund Spenser. Remarkably well preserved and restored, it currently serves as a folk museum for the area. At the eastern end of town is Vinegar Hill (390 feet). where the Wexford men of 1798 made their last stand. Now it is primarily a scenic viewing point, offering panoramic vistas of Wexford.

Fifteen miles south of Enniscorthy is Wexford, the chief town of the county (population: 15,000). Situated at the point where the River Slaney enters Wexford Harbor, this is an ancient town of narrow and winding streets. You can literally stand on the sidewalk and shake hands with a friend on the opposite side on many of Wexford's side streets and laneways.

The first reference to Wexford in history goes back to the second century, when one of Ptolemy's maps marked the site as a place called "Menapia," after a Belgic tribe who are believed to have settled here in pre-historic times. The Irish called the area "Loch Garman," but that name is so old that its origin was disputed even in early-Christian times. The modern English name of Wexford evolved from "Waesfjord" which is what the Viking sea-rovers called it when they settled here in the 9th century. It literally means "the harbor of the mud flats." Like the rest of Ireland, Wexford was under Norman control by the 12th century, and in 1649 Oliver Cromwell captured it and massacred most of the inhabitants.

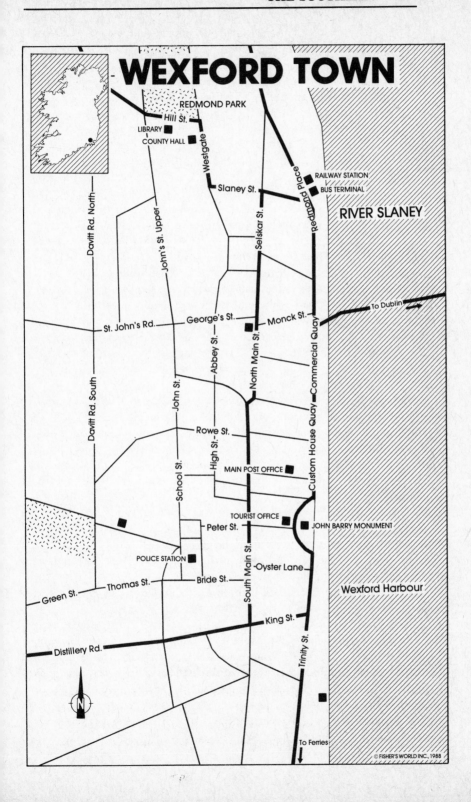

WEXFORD TOWN

REDMOND PARK

Hill St.

LIBRARY
COUNTY HALL

Westgate

Slaney St.

Redmond Place

RAILWAY STATION

BUS TERMINAL

RIVER SLANEY

Davitt Rd. North

John's St. Upper

Selskar St.

To Dublin

St. John's Rd.

George's St.

Monck St.

Abbey St.

North Main St.

Custom House Quay

Commercial Quay

Davitt Rd. South

John St.

Rowe St.

High St.

School St.

MAIN POST OFFICE

TOURIST OFFICE

Peter St.

POLICE STATION

Bride St.

South Main St.

Oyster Lane

JOHN BARRY MONUMENT

Wexford Harbour

Green St.

Thomas St.

King St.

Distillery Rd.

Trinity St.

N

To Ferries

© FISHER'S WORLD INC., 1988

Some remnants of Viking days still remain, including Westgate Tower, part of the original town walls. Nearby is the ruin of a 13th/14th century church, known as "Selskar Abbey," and now incor-★ porated into a Church of Ireland (protestant) edifice. The first Anglo-Irish treaty was signed at St. Selskar's in 1169, and it is said that Henry II spent the Lent of 1172 here doing penance for having Thomas a Becket beheaded. In the center of town is a market square called the Bull Ring. Once used by Norman nobles as a site for their sport of bull-baiting, today it is the setting for a memorial to the Irish pikemen of 1798.

Among the many 19th-century churches of Wexford are twin Gothic structures, the Church of the Assumption on Bride Street, and the Church of the Immaculate Conception of Rowe Street, both built 1851-58 to the designs of the same architect, Robert Pierce, a pupil of Augustus Pugin. Their spires are an identical 230 feet high.

On Crescent Quay is a modern statue of Commodore John Barry, born at Ballysampson, Tacumshane, ten miles southeast of Wexford town. He left Wexford while still in his teens and eventually volunteered in the cause of the American Revolution. One of the U.S. Navy's first commissioned officers, he became the captain of the "Lexington." In 1797 George Washington appointed him Commander-in-Chief of the U.S. Navy, a position which eventually earned him the title of "Father of the American Navy."

In many ways, the Barry statue has become a landmark for Wexford. It is conveniently located right on the water along the quays, with ample public parking nearby. Unless you leave your car at your hotel, it is wise to park here and walk around the rest of the town, as driving down narrow "Main Street" is a slow one-way process. Pedestrians fill this ancient thoroughfare at most times of the day, as they have for centuries.

Three miles northeast of town is the Wexford Wildfowl Reserve, part of the sloblands on the northern shore of Wexford Harbor. For seven to eight months a year, a large concentration of Greenland white-fronted geese can be found in this tiny area. More than half of the entire world population of these birds, or roughly 7,000, spend the winter here. Visitor facilities include a screened approach, car park, picnic area, observation tower, and library.

★★★ One of Wexford's newest attractions, The Irish National Heritage Park (opened in June, 1987), provides the opportunity to look back on 9,000 years of Wexford's and Ireland's history. Situated two miles north of town at Ferrycarrig overlooking the River Slaney, this park contains full-scale replicas of homesteads, burial sites, and places of worship used through the centuries. Each exhibit is laid out in an appropriate environmental setting, be it a river estuary, in the woodlands, or on a mountainside. You'll see a "crannog" (an early lake dwelling), a ring fort, and a souterrain, as well as a Viking ship, round tower, dolmen, cist burial site, horizontal mill, and "fulacht fiagh" (an ★★ ancient cooking place where hot stones were used).

Farming, vital to Wexford's history, is the focus of the Irish Agricultural Museum, which is part of the Johnstown Castle Demesne, Bridgetown Road, four miles southwest of Wexford town. Located in the old estate farmyard, the museum contains exhibits relating to rural transport, planting, and the diverse activities of the rural household. There is also an extensive display on dairying, crafts, and Irish country furniture, and a specialized book/souvenir shop. Although the 19th-century Gothic-Revival castle on the grounds is not open to the public, visitors are encouraged to enjoy the ornamental gardens which include three lakes, a tower house, hothouses, and a statue walk.

Other highlights of the Wexford countryside include a string of sandy beach resorts such as Rosslare, Courtown, Curracloe, Duncannon, and Fethard-on-Sea. Rosslare, located 11 miles southeast of Wexford, is the largest, with a wide bay and a six-mile curve of beach. The Rosslare ferry port is just five miles further south.

About 15 miles southwest is Kilmore Quay, a peaceful little fishing village, which looks out onto the Saltee Islands. These islands contain Ireland's largest off-shore bird sanctuary.

Other highlights in western County Wexford include Ballyhack, a town noted for its 15th-century castle and a ferry service which connects Wexford to Waterford (see "Hard Facts"); and New Ross, a pleasant marketing town on the River Barrow.

Lastly, we come to an attraction which links Wexford strongly with the United States. It is the John F. Kennedy Park at Dunganstown, ★★★ about 20 miles west of Wexford. As its name implies, this 600-acre park is dedicated to the memory of the 35th president of the United States. It is located near a hill known as Slieve Coilte, overlooking a simple thatched cottage at Dunganstown, one mile away, the birthplace of President Kennedy's great-grandfather. Opened in 1968, the park was a joint undertaking by a group of Americans of Irish origin and the Irish government. It is laid out and landscaped to provide for leisure, education, and research, with over 4,000 species and varieties of trees and plants from five continents. Thanks to Wexford's mild climate, that number should eventually reach 6,000. Visitor facilities include a picnic area, information center, and a hilltop observation point which presents a sweeping view of County Wexford, plus neighboring Waterford, the Saltee Islands, the Comeragh Mountains, and parts of the Rivers Suir, Nore, and Barrow.

COUNTY WATERFORD

Mention "Waterford" and most people say "glass." There's no question

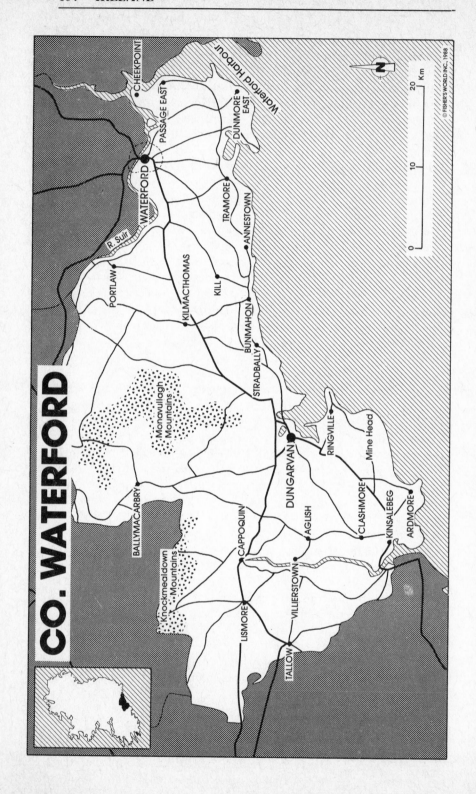

that the city's beautiful handcut crystal is known and treasured around the world. But, as you'll find out when you visit, "Waterford" is more than just the trademark of a leading industry—it is the name of a county and a city on Ireland's southeast coast, both of which have a lot to offer in their own right.

Waterford City (population: 50,000) is the main seaport of the southeast. Located 40 miles west of Wexford, Waterford has an equally proud history. Known in the Irish or Gaelic language as "Port Lairge" which means "Lairge's Landing Place," it sits on the south bank of the River Suir (pronounced "Sure"), at the point where it opens into the estuary of Waterford Harbor. The city's present name dates back to the 9th century, when it was an important Danish settlement known as "Vadrefjord."   ★★

In 1003 one of Waterford's early leaders, a Viking governor named Reginald, is said to have built the structure which still dominates the Waterford skyline today. A circular building with a conical roof and walls that are ten feet thick, Reginald's Tower, stands at the eastern end of the Quay beside the river. Over the centuries, it has been used as a fortress, prison, military stores depot, mint, air-raid shelter, exhibition center, and now is primarily a tourist attraction and photographer's delight. It is particularly striking at night, when fully floodlit.

On the nearby Mall stands Waterford's City Hall, of late 18th-   ★
century vintage. (The city's charter actually goes back as far as 1205.) This building contains a display dedicated to Waterford's local hero, Thomas Francis Meagher, born in 1823 in what is now Waterford's Granville Hotel. A leader in an 1848 Irish insurrection, he was sentenced to death, but escaped to America to earn the rank of a brigadier general in the Civil War; he eventually became acting Governor of Montana. City Hall's other treasures include an 18th-century Waterford Glass chandelier, a complete dinner service of priceless antique Waterford glasses, and a painting of Waterford City in 1736 by the Flemish master, William Van der Hagen.

Without a doubt, the number one attraction in this city is the   ★★★
Waterford Glass Company, situated on Cork Road, about two miles south of downtown. Originally started in 1783, the craft thrived, making Waterford the crystal of connoisseurs until it was forced to close in 1851, following the devastating effects of the Irish famine years. Happily, it was revived in 1947, and has since regained the lead among prized glassware. With more than 3,000 employees, Waterford is now the largest crystal factory in the world and the major industry in Waterford.

Visitors are welcome on weekdays and Saturday mornings to watch the crystal in its full process of manufacture, from the mouth-blowing and shaping of glass, to the delicate hand-cutting. A specific appointment for a guided tour is required, but that's easily arranged through

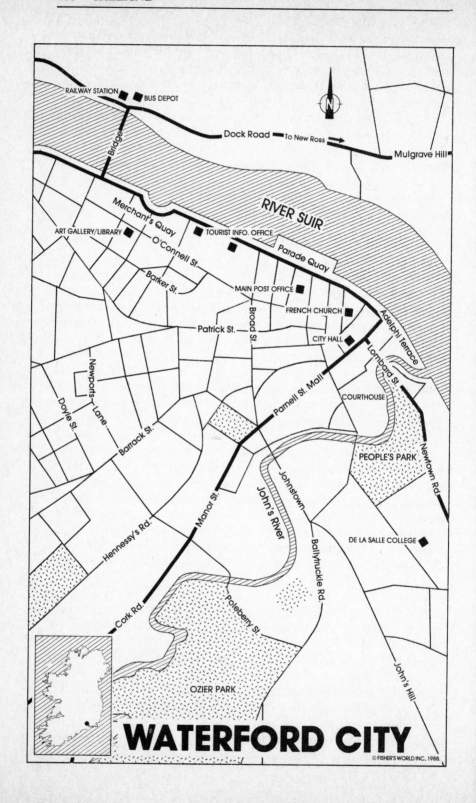

RAILWAY STATION   BUS DEPOT

Bridge

Dock Road   To New Ross   Mulgrave Hill

Merchant's Quay   RIVER SUIR

ART GALLERY/LIBRARY   TOURIST INFO. OFFICE

O'Connell St.   Parade Quay

Barker St.

MAIN POST OFFICE

Patrick St.   Broad St.   FRENCH CHURCH   Adelphi Terrace

CITY HALL   Lombard St.

Newport's Lane   Parnell St. Mall   COURTHOUSE

Doyle St.   PEOPLE'S PARK   Newtown Rd.

Barrack St.   Johnstown

Manor St.   John's River   DE LA SALLE COLLEGE

Hennessy's Rd.   Ballytruckle Rd.

Cork Rd.   Poleberry St.

OZIER PARK   John's Hill

WATERFORD CITY

© FISHER'S WORLD INC., 1988.

the tourist office, your hotel, or by contacting the factory in advance.

In addition to the tours, the factory has a new multi-level showroom with displays of all the glassware patterns, plus elaborate pieces like trophies, globes, and chandeliers. There is also a video on the complete glass-making process for those who do not care to walk through the factory or for children under 12. One point worth noting: no crystal is on sale at the factory, so don't make a special trip just to shop at the source. There are a number of good stores in the city of Waterford that specialize in selling the glassware (see "Inside Information"), but you'll find no bargains by coming here—the same prices for all Waterford items are set and maintained throughout the country. Although by no means cheap, these prices are about half of those in the U.S.

South of Waterford City is beach country. One of Ireland's premier seaside resorts, Tramore, is located just eight miles away. A favorite with Irish vacationers, Tramore has a three-mile-long sandy beach, a boardwalk, and a string of amusement arcades, ideal for families.

Other coastal highlights include Passage East, a tiny seaport from which you can catch a ferry across the harbor and cut your driving time from Waterford to Wexford in half; Dunmore East, a picturesque fishing village; Dungarvan, a major town with a fine harbor; and **★★** Ardmore, a quiet beach resort. Ardmore, which in Irish means "the great height," is also the setting for a 7th-century monastic settlement founded by St. Declan. The remains include a 97-foot-tall round tower, one of the most perfect of its kind in this part of Ireland; a 12th-century cathedral; ancient grave sites; and a holy well.

The interior of County Waterford is dotted with delightful little riverside villages such as Cappoquin and Lismore, both positioned along the salmon-rich Blackwater River. The latter is also the setting for Lismore Castle, a fairytale residence which dates back to the 12th **★★★** century. History tells us that Lismore Castle was once granted to Sir Walter Raleigh, although he never occupied it. One man who did choose to live here was Richard Boyle, whose son, Robert, was born at the castle in 1627. Robert, of course, is the celebrated chemist whose name lives on in "Boyle's Law." Currently the Irish home of the Duke of Devonshire, the castle itself is not open for tours, but can be rented in its entirety, complete with butler, maids and chef, by the week (see "Inside Information"). The splendid walled and woodland gardens are open to the public in the summer months.

COUNTY KILKENNY

County Kilkenny is the sunny southeast's inland jewel. Located west of Wexford and north of Waterford, it is primarily a farming county,

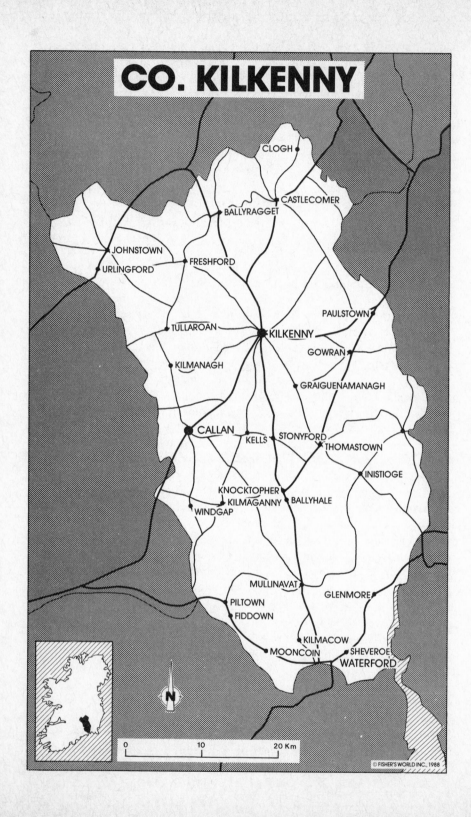

with rich river valleys, rolling pasture lands, and gentle mountains. The focus of the county is Kilkenny City (population: 11,000), fondly called "the medieval capital of Ireland." Situated along the banks of the River Nore, Kilkenny takes its name from a church founded in the 6th century by St. Canice. In the Irish language, "Cill Choinnigh" means "Canice's Church."

Like most Irish cities, Kilkenny fell into Norman hands by the 12th century, and, thanks to its central location, became a prosperous walled medieval city, serving as the venue for many parliaments during the 14th century. The town's most glorious period was from 1642 to 1648 when the Confederation of Kilkenny, which represented both the Old Irish and the Anglo-Irish Catholics, functioned as an independent Irish Parliament. In effect, Kilkenny was the short-lived capital of a united Ireland. Oliver Cromwell's army swept into the town in 1650, and the once proud capital fell.

Fortunately, much of Kilkenny's great medieval architecture has not been lost. Many of the city's most prominent buildings have been restored or preserved, and the basic town plan has not changed with the passing of the centuries. Kilkenny is still a very walkable community of narrow streets and arched laneways, many with descriptive names like Pennyfeather Lane, Horseleap Slip, Butter Slip, New Building Lane, and Pudding Lane. The main thoroughfare is High Street, which (after changing its name at mid-point to Parliament Street) runs from the grounds of Kilkenny Castle, on the southeastern corner of the city, to St. Canice Cathedral, on the northern end of town.

★★   The St. Canice's Cathedral which you see today is actually a relative newcomer, built in the 13th century, but it occupies the site of the earlier 6th century church of St. Canice. The current structure, which has benefited from much repair and restoration work in recent years, is noteworthy for many of its interior monuments dating back to 1285. The grounds include a massive round tower, 100 feet high and 46 feet in circumference and believed to be a relic of the ancient church which occupied this site, although the original conical top has been replaced by a slightly domed roof. Other highlights include the steps constructed in 1614, which lead to the cathedral, and to St. Canice's Library, containing 3,000 volumes from the 16th and 17th centuries.

★★   On the opposite end of town is Kilkenny Castle, standing beside the River Nore. First built in the 13th century, this landmark structure remained in the hands of the Butler family, the Dukes of Ormonde, from 1391 until 1967, when it was given to the Irish government to preserve as a national monument. From its sturdy corner-towers, three of which are original, to its battlements, Kilkenny Castle retains the lines of an authentic medieval fortress and duly sets the tone for the entire city. The secret to the castle's longevity is due to the fact that

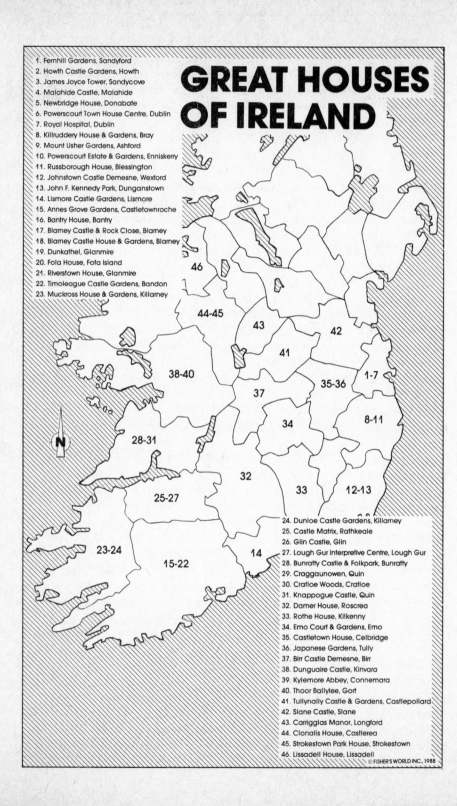

GREAT HOUSES OF IRELAND

1. Fernhill Gardens, Sandyford
2. Howth Castle Gardens, Howth
3. James Joyce Tower, Sandycove
4. Malahide Castle, Malahide
5. Newbridge House, Donabate
6. Powerscourt Town House Centre, Dublin
7. Royal Hospital, Dublin
8. Killruddery House & Gardens, Bray
9. Mount Usher Gardens, Ashford
10. Powerscourt Estate & Gardens, Enniskerry
11. Russborough House, Blessington
12. Johnstown Castle Demesne, Wexford
13. John F. Kennedy Park, Dunganstown
14. Lismore Castle Gardens, Lismore
15. Annes Grove Gardens, Castletownroche
16. Bantry House, Bantry
17. Blarney Castle & Rock Close, Blarney
18. Blarney Castle House & Gardens, Blarney
19. Dunkathel, Glanmire
20. Fota House, Fota Island
21. Riverstown House, Glanmire
22. Timoleague Castle Gardens, Bandon
23. Muckross House & Gardens, Killarney

24. Dunloe Castle Gardens, Killarney
25. Castle Matrix, Rathkeale
26. Glin Castle, Glin
27. Lough Gur Interpretive Centre, Lough Gur
28. Bunratty Castle & Folkpark, Bunratty
29. Craggaunowen, Quin
30. Cratloe Woods, Cratloe
31. Knappogue Castle, Quin
32. Damer House, Roscrea
33. Rothe House, Kilkenny
34. Emo Court & Gardens, Emo
35. Castletown House, Celbridge
36. Japanese Gardens, Tully
37. Birr Castle Demesne, Birr
38. Dunguaire Castle, Kinvara
39. Kylemore Abbey, Connemara
40. Thoor Ballylee, Gort
41. Tullynally Castle & Gardens, Castlepollard
42. Slane Castle, Slane
43. Carrigglas Manor, Longford
44. Clonalis House, Castlerea
45. Strokestown Park House, Strokestown
46. Lissadell House, Lissadell

© FISHER'S WORLD INC., 1988

parts of the structure were renewed in the 17th century and again in the 19th century. The well-preserved interior features a fine collection of Butler family portraits dating from the 14th century, and the grounds include a riverside walk and extensive gardens.

Across the street are the castle's 18th-century stables, which were restored by the Irish government in 1965. Aiming to improve the quality of Irish design, the government adapted the stables into workshops for artisans from all over Ireland, and thus the Kilkenny Design Centre was born. As the cradle of Irish industrial and craft creativity today, the design center produces merchandise ranging from fine silver jewelry to kitchenware, clothing, and pottery; a showroom/ shop is open to visitors (see "Inside Information").

Another attraction in downtown Kilkenny is the Black Abbey, a ★★ Dominican church founded in 1225. Two reasons are usually given for the origin of the abbey's name—you can choose whichever one you prefer. The first says that the abbey is called black because the Dominicans wore a black cape over their white habits, and the second blames the Black Plague which claimed eight priests' lives in 1348. The abbey's darkest days came in 1650 when it was used by Cromwell as a courthouse; by the time he left, all that remained were the walls. Reopening in 1816 for public worship, the abbey had a new nave bʏ 1866 and was fully restored in 1979.

Nearby is Rothe House, Parliament Street, built in 1594 as an ★★ Elizabethan merchant's residence, with an arcaded front, cobbled courtyards, ancient walls, and a remarkable timber ceiling. Purchased in 1961 by the Kilkenny Archeological Society, it was restored and opened to the public in 1966. The contents of the house include a museum of Kilkenny artifacts, antiquitarian books of local interest, and a costume and needlework display.

One building which really stands out on the Kilkenny streetscape is the Tholsel, with its curious clock-tower and front arcade. Otherwise known as The Town Hall or City Hall, it was erected in 1761 and served originally as the tollhouse or exchange. About 100 yards southeast, on Rose Inn Street, are the Shee Almshouses, founded in 1582 by a rich merchant to provide housing for the poor. Completely restored, this building is now home to the Kilkenny Tourist Office. It's ★★ well worth a visit, not only to pick up the latest visitor information, but also to see "Cityscope," an imaginative 20-minute presentation which blends an architectural scale model and a sound/light show to re-create the appearance and atmosphere of Kilkenny in 1640.

Nearby on St. Kieran Street is the oldest house in Kilkenny, Kyteler's Inn, once the home of Dame Alice Kyteler, a lady of great wealth who was accused of witchcraft in 1324. She escaped and forever disappeared, but her maid, Petronilla, was burned at the stake. Now restored, but still eerie, the inn is currently used as a restaurant (see "Inside Information").

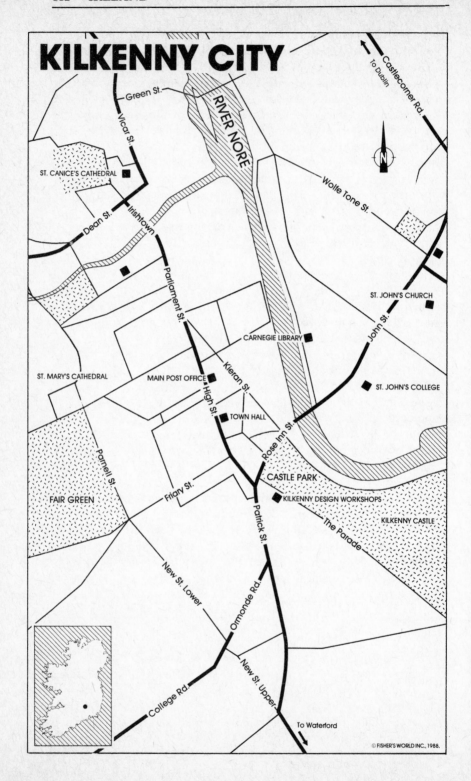

KILKENNY CITY

Green St.

Vicar St.

RIVER NORE

To Castlecomer Rd.
To Dublin

N

ST. CANICE'S CATHEDRAL

Wolfe Tone St.

Dean St.

Irishtown

Parliament St.

ST. JOHN'S CHURCH

John St.

CARNEGIE LIBRARY

ST. MARY'S CATHEDRAL

MAIN POST OFFICE

Kieran St.

High St.

ST. JOHN'S COLLEGE

TOWN HALL

Rose Inn St.

Parnell St.

Friary St.

CASTLE PARK

FAIR GREEN

KILKENNY DESIGN WORKSHOPS

KILKENNY CASTLE

The Parade

Patrick St.

New St. Lower

Ormonde Rd.

New St. Upper

College Rd.

To Waterford

© FISHER'S WORLD INC., 1988.

Before you leave Kilkenny, you should know that it is also referred to as "The Marble City." This is because fine black marble used to be quarried on the outskirts of town. Up until 1929, some of the streets also had marble pavements. In addition, Kilkenny is known for its award-winning pubs, such as Tynan's Bridge House Bar and Edward Langton's (see "Inside Information"). Be sure to try the local brew, a beer called Smithwick's (pronounced "Smith-icks"), established in 1710 by John Smithwick. The brewery occupies a site which originally belonged to a 12th-century abbey, but that's hardly surprising. Just about everything in this city has a medieval connection.

In the Kilkenny countryside are a number of interesting places to visit including Inistioge, a picture-postcard village with a tree-lined square nestled on the banks of the River Nore, about 15 miles southeast of Kilkenny City.

Another wonderful little town is Graiguenamanagh, about 20 miles ★★ to the southeast of Kilkenny City. Surrounded by vistas of Brandon Hill and the Blackstairs Mountains, this town is situated at a bend of the River Barrow and is prime salmon-fishing territory. With a name that literally means "village of the monks" in the Irish language, Graiguenamanagh is the site of 13th-century Duiske Abbey, which was suppressed in 1536, although the monks continued to occupy the site for many years. In 1774 the tower of the ruined abbey church collapsed; things took a turn for the better in 1813, however, when a large part of the building was roofed and returned to use as a Catholic church. But the abbey never aspired to its former glory until a group of local people pooled their time and talents in the 1970's to mount a major reconstruction effort. Today the abbey is completely restored and the pride and joy of Graiguenamanagh.

BALLYHACK, Co. Wexford

Restaurant

★★★★ THE NEPTUNE
Ballyhack Harbor. Tel. (051) 89284. In addition to the ruins of a 15th century castle, the main attraction of this sheltered harbor town is Pierce and Valerie McAuliffe's seafood restaurant, located in an old house on the waterfront. The interior has an airy modern motif, with paintings and pottery by Irish artisans; tables are also set up outside for sunny days. The lunch menu often includes such items as asparagus quiche, crab salad, or seafood omelets. Dinner ranges from baked turbot and filet of brill, to hot buttered lobster, Ballyhack salmon baked in cream, or the house signature dish, "hot crab Brehat" (crab

sauteed in port, and baked with mushrooms, bechamel sauce, and cheese). For meat lovers, there are T-bones and filets, as well as international favorites like Hungarian goulash. Closed Mondays and the months of January and February. You can reach this gourmet gem easily from Waterford (via the Ballyhack-Passage East car ferry) or by road from Wexford. It's worth the trip from any direction. *Moderate.*

ENNISCORTHY, Co. Wexford

Pub

★ ★ ★ ★ **ANTIQUE TAVERN**
Dublin Road (N 11). Tel. (054) 33428. On the main road between Dublin and Wexford, this Tudor-style pub makes a great refreshment stop at any time of day or night. The walls are lined with memorabilia from the Wexford area including old daggers, pikes, farming implements, lanterns, pictures, and prints. You'll also see mounted elk's heads, an antique wooden bird cage, and a glass case full of paper money from around the world.

Festival

Early July: Annual Strawberry Fair. All of Wexford turns out for this week-long open-air program of musical and cultural events revolving around the annual strawberry harvest.

FOULKSMILLS, Co. Wexford

Restaurant

★ ★ ★ **THE CELLARS RESTAURANT**
Horetown House. Tel. (051) 63706. Housed in the restored cellars of the Young family's 17th century farmhouse (which serves as a bed-and-breakfast inn), this restaurant is an attraction in its own right. The emphasis is on new Irish cuisine and the menu often includes shrimp chowder, River Slaney salmon, filets of farm trout meuniere, mignon of beef flamed in brandy, duck a l'orange, and pork chops in a rich spicy sauce. It's located about 20 miles southwest of Wexford town. Open nightly from June through August; and on Tuesday through Saturday during the rest of the year (except closed in the months of January and February). *Moderate.*

Sports

Horseback Riding

HORETOWN HOUSE HORSE AND RIDER TRAINING CENTRE
Horetown House. Tel. (051) 63633. This fully accredited facility offers indoor and outdoor horse riding throughout the year in the fertile County Wexford countryside. You can stop by and ride for an hour (about $10), but most people come to Horetown to settle in for a one- or two-week program, either at beginner's or advanced levels, with a choice of private or group instruction. If you sign up for a full riding schedule, accommodations and meals are provided in the adjacent family home which has 12 guest rooms and is surrounded by over 200 acres of farmlands and gardens. Rates average $300 to $400 per week for the room, board, and riding. In the winter months, hunting with a nearby Wexford club can also be arranged.

GOREY, Co. Wexford

Hotel

★ ★ ★ ★ **MARLFIELD HOUSE**
Courtown Road. Tel. (055) 21124. 12 rooms. Originally a dower house and then principal residence of the Earl of Courtown, this splendid Regency manor home was built around 1850. Thanks to the current owners, Ray and Mary Bowe, it has been masterfully transformed into a top notch inn with award-winning floodlit gardens, tennis court, and croquet lawn.

Although the guest rooms have every modern convenience (including fully carpeted bathrooms), they retain an old world charm with individualized decors, many with half-tester beds, four-posters, or canopies, hand-carved armoires, and one-of-a-kind antiques. The public rooms and lounge have comfortable and inviting furnishings plus gilt-edge mirrors, crystal chandeliers, and marble fireplaces. Marlfield has earned many plaudits for its cuisine, served either in the main dining area or in a fanciful skylit Victorian-style conservatory room. Located 55 miles south of Dublin, and 40 miles north of Wexford, this well-maintained inn is an ideal base for touring Ireland's southeast coast. No credit cards. *Expensive.*

ROSSLARE HARBOR, Co. Wexford

Hotel

★★★ GREAT SOUTHERN
Wexford/Rosslare Harbor Rd (N 25). Tel. (053) 33233. 96 rooms. If you are taking the ferry to/from Fishguard or LeHavre, then this two-story hotel is an ideal overnight stop. It is positioned on a cliff-top overlooking the harbor, less than a mile away from the ferry terminals.

With a bright and airy decor, this contemporary lodging has lots of wide floor-to-ceiling windows and sleek furnishings in the guest rooms and public areas. Facilities include a dining room overlooking the water, spacious lounge with evening entertainment in the summer, an indoor heated swimming pool, saunas, and tennis court. Approximately 16 miles south of Wexford town, it also makes a good base for touring the southeast coast. Open from Easter through October. *Expensive.*

WEXFORD, Co. Wexford

Hotels

★★★★ THE TALBOT
Trinity Street. Tel. (053) 22566. 103 rooms. Overlooking Wexford Harbor along the quays, this modern six-story hotel has been recently refurbished and updated. The guest rooms are outfitted with light woods and bright floral fabrics; many rooms have sea views. Among the hotel's public rooms is one of the city's best restaurants, "The Guillemot," where the menu ranges from lobster thermidor and stuffed pink trout to beef Wellington. There is also a grill room with an early Wexford theme, a lively tavern, and a leisure center with indoor heating swimming pool, gym, saunas, squash courts, and solarium; plus a large car park across the street. In the summer months, an Irish cabaret is presented on many evenings. *Moderate.*

★★★ WHITE'S
George and Main Streets. Tel. (053) 22311. 74 rooms. Dating back to 1779, this Best Western affiliate is situated right in the middle of town, with its older section facing North Main Street. Over the years, it has been expanded and updated, resulting in lots of connecting corridors and bedrooms of varying size and standards. For the most part, the public rooms reflect the aura of an old coaching inn and are a delight to browse around. Facilities include an award-winning nautical-style restaurant, "Captain White's," a coffee shop, and a lounge bar which features sing-along entertainment in the evening. There is also a large car park at the main entrance, off George Street. *Moderate.*

★★★ FERRYCARRIG

Wexford/Enniscorthy Road (N 11). Tel. (053) 22999. 40 rooms. Situated next to the Ferrycarrig Bridge about two miles north of town, this contemporary four-story hotel overlooks the River Slaney and fertile Wexford countryside. The guest rooms are furnished in bright and cheery tones, with picture windows that look out onto the river. Amenities include a full-service restaurant noted for its seafood and steaks, a lounge bar, conservatory sunroom, tennis courts, a river walk, and ample car parking. It is also adjacent to the new Wexford Heritage Park. *Moderate.*

For other Wexford area accommodations, see also Rosslare Harbor and Gorey.

Restaurants

★★★ OLD GRANARY

West Gate. Tel. (053) 23935. Located in one of Wexford's most historic sections near the old city walls, this restaurant is a rustic melange of beamed ceilings, wooden pillars, and copper kettles. The international menu ranges from Chateaubriand and duck a l'orange to chicken flamed with cream sherry, kebab of pork, or veal a la creme. Open for dinner daily. *Moderate.*

★★★ OAK TAVERN

Wexford/Enniscorthy Road (N11). Tel. (053) 22138. Dating back over 150 years, this is a combination of country pub and restaurant. It is delightfully situated two miles north of town, overlooking the River Slaney and near the Ferrycarrig Bridge. Bar lunches are served during the day, with the choices ranging from beef and vegetable hot pot to shepherd's pie. The evening menu features charcoal-grilled steaks, local salmon, river trout, and sole on-or-off the bone. Closed Monday. *Moderate.*

For nearby restaurants, see also Ballyhack and Foulksmills.

Pubs

★★★★ THE CROWN

Monck Street. Once a stagecoach inn, this tiny pub in the center of town has been in the Kelly family since 1841. Besides its historical overtones, it is well known for its museum-like collection of antique weapons. You'll see 18th century dueling pistols, pikes from the 1798 rebellion, powder horns, and blunderbusses, as well as vintage prints, military artifacts, and swords. Unlike most pubs, it may not always be open during the day, so it is best to save a visit for the evening hours.

★★★ CON MACKIN'S, THE CAPE OF GOOD HOPE

The Bull Ring, off North Main Street. Tel. (053) 22949. Long a favorite with photographers, this pub is unique for the trio of services it offers, aptly described by the sign outside the door: "Bar—Undertaker—Groceries." Hardly any visitor passes by without a second look at the windows, one displaying beer and spirit bottles, and the other featuring plastic funeral wreaths. An alehouse for centuries, "The Cape" has always been at the center of Wexford political events, and the bar walls are lined with rebel souvenirs, old weapons, and plaques.

★★★ BOHEMIAN GIRL

North Main and Monck Streets. Tel. (053) 23596. Named for an opera written by William Balfe, a one-time Wexford resident, this is a Tudor-style pub, with hanging plants on the outside wall and an interior of lantern lights, barrel-shaped tables, and matchbook covers on the ceiling. Pub lunches include fresh oysters, pates, combination sandwiches, and homemade soups.

★★★ THE WREN'S NEST

Custom House Quay. Tel. (053) 22359. A relatively new pub, it is situated along the harborfront near the John Barry Memorial. With an appropriately nautical theme, it has a bar shaped like a ship, plus a fish net ceiling and furnishings with a seagull motif. The varied pub grub includes Wexford mussel platters, house pates, soups, salads, and sandwiches.

★★★ FARMER'S KITCHEN

Rosslare Road (N 25) Tel. (053) 23295. Situated two miles south of Wexford, this is one of the few pubs in Ireland with its own squash courts and an arts/crafts gallery. The pub grub includes Wexford mussels, soups, and ploughman's platters.

Shopping

THE WEXFORD GALLERY

Cresent Quay. Tel. (053) 24400. Located in the same building as the town tourist office, this shop specializes in handmade Irish crafts including pottery by Stephen Pearce and Nicholas Mosse, paintings, knitwear, patchwork, placemats, enamels, woodwork, and herbal products. It's open daily (from noon on Sunday), year-round.

THE WOOL SHOP

39-41 South Main Street. Tel. (053) 22247. In the heart of the town's main thoroughfare, this is Wexford's best source for handknits, from caps to tams to sweaters and jackets.

Sightseeing Tours

WEXFORD WALKING TOURS

Proud of their town's ancient streets and vintage buildings, the people of Wexford spontaneously started to give tours to visitors over 20 years ago. These were local residents who worked at other jobs during the day, and volunteered informally to show the major sights to visitors during the evening hours. Eventually organized as the Old Wexford Society, this core of local folk has developed a real expertise over the years and continues to give tours on a regular basis. In the summer months, guides show up at the Talbot and White's Hotel about 7:30 P.M. and will lead a tour for whoever wishes to follow. Tours can also be arranged by request, at other times or during off-season. Just inquire at either hotel, after you check in. There is no charge, but contributions for the Old Wexford Society are gratefully accepted.

Festival

October 19-30: Wexford Festival of Opera. An annual presentation of operatic masterpieces mainly of 18th and 19th century vintage.

Directory

Wexford Tourist Office, Crescent Quay. Tel. (053) 23111.
CIE, Railway and Bus Station, Redmond Place. Tel. (053) 22522.
Sightseeing tours also leave from this depot in the summer months.

DUNGARVAN, Co. Waterford

Pub

★★★ THE SEANACHIE

Waterford/Cork Road (N 25). Tel. (058) 46285. This cozy thatched-roof pub in a farmyard setting takes its name from the Irish word meaning "storyteller." And storytelling entertainment as well as Irish music is usually on tap here, day and night. This pub is also known for its good food at lunch and dinner; choices include cheese and chutney sandwiches, seafood soups, steaks, and Irish stew. Irish coffee is a specialty here. Open April through mid-November only.

LISMORE, Co. Waterford

Castle-for-Rent

LISMORE CASTLE
Tel. (058) 54424. Dating back to 1185 when King John of England erected the first castle on this site, the multi-turreted Lismore is today the 8,000-acre Irish seat of the Duke and Duchess of Devonshire. Available for rent by the week, with full staff including butler, chef and housekeepers, it stands on a cliff overlooking the Blackwater River, with its own magnificent gardens of towering trees, clipped shrubs, a yew walk, and a rainbow of flowers, from camellias, rhododendruns, magnolias, daffodils, and azaleas to roses.

The grounds also include a nine-hole golf course, tennis court, and private salmon-fishing waters. The nine bedrooms are full of antique bedsteads, hand-carved oak armoires, dressing tables with brass fittings, marble fireplaces, and heirloom watercolors; there are six carpeted bathrooms. Previous guests have ranged from Sir Walter Raleigh to Fred Astaire, as well as a king or two. The weekly rental for parties of six to ten people is approximately $9,500, which includes the full-time staff and all meals. Contact Paul Burton, Lismore Castle, Lismore, Co. Waterford. Tel. (058) 54424.

WATERFORD, Co. Waterford

Hotels

★★★ ARDREE
Ferrybank. Tel. (051) 32111. 100 rooms. Taking its name from a Gaelic word meaning "high king," this is a modern, six-story hotel perched on a hill along the River Suir's northern banks. With such a commanding position, it's no wonder that each guest room of the Ardree enjoys a sweeping view of Waterford City that can't be matched. The dining room and lounge, which also face the river and cityscape, are decorated in a bright tweedy motif. Facilities include extensive grounds with 38 acres of well-tended gardens, ample parking area, tennis courts, and a brand new leisure center with swimming pool, saunas, and gym. *Moderate.*

★★★ GRANVILLE
Meagher Quay. Tel. (051) 55111. 55 rooms. Located along the quayside strip of Waterford's main business district, this hotel looks out onto the south side of the River Suir. Full of history, part of the Granville was originally a coaching inn, and an adjacent section was the home of Irish patriot Thomas Francis Meagher and a meeting place for Irish

freedom fighters. In 1980 it was purchased by the Cusack family who have totally restored and refurbished it. The architecture is a blend of many centuries, but the furnishings are modern and functional. The bedrooms are bedecked with bright floral fabrics and the front rooms look out onto the river. Amenities include a full-service restaurant, grill room, and a large lounge bar which is popular with a local clientele. Parking is on a first-come basis on the street. *Moderate.*

★★★ TOWER

The Mall. Tel. (051) 75801. 81 rooms. In an historic section of the city at the east end of the river, this contemporary four-story hotel is named after nearby Reginald's Tower. The bedrooms are standard but comfortable, with an eclectic mix of colors and furnishings; while the public rooms have been recently refurbished in a grand style which includes Waterford crystal chandeliers, exposed brick walls, and lots of foliage and mirrors. Amenities include a full-service restaurant, a mahogany-paneled bar, and an adjacent parking lot. *Moderate.*

Bed-and-Breakfast

★★★ BLENHEIM HOUSE

Off the Passage East Road. Tel. (051) 74115. 6 rooms. If you prefer a B & B experience, then reserve a room at this secluded home two miles south of town. Originally built in 1763 for a Quaker butter merchant family named Ridgeway, it is set on four wooded acres beside the River Suir estuary at Blenheim Heights, overlooking Waterford. Now the home of Claire and Greg Fitzmaurice, it is full of antiques and collectibles including an extensive Waterford crystal display, Belleek china, and objets d'art. The old-world charm is enhanced by Claire's helpful sightseeing suggestions and the modern comfort of private bath facilities in every guest room. No credit cards. *Bargain.*

Restaurants

★★★ JADE PALACE

3 The Mall. Tel. (051) 55611. Here you'll find two restaurants in one, both unusual for Waterford—a charcoal steak house on the ground floor, and a gourmet Chinese dining room on the upper level. The Chinese menu, which has garnered several awards, is surprisingly good for this part of the country, and is attentively served in a setting of pink linens, crystal glassware, and silver (or chopsticks, if you prefer). Dishes include king prawns, duck Cantonese, sweet-and-sour pork, steaks, and curries. Open for lunch on weekdays and dinner nightly. *Moderate.*

★★★ **GALLEY CRUISING RESTAURANT**
New Ross Quay, New Ross. Tel. (051) 21723. This is Ireland's only floating restaurant, based 15 miles northeast of the city at New Ross, Co. Wexford, but considered part of the Waterford experience. Capt. Dick Fletcher will welcome you aboard where you'll enjoy a full bar service and a meal while cruising the sylvan waters of the Rivers Suir, Nore, or Barrow. The menu is limited in choice, but the food is freshly prepared, and the views can't be equalled.

Cruises last from two to three hours, and are timed for lunch, afternoon tea, or dinner departures. Boats normally leave from New Ross, but during the summer months, trips are scheduled from both New Ross and Waterford. The Galley operates from April through September, but the hours vary, so do call ahead to make a reservation and check on specific times. No credit cards. *Moderate*.

For additional dining suggestions near Waterford City, see also Ballyhack, Co. Wexford.

Pubs

★★★★ **THE MUNSTER**
Bailey's New Street. Tel. (051) 74656. The flavor of old Waterford prevails in this 300-year-old building which also can be entered from The Mall. Often referred to as "Fitzgerald's" (the name of the family who owns it), this pub has a decor rich in etched mirrors, antique Waterford glass sconces, and dark wood walls, some of which are fashioned out of timber from the old Waterford Toll Bridge. Among the many rooms are a small oak-paneled restaurant, an original "Men's Bar," and a lively modern lounge (which often features traditional Irish music on weekends). The lunchtime fare ranges from corned beef and cabbage, or pork and apple sauce, to hot prawns in Pernod.

★★★★ **T. & H. DOOLAN**
32 George's Street. Tel. (051) 72764. Once a stagecoach stop, this 150-year-old pub in the center of town is a favorite venue for evening sessions of ballad, folk, and traditional music. It is lantern lit, with white-washed stone walls, and a collection of old farm implements, crocks, mugs, and jugs. Sandwiches and soups are served at lunchtime.

★★★ **EGAN'S**
36/37 Barronstrand Street. Tel. (051) 75619. This friendly pub is a showcase of Tudor style and decor, from its neat black and white facade to its cozy interior. A popular lunch stop, it usually has an extensive salad counter and zesty seafood platters such as smoked mackerel or curried shrimp.

★★★ **THE REGINALD**

The Mall. Tel. (051) 55611. One of the city's original walls (circa 850 A.D.) is a part of the scene at this little stone pub next to Reginald's Tower. In keeping with its Viking-inspired foundations, the Reginald is laid out in a pattern of caverns, alcoves, and arches. The cocktail list, however, is strictly geared to the 20th century, ranging from Grasshoppers and Singapore Slings to Planters Punch, Pina Colada and Tequila Sunrise. Buffet-style pub grub is available at lunchtime, and jazz is on tap on Sunday afternoons.

Shopping

JOSEPH KNOX

3/4 Barronstrand Street. Tel. (051) 75307 and 72723. For visitors to Waterford, this has long been "the place" to buy Waterford Crystal, especially since the factory does not sell to the public. This store maintains a large selection of the famous crystal, particularly in specialty items like chandeliers.

WOOLCRAFT

11 Michael Street. Tel. (051) 74082. For more than 100 years, this has been a leading source for bainin and colored Aran sweaters. It also stocks mohair and Icelandic knits, lambswool fashions, tams, and scarves.

WATERFORD CRAFT CENTRE

28 Michael Street. Tel. (051) 55733. Here you will find lots of Waterford crystal, plus another locally made product, Penrose handcut glass; also sheepskin rugs, Irish lace, ceramic jewelry, baskets, and herbal crafts.

Sightseeing Tours

WATERFORD CITY WALKING TOURS

Summerland Cottage, Morrison's Road. Tel. (051) 76198. From mid-June through mid-August, Waterford resident Margaret Cosgreve conducts walking tours of Waterford, daily at 4 P.M. All tours depart from the Tourist Office, 41 The Quay. The cost is approximately $3 per person and reservations are not necessary. At other times, tours are available by making an appointment in advance.

Perks/Sports

Polo

WHITFIELD COURT POLO SCHOOL

Waterford/Dungarvan Road (N 25). Tel. (051) 84216. Vacation in

Ireland and learn the sport of polo as a bonus. That's the theme of this establishment, Europe's only residential polo school, located eight miles west of Waterford City. The instructor is Major Hugh Dawnay, who has earned a worldwide reputation for his coaching at Palm Beach, Florida; Greenwich, Connecticut; Argentina, and Australia. Facilities include two polo grounds, wooden horses, an enclosed riding school, video equipment, 20 polo ponies, a heated swimming pool, and tennis courts. Open from May through September; advance reservations are a must. The cost, which is approximately $2,000 a week, includes accommodations and meals at a Georgian manor house on the grounds.

Getting Around

Bus Eireann operates daily bus service within Waterford and its environs. The flat fare is approximately 80 cents. Taxi ranks are located outside of Plunkett Rail Station and along Quay opposite the Granville Hotel.

Festival

September 17-October 2: Waterford Festival of Light Opera. Dozens of amateur opera companies from many countries compete for the Waterford Glass Trophy at this town's charming old Theatre Royal. The program also includes sporting and recreational activities like river cruising.

Directory

Waterford Tourist Office, 41 The Quay. Tel. (051) 75788.
CIE, Plunkett Station, at Edmund Ignatius Rice Bridge on north side of river. Tel. (051) 73401. You can arrange train and bus transportation at this depot; sightseeing tours are also operated from this point during July and August.

KILKENNY, Co. Kilkenny

Hotels

★★★★ THE NEWPARK
Castlecomer Road. Tel. (056) 22122. 70 rooms. A warm and friendly atmosphere is foremost at this lovely hotel situated about a mile north of the city center. Set on its own parklike grounds, the Newpark was opened as a small country hotel over 20 years ago by enthusiastic hotelier Bobby Kerr (formerly of Jurys in Dublin), and it has been

growing in size and gaining in reputation ever since. The latest additions include new wings of smartly decorated bedrooms and a new leisure center, including swimming pool and sun lounges, saunas, jacuzzi, gymnasium, and steam room. Other guest facilities include a first-rate restaurant, noon-to-midnight grill room, and a lounge with Irish musical entertainment, tennis courts, and ample parking. *Inexpensive to moderate.*

★★★ HOTEL KILKENNY
College Road. Tel. (056) 62000. 60 rooms. On the edge of the city in a residential neighborhood, this hotel is a combination of a gracious country house, dating back to 1830, and a modern block of rather standard bedrooms. The main house, once the private residence of Sir William Robertson, the architect who rebuilt Kilkenny Castle, is today comprised of an old world restaurant, an all-glass conservatory, and a pub with a sporting motif. The adjacent wing lacks the charm of the main building, but the bedrooms are comfortable and close to a health complex with indoor swimming pool, sauna, hot tub, sunbeds, gym, and two hard tennis courts. *Inexpensive to moderate.*

Restaurants

★★★★ LACKEN HOUSE
Dublin/Carlow Road. Tel. (056) 65611. A Georgian manor on the outskirts of Kilkenny is the culinary setting for one of Ireland's most honored chefs, Eugene McSweeney, formerly of the Berkeley Court Hotel in Dublin. Often invited to demonstrate his recipes on American TV programs, Eugene presents a new menu each evening, with such items as paupiettes of plaice with salmon stuffing; medallions of beef with blue cheese sauce; and filet of pork with apple cream sauce. Open for dinner only, Tuesday through Saturday. *Moderate.*

★★★ KYTELER'S INN
St. Kieran Street. Tel. (056) 21064. If you are in a medieval mood, it's hard to beat this stone-walled tavern in the center of town. An inn since 1324, it was once the home of Dame Alice Kyteler, a colorful character who was accused of witchcraft. The dining chambers, with a candlelit setting of caverns and arches, are bewitchingly below ground level. The menu, however, is attuned to 20th century tastes, with such dishes as beef stroganoff, giant langoustines, coquilles St. Jacques, and veal Cordon Bleu. Open for buffet lunches and full dinners, daily year-round. *Moderate.*

Pubs

★★★★★ TYNAN'S BRIDGE HOUSE

2 Horseleap Slip. Tel. (056) 21291. A classic establishment, situated next to St. John's Bridge, along the River Nore, on a street that was once used as an exercise run for horses. Proud owners Michael and Frieda Tynan cheerfully welcome all comers to their award-winning 220-year-old pub, with its horseshoe-shaped marble bar, gas lamps, shiny brass fixtures, and silver tankards. Side drawers marked "mace," "citron," and "sago," are not filled with exotic cocktail ingredients, but remain from the years when the pub also served as a grocery and pharmacy. Shelves display 17th century weighing scales, shaving mugs, and teapots; there is even a tattered copy of Chaucer's "Canterbury Tales" for rainy days. The decor is so fascinating, you might even forget to order a drink.

★★★★ EDWARD LANGTON

69 John Street. Tel. (056) 21728. A recent "Pub of the Year" winner, this well-kept establishment is a pub-enthusiast's delight—from its rich wood tones, etched mirrors, and stained glass windows, to the brass globe lamps, green velour banquettes, and a warming hand-carved limestone fireplace. For summer days, there is also a conservatory/ garden area, backed by the old city walls dating from the 14th century. Pub meals are a specialty here, with choices ranging from homemade soup with crispy crusted brown bread, to beefsteak and mushroom pies.

★★★ MARBLE CITY BAR

66 High Street. Tel. (056) 62091. One of the best shopfront facades in Ireland belongs to this pub in the middle of town. It is a showcase of carved wood, polished brass, and globe lamps, with flower boxes overhead. Needless to say, the interior is equally inviting. Even if you don't stop for a drink here, you'll certainly want to take a picture.

Shopping

KILKENNY DESIGN CENTRE

The Parade. Tel. (056) 22118. The former stables of Kilkenny Castle were adapted in 1965 into a workshop area to encourage new designs and creativity among craftspeople from all over Ireland. The adjacent shop has since become a showcase for the country's top hand-crafted products, from jewelry, glassware, and pottery, to clothing, candles, linens, books, leatherwork, and furniture. (Although many people plan a trip to Kilkenny just to visit this center, it is good to know that a branch of this "all Irish" emporium is also located in Dublin on Nassau Street.)

ROTHE CRAFTS
Parliament Street. Tel. (056) 21066. Located in historic Rothe House, this shop offers a good selection of local knitwear, handwoven tweeds, hats, candles, dolls, banners, posters, souvenirs, and Kilkenny-made crystal and pottery.

LIAM COSTIGAN
Colliers Lane, off High Street. Tel. (056) 62408. Handcrafted silver and gold jewelry are produced in this tiny shop by an alumnus of the Kilkenny Design Centre. As you browse here, you can also see Liam at work.

THE WEAVER'S CRAFT SHOP
92 High Street. Run by Peter Mulhern, a weaver formerly associated with the Kilkenny Design Centre, this second floor shop features a wide variety of tweeds and hand-woven products, using unusual materials ranging from alpaca to brush wool. Visitors are welcome to see Peter at work on his authentic double-width Donegal mill.

Sightseeing Tours

TYNAN'S WALKING TOURS
Tel. (056) 61348. Walk the streets and lanes of medieval Kilkenny, accompanied by local historian/guides Pat or Martin Tynan. Tours depart from the Tourist Office, Rose Inn Street, at 10:30 A.M., 12:15 P.M., 3 P.M., 4:30 P.M., and 7 P.M., daily except Sunday mornings. The cost is approximately $3, and no advance reservation is required.

Festival

August 20-27: Kilkenny International Arts Week. A selection of instrumental and vocal recitals, chamber music, poetry readings, and art exhibitions.

Directory

Kilkenny Tourist Office, Shee Alms House, Rose Inn Street. Tel. (056) 21755.
    CIE, McDonagh Station, John Street. Tel. (056) 22024. For buses and trains.

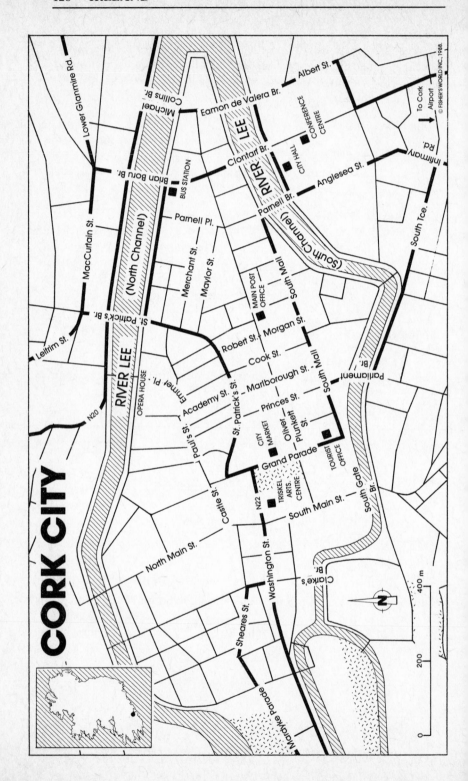

CORK CITY

County Cork

CORK CITY AND ENVIRONS, AND THE WEST CORK COAST

Dublin's Fair City may merit first place as the largest of Ireland's cities, but when it comes to ranking the counties, Cork is number one. In addition to its size, County Cork has many other claims to fame, starting with the Blarney Stone, Ireland's most popular tourist attraction. It is also the home of the transatlantic port of Cobh and the world's oldest yacht club at Crosshaven, as well as Mizen Head, the most southerly point in the whole country. And that's just for starters.

Situated between the Atlantic Ocean and the Celtic Sea, Cork shares the southwest coast of Ireland with Kerry. As neighbors, they have many things in common, such as craggy coastlines, mighty mountains, and gentle Gulf Stream breezes, but Cork is still unique. Nowhere but in Cork do you find familiar placenames like Baltimore and Long Island side-by-side with fanciful ones like Leap, Ovens, Owenahincha, Dripsey, Crookhaven, Barleycove, and Ballycotton. Cork is indeed an adventure, and what better place to start than in the hub of it all, Cork City?

CORK CITY

It has been said that Cork is the Irish version of Manhattan, and indeed it is built on an island. But that's about the extent of the similarity.

Cork sits between two channels of the River Lee, but unlike Manhattan, Cork's "midtown" area spills over onto the elongated

north and south banks of its river, with no less than 16 bridges
spanning the narrow strips of water. Many of the bridges are so short
you hardly know that you have crossed over the water at all, so Cork
seems unified and walkable.

Getting around the city, however, does mean frequent criss-crossing
from one side of the river to the other, and following a pattern of
mostly one-way streets. This makes driving a challenge, to put it
mildly, especially if you are not familiar with the layout. Our best
advice is to park the car at your hotel or at the centrally located
enclosed municipal car park (on Lavitt's Quay), and either take a
guided tour or walk around yourself to get the feel of the city.

The best place to begin is on the south bank of the river; at least
that's what St. Finbarr thought. He is credited with laying the foundation of the city by starting a church and school here in the 6th century.
At that point, the area was a marsh and St. Finbarr identified it as
"Corcaigh" or "marshy place." In time, the school flourished and a
considerable town grew up.

By the 9th century, Cork was a Danish stronghold; it fell to an
Anglo-Norman invasion in 1172. The city's first charter was granted
by King Henry II in 1185. Because of its relatively remote location and
the spunky attitude of its citizens, Cork asserted a remarkable independence from outside authority over the years, and gradually earned
itself the title of "Rebel Cork." This was carried through to the 1919-
21 Irish War of Independence, when Corkmen figured prominently in
the struggle.

★★.   Today, on the site of St. Finbarr's settlement, there is a Church of
Ireland cathedral in his name. Dominating the city skyline with three
giant spires, the current building dates back to 1880. It is early French
Gothic in style, with a highly ornamented interior and unique mosaic
work; the bells were transferred from a previous 1735 church which
had been on this site. Just west of St. Finbarr's starts the campus of
University College-Cork, founded in 1845.

★   Further eastward along the south bank is Cork's City Hall, on
Albert Quay. Built in 1936, it is Cork's chief administrative center, but
is of particular interest to visitors because of its 2,000-seat concert hall,
usually the centerpiece of the annual October Jazz Festival.

From City Hall, you can easily cross over Parnell Bridge to Cork's
central island or main commercial section. To your left will be the
South Mall, the business heart of Cork. This is a wide tree-lined street,
with mostly Georgian architecture and a row of banks, insurance
companies, legal offices, and the like. Follow the South Mall to the
Grand Parade, a spacious thoroughfare which blends the remains of
the old city walls and 18th-century bow-fronted houses with modern
offices and shops. You'll also find a welcome patch of greenery, the
★ Bishop Lucey Park, a fairly new (1986) addition to the cityscape.

Meander along the Grand Parade, past Oliver Plunkett Street on the right, and next you will see the entrance to the City Market, a ★★ Cork tradition going back to 1610. Housed in a relatively recent (1786) building, this is a colorful trading place, with stands for meats, fish, vegetables, and fruit. You'll also see such traditional Cork foods as tripe (animal stomach), crubeens (pig's feet), and drisheens (local blood sausage). From the market, you can exit onto St. Patrick Street, Cork's main thoroughfare.

Referred to simply as "Patrick Street" by Corkonians, this broad avenue was formed in 1789 by covering in an open channel in the river. It is primarily a shopping street, but it is also a place for the Cork folks to stroll and be seen. Patrick Street is also the site of one of the city's best known meeting places, a statue of a 19th-century priest, Fr. Theobald Matthew, a crusader against drink who is fondly called "the apostle of temperance." The statue, or "the stacha," as the locals call it, stands at the point where Patrick Street reaches St. Patrick's Bridge, and is considered the city's central point of reference.

St. Patrick's Bridge (or Patrick's Bridge), opened in 1859, leads over the river to the north side of the city, a hilly and terraced section where the continuation of Patrick Street is called St. Patrick's Hill. And is it ★★ ever a hill—with an incline so steep that it is usually compared to San Francisco! If you have the desire (and stamina) to climb the stepped sidewalks of St. Patrick's Hill, you will be rewarded with a sweeping view of the Cork skyline.

Before you go climbing, however, you may wish to make your first right turn and stroll along the main business thoroughfare on this side of the bridge, MacCurtain Street, which is on the lower ground, running parallel to the river. It is named for a former Lord Mayor of the city, Thomas MacCurtain, who was murdered by British forces in 1920 during the Irish struggle for independence.

MacCurtain Street, which goes one-way in a easterly direction, will lead you to N 8, the main road along the River Lee, to the Tivoli section of Cork and to Dublin and points east. From MacCurtain, you can also bear to the left and climb Summerhill Road into the Cork hills to the residential districts of St. Luke's and Montenotte (where you will find a classic pub, Henchy's, and a great hotel/restaurant, the Arbutus Lodge—see "Inside Information").

After looking at MacCurtain Street and the hilly residential areas, save some time for exploring the section of Cork west of St. Patrick's Hill, one of the city's oldest neighborhoods. Turn left at Camden Quay and follow Upper John Street to John Redmond Street—this will lead you right to the corner of Exchange Street and St. Anne's Shandon ★★ Church, famous in story and song for its giant pepperpot steeple and its eight melodious bells.

Cork's prime landmark, the Shandon Church, dates back to 1722 and dominates the north side of the city. From almost anywhere downtown, you can see the church's tower, two sides of which are made of limestone and two of sandstone, with a top crowned by a gilt ball and a fish weathervane. Visitors are often encouraged to climb to the belfry and play a tune, so you are apt to hear the bells of Shandon ringing at all times of the day.

This church is situated next to the site of Cork's original Butter Market, a commercial exchange which was begun in 1730 and flourished for many years in this section. At the site today you will find a very fine merchants' hub of a different sort, the Shandon Craft Centre, an enclosed emporium where 20th-century artisans practice a range of traditional trades and display their wares for sale (See "Inside Information").

Before you leave this bustling city of 140,000 fast-talking people, do visit a few of the interesting pubs (for some specific recommendations, see "Inside Information"). Be sure to taste the local brews, Beamish and Murphy's. If you are a teetotaler, ask for Barry's Tea, blended in Cork since 1901, and Hadji Bey, the city's own sweet version of Turkish Delight.

CORK CITY ENVIRONS

★★★ In many ways, the Blarney Stone is to Ireland what Big Ben is to Britain or the Eiffel Tower to France. Just about everyone in the western world has heard of the Blarney Stone and associates it with the Emerald Isle.

Located six miles northwest of Cork City, the famous stone is a part of 15th-century Blarney Castle, the centerpiece in a village of the same name. Originally the stronghold of the MacCarthys, all that remains of the castle today is a massive square keep, or tower, with a battlemented parapet rising 83 feet. The fabled stone is wedged underneath the battlements, and, in order to kiss it, visitors must lie down and bend backwards down into a trench; but have no fear—the area is fully protected and a trained guide supervises all the kissing. The hardest part of the whole experience is climbing the ancient curved steps up to the parapet.

Legend has it the reward is great for those who make the effort, since kissing the Blarney Stone is supposed to convey the "gift of eloquence." The basis for this belief harks back to the days of Queen Elizabeth I. The story goes that the then-Lord of Blarney, Cormac MacDermott MacCarthy, became a bit evasive when asked by the Queen's deputy, Carew, to renounce the traditional system by which the clans elected their chief, and to take the tenure of his lands from the Crown. While seeming to agree to this proposal, he put off the

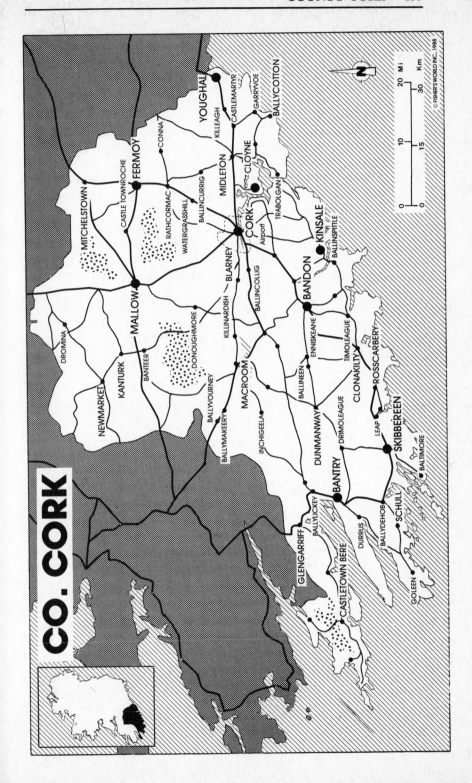

fulfillment of his promise from day to day with "fair words and soft speech." Finally the Queen is reputed to have declared "This is all Blarney—what he says, he never means!" And thus the word "blarney" came to mean pleasant talk intended to deceive without offending, and in its modern connotation, a clever form of flattery.

★★ After kissing the storied stone, you may wish to stroll through the gardens and a nearby dell beside Blarney Lake. You can also visit the adjacent Blarney House, a Scottish baronial mansion dating from 1874, which has been recently restored. It contains a fine collection of ancestral paintings and heraldic decorations.

In addition to the suburb of Blarney, the Cork area is well known for its harbor town of Cobh (pronounced "Cove" and meaning "haven" in the Irish language). In the days before airline travel, Cobh was Ireland's chief port of entry, with up to three or four transatlantic liners calling here a week. For thousands of Irish emigrants, particularly in the famine years and the early part of this century, Cobh was also their last sight of Ireland.

The coming of the jet age has changed all of that, and Cobh is much quieter now, although it is still a picturesque port and a favorite with yachtsmen. A relatively modern town, Cobh is located on the eastern side of the harbor, 15 miles from Cork City. With a landscape of terraces rising from the sea, the Cobh skyline is dominated by the ★★ magnificent St. Colman's Cathedral, a Gothic-Revival structure with elaborate flying buttresses, columns of polished marble, mosaic flooring, and moulded arches. The fine-tuned cathedral carillon of 47 bells is said to be one of the best in the world.

★★★ About five miles north of Cobh is one of the Cork area's major attractions, Fota Island, a 70-acre harborside ornamental estate. Owned by the University College of Cork, Fota has recently won the European Museum of the Year Award. The centerpiece is the Regency-style Fota House, built in the 1820's for the Smith-Barry family, once the Earls of Barrymore. With fine neo-classical interiors, the house is full of 18th- and 19th-century furnishings, wallpapers, and draperies, but the prime draw is a very comprehensive collection of Irish landscape paintings dating from the 1750's to the 1870's.

The Fota gardens and arboretum, first planted in the 1820's, contain trees and shrubs from the temperate and subtropical regions of the world including China, Japan, New Zealand, Australia, North and South America, and the Himalayas. The adjacent wildlife park is home to rare and endangered species of giraffe, zebra, ostrich, antelope,

Moving further to the southeast of Cork City, you will approach Ballycotton Bay, about a 25-mile drive, and the little village of

Shanagarry. This is the home of Ballymaloe House, one of Ireland's most comfortable country inns and the headquarters of the Ballymaloe Cooking School, a culinary trend-setter for the entire country. (See "Inside Information.")

The county's major coastal town near the Waterford border is Youghal (pronounced "Yawl"), 30 miles to the east of Cork City. A leading beach resort and fishing port, Youghal is loosely identified with Sir Walter Raleigh, who was once the town mayor. According to tradition, it was here that Raleigh smoked the first tobacco and grew the first potatoes in Ireland. His house, Myrtle Grove, still stands, but is not open to visitors.

Another highlight in the Cork environs, 22 miles north of the city, is Mallow, a thriving agricultural town and a leading Irish sugar producer. Mallow sits on the banks of the River Blackwater, a long stretch of water particularly favored by salmon fishermen. Here you will find Longueville House, a top-notch country inn and restaurant with a huge farmland estate that even has its own winery. It produces a very drinkable white wine, unique in this land known for its beers and whiskies.

Along the banks of the river you will also find Mallow Castle, a 400-year-old baronial mansion which can be rented, complete with staff and a resident herd of rare white deer, on a weekly basis (See "Inside Information").

THE WEST CORK COAST

Kinsale is the gateway to the western Cork seacoast. Located about 18 ★★★ miles south of Cork City, this compact little town of 2,000 residents has made a big name for itself as the "gourmet capital" of Ireland. Home to more than a dozen award-winning restaurants and pubs, Kinsale draws lovers of good food year-round but particularly each October, when the whole town is the focus of a three-day Gourmet Festival.

Part of the secret to Kinsale's success is that it also fits the picture postcard image of what a charming little seaport should look like—narrow winding streets, well-kept 18th-century houses, imaginatively painted shopfronts, windowboxes and street stanchions brimming with colorful flowers, and a harbor full of sailboats. Just for good measure, Kinsale also boasts one of the best-equipped sea fishing centers on the south coast, plus a medieval church, a 16th-century castle, and two 17th-century star-shaped fortresses.

A mecca for history buffs, in 1602 Kinsale was the scene of the Battle of Kinsale, a great turning point in Irish history. A defeat for the natives, it helped to establish English domination over Ireland, setting in train the inevitable process of "plantation" and putting an end to the Irish clan system. This also brought to the town a new governor representing the British crown, William Penn. For a time, Penn's son served the town as clerk of the admiralty court, but William Penn Jr. did not stay long—he was soon off to the New World to found the commonwealth of Pennsylvania.

Kinsale's other rendezvous with history was a much more tragic note. It was just off the coast of the Old Head of Kinsale, about five miles west of the town, that the "Lusitania" was sunk by a German submarine in 1915, with a loss of over 1,500 people, many of whom are buried in a local cemetery.

From Kinsale, you can enjoy a full day's drive along Cork's coast into an area simply referred to as "West Cork." In many ways, West Cork has its own personality, with a string of interesting little harbor towns, all with very memorable and multi-syllabic names, such as Courtmacsherry, Clonakilty, Rosscarbery, Castletownshend, Skibbereen, and Owenahincha. Although you'll want to meander down some of the country roads, you can do most of this drive by sticking to the major N 71 route.

Of all of the towns in West Cork, Castletownshend has probably received the most prominence because it was the home of Edith Somerville and "Martin" (Violet Florence) Ross, the 19th-century writing team who produced "The Experiences of an Irish R.M.," a classic book turned into a recent television story.

Our favorite stop on the West Cork circuit, however, is Ballydehob, a small town pleasantly plunked between Mt. Gabriel and Roaringwater Bay. In spite of its unsophisticated name, it is home to an international enclave of artisans and craftspeople—painters, potters, sculpturers and calligraphers, from all over Ireland, the U.S., Canada, Britain, the Netherlands, Germany, and Denmark, to name a few. Ballydehob's creative residents often exhibit their award-winning works in Dublin, London, the U.S., and throughout Europe.

Best of all, the artistic atmosphere even shows up on the merchants' gaily painted shopfronts. O'Sullivan's butcher shop displays drawings of cattle, pigs, chickens, etc., rather than signs listing the meats available. Coughlan's grocery features a tableau of fruits, vegetables and other popular products, and Vincent Coughlan's pub has an outside wall mural depicting a spirited group of singing musicians. It's extremely inviting.

Although Ballydehob will probably win your heart, you'll find a different kind of enchantment at Schull, an old-world yachting town, and at Barleycove, a remote windswept resort which is the last stop ★★★ before you reach Mizen Head and the sheer cliffs which signal the southernmost tip of the Emerald Isle.

Once you have filled your lungs with the bracing air of Mizen Head, you should aim to return to the N 71 road and head for Bantry.

If time permits, you might like to do the 20-mile circuit around the Sheep's Head Peninsula, just south of Bantry. It's a relatively undiscovered beauty spot, with narrow roads and luscious views of Dunmanus Bay on one side and Bantry Bay on the other. You'll also find a surprise here—an authentic Japanese restaurant at Ahakista (see "Inside Information").

In the village of Bantry you will not only have expansive views of one of the most beautiful bays on the Irish coast, Bantry Bay, but you ★★ can also visit Bantry House, the home of Mr. and Mrs. Egerton Shelswell-White and formerly the seat of the Earls of Bantry. Set right on the bay on the edge of town, this house was built around 1750, and has a mostly-Georgian facade with Victorian additions. Open to the public since 1946, it contains many items of furniture and objets d'art from all over Europe; the gardens are beautifully kept and well worth a stroll.

Just outside of Bantry is the tiny village of Ballylickey, a sheltered spot on Bantry Bay and home to two fine lodging establishments, in case you decide to stay a day or two in this area (see "Inside Information").

The N 71 route will next bring you to Glengariff, a village in a beautiful glen, thickly wooded with oak, elm, pine, yew, holly, and palm trees. Glengariff also faces Bantry Bay, and looks out onto a ★★★ subtropical island called Garnish (sometimes spelled "Garinish"). Once a barren island, in 1919 it was transformed into an elaborately planned Italianate garden with classical pavilions and a myriad of unusual plants and flowers from many continents. Local boatmen eagerly await a chance to take you to this balmy island. Unfortunately, herein lies the one "tourist trap" drawback of a visit to Glengariff. The boatmen can be so anxious for business that they have been known to flag down cars driving through the village. Just be prepared. If you want to visit Garnish Island, the zealous boatmen provide the only means of transport. However, if you prefer to see the island from the shore and to soak up the ambience of Glengariff on foot, just ignore the sales pitches.

Glengariff is also the gateway to the Beara Peninsula, a 30-mile finger of land extending out into the Atlantic between Bantry Bay and the Kenmare River. The Caha Mountains stretch almost the entire ★★★ length of the peninsula and a narrow road rims the edge along the north and south shores. If you are pressed for time, this drive can be cut in half by following the Tim Healy Pass across the mountains. This not only saves an hour or more but provides some of the most beautiful panoramas of West Cork scenery that you will find. The Beara Peninsula also brings you to the County Kerry border (at Lauragh) and leads you into Kenmare, on the Ring of Kerry circuit (see the "County Kerry" chapter).

Alternatively, if you wish to see some of the inland highlights of
★★ West Cork, you should travel from Glengariff to Ballylickey and
follow the scenic road northeast through the Pass Of Keimaneigh to
Gougane Barra. The River Lee has its source at Gougane Barra, a
dramatic corrie lake in a wooded setting. The local legend says that St.
Finbarr had a hermitage on an island in this lake before he moved
downriver to Cork to found his great monastery.

Be that as it may, Gougane Barra today is a peaceful mountain
retreat with forest walks, nature trails, and lakeshore paths, tucked in
a pocket of West Cork where Irish (or Gaelic) is the everyday language
of the people.

The nearest major point is Macroom, a marketing town on the
main Killarney/Cork road (N 22). Like Kinsale, this place has a
connection with William Penn, as history tells us that for a while in
the mid-17th century Penn's father owned both the town and its castle,
the latter of which has since fallen into ruin. From Macroom, you are
in a good position to return to Cork, or to travel onward to Killarney
and Co. Kerry.

AHAKISTA, Co. Cork

Restaurant

★★★★ SHIRO

Kilcrohane Road. Tel. (027) 67030. The secluded Sheep's Head Peninsula may seem an unlikely place to find a great restaurant, much less
one in authentic Japanese style. But, here, on the northern shore of
Dunmanus Bay, is the remarkable culinary outpost of Werner and Kei
Pilz, a German/Japanese couple.

A favorite with the locals, including actress Maureen O'Hara who
has a home nearby, this country-house restaurant offers such dishes as
authentic sashimi (rare in this part of Ireland), suimono soup, prawn
tempura, spicy minced meat in pastry puff (Gyo-za), pork in ginger
sauce and fresh vegetables (Buta-Shogay-ki), and Japanese pork cutlets
with different sauces and vegetables (Tun-katsu). Open year-round for
dinner, with seating for only 16, reservations are essential. Located
about 15 miles southwest of Bantry. No credit cards. *Expensive.*

BALLYDEHOB, Co. Cork

Restaurant

> ★★ ANNIE'S (Best in Town)
> Main Street. Tel. (028) 37292. This small shopfront wine bar and
> restaurant is ideal for a lunch or dinner stop when you are touring
> the West Cork area. It's small and homey, with a menu that
> features liver and bacon pate, homemade cider-marinated ham,
> escalop of pork with orange sauce, beef kebab with mustard
> sauce, roasted almond ice cream. Closed Sunday and Monday;
> and the month of November. *Moderate.*

Pub

★★ V. COUGHLAN'S PUB
Main Street. The colorful exterior mural of fiddlers and accordianists
on the side wall of this old building is a preview of the music sessions
which are held here nightly. By day, it's a pleasant place to stop for a
drink or cup of coffee, seek some sightseeing advice, or chat with the
locals.

Shopping

THE BRIDGE GALLERY
The Bridge. "Small is beautiful" is the theme of this gallery which
displays the miniature art designs of A. Edward Webb. The works
mainly focus on scenes of the West Cork area and are painted on small
canvasses as well a pieces of wood, rocks, and cameos, all lovely
souvenirs of this enchanting corner of Ireland.

BALLYLICKEY, Co. Cork

Hotels

★★★★ SEA VIEW
Bantry/Glengariff Road (N 71). Tel. (027) 50073. 13 rooms. Like a
dove proudly spreading its wings on the horizon, this snowy white
structure stands tall amid verdant gardens rimming the shores of Bantry
Bay. Aptly named, Sea View is homey and full of heirlooms, antiques,
lots of tall windows, and a cheery decor. It is best known, however, for
the award-winning cuisine of proprietor Kathleen O'Sullivan. The
house specialties include mussel soup, filets of John Dory, escalopes of
veal, cider-baked ham, and praline pancakes. Besides the restaurant,

there is also a cozy lounge bar and an outdoor patio. Located three miles from Bantry; open mid-March through October. *Moderate.*

★★★ BALLYLICKEY MANOR

Bantry/Glengariff Road (N 71). Tel. (027) 50071. 11 rooms. Overlooking Bantry Bay in a 10-acre setting of lawns and gardens, this well-established retreat offers a choice of accommodations in a 300-year-old manor house or in modern wooden cottages which surround the swimming pool. A member of the Relais and Chateaux association, this inn has an international ambience, thanks to the influence of its owners, the French-Irish Graves family, and a largely European clientele. Open from mid-March through October. *Moderate to expensive.*

BANTRY, Co. Cork

Bed-and-Breakfast

★★★ SHANGRI-LA

Glengariff/Skibbereen Road (N 71). Tel. (027) 50244. 6 rooms. Over 15 years ago, the Muckleys converted their modern split-level home into a guest lodge in the "town and country house" category. As private homes go, it's a standout, offering hotel-style facilities including five rooms with private bath, and a restaurant with wine license on the premises. Perched on a hill overlooking Bantry Bay, this friendly oasis also has its own gardens and parking lot. *Bargain.*

For other accommodations and restaurant listings in the Bantry vicinity, see also Ballylickey, Ahakista, Durrus, Schull, and Ballydehob.

CORK CITY, Co. Cork

Hotels

★★★★ JURYS

Western Road (N 22). Tel. (021) 966377. 190 rooms. Situated on the western edge of town, Jurys is the top hotel in this busy southern coastal city. It is well positioned in its own gardens, with ample car parking, next to University College-Cork and along the banks of the River Lee, yet just a five-minute walk from the city center.

Basically a modern two-story multi-winged structure, it's formerly an Inter-Continental Hotel, like its sister hotels in Dublin and Limerick. Recently refurbished to the tune of $4 million, it has a nautical-theme restaurant, sleek new bedrooms facing the riverfront, a skylit atrium-like pavilion housing an indoor-outdoor swimming pool and fitness center, and a trendy new pub which combines views of the river with an "old Cork" ambience. *Expensive.*

★★★ IMPERIAL HOTEL—QUALITY INN

South Mall. Tel. (021) 965333. 80 rooms. Of the major Cork hotels, this vintage four-story lodging is the most conveniently situated in the heart of the city's business district. The location is ideal, especially if you want to walk around Cork, or if you have arrived by train and do not have a car. (On the other hand, if you have a rented car, you'll have to park it on the street.)

With Waterford crystal chandeliers, marble floors, and brass fittings, this property exudes an aura of grandeur in its reception area and public rooms. The bedrooms, however, tend to be more "art deco moderne," with a black and white lacquered look. Other facilities include a coffee shop, nautical bar, and a very good restaurant, "La Duchesse," with a pianist adding to the ambience each evening. *Expensive.*

★★★ ARBUTUS LODGE

Montenotte. Tel. (021) 501237. 20 rooms. The views of Cork City are hard to beat from the Arbutus Lodge vantage point, perched high in the hills overlooking the north bank of the River Lee. Taking its name from the arbutus tree which grows in its prize-winning gardens, this is an old Georgian town house, once the home of the Lord Mayor of Cork, and converted by the Ryan family into a comfortable hotel with antique furnishings, modern Irish art, and Wedgwood trim. The extensive grounds include plenty of car parking, a blessing if you prefer to walk around Cork (since driving in the city center can be a bit confusing, with lots of one-way streets and bridges).

The main claim to fame of the Arbutus Lodge, however, is its award-winning restaurant, which easily merits a ★★★★★ rank. The menu includes such entrees as roast quail a l'Armagnac, veal kidney with mustard sauce, chicken in tomato and basil, or rib of beef with sauce Beaujolais, as well as your choice of lobster from the tank. If you can gather together a few couples, the chef also prepares a "tasting menu," eight courses incorporating the best of many dishes. Price-wise, the hotel is *Expensive* and the restaurant can be *Very expensive.*

Guesthouse

★★★ LOTAMORE HOUSE

Dublin/Waterford Road (N 8/25), Tivoli. Tel. (021) 822344. 20 rooms. If you prefer a guesthouse experience, this Georgian manor is located two miles east of Cork City, overlooking the River Lee on four acres of wooded grounds and gardens. Furnished with antiques, crystal chandeliers, and a fireplace dating back to 1791, this is an exceptionally well-run facility, owned by two doctors, Mareaid and Leonard Harty. The bedrooms, all of which have private baths and orthopedic beds, are fully carpeted, with TVs and direct-dial phones in all rooms, a rarity for guesthouses. Only breakfast is served, but even that is exceptional, with freshly squeezed orange juice on the menu every day. *Inexpensive.*

For other lodgings in the Cork City environs, see also Kinsale, Mallow, Shanagarry, and Kanturk.

Restaurants

★★★★ LOVETTS

Churchyard Lane, off Well Road. Tel. (021) 294909. In addition to the Arbutus Lodge, the most highly regarded restaurant of Cork City is not in the downtown area at all, but in the affluent southside suburb of Douglas. To reach this celebrated spot, follow the signs for Rte. 609 and stay on the Douglas Road for five minutes. Make a left when you come to Well Road, and soon you will see the iron gates of Lovett's, an impressive Georgian house on its own grounds.

Proprietor/chef Dermod Lovett specializes in seafood such as monkfish in prawn sauce, whole black sole on the bone, brill poached in Dubonnet, or grilled mussels. This kitchen is also known for well-aged steaks and local lamb, as well as unique desserts like brown bread ice cream. Open for lunch and dinner, with lighter choices at midday. *Expensive.*

★★★ JACQUES

9 Phoenix Street. Tel. (021) 502387. This small and unique bistro is in the heart of town, near the South Mall and General Post Office. The creation of two sisters, Eithne and Jacqueline Barry, it is a self-service snack bar during the day and a full-scale restaurant and wine bar at night.

Innovative cuisine is the keynote at dinner, with featured dishes such as crab claws and scallops beurre blanc; pork en croute; roast quail with port cream and grapes; duck with potato stuffing and apricot sauce; and beef filets flamed in brandy, as well as a vegetarian dish of crunchy vegetables and nut roast. Don't miss the signature dessert, almond merengue cake. Jacques is remarkably good value, considering its city center location, plus the high standard of cuisine and attentive service. Open Tuesday through Saturday for dinner. *Moderate.*

★★★ OYSTER TAVERN

Market Lane, off 56 St. Patrick Street. Tel. (021) 272716. In the heart of the old city, this Cork institution is known for its seafood. It's very popular with the locals, and, as its name implies, oysters are a favorite here, as are prawn dishes, crab mornay, salmon, sole, and turbot. Be prepared to sip an aperitif and wait in the old world bar area, even if you have a reservation; it's part of the tradition. Lunch and dinner. *Moderate.*

For fine dining near Cork City, see also the restaurants of Kinsale, plus Longueville House at Mallow, and Ballymaloe House, Shanagarry.

Pubs

★★★★★ HENCHY'S
40 St. Luke's. Tel. (021) 501115. It's worth a walk up the steep Summerhill Road, a northeast continuation of busy MacCurtain Street, to reach this classic and well-maintained pub (near the Arbutus Lodge Hotel). Originally established by John Henchy in 1884, it looks just the same as it did then, with lots of polished brass fittings, leaded glass windows, silver tankards, thick red curtains, and a small snug. Even the pub grub, which includes shepherd's pie and sausage rolls, is a reflection of earlier times. The original Henchy family grocery store still operates adjacent to the pub.

★★★★ MUTTON LANE INN
3 Mutton Lane, off St. Patrick Street. Tel. (021) 273471. Old Cork is alive and well at this tiny pub down an alley which was first trod as a pathway for sheep going to market. Begun in 1787 as a public house by the Ring family, who used to make their own whiskey, it is now the domain of Maeva and Vincent McLoughlin, who have preserved the exposed beam ceilings, and an antique cash register. A good spot for a hearty lunch of soup, shepherd's pie, or roast beef sandwiches.

★★★ THE OFFICE
5 Sullivan's Quay. Tel. (021) 967652. This pub is a favorite after-work stop for Cork businessmen who have been known to phone home late in the evening and use the excuse, "I'm delayed at the Office, Dear." It has a neat black and white (and very photogenic) facade, complete with hand-carved sign of a gentleman with a quilled pen, and an interior which has been recently up-dated but still retains a hint of an office-like decor with vintage benches and desks. Baskets of tasty Irish sausages are often served in place of peanuts as a bar snack. It's conveniently located on the south side of Parliament Bridge, opposite the South Mall.

★★★ LeCHATEAU
93 St. Patrick Street. Tel. (021) 203701. Established in 1793, this is one of Cork's oldest pubs of great character, located right in the middle of the city's main thoroughfare. As pubs go, it's a large specimen, with a choice of various rooms and alcoves filled with Cork memorabilia. The pub grub ranges from simple sandwiches, salads, and soups to the

more exotic—pizzas, quiches, and lasagne, as well as a hearty Irish stew. Irish Coffee is also a specialty here.

★★★ MAGUIRE'S PENNYFARTHING INN
Daunt Square, Grand Parade. Tel. (021) 502825. An inviting buffet counter of hot and cold meats and a full-scale salad bar make this Edwardian-style pub a lunchtime favorite with Cork office workers and shoppers. Located just off St. Patrick Street in the heart of town, it has a conversation-piece decor of vintage bicycles, unicycles, and lots of old brass fixtures.

★★★ DeLACY HOUSE
74 Oliver Plunkett Street. Tel. (021) 270074. If it's Irish music you are looking for, then there's no better place in Cork than this midtown pub, located between St. Patrick Street and the South Mall. Entertainment is scheduled nightly.

Theatres/Entertainment

CORK OPERA HOUSE
Emmet Place. Tel. (021) 276357 or 270022. A modern theatre near Lavitt's Quay along the River Lee, this is a major stage in southwest Ireland for an ever-changing program of opera, drama, musicals, comedies, dance, concerts, and variety nights. Curtain is normally at 8 P.M.; there are also matinees frequently on Saturday afternoons. Depending on the event, ticket prices range from $3 to $30, but average around $8.

EVERYMAN PLAYHOUSE
Father Matthew Street, off South Mall. Tel. (021) 276287. This theatre is well known as a showcase for new plays; the Irish National Ballet also performs here regularly. Curtain is usually at 8 P.M., and tickets range from $3 to $7.50.

IVERNIA THEATRE
Grand Parade. Tel. (021) 272703 or 273156. Located adjacent to the Tourist Office, this is the home of the Cork Theatre Company and a good place to see Irish and international drama. In the summer months, lunchtime performances are often scheduled, in addition to the evening programs. Prices average $5 to $7.

Shopping

SHANDON CRAFT CENTRE
John Redmond Street, Cork Exchange. Tel. (021) 508881. Located in a restored building within a block of the famous St. Anne's Shandon Church, this is a unique sightseeing and shopping experience. Here you can not only purchase hand-made crafts, but you can watch potters, weavers and other artisans at work and chat with them about their wares. Open Monday through Friday only.

HOUSE OF DONEGAL
Paul Street. Tel. (021) 272447. "Tailoring to please" is the theme of this showroom/workshop, located one block north of St. Patrick Street, off the Grand Parade. You can buy ready-made or specially tailored raincoats, classic trench coats, jackets, suits, and sportwear, for men and women. The handsome rainwear, with Donegal tweed linings, are a special find.

STEPHEN PEARCE
Paul Street. Tel. (021) 272324. One of Ireland's most well-known potters, based at nearby Shanagarry, has given his name and his wares to this shop just off St. Patrick Street. The store itself, formerly a tea warehouse and candy factory, is an artistic multi-level showcase for the products of at least 50 other local craftspeople—from tweeds and tiles to candles and cards, not to mention wooden toys and natural soaps.

IRISH HOME CRAFTS
7 Marlborough Street. Tel. (021) 273379. Individually-made craft items are the main attraction of this small shop, located between St. Patrick Street and the South Mall. You'll find crochet work, handmade dolls, knitware, pottery, patchwork, ceramic and enamel jewelry, tea cozies, shamrock-shaped rings, and mohair jackets.

CASH'S
18 St. Patrick Street. Tel. (021) 276771. Dating back to 1830, this is the "Saks Fifth Avenue" of Cork, the premier department store on the city's main thoroughfare. A convenient source for all types of knitwear, tweeds, linens, glassware, and other gift items, it is affiliated with Dublin's Switzers and Todd's of Limerick.

BLARNEY WOOLLEN MILLS
Blarney. Tel. (021) 385280. Located about five miles northwest of Cork City near the famous castle of the same name, this Kelleher family enterprise is housed in an old mill dating back to 1824. It is a one-stop source for all kinds of Irish products, from cashmeres to crystal glassware, hats to heraldry, and tweeds to tee shirts, as well as the distinctive Kelly green Blarney Castle-design wool sweaters, made on the premises. Best of all, it's open daily, and until 10 P.M. every night in the summer.

Sightseeing Tours

BUS EIREANN
Parnell Street, off St. Patrick Street. Tel. (021) 503399, ext. 318. In the summer months, this office operates a full schedule of full-day and half-day sightseeing trips around Cork, as well as to Bantry Bay, Killarney, the Ring of Kerry, and Bunratty.

WALKING TOURS
Guided tours of Cork City for visitors are scheduled every Tuesday and Thursday evening, free of charge, during July and August. Assemble at the Cork Tourist Office, Grand Parade, at 7:30 P.M.

RIVER CRUISES
Marine Transport, Cobh. Tel. (021) 811485. From mid-May through mid-August, there are afternoon and evening cruises around Cork Harbor and excursions to Fota Island. Details of schedules and rates can be obtained from the tourist office.

Sports

Golf

THE DOUGLAS GOLF CLUB
Maryboro Hill, Douglas, Tel. (021) 291086. This 18-hole course is located three miles south of Cork City center. It's a challenging inland course, with a layout that includes sloping fairways, streams, quarries, and palm trees. Greens fees are approximately $13; clubs can be hired for $6 and caddie carts for $1.50. To arrange a starting time, phone the club secretary/manager, Mrs. Grace Buckley.

Getting Around

Bus Eireann provides regularly scheduled bus service throughout Cork City and its environs, from 7 A.M. to 11 P.M. on Monday through Saturday, and slightly shorter hours on Sunday. The flat fare is approximately 80 cents. Transfers to/from Cork Airport are available for about $2 each way. For further information, call (021) 503399.

Taxis are readily available throughout Cork. The chief taxi ranks are located along St. Patrick's Street, the South Mall, and outside of major hotels.

Festivals

April 27-May 1: International Choral and Folk Dance Festival. Ever since 1954, this gathering has attracted the leading professional and amateur choirs and dance groups from all over the world.

October 28-31: Guinness Jazz Festival. Top names from the international jazz world converge on Cork for concerts, impromptu sessions, and "jazz on tap" pub gigs.

Directory

The Cork Tourist Office, Grand Parade. Tel. (021) 273251.
Irish Rail, Kent Station, Lower Glanmire Road. Tel. (021) 504422.
Bus Eireann, Parnell Place, off St. Patrick Street. Tel. (021) 503399.
Cork Airport, Kinsale Road. Tel. (021) 965414.

Religious Services

Roman Catholic:

Sts. Peter and Paul Church, Paul Street. Tel. (021) 276573.
St. Francis Church, Liberty Street. Tel. (021) 270301.

Church of Ireland:

St. Luke Church, St. Luke's Cross. Tel. (021) 501672.
St. Michael Church, Blackrock. Tel. (021) 891539.

Synagogue:

Cork Hebrew Congregation, 10 South Terrace. Tel. (021) 291116.

DURRUS, Co. Cork

Restaurant

★★★★ BLAIR'S COVE
Barley Cove Road. Tel. (027) 61127. A grassy country lane leads you
to this romantic restaurant overlooking Dunmanus Bay, situated less
than ten miles from Bantry in West Cork. Owners Philip and Sabine
de Mey have converted a stone barn with a 250-year-old Georgian
courtyard and terrace into one of the best dining experiences in southwest Ireland. Each meal starts with a buffet of appetizers (from salmon
fume to prawns, pates, oysters, and mousses). Entrees, such as beef,
lamb, or seafood, are cooked-to-order over a wood-burning fireplace
in the dining room. For dessert, step up to a grand piano that doubles
as a sweet trolley. Open Easter to mid-October for dinner, and on weekends only during the rest of the year (except January and February).

KANTURK, Co. Cork

Guesthouse

★★★ ASSOLAS HOUSE
Tel. (029) 50015. 10 rooms. About four miles east of the village, this is
an ivy-covered country house located in north County Cork, within
an hour's drive of Cork City, Killarney, Tralee, or Limerick. Owned

by the Bourke family, it is nestled beside a river and is named after the Gaelic word meaning "ford of the light."

Built over several centuries, it has a Jacobean section, a 17th century wing, and a Queen Anne addition dating from the early 18th century. As might be expected, it is tastefully furnished with antiques and family heirlooms; the bedrooms are large and airy, with colorful floral motifs. Picturesquely set on its own grounds with award-winning gardens, Assolas offers guests facilities for tennis, croquet, boating, and fishing, plus a highly praised restaurant. Open from mid-April through October. *Moderate.*

KINSALE, Co. Cork

Hotels

★★★★ THE BLUE HAVEN

Pearse Street. Tel. (021) 772209. 10 rooms. To ease into the stride of the laid-back fishing port of Kinsale, there's no better place to stay than the Blue Haven. Positioned right on the main thoroughfare, this ★★★ old-world inn is the town focal point. It is meticulously operated by Brian and Anne Cronin, a hard-working duo who first built an award-winning reputation on the merits of their top notch seafood restaurant, and then gradually up-dated and enhanced the rest of the inn. (As a testimony to their culinary efforts, Bloomingdale's, the trendy New York emporium, brought the Cronins across the Atlantic to demonstrate their recipes as part of a 1981 store-wide "Ireland" promotion.)

Today the restaurant is still a major drawing card for the Blue Haven, with such varied dishes as prawn tails with salmon mousse, oysters au gratin, lobster flambe, spring lamb in puff pastry, and farmhouse duckling. The inn also has a leafy new outdoor sun room with glass roof and a cozy pub, both of which serve light lunches (such as seafood pancakes and quiches, pizzas, and homemade lasagne). The pleasant guest rooms upstairs, many of which overlook the back garden, are decorated with light wood furnishings, local crafts, and artwork; some rooms even have well-stocked mini-bars. All that is lacking is an elevator and private parking, although on-street parking outside the front entrance is usually available. Open March through December. *Inexpensive* for the hotel and *Moderate* for the restaurant.

★★★ ACTON'S

The Waterfront. Tel. (021) 772135. 55 rooms. Built over the years, this Trusthouse Forte hotel is actually six three-story harborfront houses which have been joined, renovated, expanded, and refurbished. Consequently, the guest rooms vary in size, but most are large and airy, with standard furniture; the best part is that most of the rooms overlook the marina and the well-tended rose gardens. Amenities include a full-service restaurant, a nautical-theme tavern, and a brand new adjacent health center and leisure club with swimming pool, saunas, sunbeds, and billiard room. *Moderate.*

Restaurants

★★★★ THE VINTAGE
Main Street. Tel. (021) 772502. Marie and Michael Riese, from Cork and Hamburg respectively, enliven this charming 200-year-old house in the heart of town with a repertoire of Irish and German recipes. Some of the specialties include weiner schnitzel, hot oak-smoked salmon steak, brace of quail, free-range goose, veal Calvados, sirloin steak in Irish whiskey sauce, and noisettes of local lamb rolled in spinach and mushrooms. Be sure to top off your meal with the Rieses' unique rum and brandy truffles. Open for dinner nightly, March through December, except Sunday. *Moderate.*

★★★★ MAN FRIDAY
Scilly. Tel. (021) 772260. Situated in a hilly area overlooking Kinsale harbor, this restaurant is as close to "Trader Vic's" as you'll get in these parts. Start by following the steps through a bamboo tunnel and an almost tropical garden entrance. The rustic bar area is a blend of exposed beam ceilings, stone walls, and tree stump stools, while the dimly-lit pine-paneled restaurant has a romantic display of fine art work. The menu, concocted by chef-owner Phillip Morgan, features international cuisine, ranging from prawns Napolean and Polynesian chicken, to Kinsale seafood platter or veal stuffed with brie, mushrooms, and ham. Open for dinner nightly, year-round. *Moderate.*

★★★★ COTTAGE LOFT
Castlepark. Tel. (021) 772803. This is one of the few fine restaurants in Kinsale which offers views of the water. Situated slightly out of town, on the James Fort Road, it overlooks the sailboat-studded inner harbor. The cottage-style decor of this upstairs eatery includes caned-chairs, leafy hanging plants, and wooden ceiling beams. The eclectic menu ranges from sole on the bone and farmyard duck, to Peking beef, mussels in champagne sauce, curried seafood kebab, and cod stuffed with chutney. Open for dinner nightly (except Sunday and Monday in the winter months). *Moderate.*

★★★ LE BISTRO
Market Street. Tel. (021) 772470. As its names implies, this colorful building in the middle of town has a French atmosphere and decor. The fairly straight-forward menu features pastas, steaks, and seafood

dishes like calamari and prawns in garlic. Open for dinner nightly and
for lunch on Thursday through Saturday. *Moderate.*

★★★ MAX'S WINE BAR
Main Street. Tel. (021) 772443. Located just a few doors from the
Vintage, this old-world townhouse with an outdoor patio is ideal for a
light snack as well as a full meal. The emphasis is on low calorie and
high fibre salads, nut and fruit dishes, and vegetarian platters. Other
choices include pancakes with spinach and bacon, beefburgers, lamb's
liver, chicken with orange and ginger, and platters of Kinsale mussels
or oysters. Open for lunch and dinner, March through September,
except Tuesday. *Inexpensive to moderate.*

Pubs

★★★★ THE SPANIARD
Scilly. Tel. (021) 772436. Named for Don Juan de Aguila who rallied
his fleet with the Irish in an historic but unsuccessful attempt to defeat
the British in 1601, this old pub is full of local seafaring memorabilia.
With a much photographed black and white facade, it has a great
location in the hills overlooking Kinsale, with tables outside for sunny
day snacks. The Spaniard draws large crowds for live music nightly in
the summer months, and on weekends at other times of the year.

★★★ THE DOCK
Castlepark. Tel. (021) 772522. Located next to the Cottage Loft
Restaurant, this pub has one of the nicest locations in town, overlooking the inner harbor. The walls are lined with fishing-theme posters
and equipment, and the windows look out into the water. If the
weather is nice, you can step out onto the front deck with its row of
inviting tables and chairs.

★★★ JIM EDWARDS
Off Emmet Place. tel. (021) 772541. A classy nautical theme dominates
the decor of this pub, with colored glass windows and plush red
cushioned seating. Located in a lane between the Methodist Church
and the Temperance Hall, it is known for its good food including such
dishes as fricasse of seafood, king prawns, and steaks.

★★★ THE WHITE HOUSE
End of Pearse Street. Tel. (021) 772125. With its snowy Georgian facade
and distinctive name over the front entrance, this is one pub that tempts
nearly every American visitor to take a photograph. The inside is more
pubby, with a motif that focuses on local sporting memorabilia.

★★★ THE GREYHOUND
Marian Terrace. Tel. (021) 772889. Photographers are also enchanted
with the exterior of this pub, with its neat flower boxes, rows of stout

barrels, and handmade signs depicting the swift Irish racing animal. The interior rooms are cozy and known for hearty pub grub, such as farmhouse soups, seafood pancakes, shepherd's pie, and Irish stew.

★★★ LORD KINGSALE

Main Street. Tel. (021) 772371. A touch of elegance prevails at this handsome pub, decorated with lots of polished horse brass and black and white Tudor-style trappings. It takes its name (and ancient spelling) from the first Anglo-Norman baron who took charge of this Irish port in 1223. You'll often find evening sing-alongs here, and the soup-and-sandwich pub grub is very good.

★★★ THE SHANAKEE

Market Street. With an Anglicized name (derived from the Irish word "seanachie," which means storyteller), this vintage pub is known for its music, from sing-alongs on Sundays, to traditional ceili dancing on Thursdays.

Sports/Perks

Fishing

KINSALE MARINE SERVICES

Lower O'Connell Street. Tel. (021) 775241. If you'd like to try your hand at deep sea fishing off Kinsale, you can cast a line for blue shark, ocean pollock, ray, ling, whiting, conger, eel, and mackerel. The 36-foot "Peggy G" goes out each day at 9:30 A.M. Prices range from about $25 per person for a day's fishing including the rods, bait, and crew. If you have a small group, you can charter the whole boat for about $150 a day. Arrangements can also be made directly at the Blue Haven Hotel.

Shopping

BOLAND'S IRISH CRAFT SHOP

Pearse Street. Tel. (021) 772161. This is just the spot to buy a traditional Kinsale smock, as well as Aran knit vests, local pottery, ogham plaques, wooly and ceramic sheep, quilts, and miniature paintings by Irish artists.

Festival

August 6-7: Annual Regatta. A colorful display of boats in Kinsale harbor, with festive doings in all the local pubs and restaurants.

October 1-2: Kinsale Gourmet Festival. A gastronomic and culinary weekend, with special meals prepared by Kinsale's "gourmet circle" of fine restaurants.

MALLOW, Co. Cork

Hotel

★★★★ LONGUEVILLE HOUSE
Killarney Road (N 72). Tel. (022) 27156. 18 rooms. Built about 1720, this convivial country retreat is the pride and joy of the O'Callaghans—Michael (proprietor) and Jane (chef). Most of the bedrooms look out onto leafy greens, vineyards, or the open grazing fields of this 500-acre farmland/estate. Guest privileges include three miles of salmon and trout fishing on the River Blackwater and free golf at the nearby 18-hole Mallow Golf Course. At Longueville, you can also tour Ireland's only country inn winery and sample some of its pleasant all-Irish-made dry white vintages. Guest rooms are furnished in the old-world style, with family heirlooms and period pieces. A new addition to the premises is a craft shop with features antique jewelry, handmade porcelain, and other one-of-a-kind items.

This house is also distinguished by its ★★★★★ restaurant, "The Presidents' Room," decorated with portraits of Ireland's past heads of state, and featuring an award-winning menu, ranging from Longueville-raised lamb, and river-fresh salmon to stuffed porksteak and local roast quail, as well as crunchy green asparagus and other vegetables from the hotel's own garden. In the summer months, meals are also served in a festive and skylit Victorian conservatory. A member of the prestigious Relais and Chateaux group, Longueville is situated 20 miles north of Cork City, making it an ideal touring center for the southern coastal area. Open April through December; the restaurant serves all meals for hotel guests daily, but dinner only, Tuesday through Saturday, for those not overnighting. *Expensive.*

Castle-for-Rent

MALLOW CASTLE
Tel. (022) 21469. Once the Elizabethan seat of the Lord President of Munster (one of the four Irish provinces), Mallow was also the residence of the Norreys-Jephson family for almost 400 years, until it was purchased in 1984 by Michael and Judy McGinn of Washington, D.C. The McGinns occupy the castle only periodically, and rent it by the week at other times.

With an exterior of turrets and gables, the house inside is an impressive array of floor-to-ceiling elm paneling, mullioned windows, ornate white sandstone fireplaces, and castle heirlooms including the original 90-page sheepskin deed to the land signed by King James I of England. The six bedrooms (with six bathrooms) are all individually furnished, with antiques from many lands, and can accommodate 8 to 12 people. Sitting along the banks of the River Blackwater, with 40 acres of grounds, Mallow Castle also boasts a rare herd of 70 white fallow deer, all descended from a pair presented by Queen Elizabeth I to the then-lady of the house almost 400 years ago. The weekly rental, with a full complement of staff, is approximately $6,500; food is extra. For details and reservations, contact Michael McGinn, 319 Maryland Ave., N.E., Washington, D.C. 20002. Tel. (202) 547-7849.

SCHULL, Co. Cork

Hotel

★★★ ARD NA GREINE

Goleen Road. Tel. (028) 28181. 7 rooms. One of the highlights of touring Ireland's southwest coast is Schull, a small fishing and yachting port, and one of the main delights of the Schull area is the Ard na Greine Inn, located about a mile west of town. Facing the Fastnet Lighthouse on Roaringwater Bay, this 18th century farmhouse was converted into a country inn about a dozen years ago. Although the house offers every modern comfort, a large measure of rustic charm has been preserved by the enthusiastic owners, Frank and Rhona O'Sullivan. Guest rooms are individually decorated in a homey style; many offer views of the gardens or nearby mountains. Guest facilities include a pubby lounge with an open hearth and a full-service restaurant. Open April to late October. *Moderate.*

Pub

★★★ BUNRATTY INN

Main Street. If you are just passing through the area, this award-winning pub is a good place to know about for a light meal or refreshment. Located in the center of town, it has a mostly nautical decor, with agrarian touches, such as bar stools made from old milk cans. In the summer, an adjacent stableyard is outfitted with picnic tables for outdoor imbibing and snacks. Try the crab sandwiches or ploughman's platter (Irish farm cheeses with country pate, pickles, and crusty bread).

SHANAGARRY, Co. Cork

Hotel

★★★★ BALLYMALOE HOUSE

Ballycotton Road (L 35). Tel. (021) 652531. 30 rooms. Combining a Georgian farmhouse facade with the tower of a 14th century castle, this ivy-covered enclave of hospitality run by the Allen family is situated on a 400-acre farm, with grazing sheep and cows. The only road sign you'll see is one which alerts you to the importance of four-legged traffic: "Drive Slow: Lambs crossing." The bedrooms are furnished in an informal, comfortable style, and the guest facilities include a heated outdoor swimming pool, hard tennis courts, trout pond, nine-hole golf course, and a craft shop emphasizing local wares. The biggest draw to Ballymaloe, however, is the Yeats Dining room, praised by countless visitors, as well as "Gourmet," "The N.Y. Times," and "Travel and Leisure," to name but three. This ★★★★★ restaurant, the domain of Myrtle Allen, has set the standard for much of Ireland's new wave of imaginative cookery. Relying on local seafood and produce, the menu includes mousseline of mussels on an artichoke heart, cockles au gratin, salmon meuniere, hot buttered lobster, chicken Gruyere, steak-and-oyster pie, and a classic Irish Stew. All entrees are accompanied by fresh vegetables from the garden.

The success of the kitchen has also spawned Ireland's first year-round country inn cooking school, and Myrtle's own cookbook. Ballymaloe is located about 20 miles southeast of Cork City, less than two miles from Ballycotton Bay. *Expensive.*

YOUGHAL, Co. Cork

Restaurant/Pub

★★★★ AHERNE'S

162/163 N. Main Street. Tel. (024) 92424. The best of the local catch is a key to the success of this award-winning nautical restaurant, owned by Capt. Ger Fitzgibbon and family. It's located in the middle of Youghal, a fishing port/seaside resort 30 miles east of Cork City. If you are driving the southern coastal route, this spot makes a great stop for a meal or light refreshment. It is also close enough to Cork to be a favored dinner choice.

Lunchtime bar food includes seafood pies, chowders, crab sandwiches, and crisp salads, while the main dining room's menu offers lobsters from the tank, rock oysters, coquilles St. Jacques, black sole meuniere, Blackwater salmon, chicken Kiev, rack of lamb, or steak. At any time of day, you can also order the best prawn cocktail in Ireland (according to our own opinions and succulent samplings). Open daily in July and August, and closed Monday during the rest of the year. *Moderate to expensive.*

Pub

★★★ MOBY DICK

Market Square. Tel. (024) 92756. To enjoy the seafaring nature of this town, amble into the Moby Dick. It takes its name from the classic movie, starring Gregory Peck, which was partly filmed in Youghal years ago. Appropriately decorated with nautical artifacts, this pub offers views of the adjacent harbor.

Festival

June 24-July 2: The Gourmet Potato Festival. Celebrations commemorating the introduction of the potato to the Cork area by Sir Walter Raleigh, onetime mayor of Youghal, over 400 years ago.

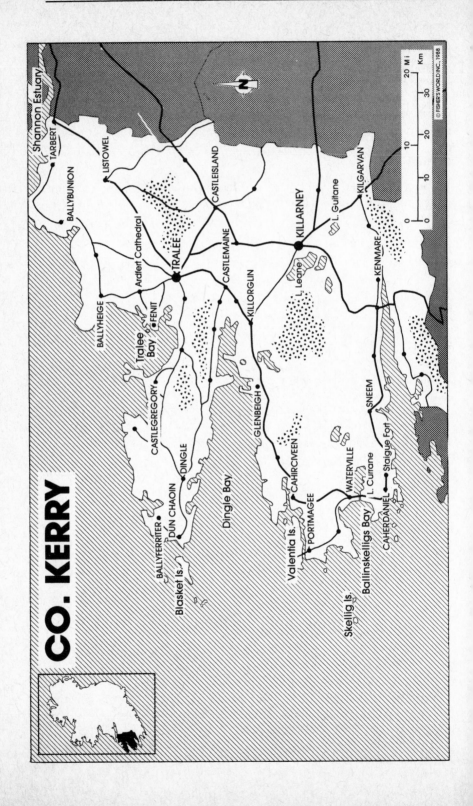

County Kerry

KILLARNEY, RING OF KERRY, AND DINGLE PENINSULA

County Kerry is in a class by itself. Not only does it shelter Ireland's number one scenic attraction—Killarney—but it also boasts the highest mountain peaks in Ireland, Macgillycuddy's Reeks and Mount Brandon, and it is the home of the two most heralded touring routes, the Ring of Kerry and the Dingle Peninsula. No wonder it is the only place in the Emerald Isle where you'll hear the residents referring to their county as "the kingdom."

Situated on Ireland's extreme southwest coast, Co. Kerry extends out into the Atlantic, with a coastline dominated by two finger-shaped peninsulas as well as a series of smaller curves and projections. It is warmed by the Gulf Stream, and temperatures average from 40 to 45 degrees F. in winter and from 55 to 65 F. in summer.

Actually, it is said that there is not much climate in Co. Kerry, just weather. And thanks to the strong winds blowing off the Atlantic, there is a great deal of weather, and it is weather that can best be described as "changeable." It can be beautiful in the morning and very wet in the afternoon, and vice versa, and, in many ways, especially in the winter, it can feel like four seasons in one day. You can start out the day with misty rain in Killarney and travel 50 miles to the Dingle Peninsula and find the sun shining. Of course, after the rain and mist, you'll appreciate the sunshine and brilliant colors twice as much. If Kerry did not have its rain, it would not be nearly as lush and colorful, nor would there be the dramatic cloud formations which shroud the tops of the mountains, dot the skies, and hover over the lakes and bays.

Thanks to its remoteness, Co. Kerry has always been an outpost of Gaelic culture. Poetry and music are intrinsic to Kerry lifestyle, as is a love of the outdoors. The native sport of Gaelic football is an obsession in this county, as evidenced by the fact that Kerry wins most of the national championships. You'll also find some of Ireland's best golf courses here, and the fishing for salmon and trout is unbeatable.

KILLARNEY

Celebrated in copious prose, poetry, and song, Killarney is a bit of ★★★ Nevada's Lake Tahoe, Pennsylvania's Poconos, and New York's Central Park, all wrapped up in one glorious package. You'll find three storied lakes, medieval castles, floating islands, craggy mountains ancient trees, lush foliage, cascading waterfalls, and rare wildlife

Above all, the lakes are Killarney's main focus. The first of these, the Lower Lake is sometimes called "Lough Leane" or "Lough Lein" which means the "lake of learning." The largest at over four miles long, it is dotted with 30 small islands. The second lake is aptly called the Middle Lake or Muckross Lake, while the third is simply known as the Upper Lake. The latter is the smallest of the three lakes and is also replete with islands that are covered with a variety of trees ranging from evergreens to cedar of Lebanon, oak, juniper, holly and mountain ash.

The lakes and the surrounding woodlands are all part of the 23-square-mile Killarney National Park. This park includes two major estates, the Muckross and Knockreer demesnes, and most of the land which rims the three lakes, plus a profusion of foliage such as rhododendrons, azaleas, magnolia, camelias, hydrangeas, and tropical plant ferns. At almost every turn, you will also see Killarney's own botanical wonder, the arbutus or strawberry tree, plus eucalyptus, redwoods, and native oak. The wildlife includes rare red deer, the only native Irish herd, plus fallow and Japanese shika deer, unusual all-black Kerry cattle, and 114 species of birds.

Just outside of the parkland's perimeter is the town of Killarney (population: 7,000), located at the junction of the Kenmare and Killorglin roads. It sits at the edge of the largest of three lakes, and is surrounded by mountains with names like Purple, Torc, Mangerton, and Tomie.

Surprisingly, the town center has no great charm or particularly idyllic views, but it does offer a cornucopia of craft shops and a few interesting sights. Above all, it is the base for an extensive fleet of jaunting cars. Dating back to Victorian times, these one-horse open carriages are the traditional mode of transport in the Killarney Lake District, parts of which are closed to vehicular traffic. Unless you

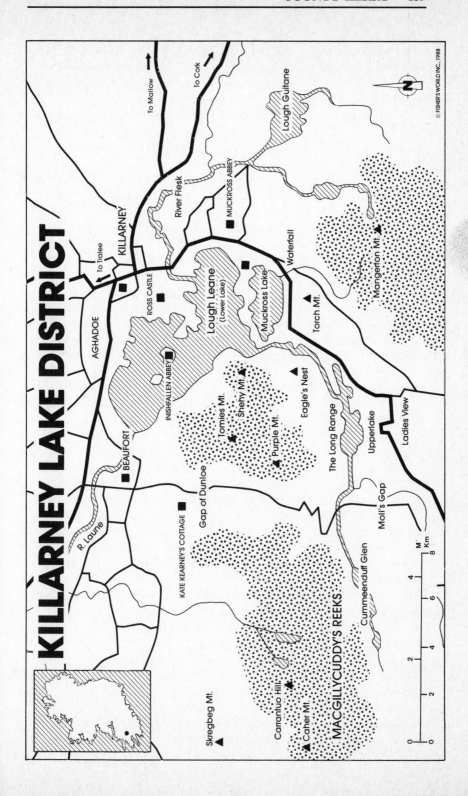

KILLARNEY LAKE DISTRICT

© FISHER'S WORLD INC., 1988

To Mallow

To Cork

KILLARNEY

To Tralee

River Flesk

MUCKROSS ABBEY

Lough Guitane

Mangerton Mt.

AGHADOE

ROSS CASTLE

Lough Leane
(Lower Lake)

Muckross Lake

Waterfall

Torch Mt.

INISHFALLEN ABBEY

Tomies Mt.

Shehy Mt.

Purple Mt.

Eagle's Nest

The Long Range

Upperlake

Ladies View

BEAUFORT

R. Laune

KATE KEARNEY'S COTTAGE

Gap of Dunloe

Moll's Gap

Cummeenduff Glen

MACGILLYCUDDY'S REEKS

Skregbeg Mt.

Carrantuo Hill

Caher Mt.

Mi.
Km
8

4

6

2

4

2

0

prefer to walk or rent a bike, you'll need to take a jaunting car ride to see the prime scenic attractions around the three lakes. The drivers of these jaunting cars, called "jarveys," will anxiously pursue you until you agree to take a ride (see "Inside Information"). Once you board a jaunting car, you'll have a tartan blanket tucked on your lap, "just in case" there's a mist or a cool breeze. To help you appreciate the sights along the way, the jarvey will give you a running commentary, complete with local legends, and, with the slightest encouragement, an appropriate song or two.

Some jaunting cars will concentrate on the sights of the Lower Lake, while others will take you to see the highlights of the Middle Lake, or a combination of the two. The main attraction of the Lower Lake is Ross Castle, a 15th-century fortress which distinguished itself in 1652 by being the last in Ireland to surrender to Cromwell's forces. All that remains today is a tower house, surrounded by a fortified bawn (courtyard) with rounded turrets.

From Ross Castle, you can also see (and visit) Innisfallen Island, peacefully floating in the Lower Lake. It's the site of a monastery, founded by St. Fallen in the 7th century, which flourished for 1,000 years. It is said that Brian Boru, the great Irish chieftain, and St. Brendan the Navigator were both educated here. In addition, the *Annals of Innisfallen*, a chronicle of early Irish history, was written here during the years 950 to 1320; it is now in the Bodleian Library at Oxford University. Although not much remains today, you can still see traces of an 11th-century church and a 12th-century priory. The island is open to the public, and men with rowboats are available at Ross Castle for hire if you wish to make the trip. It takes about a half-hour of rowing to reach the island, a delightful trip on a clear day.

Near the point where the Lower Lake meets the Middle Lake is Muckross Abbey, a 'medieval monastery founded in 1448 and sup- **★★** pressed in 1652. Designed in the Irish Gothic style, it has a cloister with 22 arches, each one framing a view of a giant yew tree which is said to have been growing in the center of the court since the abbey was built. This abbey is noteworthy as the burial place of Co. Kerry's great early chieftains, the MacCarthys, O'Donoghues, and O'Sullivans (surnames which still predominate in the county). It is also the final resting place for four of the county's most cherished 17th- and 18th-century poets, Egan O'Rahilly, Geoffrey O'Donoghue, Owen Roe O'Sullivan, and Pierce Ferriter.

The centerpiece of the Middle Lake, and, in many ways, of the entire national park, is the Muckross Estate, often called "the jewel of **★★★** Killarney." It consists of a gracious ivy-covered Elizabethan-style residence with colorful and well-tended gardens, all facing a panorama of lake and mountain scenery. Dating back to 1843, this 20-room house has been converted into a museum of Co. Kerry folklife

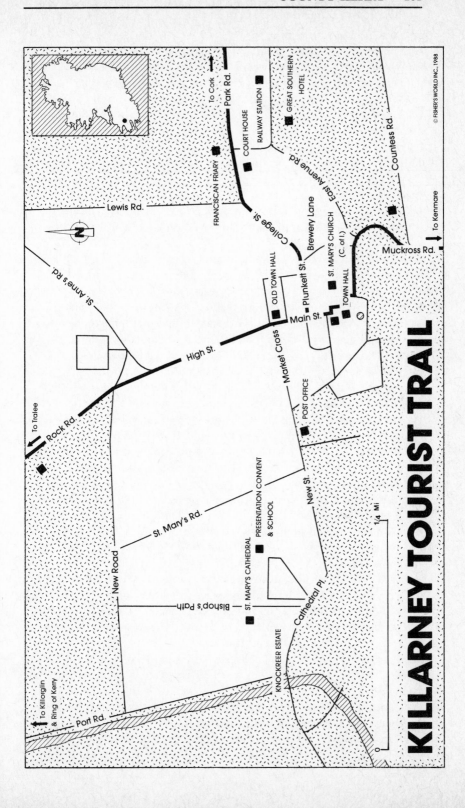

KILLARNEY TOURIST TRAIL

spanning the last two hundred years. It is a showcase of locally carved furniture, prints, maps, paintings, and needlework, as well as many imported treasures like Oriental screens, Venetian mirrors, Chippendale chairs, curtains woven in Brussels, and Turkish carpets.

The former cellars have been converted into a cluster of working craft shops, with 20th-century artisans demonstrating 18th- and 19th-century trades, such as shoemaking, printing, woodcarving, harness-making, bookbinding, spinning and weaving, pottery, and basketry. Many of the craft items produced here are also on sale in the adjacent shop. The house and the luxuriant gardens are open to the public year-round.

Nearby in a forest setting is the Torc Waterfall, a roaring cascade of ★★ waters falling down a 60-foot arc to the Middle Lake. If you climb the adjacent footpath to the top, there is a fine view of the lake district. Most jaunting car trips end at this point and return you to Killarney town or wherever you commenced your ride.

To see the Upper Lake, you'll need to drive along the Kenmare Road (N 71), about six or seven miles outside of town. There is a walking trail along the lake or you can follow the main road up into the hills, about 12 miles from Killarney. Here you will come to a spot known as "Ladies View," a look-out point which gives a broad survey ★ of all three lakes and the surrounding mountains. It earned its name in 1861 at the time of Queen Victoria's visit to ireland, when her ladies-in-waiting expressed great delight with the view from this spot.

As you can calculate, all of this sightseeing in the Killarney environs can easily fill a day. You will also want to save some time for the highlights of the downtown area. In addition to the many shops along the principal streets (Main, High, New, College, and Plunkett), there are some attractions which offer "indoor" sights in case it should be raining. These include an impressive cathedral, St. Mary's, designed in ★ the Gothic Revival style by Augustus Pugin. Situated at the edge of town on the far end of New Street, it was begun in 1842, interrupted by the Irish famine years, and finished in 1855; the magnificent central spire was added in 1912.

On Main Street in the town center is the neo-Gothic St. Mary's Church, now a Church of Ireland structure, dating back to 1870. The most significant thing about this edifice is that it is located on a site where there have been a succession of places of worship spanning at least eight centuries. The common belief is that this was the original "Cill Airne" (which means "church of the sloe woods" in the Irish or Gaelic language). And this is how the town got its name, which has since been anglicized to "Killarney."

Killarney's only museum is an unusual one, the Transport Treasures of Ireland, located on East Avenue Road, just off Main Street. It is a ★★ collection of historic veteran cars, cycles, carriages, and automobilia, including Ireland's oldest car.

★★ You can also enjoy fine views of the Lower Lake by visiting the Knockreer Estate, a part of the National Park grounds most recently opened to the public (1986). The main access to Knockreer is via a gate opposite the cathedral, off New Street, so you can easily walk to this site. Once the home of Lord Kenmare, it includes a turn-of-the-century house, a pathway along the River Deenagh, and gardens which are a mix of 200-year-old trees with flowering cherries, magnolias, and azaleas.

Hopefully, you'll be staying in Killarney more than one day, enabling you to devote at least a morning or afternoon to the Ring of Kerry drive. You'll need still another day for Dingle Peninsula.

★★★ In addition, if you are fond of outdoor activity, do consider taking a local excursion known as the "Gap of Dunloe" trip. You'll ride horseback (or in a horse-drawn cart, if you prefer) through a seven-mile mountain pass, have a picnic lunch, and then take a rowboat trip across the three Killarney Lakes. Your muscles might be sore at day's end, but you'll never forget the exhilarating experience or the sights (see "Inside Information").

Lastly, perhaps as you leave the area to travel onward, you should venture two miles north, off the main Tralee Road (N 22), to a place known as Aghadoe Heights. Surpassing "Ladies View" in some respects, this 400-foot hill looks out onto the whole Killarney spectrum—the lakes, mountains, parklands, the entire town, and the surrounding farmlands.

THE RING OF KERRY

★★★★ Undoubtedly Ireland's most popular scenic drive, the "Ring of Kerry" is a 110-mile panorama of seacoast, mountain, and lakeland vistas. For the most part, it follows the N 70 road which circles the Iveragh Peninsula, starting and finishing at Killarney (but you can also use Kenmare as a base). Although a little rain or passing showers should not deter you from embarking on this drive, it is best not to set out in heavy sea mist or continuous rain. If the clouds are moving, however, that usually means you'll have a good day for the Ring.

The drive can be undertaken in either direction, but we recommend a counter-clockwise route. The duration can be anything from four hours to a full day, depending on how many stops you make for picture-taking, beach-walking, hill-climbing, pubbing, shopping, and diversions down side roads.

Departing Killarney, follow the signs for Killorglin. When you reach this little town, you are now on the N 70 road. You may wish to stop and walk around Killorglin, a spot which is known far and wide for its annual mid-August horse, sheep, and cattle fair. It's officially called the "Puck Fair," because the local residents capture a wild goat from the mountains and enthrone it in the center of town as a sign of unrestricted merrymaking.

Continue on the N 70 road and soon vistas of Dingle Bay will appear on your right and Carrantuohill, Ireland's tallest mountain (3,414 feet) to your left. Another sight which will constantly come into view is the open bogland, from which the local residents dig pieces of peat or "turf" to burn in their fireplaces for warmth. These boglands, formed thousands of years ago, are mainly made up of decayed trees, and tend to be bumpy if you attempt to drive over them too speedily, so do be cautious.

You'll also find that the road winds around cliffs and the edge of mountains, with nothing but the sea below—another reason that you will probably average only 30 miles an hour at best. The remains of many abandoned cottages date from the famine years, in the mid-1840's, when the Irish potato crop failed and millions of people either starved or were forced to emigrate. You'll see reminders of the famine all over Ireland, but especially in Galway, Mayo, Donegal, and in the remote parts of Kerry. This peninsula alone lost three-fourths of its population.

The next town is Glenbeigh, a palm tree-lined fishing resort, with a lovely dune-filled beach called Rossbeigh Strand. You may wish to stop here or continue the sweep through the mountains and along the sea's edge to Cahirciveen. From here, you can make a slight detour to see Valentia, an offshore island seven miles long and one of the most westerly points of Europe. Connected to the mainland by a bridge at Portmagee, this was the site of the first telegraph cable laid across the Atlantic in 1866. In addition, the Valentia harbor was famous in the 18th century as a refuge for smugglers and privateers; it is said that John Paul Jones also anchored here quite often.

Head next for Waterville, an idyllic spot wedged between Lough Currane and Ballinskelligs Bay off the Atlantic. For years, it was known as the favorite retreat of Charlie Chaplin, but today it is a mecca for golfers (see "Inside Information"). It is also a prime spot for salmon and trout fishing.

If you follow the sea road north of town out to the Irish-speaking village of Ballinskelligs at the mouth of the bay, you can also catch a glimpse of the two Skellig Rocks. The smaller Skellig is home to ★★ thousands of gannets, and is recognized as one of the great bird sanctuaries of the world. The larger rock, known as the Great Skellig or Skellig Michael, is the site of a monastic settlement which was a great center of pilgrimage between the 6th and 12th centuries.

Continuing on the N 70 route, the next point of interest is Derrynane, the home of Daniel O'Connell, remembered in Ireland as "The

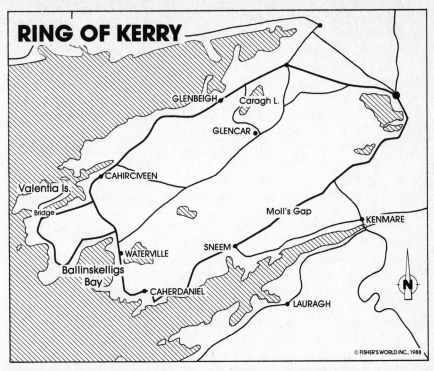

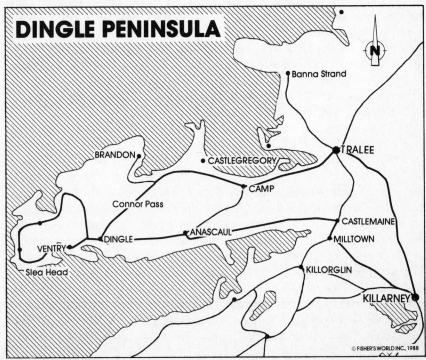

Liberator" because in 1829 he freed Irish Catholics from the last of the discriminatory penal restraints. The site is now a national monument and park, and a major center of Gaelic culture.

Watch for signs to "Staigue Fort," about two miles off the main ★★ road. One of the best preserved of all Irish ancient structures, this circular fort is constructed of rough stones put into position without mortar of any kind. The walls are 13 feet wide at its base, and the diameter is about 90 feet. Not much is known of its history, but experts think it probably dates back to around 1,000 B.C.

Sneem is the next village on the circuit. It's a colorful little hamlet, with twin parklets and houses painted in vibrant shades of blue, pink, yellow, purple, and orange, almost like a Mediterranean cluster. Because this area is a good fishing spot, the local church even sports a salmon-shaped weather vane on its steeple.

As you continue on the road, the foliage becomes richer and more extensive thanks to the warming waters and winds of the Gulf Stream. When you begin to see lots of palm trees and other subtropical vegetation, you'll know you are in Parknasilla, once a favorite haunt of George Bernard Shaw. Today Parknasilla's main claim to fame is its splendid resort hotel (see "Inside Information").

The final town on the Ring of Kerry route is by far the most enchanting. Originally called "Neidin" which in the Irish language means "Little Nest," Kenmare is indeed a little nest of lush foliage nestled between the River Roughty and Kenmare Bay. Well laid out and immaculately maintained by its proud residents, it easily rivals Killarney as an alternative base for County Kerry sightseeing. Kenmare is also the home of the Park Hotel, a chateau-like lodging which many people consider to be the best hostelry in all of Ireland (see "Inside Information").

On the return to Killarney, the final lap of the Ring road takes you through a scenic mountain stretch known as Moll's Gap.

THE DINGLE PENINSULA

Situated twenty miles northwest of Killarney, the Dingle Peninsula is ★★★ similar to the Ring of Kerry, but its appeal is more rugged and remote. The movie "Ryan's Daughter," which won rave reviews for its scenery rather than its story, was filmed here. You can enter the Dingle Peninsula at Castlemaine or Tralee. Many people choose to stay at or visit Tralee first and then venture out on the westward drive.

The chief town of County Kerry, Tralee (pronounced "Trah-lee"), has a population of 22,000 and lies in the center of a rich limestone farm belt appropriately known as the Vale of Tralee. As you might have guessed, it served as the inspiration for the song, "The Rose of

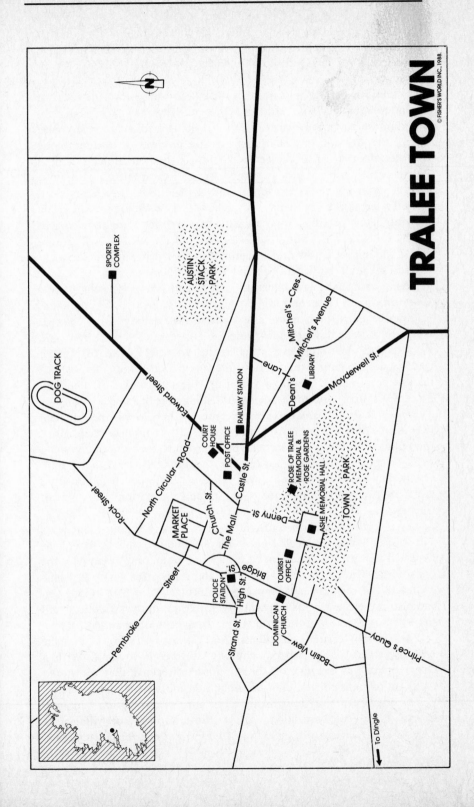

Tralee," composed by local resident William Mulchinock over 100 years ago. Tralee is also the setting for the country's largest annual festival, and for the National Folk Theatre of Ireland (see "Inside Information").

The harbor of Tralee is located four miles northwest of the town, at Fenit. A major sailing center, this is the spot where legend says that St. Brendan the Navigator was born in 484; he is credited by many with sailing the Atlantic in a leather boat and discovering America long before Columbus. The Tralee Golf Club, a new creation of Arnold Palmer, is also located near here (See "Inside Information").

When you are ready to venture into Dingle, take the Camp Road from Tralee along Tralee Bay, with the Slieve Mish Mountains rising on your left. Although the peninsula is narrower than the Ring of Kerry, it also reaches about 40 miles out into the sea and will require about 100 miles of slow and sometimes tedious driving (counterclockwise) to see it all, but it will be a day to remember.

From Camp, the road hugs the shore and provides vistas of Mt. Brandon, Ireland's second highest mountain, named for St. Brendan. ★★★ Follow the signs for Conor Pass, a spectacular drive up to 1,500 feet which on a clear day provides views of Tralee Bay, north Kerry, and the mouth of the Shannon as it meets the Atlantic. Rising steeply, the road includes a panorama of rocky mountain slopes and cliffs, including one point named "Faill na Seamrog," the shamrock cliff. The final descent will bring you to the sheltered fishing port of Dingle.

With a charter dating back many centuries, Dingle was the principal harbor in County Kerry during medieval times. Today it is the focus of the Dingle Peninsula and a great spot to spend an afternoon, a day, a week, or more. Even though it is just a small town (population: 1,500), Dingle has more fine restaurants than most of Ireland's major cities and dozens of interesting pubs (See "Inside Information" for a few of the best).

Beyond Dingle are a trio of remote towns where Irish (or Gaelic) is the spoken language, including Ventry, Dunquin, and Ballyferriter. You will also want to pause at Slea Head, a mountainous curve at the ★★★ end of the peninsula which has been the setting for many a scenic postcard and sea-splashed landscape painting. From Slea Head, you can also see the seven Blasket Islands sitting out in the Atlantic. Until the 1950's the largest of these, the Great Blasket, was inhabited.

East of Ballyferriter you will also find Gallarus Oratory, one of the ★★ best preserved early-Christian church buildings in Ireland. With a shape much like an inverted boat, it is constructed of unmortared stone yet remains completely watertight after more than 1,000 years.

The road eventually returns inland to Dingle town. From here, you ★★★ should travel eastward along Dingle Bay through the villages of Lispole and Annascaul to Inch, one of Dingle's most beautiful sights.

This is a four-mile stretch of sandy beach, with distant views of the Ring of Kerry and Killarney. From Inch, you can return via Camp to Tralee or continue to Castlemaine and onward to Limerick or other parts of Kerry and Cork.

DINGLE, Co. Kerry

Hotel

★★ THE NEW SCEILIG—QUALITY INN (For Location)
Annascaul Road. Tel. (066) 51144. 79 rooms. Named for the fabled Sceilig Rocks off the coast, this modern motor inn was re-opened in 1987 under new management after a hiatus of two years. Even though it has always had a lot going for it (including up-to-date facilities and an idyllic location next to Dingle Bay on the eastern edge of town), it has had a checkered past of changing hands often. At the present time, happily, it looks like things will stay on the upswing. Promising evidence includes a recent $1.5 million refurbishment and the addition of a new leisure center with an indoor heated swimming pool, sauna, and tennis court.

At the moment, the Sceilig is the only full-scale hotel in town and a logical place to stay, although the Doyle family (see "Restaurants" below) has big plans for a new Dingle lodging choice by March of 1988. *Moderate.*

Restaurants

★★★★★ DOYLE'S SEAFOOD
John Street. Tel. (066) 51174. Located in a small fishing port with a dozen fine restaurants, Doyle's was the first to achieve international acclaim and it remains the benchmark of them all. Many people make a special trip to Dingle from Killarney, Tralee, Limerick, or points beyond, just to eat at Doyle's. Now in its 16th year, this award-winning spot is the creation of John and Stella Doyle, formerly of Dublin.

With walls and floors of stone, sugan chairs, tweedy placemats, and old Dingle sketches, this 30-seat gem has a homey country town atmosphere. All the ingredients come either from the sea, the Doyles' own gardens, or nearby farms. Specialties include cockle and mussel soup, nettle soup (an old Irish recipe somewhat like spinach soup), brown trout with mushroom sauce, crab claws beurre blanc, scallops with light orange sauce, seafood mornay (crab, salmon, mussels, scallops, prawns, and more), filet of salmon en papilotte, and rack of lamb, all accompanied by a divine homemade brown bread, and a selection of wines which the Doyles have personally gathered from all corners of the globe. Open for lunch and dinner, mid-March through mid-November, except Sunday. *Moderate.*

Note: As we go to press, the Doyles have just announced the acquisition of the building adjoining the restaurant, which they are going to convert and refurbish into an eight-room town house inn. It opened on schedule in March, 1988, and, judging from the Doyles' past endeavors, it should become "the place" to stay in Dingle.

★★★★ THE HALF DOOR
John Street. Tel. (066) 51600. It isn't easy being the restaurant next door to Doyle's, but John and Celeste Slye hold their own very nicely on the Dingle culinary scene. Also specializing in seafood, the Slyes aim to create inventive dishes, frequently coupling fish with fresh fruits. Some of the featured entrees include pears and shellfish in tarragon dressing, sole with banana and chutney, trout in blackberry and vermouth sauce, and salmon in ginger butter sauce. Open for lunch and dinner, mid-March through mid-November. Closed Tuesday. *Moderate.*

★★★ WHELAN'S
Main Street. Tel. (066) 51622. For those who crave a good old fashioned Irish stew, this is the place. In this versatile 40-seat restaurant, you'll also find an eclectic blend of dishes from seafood pancakes and salmon over seaweed, to prawns in brandy cream and asparagus mousse, not to mention a juicy Gaelic steak. It's in the middle of town, run by John Whelan. Open for dinner only, April through October. *Moderate.*

★★★ GREET'S
The Wood. Tel. (066) 51214. Of all the Dingle restaurants, this one has the most scenic location, on a hillside west of town overlooking Dingle harbor. Owned by the same Flemish family who have made Gaby's such an outstanding Killarney success, Greet's has a modern ranch-style layout with expansive windows, and indoor/outdoor seating, depending on the weather. The menu includes beef or pork steaks, chicken breast in raspberry sauce, haddock in wine, hot smoked trout, or lobsters from the tank. Open April to October, for lunch and dinner daily (except no dinner Monday). *Moderate.*

Pubs

★★★ O'FLAHERTY'S
Bridge Street. Tel. (066) 51461. The true flavor of the Dingle Peninsula

is reflected in this rustic pub. The walls are lined with old posters, prints, clippings, and photos of Irish literary figures of long ago. You'll also see poems on the Dingle area by local authors and favorite Gaelic phrases, many of which are just tacked up and curling at the edges. In the evenings, traditional music sessions are usually on tap.

★★★ **RICHARD MacDONNELL**
Green Street. You can do a bit of craft-hunting by visiting this unique pub. Once inside, turn left and you'll see a counter for leather goods and groceries; then cross over to the right, and you'll be at the tiny bar. This multi-purpose enclave is a favorite with the locals, who stop by mostly to hear owner "Dick Mack" reminisce about the last 80 or so years. In the course of the chat, Dick will serve the drinks, and then move to the other side of the room where he'll handily emboss initials or a shamrock on a belt, key fob, or a pair of boots.

Shopping

AN CAFE LITEARTHA
Dykegate Street. Tel. (066) 51380. A cross between a book store and a cafe, this is a treasure-trove for all types of books and maps of Irish interest, and particularly on life in this corner of County Kerry. The cafe at the rear features freshly baked goods, salads, and seafoods. It's an ideal spot to browse and to enjoy a quick lunch or snack in the middle of town.

GLENBEIGH, Co. Kerry

Hotel

★★ **TOWERS** (For Ambience)
Ring of Kerry Road (N 70). Tel. (066) 68212. 22 rooms. This vintage country inn is right in the middle of a small fishing village, yet within a mile of the sandy Rossbeigh strand and 20 miles west of Killarney. Recently refurbished and up-dated, it is best known for its lively pub and good seafood restaurant. Open April through October. *Inexpensive.*

KENMARE, Co. Kerry

Hotels

★★★★★ **THE PARK**
Tel. (064) 41200. 48 rooms and suites. If we could give one hotel in

Ireland ten stars, this would be the place. A haven of impeccable service and luxurious living, this chateau on Kenmare Bay is a showcase of antiques, oil paintings, tapestries, and plush furnishings.

Originally opened as a Great Southern hotel in 1897, it was totally restored and refurbished eight years ago, and has since been under the masterful management of Francis Brennan. Bedrooms have individual character, many with four-poster or canopy beds, hand-carved armoires, china lamps, curios, and little extra touches like telephones in the bathroom and towel warmers. Outdoor facilities include a nine-hole golf course, joggers' trail, tennis courts, and salmon fishing.

The elegant dining room, with romantic views of the water and palm tree-lined gardens, is the most highly acclaimed hotel restaurant in Ireland; signature dishes include breast of chicken stuffed with salmon in lobster sauce, baby rack of lamb with garden vegetables, duckling en croute, and Irish Mist souffle. A member of the prestigious Relais and Chateaux group, the Park is situated on the Ring of Kerry, about 20 miles from Killarney, set on its own grounds at the top of the town. Open April through December. *Very expensive.*

★★★ KENMARE BAY
Sneem Road. Tel. (064) 41300. 68 rooms. This is a modern motor inn at the edge of town, just off the main road which winds around the Ring of Kerry. The motif is tweedy and modern, with large windows which look out onto the mountainous countryside. Facilities include a full-service restaurant and a spacious lounge bar which is the setting for traditional Irish music sing-alongs on most evenings. Open April through October. *Inexpensive.*

Bed-and-Breakfast

★★ MUXNAW LODGE (For Ambience)
Castletownbere Road. Tel. (064) 41252. 4 rooms. If you prefer staying at a private residence, you can't go wrong at this gabled Victorian country house built in 1801 and named after a nearby mountain. Set in its own grounds overlooking the bay, this peaceful retreat is the home of the Boland family. The front rooms boast views of the water, brass beds, and private facilities; the two back rooms are less elaborate and share a bathroom. A tennis court and three acres of mature garden walks are part of the grounds. No credit cards. *Bargain.*

Restaurants

★★★★ LIME TREE
Shelbourne Road. Tel. (064) 42225. Innovative Irish cuisine is the

focus at this new restaurant in a renovated schoolhouse landmark (1821), next to the grounds of the Park Hotel. The decor includes a skylit gallery and stone walls lined with paintings by local artists. The menu includes such items as oak-smoked chicken, West Cork ham, Kenmare Bay scallops, wild trout with leeks and cream, and rack of lamb with spicy plum sauce. Open for dinner only, March through October. No credit cards. *Moderate to expensive.*

★★★ REMY'S HOUSE
Main Street. Tel. (064) 41589. Remy Benoit has brought a touch of France to a 19th century bank building at the top of the street. Entrees range from pork rib and rack of lamb to a puff pastry filled with mussels and spinach in a creamy sauce. Open for dinner only, mid-March through mid-October. Closed Tuesday. *Moderate.*

★★★ JUGS
Sneem Road, Gortamullen. Tel. (064) 41099. Dutch chef/owner Peter Ringlever has brought an international flair to this modern bungalow bistro, on the edge of town. The menu includes local salmon, rainbow trout amandine, turkey a la Vienna, and fruitnut ice cream. An innovative touch is a teppanyaki-style portable grill which allows guests to cook a selection of lean meats and steaks at tableside. Open for lunch and dinner daily, from April through October, except Monday from mid-April to the end of May.

Pub

★★ LANSDOWNE ARMS
Main Street. Tel. (064) 41368. In the heart of town, this pub lounge is an oasis of country charm with nightly programs of music, song, or poetry.

Shopping

CLEO
2 Shelbourne Road. Tel. (064) 41410. A branch of the long established Dublin store of the same name, this trendy shop is known for its colorful tweed and linen fashions, as well as specialty items like Kinsale cloaks.

D.J. CREMIN AND SONS
Main Street. Tel. (064) 41597. Founded in 1906 as a general drapery store, this family-run business is a haven for limited Waterford Crystal items like lamps, globes, candelabras, wall brackets, and chandeliers. You will also find unusual Irish dolls, locally-made handknits and other giftware. (Also maintains a branch on East Avenue in Killarney.)

SPINDLE AND TREADLE
The Square. Tel. (064) 41060. As you shop in this tiny store, you can watch craftsperson Olive Donovan knitting and weaving scarves, stoles, table mats, tweed lengths, and blanket rugs on the premises.

KILLARNEY, Co. Kerry

Hotels

★★★★ THE GREAT SOUTHERN
Railway Road. Tel. (064) 31262. 180 rooms. Built in 1854 and recently up-dated and refurbished, this ivy-covered four-story landmark is the "grande dame" of Killarney hotels. Enlarged in stages over the decades, some of the older rooms have tall ceilings, huge windows, and period furnishings, while the newer units are sleek and modern. Situated right on the eastern edge of town and surrounded by lush foliage and mountain vistas, the Great Southern was first opened around the time of Queen Victoria's visit to Killarney and has since been host to presidents, princes, and personalities from all over the world.

The classic main dining room overlooks the gardens, while the smaller Malton Room provides a la carte service in a clubby setting of banquette seating, candlelight, Irish silver, Cavan Crystal, and 19th century prints. Guest facilities include an indoor heated swimming pool, saunas, tennis courts, boutique, nightly entertainment in the summer months, and plenty of parking. Open mid-March through December. *Expensive.*

★★★★ EUROPE
Fossa, off the Killorglin Road. Tel. (064) 31900. 188 rooms. The award for the most idyllic location of a Killarney hotel has to go to the Hotel Europe. Located three miles west of town, it sits right on the shores of the Lower Lake, next to Killarney's two 18-hole golf courses, and surrounded by dozens of mountain peaks.

Modern and spotless, this German-owned hotel is a favorite with continental European visitors and with American convention and tour groups. With spacious and open public areas and stereotyped guest rooms, it does lack a certain Irish ambience, but it's hard to beat the views and the efficiency. Dining facilities include the aptly named "Panorama Restaurant" and an alpine-themed "Tyrol" cafe for light meals. Other amenities range from an indoor heated pool and health center, plus horseback riding, boating, fishing, tennis, and bicycling, to evening entertainment and ample parking. Open during March and from May through October. *Expensive.*

★★★★ DUNLOE CASTLE

Beaufort, off the Killorglin Road. Tel. (064) 44111. 140 rooms. Located on its own extensive tropical grounds about six miles west of town near the entrance to the Gap of Dunloe, this is not really a castle, in the medieval sense. Instead it is a contemporary-style hotel which takes its name from a ruined 15th century fortress nearby. Like its sister hotel, the Europe, it is German-owned and a favorite with Europeans.

Surrounded by broad mountain vistas, the Dunloe has a certain agrarian ambience, with horses, ponies, and cows grazing in the adjacent fields. Facilities include a full-service restaurant, heated indoor swimming pool, sauna, tennis courts, horseback riding, fishing, croquet, putting green, fitness track, and nightly entertainment. It's a place to come to unwind and to spend a few days; you'll need a car to get to town or to sightsee in the area. Open April through October. *Expensive.*

★★★ AGHADOE HEIGHTS—QUALITY INN

Aghadoe, off N 22. Tel. (064) 31766. 60 rooms. For a total Killarney perspective—overlooking the town, lakes, mountains, and surrounding countryside, this modern two-story hotel couldn't be in a better spot. Situated on high ground two miles northwest of Killarney, the Aghadoe Heights is owner/managed by personable Louis O'Hara and newly affiliated with the Quality Inn group.

Recently refurbished, it combines a tweedy motif with floor-to-ceiling window views of the Killarney kaleidoscope. Guest facilities include a rooftop restaurant which specializes in local seafoods, and a lounge with musical entertainment on summer evenings, plus salmon fishing on a private stretch of river, and golfing privileges on Killarney's two 18-hole courses. Closed mid-December to mid-January. *Moderate.*

★★★ CAHERNANE

Muckross Road (N 71). Tel. (064) 31895. 36 rooms. Originally built in 1877 as a manor home for the Herbert family (the Earls of Pembroke), this country house hotel is situated less than a mile from town, along the shores of the Lower Lake in a sylvan setting of ancient trees and well-tended rose gardens. As befits its Victorian heritage, the house is furnished with antiques and period furniture both in its public areas and most of its guest rooms. Amenities include a gracious old-world dining room, piano bar, tennis courts, pitch and putt, croquet, and fishing privileges for salmon and trout. Closed November through March. *Expensive.*

★★★ THE TORC GREAT SOUTHERN

Cork Road. Tel. (064) 31611. 96 rooms. This contemporary motor inn is positioned on its own grounds in a prosperous residential area less than a mile east of town. The guest rooms are sleek and bright, with large window views of the adjacent gardens and nearby mountains. There is a full-service restaurant and cocktail lounge, plus a health center with indoor heated swimming pool, saunas, and tennis courts. Open mid-April through September. *Moderate.*

★★★ CASTLEROSSE

Killorglin Road. Tel. (064) 31114. 40 rooms. A Best Western affiliate, this one-story ranch-style inn is set on its own parklands overlooking the lakes and mountains. It's two miles from the heart of town, and next to Killarney's two golf courses. For those who prefer a motel-style of accommodations, this is good value. There is a full-service restaurant, outdoor swimming pool, tennis courts, and croquet lawn. Open from April through October. *Inexpensive to moderate.*

Guesthouse

★★★ KATHLEEN'S COUNTRY HOUSE

Madam's Height, Tralee Road (N 22). Tel. (064) 32810. 10 rooms. Of the many guesthouses and B & B homes in this area, this one stands out. Located about a mile north of town on its own grounds, with ample parking and next to a dairy farm, it is a two-story contemporary house, with a modern mansard-style roof and many picture windows. Enthusiastic and efficient hostess Kathleen O'Regan-Sheppard has also outfitted all the bedrooms with private baths and orthopedic beds. Open from March through October. *Bargain to inexpensive.*

For other accommodations within a 20-mile radius of Killarney, see also Kenmare, Tralee, and Glenbeigh.

Restaurants

★★★★ GABY'S

17 High Street. Tel. (064) 32519. This informal seafood restaurant is wedged among a string of shops along one of Killarney's busiest streets. Long and narrow, with a nautical decor, it is configured to hold about 50 diners, mostly in booth-style seating. Quarters are cramped, reservations are not accepted, but no one ever minds, since the food is the best in town. Run by the Maes family who bring a Flemish influence to the Irish seafood specialties, this restaurant is known for its succulent lobster, served grilled or in a house sauce; other choices include turbot, haddock in wine, local salmon, and a giant Kerry shellfish platter—a veritable feast of prawns, scallops, mussels, lobster, crayfish, and oysters. Open for lunch and dinner, mid-March through November, except Monday for lunch and Sunday all day. *Expensive.*

★★★ DINGLES

40 New Street. Tel. (064) 31079. Located on one of Killarney's fastest developing streets, near the Knockreer Estate, this is an enchanting

bistro-style restaurant run by congenial host Gerry Cunningham. The decor is a cozy blend of an open turf fireplace, surrounded by arches and alcoves, with wooden benches, leather cushions, recycled church pew benches and cathedral choir stalls. The international menu includes such dishes as chicken curry, chili con carne, beef Stroganoff, Irish stew, and seafood dishes such as giant prawn tails in garlic butter, or crab and shrimp au gratin. Open daily for dinner only, except the end of December through February. *Moderate.*

★★★ FOLEY'S
23 High Street. Tel. (064) 31217. A Georgian country home atmosphere prevails at this seafood and steak restaurant, a few doors down from Gaby's. The ever-changing menu features such items as mussel soup, Dingle Bay scallops mornay, rainbow trout, and fresh salmon, as well as prime steaks and Kerry mountain lamb. Don't miss the home-baked brown bread scones which accompany each meal. This restaurant has a full bar, and a resident pianist who adds to the ambience by playing a repertoire of tunes from contemporary and classical to traditional Irish. Open for lunch and dinner daily, year-round except Christmas Day. *Moderate.*

For additional nearby dining accommodations, see also Kenmare, Tralee, and Dingle.

Pubs

★★★★ BUCKLEY'S
2 College Street. Tel. (064) 31037. For a quiet drink and some convivial conversation, don't miss this well-kept pub. Established in 1926, it has a neat Georgian facade, and an interior which focuses on Kerry's great sporting traditions. You'll see football trophies, uniforms and team photos, plus some intriguing pictures and paintings of old Killarney.

★★★ DUNLOE LODGE
Plunkett Street. Tel. (064) 32502. This simple local pub in the heart of town has a friendly and comfortable atmosphere. Don't be surprised if someone spontaneously pulls out a harmonica, accordian, banjo, or fiddle, and starts to play.

★★★ THE LAURELS
Main Street. Tel. (064) 31149. Music, music, music is the focus here each evening, with mostly Irish tunes on tap. Hearty meals of Irish stew and other traditional dishes are also served.

★★★ DANNY MANN
97 New Street. Tel. (064) 31640. Also known for its music, this pub attracts a younger crowd and offers disco dancing later in the evening.

★★★ **KATE KEARNEY'S COTTAGE**
Gap of Dunloe. Tel. (064) 44146. Of all the Killarney pubs, the one that enjoys the best scenery is this secluded white-washed outpost nine miles west of the town center. Almost everyone who ventures through the famous Gap on horseback or via a horse-drawn cart first makes a customary visit to this former coaching inn. It is named after a woman who was thought to be a witch long ago, but today it is quite civilized, more of a comfort and refreshment stop, with souvenirs on sale as well.

Shopping

THE ARTIST GALLERY
5 Plunkett Street. Tel. (064) 32273. The colorful paintings, drawings, prints, and graphics in this shop reflect the designs of Celtic Ireland. Local artist Stephen Doyle produces most of the work himself on the premises.

KERRY GLASS
Fair Hill. Tel. (064) 32587. This is the home of Killarney's distinctive colored glass. Visitors are welcome to watch and photograph the craftsmen firing, blowing, and adding the color to the glass as it is shaped into vases, paperweights, and figurines. The factory and shop are open year-round, Monday through Friday. If you should be in town on a weekend, there is an outlet store located on College Street; Kerry Glass items are also usually stocked at most other craft shops in town. Conveniently located opposite the Great Southern Hotel.

QUILL'S WOOLLEN MARKET
1 Fairhill. Tel. (064) 33763. Quill's is one of the best spots in town for handknit sweaters of all colors, sizes, and types, plus tweeds, mohair, and sheepskins. If you miss this one, there are also branches in Ballingeary, Co. Cork, Sneem and Kenmare in Co. Kerry.

THREADS AND CLAY
Down Lane off College Street. Tel. (064) 33433. This is a working shop displaying the handcrafts of a husband and wife team. John Joe Murphy weaves beautiful scarves and shawls, while spouse Mary turns out pottery creations ranging from vases and tea pots to goblets.

SERENDIPITY
15 College Street. Tel. (064) 31056. The shelves of this tidy shop feature a wide range of unusual crafts from local artisans, such as copper leprechauns mounted on aged bogwood and ceramic sheep and goats, to miniature oil paintings, pressed flowers and shamrocks, crochet work, and lace.

MUCKROSS HOUSE CRAFT SHOP
Kenmare Road. (064) 31440. After you have seen the weaver, potter,

bookbinder, basket-maker, and blacksmith, all plying their trades in the Muckross Folk Museum workshops, you can buy the products in the on-premises shop. The wares range from scarves and stoles to table mats, goblets, jugs, door knockers, and photo albums.

KILLARNEY ANTIQUES SHOP
16 College Street. Tel. (064) 31351. An orderly collection of nick nacks and curios fills this tiny shop, along with a sprinkling of wall clocks, silverware, china, and pictures of the Killarney area. After you browse, you can also enjoy a snack at the homey Kitchen Garden, a cafe/wine bar tucked at the rear of the shop. It's open throughout the day, specializing in smoked meats, fish, and cheese, plus crusty home-baked breads and unusual soups.

Sightseeing Tours

Horse-drawn Carts and More

JAUNTING CAR RIDES
Undoubtedly the official mode of transport in Killarney, these one-horse-drawn touring carts are more plentiful than taxis. You'll find them lined up along Main Street and Kenmare Place, outside of the major downtown hotels, in front of the Tourist Office, and at sightseeing attractions such as Muckross House and Ross Castle.

In order to get the best views of the lakes, you and your companions sit side-ways facing the scenery, while the driver (known locally as "a jarvey") commentates on the sights, often interjecting a local legend or song along the way. Since autos are not permitted in the Muckross Estate and in much of the National Park expanse, a jaunting car ride is not to be missed. You might say that a jaunting car ride is to Killarney what a cable car is to San Francisco or a gondola to Venice.

Be warned that the jarveys can be a bit aggressive in soliciting your business; but if you prefer to walk or bicycle around the lakes, a polite but firm "No, thank you" is all you need to say. Take comfort, however, in the fact that jaunting car rates are set and carefully monitored by the local tourist office, so you won't be overcharged. The current rate is about $15 for a two-hour excursion, but do check in advance.

THE GAP OF DUNLOE
If you have an extra day to spare, a trip through this winding and rocky gorge will show you the best of lakeside and mountain scenery, and give you a day's touring in the fresh air. The excursion starts at Kate Kearney's Cottage, about 9 miles west of Killarney. From there, you either mount a pony or climb into a horse-drawn cart for the seven-mile trek through the Gap to the shores of the Upper Lake; if you're hale and hearty, you can also walk or sprint along.

The route is a constant panorama of craggy rocks, massive cliffs, meandering streams, and deep valleys. You'll pass Serpent Lake, the spot where St. Patrick is said to have drowned the last snake in Ireland; to this day, it is without fish. As you approach the lakeshore, a stop is made for a picnic lunch at Lord Brandon's Cottage.

The next phase of the journey is on water, as you board open boats for a return trip across the Lakes of Killarney. What better way to appreciate the beauty of these three storied lakes, than to sit back and enjoy the gentle gliding as the oarsmen row in unison. The tour ends at 15th century Ross Castle, where jaunting carts are lined up to take passengers back to Killarney town. The total price of this day-long excursion is about $30, but check with the tourist office in advance, to see what the set rate is before you sign up at your hotel. (The price usually includes a packed lunch supplied by your hotel.)

Cruising the Lakes

LAKE TOURS
College Street. Tel. (064) 32911. Cruise the Lakes of Killarney in an all-weather motorized waterbus. A 90-minute sightseeing excursion with commentary costs about $6; boats depart Ross Castle during the summer season, approximately every two hours.

ROSS CASTLE BOATS
Ross Castle, Kenmare Road. Tel. (064) 32252. For sightseeing or fishing, with or without a boatman, you can traverse the waters of Killarney's Lakes, by the hour, half-day or full day. Prices range from about $10 to $20.

Sports

Golf

KILLARNEY GOLF CLUB
Killorglin Road. Tel. (064) 31034. Visitors are welcome any day and especially on weekdays at the twin 18-hole championship courses of Killarney's lakeside golf club, located three miles west of the town center. Widely praised as the most scenic golf setting in the world, these courses, known as "Killeen" and "Mahony's Point," will also challenge your golfing skills. Greens fees, which cover a day's play on both courses, are about $20. You can rent clubs for $9 per round and caddie carts for about $2. To arrange a day's outing, contact Capt. D.D. O'Connell, the manager for both courses.

For other nearby Co. Kerry golf courses, see also Tralee and Waterville.

Festivals

May 14-21: Pan Celtic Festival. A celebration of music, song, language, and sport, by the Celtic peoples of Ireland, Scotland, Isle of Man, Wales, Brittany, and Cornwall, and spectators from around the globe.

July 11-15: Killarney Racing Week. A colorful mid-summer program of horse races and social events.

Directory

Killarney Tourist Office, Town Hall, Main Street. Tel. (064) 31633.
CIE, Railway Station, next to the Great Southern Hotel. Tel. (064) 31067, for trains, buses, and local sightseeing tours.

PARKNASILLA, Co. Kerry

Hotels

★★★★ GREAT SOUTHERN
Ring of Kerry Road (N 70). Tel. (064) 45122. 60 rooms. Facing one of the loveliest seascape settings in Ireland, this hotel is nestled amid 300 acres of lush subtropical foliage, palm trees, and flowering shrubs. Thanks to the warming influence of the Gulf Stream, it enjoys a year-round temperate climate.

The present structure, an outgrowth and expansion of a former private mansion, was built with a fanciful Victorian stone facade in 1896. Over the years, it has been a favorite with visiting royalty and celebrities, including Nobel Prize-winning dramatist, George Bernard Shaw. It's not surprising that he found the inspiration here to write much of his play "St. Joan." Today's traveler is inspired, most of all, to have a memorable vacation, thanks to such amenities as a private nine-hole golf course, heated indoor salt-water swimming pool, saunas, horseback riding, tennis, fishing, boating, outdoor and indoor sundecks, a pubby lounge bar, and an award-winning restaurant. The bedrooms, which vary in size, are individually furnished with reproduction pieces; most look out onto broad vistas of the Kenmare River and the Atlantic. Open mid-April through October. *Expensive.*

SNEEM, Co. Kerry

Pub

★★ THE BLUE BULL
Ring of Kerry Road (N 70). Tel. (0664) 45231. As you drive the scenic route around the Iveragh Peninsula, you'll find this old pub in a

colorful village between Waterville and Kenmare. With a blue straw bull's head resting over the doorway, there are three small rooms, each with an open fireplace and walls lined with old prints of Co. Kerry scenes and people. Snacks are available throughout the year, and seafood in the summer season; and there's music on most weekends.

TRALEE, Co. Kerry

Hotels

★★★ BRANDON
Princess Street. Tel. (066) 21311. 154 rooms. Named for nearby Mount Brandon, this is a modern and dependable five-story hotel at the west edge of the town, with vistas of the Dingle Peninsula in the distance. There is nothing unique about the guest rooms, but they are functional and well kept. The guest facilities include a pleasant dining room, coffee shop, lounge bar, disco-style night club, and a large parking lot across the street. Best of all, the hotel is just a block from the town theatre and tourist office, and within easy strolling distance of all the shops and downtown restaurants. Convenience is its forte. *Expensive.*

★★★ BALLYGARRY HOUSE
Tralee/Killarney Road, Leebrook. Tel. (066) 21233. 16 rooms. Located one mile south of town, this country inn is on the edge of a residential neighborhood, surrounded by well-tended gardens and sheltering trees. Recently updated, the bedrooms vary in size; each is individually furnished and decorated to reflect different aspects of County Kerry, with names on the doorways that characterize the interiors, such as Arbutus, Muckross, Valentia, or Slea Head. The public areas have a horsey theme, with pictures of prize-winning thoroughbreds, horse brass, and other equestrian touches. Amenities include a full-service restaurant, old world lounge bar, and ample car parking. *Moderate.*

Restaurants

★★★ BARRETT'S CORDON BLEU
The Square. Tel. (066) 21596. In the heart of one of Tralee's oldest sections, this little shopfront restaurant has a cozy atmosphere, with beamed ceilings and a log-burning fireplace. Owned by Tom and Geraldine Barrett, the cooking is European/Irish, with such dishes as baked Brandon sea trout, seafood in puff pastry, black sole on the bone, homemade lasagne, T-bone steaks, and, of course, veal Cordon Bleu. Open for lunch and dinner. *Moderate.*

★★★ OCEAN BILLOW
29 Lower Castle Street. Tel. (066) 21377. This second floor bistro is decorated with sea scenes and various shades of blue, about as nautical as you can get on the main thoroughfare of Tralee. The mostly-seafood menu concentrates on such specialties as cream of salmon soup, hot seafood souffle, pineapple seafood curry, scallops mornay, and surf and turf. Open for lunch Tuesday through Friday and dinner Monday through Saturday. *Moderate.*

★★★ THE TANKARD
Kilfenora, Fenit. Tel. (066) 36164. Located six miles west of Tralee, this is one of the few restaurants to capitalize on sweeping views of Tralee Bay. Situated right on the water's edge, it is outfitted with wide picture windows and a sleek contemporary decor. The straight-forward menu primarily features local shellfish, as well as duck, quail, and a variety of steaks. Open for lunch and dinner daily. *Moderate.*

For fine dining in the Tralee area, see also Dingle.

Pubs

★★ KIRBY'S BROGUE INN
Rock Street. Tel. (066) 22126. This pub has a barn-like layout, with an interior that incorporates agricultural instruments, farming memorabilia, and rushwork tables and chairs. Snacks and light lunches are served.

★★ SLATT'S BAR
79 Boherbee. Tel. (066) 21161. Situated on the eastern approach to the town center, this pub is known for its open hearth, piano bar, and hearty meals.

★★ OYSTER TAVERN
Spa. Tel. (066) 36102. The nicest location of any pub in the Tralee area belongs to this tavern, just three miles west of downtown, overlooking Tralee Bay. The pub grub available includes seafood soups and platters.

Entertainment

SIAMSA TIRE THEATRE
Godfrey Place. Tel. (066) 23055. "Siamsa" (pronounced: "Sheem-sha") is the national folk theatre of Ireland, offering a form of entertainment which portrays an age when Irish (or Gaelic) was the spoken language of the land. A mixture of music, dance, and mime, the program includes scenes depicting the thatching of a cottage roof, flailing a sheaf of corn, twisting a sugan rope, and making a butter churn. The

cast members wear traditional costumes and dance to the music of pipes, flutes, and fiddles. Scheduled on Monday and Thursday nights, June through September, with additional performances on Tuesday and Friday during July and August; curtain time is 8:30 P.M. Admission charge is approximately $6.

Sports

Golf

TRALEE GOLF CLUB
Fenit/Churchill Road, West Barrow, Ardfert. Tel. (066) 36379. Situated overlooking the Atlantic eight miles northwest of Tralee, this is the first Arnold Palmer-designed golf course in Europe. One of Ireland's newest courses, it has already been acknowledged as an outstanding layout and is expected in time to rank among the great courses of the world. Greens fees are $15 and caddie pull-carts can be hired for about $1 per round. Visitors are welcome any day; just phone the club secretary, Jacques Kleynhans, to arrange a game.

BALLYBUNION GOLF CLUB
Tel. (068) 27146. This facility offers visitors the chance to play on two challenging 18-hole seaside links, both laid out on the cliffs overlooking the Shannon River estuary and the Atlantic. The "old course" is rated by Tom Watson as one of the finest in the world, while the "new" one was designed by Robert Trent Jones Sr. A greens fee of approximately $22 will entitle you to play both courses; club hire is $7.50 and caddie pull-carts are about $1.50 per round. To make arrangements, call club manager Sean Walsh. Ballybunion is situated about 25 miles north of Tralee, in the northwest corner of Co. Kerry.

Festival

August 26-September 2: Rose of Tralee International Festival. A carnival-like atmosphere prevails here for a week, with the highlight being the selection of the 1988 "Rose of Tralee." Other events include a variety of concerts, five days of horse races, and an array of free street entertainment.

Directory

Tralee Tourist Office, Godfrey Place, on Princess Street. Tel. (066) 21288.

WATERVILLE, Co. Kerry

Hotels

★★★★ WATERVILLE LAKE

Off the Ring of Kerry Road (N 70). Tel. (0667) 4133. 50 rooms. Sports enthusiasts as well as sightseers are drawn to this contemporary inn on western sweep of the Iveragh Peninsula. Located just south of the village of Waterville on the shores of Lough Currane, it is a well-kept and up-to-date two-story hotel with a bright and airy decor, and lots of wide windows to show off the surrounding lake and mountain views.

The facilities include an 18-hole championship golf course (free to guests who stay a minimum of two nights; see "Sports" below), heated indoor swimming pool, thermal spa pool, sauna, solarium, full-service restaurant, and lounge bar. The Waterville Lake also enjoys exclusive rights to some of the best salmon and seatrout fishing in Ireland including the famous Butler's Pool. Open from April to mid-October. *Expensive.*

★★★ BUTLER ARMS

Tel. (0667) 4144. 29 rooms. Once a favorite vacation retreat of Charlie Chaplin, this grand old inn is now run by the third generation of the Huggard family. Located on the edge of town and partially facing the sea, it has a sprawling and semi-turreted white facade. The refurbished guest rooms are functional and pleasant; many have views of the water or the palm tree-studded gardens. An old-world charm emanates from the public rooms and bars, most of which have open turf fireplaces. Other facilities include a full-service restaurant, sun lounge, hard court tennis, free salmon and seatrout fishing. Open mid-April through mid-October. *Expensive.*

Restaurants

★★★★ THE HUNTSMAN

Tel. (0667) 4124. It's worth a trip to Waterville just to dine at this contemporary restaurant on the shores of Ballinskelligs Bay, with sweeping vistas of the Atlantic. Recently enlarged and re-modeled, the Huntsman has a plush red-cushioned motif, with wrought iron fixtures and lots of leafy plants, but the prime emphasis here is on romantic picture-window views and fine cuisine.

Chef-owner Raymond Hunt, who trained at the Plaza Athenee in Paris, offers a mostly-seafood menu, using the freshest of the local catch. Specialties include Skellig lobster, Kenmare Bay scampi, black sole bonne femme, filet of John Dory, and red sea bream, as well as veal marsala, supreme of turkey, and rack of lamb. Open daily for lunch and dinner, mid-March through October. *Moderate to expensive.*

★★★ THE SMUGGLER'S INN

Cliff Road. Tel. (0667) 4330. Positioned a mile north of the town along the Ballinskelligs Bay beach, this renovated farmhouse is across the road from the entrance to the Waterville Golf Course. As could be expected, the decor is nautical, with fine sea views from the dining room windows. The chef/owner is Harry Hunt (brother of Raymond, of "The Huntsman" above), who offers a varied menu ranging from lobster newburg, Lough Currane salmon, Valencia scallops St. Jacques, and crab claws au gratin, to chicken Kiev, veal Cordon Bleu, beef stroganoff, and steaks. Open daily for lunch and dinner, March through October. *Moderate.*

Sports

Golf

WATERVILLE GOLF CLUB

Tel. (0667) 4237. Laid out on huge sand dunes and bounded on three sides by the Atlantic, this 18-hole championship golf links is one of the longest courses in Ireland (7,234 yards), but its large and varied teeing areas provide a choice of playing distances (such as a mere 6,039 yards). Visitors are welcomed every day; greens fees are approximately $23, and club rental is $7.50 per round. Although caddie pull-carts are available for $1.50, the big attraction here is a fleet of motorized golf carts, similar to those used on American courses; the rental charge is $24 per round. To arrange a game, phone the club professional, Liam Higgins. The club is situated one mile north of the village and is well sign-posted.

Visiting Houses and Castles
in Southern Ireland

by
The Knight of Glin

Visiting country estates first became fashionable in eighteenth century England. On any fine day, one might see a party of well-dressed ladies and gentlemen climb into a carriage for a trip to such famous establishments as Chatsworth, Woburn, or Kedleston. Ostensibly, these early tourists went to view historical treasures. However, considering the mentality of the age, it's far more likely that the visitors wanted to add such phrases as "on my visit to Badminton" to their conversation, a visit it was doubtful they would make in any other way. Did they come away satisfied? It's difficult to say. Armed with the guide books of the day, the tourists were herded along miles of dusty stone corridor while an ill-informed upper servant intoned the history of the house. Frequently, the information was incorrect; sometimes, it was hilarious, as when one of the staff guides at Strawberry Hill pointed out paintings of Cleopatra and Lucretia and described them both as Charles II's mistresses.

Regardless of the problems, the fascination for visiting mansions soon spread to Ireland. C. P. Bowden, an English tourist, was greatly impressed by Russborough's Palladian glories in 1791 and wrote, "Such is the urbanity of Lord Milltown that he takes a pleasure in showing his house and paintings himself, to all who have curiosity to view them." A minor Irish poet, William Preston, wrote a rollicking verse to demonstrate the determination of certain visitors to gain entrance to Slane Castle in 1793.

> Meantime they posted on pell mell,
> The Castle to survey!
> And tho' a giant there shou'd dwell
> They mean to force their way!

The house was being rebuilt at the time and the owner was away. However, after much ringing they roused a servant.

> Then, from the vault a damsel came
> With modest pace and slow;
> And in she let each knight and dame
> By postern door so low;
> The wonders having then surveyed
> Within the Castle stor'd
> They sought their Inn, the cloth was laid. . . .

What followed appears to have been a bacchanal which is better left to the imagination!

The tradition of opening the great houses continued into the nineteenth century when Howth Castle threw back its doors. Boasting such wonders as William III's bed and a painting of the pirate queen, Grace O'Malley, it became a popular tourist stop. Soon, Malahide Castle joined in, and then Birr, where one could see the fourth Lord Rosse's telescope and scientific equipment.

Political unrest and land wars had closed many of these massive portals by the 1880's, and they were to remain closed for three quarters of a century. Then, in 1958, in response to the resurgence of interest in the great houses and castles, the Hon. Mr. and Mrs. Desmond Guinness founded the Irish Georgian Society. Surprised landowners suddenly found themselves innundated by enthusiastic bands of Georgians who wanted to study every cornice and turned wood leg. Encouraged by the society, Mrs. Clodagh Shellswell-White opened Bantry to the public; it was the first Irish house to be open on a regular basis. Lord Altamont at Westport followed suit. By 1971, there were fourteen properties open for visitation, and the Historic Irish Tourist Houses and Gardens Association was formed. The organization has grown to include forty-nine estates which now host some million visitors each year. It is often difficult to keep these great houses in condition for viewing. Except for a few tax concessions, limited to landowners who open their houses at least thirty days a year, government support is virtually non-existent. Outside agencies lend assistance when possible. Bord Failte, the Irish Tourist Board, helps the HITHA properties obtain the few grants available for repairs and support facilities of historic sites. Its main purpose, however, is to promote the properties, thereby increasing tourist volume, and subsequently, visitation fees. *Ireland's Heritage,* the guidebook published by the Bord, is a comprehensive volume describing the houses, gardens, national monuments, and parks. HITHA also produces an informative booklet on the member properties.

A good place to begin a tour of Irish history is in Dublin, since there is a marvelous variety of sites within easy driving distance. HOWTH and MALAHIDE castles blend medieval and Georgian architecture. The former is renowned for its mysterious stonework designs; the latter boasts rococo ceilings and a great hall hung with a valuable collection of Talbot portraits in addition to the National Gallery of Ireland's portrait collection. Over the estuary at Donabate stands NEWBRIDGE, a mid-Georgian house which has been lovingly restored over the last two years. A magnificent, high-ceilinged ballroom is hung with original Regency draperies and crimson wallpaper. The layout of kitchen, laundry, offices, and stables provides a vivid impression of the huge community once centered about the house. SLANE, situated to the northwest on the Boyne River, combines history with romance. The highlight is a splendid circular ballroom with a vaulted ceiling and filigree decoration, which was built especially to entertain George IV, the former Prince Regent of Regency novels, on the occasion of his visit to Lady Conyngham, one of his many mistresses, in 1821.

Traveling west from Dublin some thirteen miles, one encounters CASTLETOWN, Ireland's first and most imposing Palladian house. The central block, done in Palazzo Farnese style, was designed in 1722 by architect Alessandro Galilei, for Speaker William Conolly of the Irish House of Commons, and was completed by Edward Lovett Pearce, who designed the Parliament House. Pearce's pupil, Richard Castle, designed both POWERS-COURT and RUSSBOROUGH in County Wicklow in the 1740's. Tragically, the main block of Powerscourt was destroyed by fire, but the formal baroque gardens with a view of the big sugarloaf mountain are maintained in elegant style. Russborough offers the Beit art collection and outstanding plasterwork by the La Franchini brothers, who also decorated the grand staircase of Castletown. KILRUDDERY, near Bray, features seventeenth-century formal gardens and two Regency-era state apartments.

Furthe afield, but still within driving distance of Dublin, is TULLYNALLY Castle. Set in a charming park north of Mullingar, it is the home of the literary Pakenham family and features a museum collection of domestic appliances and a range of early nineteenth-century greenhouses.

A southwesterly heading toward Limerick brings one to the town of Roscrea and the DAMER house, recently restored by the Irish Georgian Society. A fine early eighteenth-century carved pine staircase leads the way to numerous exhibition areas. The Roscrea Heritage Center is based there and exhibits items of local and archaeological interest. A few miles away is BIRR Castle, famous for its gardens and arboretum.

The Limerick and Shannon area has the Clare castles, BUN-RATTY, KNAPPOGUE, and CRAGGAUNOWEN, all of them loaded with fifteenth- and sixteenth-century artworks. In County Limerick is CASTLEMATRIX, another newly renovated tower house and a treasure trove of old furnishings and documents. Spencer and Raleigh are reputed to have met here, and legend claims that the first Irish potato was grown in the gardens.

190

Not far away, on the banks of the Shannon, is GLIN Castle, a pasteboard Gothic fantasy, surrounded by pepper-pot lodges and follies. The interior has elegant Adam style ceilings, a flying staircase, and an important collection of eighteenth-century Irish furniture and portraits. The Fitz-Gerald family has been in residence for over seven hundred years.

In the southwestern counties of Kerry and Cork are such treasures as English architect William Burn's Tudor revival MUCKROSS, and romantic BANTRY with its French furniture and tapestries. RIVERSTOWN, near Cork, has another historically important room, decorated in 1745 by the La Franchini brothers for the Bishop of Cork.

The most recent restoration of a great house is at FOTA, on the way to Cobb. Like Kilruddery, it was designed by Richard Morrison, and the newly-renovated Neo-Classical interior makes a superb backdrop for a collection of Irish paintings and furnishings collected during the last decade by Richard Wood.

At Blarney, near the famous stone in the old castle, is a new restoration of the VICTORIAN SCOTTISH BARONIAL Castle, the home of the Colthurst family since they abandoned the seventeenth- and eighteenth-century additions to the old keep.

There are many more properties worth visiting far afield from the big cities. CLONALIS in County Roscommon, seat of the O'Conor chiefs, has archives filled with manuscripts which date back nearly 2,000 years. STROKESTOWN, also in County Roscommon, is a Palladian house with wings incorporating the original kitchen with the ballustraded gallery and vaulted stables, and dates from the 1730's. The rather forbidding Scottish baronial exterior of Castle LESLIE in County Monaghan hides some truly charming Italianate reception rooms. Providing contrast is KYLEMORE ABBEY in Connemara, with its Victorian battlements, towers, and oriel windows. For picturesque, one might visit LISMORE Castle in County Waterford. Its battlemented towers rise above the Blackwater River and shield a seventeenth-century garden.

Without question, Ireland provides the tourist with a century-spanning collage of architectural styles. In a very small space, one might have a medieval tower frowning disapprovingly down at four-square Georgian block, while just o'er the hill, a prime specimen of Gothic revival fantasy laughs at them both.

The KNIGHT OF GLIN is a past chairman of the Historic Tourist Houses Association.

The Shannon Region

COUNTIES CLARE, LIMERICK, AND TIPPERARY

Contrary to popular American belief, Shannon is not an Irish city. It is, first of all, a river, the longest in Ireland and Britain. In 1945, this river lent its name to an airport which served for many years as the first landing point for most transatlantic flights. In 1947, Shannon International Airport became the world's first duty-free airport.

As the airport grew, the surrounding counties, especially Clare, Limerick, and Tipperary, prospered. Hotels were built, new industries established, craft centers encouraged, and ancient sites were re-discovered and restored. The airport itself has gained in popularity as a gateway, not just as a re-fueling stop. Today the Shannon region is exceeded only by Dublin and Killarney in attracting the most overnight visitors.

COUNTY CLARE

Step off the plane at Shannon, hire a car or board a tour bus, and your first sights of Ireland are the vistas of County Clare. Rich green fields and rolling hills are parted by the meandering Shannon River forming a pastoral tableau. Turn left, and the rocky Atlantic coast of Clare awaits you; turn right, and you'll be heading into the historic city of Limerick.

After an overnight flight, most people make a beeline for a local hotel to cure their jet lag. Remember that Ireland is five hours ahead

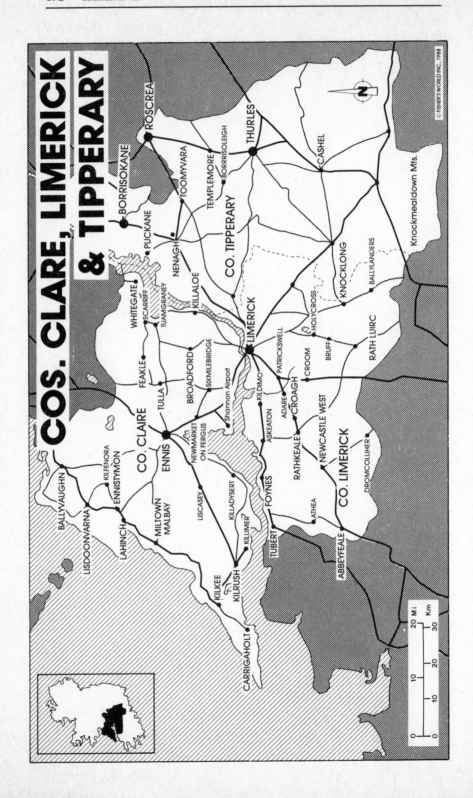

COS. CLARE, LIMERICK & TIPPERARY

of the U.S. East Coast time zone and eight hours ahead of the West Coast. The majority of transatlantic planes arrive in the early morning (Irish time), which will be middle-of-the-night time to your body's time clock. So don't plan too much activity for your first day. If you are flying into Shannon from Britain or Europe, you'll be fairly well attuned to the local time.

A good place to start sightseeing is Bunratty Castle, a striking 15th-century fortress located just five miles south of the airport beside the O'Garney River in the village of Bunratty. The most complete medieval castle in Ireland, this ancient stronghold has been carefully restored with authentic furniture, armorial stained glass, tapestries, and works of art. By day, the building's inner chambers and grounds are open for public tours, while at night the castle's Great Hall serves as a candlelit setting for medieval banquets and entertainment (see "Inside Information").

Bunratty Castle is the focal point of a 20-acre theme park, appropriately known as Bunratty Folk Park, which is a re-creation of a typical 19th-century Irish village. The park includes thatched cottages, farmhouses, and an entire village street with school, post office, pub, grocery store, print shop, and craft shops, all open to browsing and shopping. Fresh scones are baked in the cottages, craftsmen ply their trades, and a blacksmith is busy at his forge. For a glimpse of the grander side of Irish lifestyle of the period, you can also tour Bunratty House, a restored Georgian manor (1805), built on a hillside overlooking the rest of the village. The wine cellars of the house have been converted into one of the area's top restaurants. (See "MacCloskeys'" in the "Inside Information" section.)

Adjacent to the folk park is a popular 17th-century landmark pub, called "Durty Nelly's" (see "Inside Information") and a winery, but not in the mode of the Napa or Loire Valleys. This is a winery that produces mead, a medieval drink made from honey, fermented grape juice, water, matured spirits, and a selection of herbs. Long ago, it was served by the jugfull at regal gatherings and at weddings. In fact, the custom required that a bride and groom continue to drink mead for one full moon in order to increase the probability of a happy marriage. (Legend has it that this is how the word "honeymoon" originated.) Today the Bunratty Winery produces mead primarily for consumption at the medieval-style banquets at Bunratty Castle. Visitors are welcome to stop by this working winery, housed in a converted coach house, and taste the brew.

In addition, mead can be sampled at another restored fortress, Knappogue Castle at Quin, also the scene of nightly medieval banquets, in the summer season (see "Inside Information"). Located approximately ten miles from Bunratty, Knappogue was built in 1467 and for centuries was the home of the McNamara Clan. The original Norman structure now includes elaborate late-Georgian and Regency wings

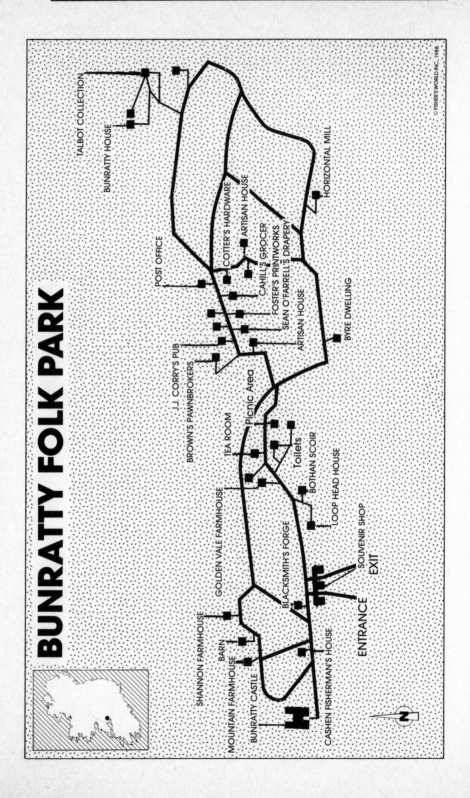

BUNRATTY FOLK PARK

TALBOT COLLECTION

BUNRATTY HOUSE

HORIZONTAL MILL

POST OFFICE

COTTER'S HARDWARE

ARTISAN HOUSE

CAHILL'S GROCER

FOSTER'S PRINTWORKS

SEAN O'FARRELL'S DRAPERY

ARTISAN HOUSE

BYRE DWELLING

J.J. CORRY'S PUB

BROWN'S PAWNBROKERS

TEA ROOM

Picnic Area

Toilets

BOTHAN SCOIR

LOOP HEAD HOUSE

GOLDEN VALE FARMHOUSE

SHANNON FARMHOUSE

BARN

MOUNTAIN FARMHOUSE

BUNRATTY CASTLE

BLACKSMITH'S FORGE

CASHEN FISHERMAN'S HOUSE

SOUVENIR SHOP

ENTRANCE

EXIT

N

© FISHER'S WORLD INC. 1988.

which were added in the mid-19th century. This castle is also open to the public during the day.

Continue to tour in this neighborhood, and, six miles east of Quin, you'll come to a unique development known as Craggaunowen. ★★ Although it looks like something you might find in the jungles of Africa, this is a reconstruction of a Irish "crannog," a Bronze Age lake dwelling. You'll also see a ring fort from the early-Christian period and a "Fulachta Fiadha" (ancient cooking place). Jumping to more recent history, the Craggaunowen grounds also shelter the history-making hide boat, "The Brendan." This is the vessel in which explorer/author Tim Severin sailed across the Atlantic from County Kerry to Boston in 1976, to prove that St. Brendan could have discovered America in the 6th century, long before Columbus.

The main town of County Clare is Ennis, a busy marketing center (population: 6,000) with narrow winding streets and a Franciscan ★★ Abbey dating back to 1241. A famous seat of learning in medieval times, the abbey made Ennis a focal point of western European scholarship for many years—records show that in 1375 it buzzed with the activity of no less than 350 friars and 600 students. Although it was finally forced to close in 1692 and fell into ruin, the abbey still contains many interesting sculptured tombs and decorative fragments. Located just fifteen miles from the airport, Ennis offers a number of good lodging and/or restaurant choices for the Shannon area, as do the nearby towns of Newmarket-on-Fergus, Bunratty, Quin, and Corofin (see "Inside Information").

Moving westward from Ennis into the heart of County Clare, you'll come to an amazing district of 100 square miles called "The Burren," ★★★ which means "great rock." It is a strange lunar-like region of bare carboniferous limestone, bordered roughly by the towns of Corofin, Ennistymon, Lahinch, Lisdoonvarna, and Ballyvaughan. Massive sheets of rock, jagged and craggy boulders, caves, and potholes are visible for miles in a moonscape-like pattern, yet this is also a setting for little lakes and streams and an amazing assemblage of flora. Experts say there is always something in bloom, even in winter, from the fern and moss, to orchids, rockroses, milkworts, wild thyme, geraniums, violets, and fuschia. If you have questions, there is an interpretive display/information office in the center of the region at Kilfenora.

One of the most scenic Burren drives is the corkscrew-shaped road which leads to Ballyvaughan, a delightful little village which overlooks Galway Bay. Nearby is the Aillwee Cave, one of Ireland's oldest under- ★★ ground sites, formed millions of years ago but discovered just forty years ago by a local farmer. The cave has over 3,000 feet of passages and hollows running straight into a mountain of rock. Guided tours are conducted year-round. The facilities include a cafe and craft shop, as well as a unique farmhouse cheese-making enterprise near the cave's entrance.

★★★ If you head out toward the Atlantic Coast, you can also see Co. Clare's foremost natural wonder, the Cliffs of Moher, about five miles north of Lahinch. Rising to nearly 700 feet and extending about five miles along the coast, these sheer cliffs offer panoramic views, especially from O'Brien's Tower at the northern end. On a clear day you can see the Aran Islands and Galway Bay.

Other highlights of the Clare Coast include the world-renowned golf resort at Lahinch, the secluded fishing village of Doolin, and Lisdoonvarna, a town known for its spa. Although it can't compare to Safety Harbor in Florida or Margaret Island in Budapest, Lisdoonvarna draws thousands of bathers to its therapeutic waters of sulphur, chalybeate (iron), and iodine.

The Clare Coast also offers a number of seaside resorts particularly popular with Irish families, such as Kilrush, Kilkee, and Ennistymon. If you are driving in this section and plan to move on to County Kerry, you should also be aware that there is a regular car ferry service across the Shannon estuary which will take you from Killimer, Co. Clare, to Tarbert, in north County Kerry. The trip, which takes less than a half-hour, operates on a drive-on/drive-off basis, with no reservations required. In addition to being a very pleasant diversion, it's a time-saver and a mileage-saver (see "Hard Facts" section for details).

COUNTY LIMERICK

Lying east and south of Clare, County Limerick is divided into two parts by the Shannon River. The chief city, also named Limerick, is likewise divided by the river, and is the major urban center (population: 101,000) of the Shannon region.

★ Because of its position on the Shannon, Limerick City has always been an important port, dating back at least to the 9th century when the Danes made it a base for plundering the hinterland. In subsequent years, Limerick was variously in the hands of the Irish and the Anglo-Normans. In 1210 King John of England visited Limerick and was so taken with the site that he ordered a "strong castle" to be built here. So sturdy was it, that parts survive to this day. It is one of the oldest examples of medieval architecture in Ireland, with rounded gate towers and curtain walls.

★ Just across the bridge from the castle is Limerick's symbolic "Treaty Stone," a rock on a pedestal overlooking the Shannon. It is the site of an historic 1691 treaty between England and Ireland which guaranteed religious tolerance, but which was never ratified by the British Parliament. Afterwards Limerick was often referred to as "the city of the violated treaty."

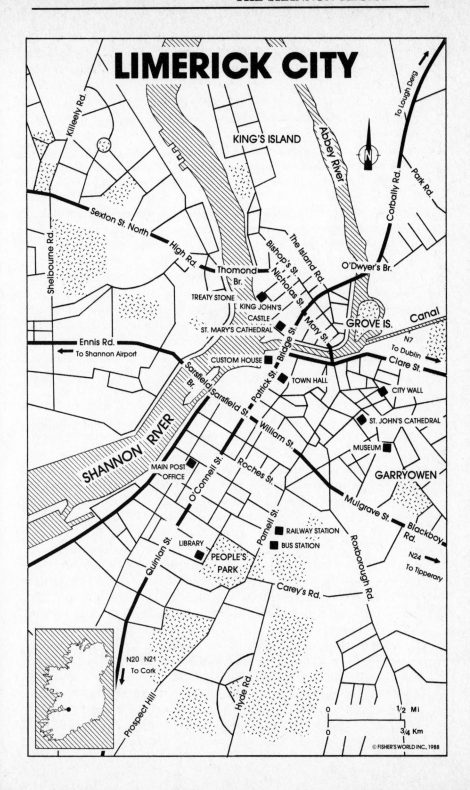

LIMERICK CITY

★★   Another of the city's landmarks is St. Mary's Cathedral, built in
1172 on the site of a former palace. Parts of the palace, including a
Romanesque doorway, were incorporated into this ecclesiastical edifice.
Features added in later years include 15th-century misericords carved
in black oak. Now a Church of Ireland property, St. Mary's is the site
of nightly "Son et Lumiere" presentations during the summer season
(see "Inside Information").

Limerick City lends itself to walking, its wide streets similar to
Dublin's. Like the Irish capital, its main thoroughfare is also called
O'Connell Street, and much of the architecture dates back to the
Georgian period. Limerick is not quite as polished as Dublin's Fair
City, but a lot of restoration and improvement is currently in progress.

Some of Limerick's top visitor attractions lie on the rim of the city,
★★ such as Lough Gur, fifteen miles to the south. One of the most
important archeological sites in Ireland, Lough Gur contains an
extraordinary collection of ancient monuments, from stone circles,
stone forts, dolmens, and megalithic tombs, to standing stones and
house sites. Excavations have shown that Lough Gur was continuously
occupied from the Neolithic period to late medieval times, and the
natural caves nearby have yielded the remains of now extinct or no
longer indigenous animals, such as reindeer, giant Irish deer, and bear.
The site includes a visitor center with a display on the archeology and
5,000-year history of the area.

★★   Traveling ten miles southeast of Limerick, you will come to Adare,
a favorite with photographers who generally refer to it as "the prettiest
village in Ireland." Situated on the main road to Killarney/Tralee (N
21), this is an old-world community of thatched cottages and ivy-
covered medieval churches in wooded surroundings on the west bank
of the River Maigue. Adare is also in the heart of County Limerick's
hunt country, and one of Ireland's chief fox hunting centers is headquartered here at the Dunraven Arms Hotel (see "Inside Information").

From Adare it is about 12 miles to Rathkeale and a district long
known as the "Palatine," because early in the 18th century it was
settled with a colony of German refugees who had been driven from
the Palatinate by the French. These people worked hard in their new
surroundings and preserved many of their national customs until late
★★ in the 19th century. Rathkeale is also the setting for Castle Matrix,
built in 1440 by the Earl of Desmond. It was here in 1580 that
Edmund Spenser and Walter Raleigh met and began their lifelong
friendship. Fully restored, the castle is the headquarters of the Heraldry
Society of Ireland and contains authentic furnishings, objets d'art, and
historical documents. Open to the public in the summer months, it is
also available as a bed-and-breakfast (see "Inside Information").

Another famous castle is located in the dairy-farming village of Glin
along the shores of the Shannon estuary in western County Limerick.

A fairytale Georgian-Gothic building, Glin Castle is the seat of the ★★★
Knight of Glin, whose family (the Fitzgeralds) has maintained almost
continuous possession for 700 years. Noted for its interior neoclassical
plasterwork, unique staircase, and collection of 18th-century furniture,
this splendid castle can be toured in the mid-May/mid-June period;
the contemporary gate lodge also contains a cafe and craft center. For
a special week-long splurge, Glin Castle can also be rented, complete
with staff. (See "Inside Information.") Note: If you are taking the
Killimer/Tarbert car ferry, Glin is only four miles from the Tarbert
dock.

COUNTY TIPPERARY

Once you arrive at Shannon Airport, it's not such a long way to
Tipperary; in fact, it's only about 25 miles.

Like Clare and Limerick, County Tipperary is also rimmed by the
Shannon River, on its northwest corner. As Ireland's largest inland
county, Tipperary is rich in pastoral scenery, with green hills and
fertile river valleys. The Tipperary tableau also includes the Galtee and
Knockmealdown Mountains, and in the middle of the county a broad
plain is traversed by the River Suir (pronounced "Sure").

As might be expected, Tipperary rivals County Kildare as the home
of the horse. There are three race tracks in the county (at Clonmel,
Thurles, and Limerick Junction), and stud farms dot the countryside.
One of Ireland's foremost racing-horse trainers, Vincent O'Brien,
operates a vast horse farm in the middle of the county. There is even a
town, mid-way between Cashel and Thurles (on N 8), called Horse and ★★★
Jockey.

Although Nenagh (pronounced "Neen-ah") is the chief town in
Tipperary, by far the premier attraction of this county is the little town
of Cashel with its famous "Rock." Basically, the "Rock" is an outcrop
of limestone reaching 200 feet into the sky, but what makes it special is
sixteen centuries of history. Dating back at least to 360 A.D., the Rock
of Cashel was the seat of the kings of the province of Munster, in
many ways comparable to Royal County Meath near Dublin. A castle
was first built on this site and it remained a royal fortress until 1101,
when King Murtagh O'Brien ceded it to the church. Among Cashel's
many great moments was the baptism of King Aengus by St. Patrick
in 448.

Although in ruins, Cashel still dominates the Tipperary countryside.
The remains include a two-towered chapel, cruciform cathedral, a 92-
foot-tall round tower, and a cluster of other medieval monuments. The
town at the foot of this great monument is also noted for its fine
lodgings and restaurant (see "Inside Information").

Another noteworthy medieval structure in the Tipperary country-
★★ side is Cahir Castle, in the village of Cahir (pronounced "Kair") on the
banks of the River Suir. One of Ireland's largest fortresses, this 15th-
century castle has a massive keep, high walls, spacious courtyards, and
a great hall, all fully restored. So impressive is this site that it has been
used often as a movie location, for the film "Barry Lyndon," for
example.

At Cahir you can also embark in a northerly direction on one of the
county's most scenic drives, through the Galtee Mountains and the
Glen of Aherlow.

If you prefer to head south, there is another drive which is possibly
★★★ even more rewarding on a clear day, from Clogheen, through the
Knockmealdown Mountains and the "Vee" Gap. It is so named
because the horizon looks like a V-shaped formation as you drive a
zig-zag course from a height of 1,114 feet downward to Lismore and
Cappoquin (both in County Waterford). This road offers a series of
magnificent views at different levels, and it is said that you can see five
counties at various points along the drive.

BALLYVAUGHAN, Co. Clare

Hotels

★★★ GREGAN'S CASTLE
Foot of Corkscrew Hill. Tel. (065) 77005. 14 rooms and 4 mini-suites.
Located in the northern part of County Clare, about an hour's drive
from Shannon, this fine country house is in the heart of the famous
rocky "Burren Country," with distant views of Galway Bay. Although
not strictly a castle in the architectural sense, it is built on the site of
the ancient family estates of the Martyn family and the O'Loughlins,
Princes of the Burren. Owner-managed by Peter and Moira Hayden,
this delightful inn is cheerily furnished with designer fabrics, copper
and brass hangings, with many antiques. The restaurant has a reputation for fine seafood and creative cookery. Open April through
October. *Moderate.*

Restaurant

★★★ CLAIRE'S
Main Street. Tel. (065) 77029. With candlelight dining and piano
music in the background, this is a homey and intimate 28-seat restaurant, the domain of Claire Walsh whose husband Manus operates a
craft shop overhead. It's located in the middle of the village, near the

shores of Galway Bay. Open for dinner only, from April through September, the menu often includes such dishes as baked Kinvara crab, chicken Kiev, and cod with prawns and mussel sauce. *Moderate.*

Shopping

MANUS WALSH CRAFT WORKSHOP AND GALLERY

Main Street. Tel. (065) 77029. Located on the upper level of Claire's Restaurant, this shop features a wide range of colorful hand-crafted enamel jewelry of Celtic and early Irish designs. Visitors are welcome to watch Manus work as they browse or buy. Items for sale include pendants, brooches, earrings, ornate boxes, dishes, and plaques.

BUNRATTY, Co. Clare

Hotel

★★★★ FITZPATRICK'S SHANNON SHAMROCK HOTEL

Limerick/Ennis Road (N 18). Tel. (061) 61177. 110 rooms and suites. A sister hotel to Dublin's Fitzpatrick Castle, this rambling ranch-style inn is ideally located right next to Bunratty Castle and Folk Park, and just four miles from Shannon Airport. The guest rooms are modern, decorated with Irish fabrics and furnishings, and with views of the lovely grounds and gardens. Amenities include a sunlit and plant-filled conservatory, indoor heated swimming pool, saunas, a lively cocktail lounge with musical entertainment, a French/Irish restaurant, and the pervasive Fitzpatrick family finesse and hospitality. The Shannon Shamrock also offers its guests a courtesy minibus service to/from the airport, making it an ideal base if you don't rent a car, but want to be in walking distance to all the Bunratty area attractions and shops. *Moderate.*

Restaurants

★★★★★ MacCLOSKEY'S

Bunratty House, Bunratty Folk Park. Tel. (061) 74082. Located in the former mews and wine cellars of a restored 1804 Georgian mansion, this award-winning candlelight restaurant is the creation of a hard-working duo, Gerry and Marie MacCloskey. There are four dining rooms, each with original whitewashed walls, archways, and polished slate floors. Rack of lamb, black sole, mussels in champagne, duck a l'orange, crab crepes, and wild salmon are specialties. You can also get a masterful Caesar salad or pickled herring here, and desserts which range from hot Cointreau souffle to chocolate mousse with brandy, or baked pear puffs. Closed Sunday and Monday, and all of January. Dinner only. *Expensive.*

★★★ THISILLDOUS

10 Firgrove, Hurlers Cross. Tel. (061) 74758. Although the name sounds a little Greek, this homey bistro is run by Tony and Waltraud McMahon, an Irish/Austrian couple who looked at their own living room when searching for a restaurant venue and decided "This'll do us." Just a mile from Shannon Airport, it is known for its mostly seafood and veal menu, served in a comfortable setting with a glowing fireplace and soft easy chairs. Dinner only. Closed mid-December to mid-January. *Moderate to expensive.*

Pub

★★★★ DURTY NELLY'S

Limerick/Ennis Road (N 18). Tel. (061) 74861. Established in 1620, and located next door to Bunratty Castle, this cottage tavern was originally a watering hole for the castle guards. Now, with a mustard colored facade and palm trees at its entrance, it is a favorite haunt of local folk and of tourists who pour into the nightly medieval banquets at the castle. With mounted elk heads and old lanterns on the walls, sawdust on the floors, and open turf fireplaces, the decor hasn't changed much over the centuries. This is a good spot for a soup and sandwich lunch; spontaneous Irish music sessions also erupt here on most evenings. If you crave a more substantial meal, the recently expanded "Oyster" restaurant at the rear of the pub is a good place for seafood and steaks.

Evening Entertainment

BUNRATTY CASTLE

Limerick/Ennis Road (N 18). Tel. (061) 61788. Built in 1469, this splendid structure is the most complete and authentic example of a medieval castle in Ireland. Each evening, at 6 P.M. and 9 P.M., a full medieval banquet is re-created with music, song, and merriment. Seated at long tables in the castle's magnificent baronial hall, you'll feast on spare ribs, roast chicken, a garden salad, and fresh vegetables— all served in strictly medieval use-your-fingers style. To wash down your meal, there's mulled wine, claret, or mugs of mead (the traditional honey-based drink of old). Now celebrating its 25th season of success, this is a great evening of good food, camraderie, and entertainment, all for approximately $35. Open year-round; for other castle banquets on a seasonal basis, see also Knappogue Castle at Quin, Co. Clare, and Dun Guaire Castle, at Kinvara, Co. Galway.

SHANNON CEILI
Bunratty Folk Park, off the Limerick/Ennis Road (N 18). Tel. (061) 61788. Irish country life of yesteryear is the focus of this "at home" evening in a thatched farmhouse cottage. There is a traditional meal of Irish stew, homemade breads, apple pie and fresh cream. Then the music begins: the flute and fiddle, accordian, bodhran and spoons—all to a spirited, foot-tapping pace. Nightly at 6 P.M. and 9 P.M., from mid-May through September. The cost for meal and entertainment is approximately $30.

Shopping

VONNIE REYNOLDS
Limerick/Ennis Road (N 18). Tel. (061) 74321. Located across the street from Bunratty Castle, this shop was originally used as a black-smith's forge and then a post office before it was turned into a slate-floor high fashion boutique by Vonnie Reynolds, a dressmaker and designer. With a customer list ranging from Vanessa Redgrave and Katherine Hepburn to Jeane Kirkpatrick, this trendy shop features one-of-a-kind gowns, lace blouses, tweed capes, coachmen's coats, and handknit farmer hats, as well as Celtic design jewelry, fine linens, crochet work, crystal, and other crafts. Open daily.

AVOCA
Limerick/Ennis Road (N 18). Tel. (061) 364029. This thatched-roof cottage shop is a branch of the legendary Avoca Handweavers, the oldest company of its kind in Ireland, dating back to 1723. It carries all the colorful tweeds and mohairs which have made the Avoca line famous, plus linen-cotton fashions, stylish sweaters, tweed totes, and a wide array of hats. Open daily.

BUNRATTY DUTY-FREE EXPORT SHOP
Limerick/Ennis Road (N 18). Tel. (061) 364401. Just over the bridge from Durty Nelly's Pub, this well-stocked emporium carries a wide array of crystal and tweeds, as well as more unusual items like hand-crocheted bedspreads, lace accessories, and full-size harps. Catering exclusively to foreign visitors, this shop has pioneered in a new system of deducting the VAT (sales tax) at the time of purchase (relying on customers to mail back the stamped customs form after leaving the country). This saves shoppers the bother of waiting for a VAT refund by mail. Open daily.

COROFIN, Co. Clare

Restaurants

★★★★ MARYSE AND GILBERT'S

Tel. (065) 27660. You'll find this well sign-posted oasis of French/Italian cuisine in the heart of the famous Burren country, a nine-mile drive from Ennis and a half-mile west of Corofin. It's a charming farmhouse-style restaurant on its own grounds, with a menu that includes chicken cacciatore, filet of beef en moutarde, pork steak with lemon sauce, pasta carbonnara, and tagliatelle with smoked salmon and cream. Dinner only, open from April to September; closed Sunday and Monday from April through June, and on Monday only during July and August. *Moderate.*

★★★ BOFEY QUINN'S VILLAGE INN

Main Street. Tel. (065) 27627. An informal atmosphere prevails at this popular steak and seafood restaurant in the center of town. A seawater tank holds the fresh lobster which, served broiled or steamed, is one of the most popular dinner choices. You can also have your lobster prepared thermidor or newburg style. Other specialties include seafood chowder, mussels in white wine, whole black sole on the bone, and surf-and-turf. Pub-style lunches are also available throughout the day, and there is music most weekend evenings. *Moderate.*

DOOLIN, Co. Clare

Restaurants

★★★ KILLILAGH HOUSE

Roadford. Tel. (065) 74183. Located in a modern wide-windowed cottage, this award-winning restaurant near the Cliffs of Moher features fresh seafood and produce. In addition to fine food, it is also known for its display of local handcrafts, making it a sort of restaurant-cum-gallery. Open for dinner only, from April through September.

★★★ IVY COTTAGE

Tel. (065) 74244. Located just a few doors from Gus O'Connor's famous pub, this restaurant, also known as Ilsa's Kitchen, is housed in an ivy-covered stone cottage (dating back to 1901), with turf for the fireplace piled high outside the main doorway. The simple menu concentrates on wholefood and local seafood. Open for dinner only, May to October (except Monday and Tuesday).

Pub

★★★ GUS O'CONNOR

Tel. (065) 74168. In a row of thatched fishermen's cottages less than a mile from the roaring waters of the Atlantic, this simple pub beckons people from many miles away each evening. Besides the historic charm (dating back to 1832), its big draw is music—from the flute and fiddle to the bodhran and concertina, this is "the spot" to gather in western Co. Clare for Irish traditional music sessions.

ENNIS, Co. Clare

Hotels

★★★★ OLD GROUND

O'Connell Street. Tel. (065) 28127. 60 rooms. Less than a half-hour drive from Shannon Airport and in the heart of a busy marketing town, this gracious ivy-covered two-story hotel dates back to 1749. According to a citation at the front entrance, it has been known variously as the Great Inn of Jayl Street and the Kings Arms; part of the hotel was once used as the Town Hall and the Town Jail.

Many of the furnishings are antiques—you'll find vintage tea chests in the halls and there's even a 1553 fireplace which once warmed the interior of nearby Lemaneagh Castle. Most of the guest rooms of this Trusthouse Forte property have a more modern decor with up-to-date facilities and little extras like in-room coffee/tea makers. Amenities include a restaurant, grill room, and a very charming pub called "The Poet's Corner." In the summer months, there is also cabaret-style entertainment on many evenings. *Moderate.*

★★★ WEST COUNTY INN

Clare Road (N 18). Tel. (065) 28421. 109 rooms. A Best Western affiliate, this modern motor inn is set on its own grounds on the southern edge of Ennis, about 15 miles from Shannon. The decor makes use of wide-windowed facades and skylights in many of the public areas, and the guest rooms are roomy and functional; many units have views of the nearby Clare hills. Facilities include a candle-light restaurant, a piano bar, nightclub, and a cabaret-dinner show in the summer months. *Inexpensive.*

For additional accommodations suggestion near Ennis, see also Quin.

Restaurant

★★★★ THE CLOISTER

Abbey Street. Tel. (065) 29521. Located next to the remains of a 13th century abbey, this old-world gem offers innovative Irish cuisine, to the accompaniment of a pianist or harpist in the evenings. The menu includes such items as salmon in champagne sauce, spiced braised duckling, filet of lamb en croute with mint pea mousse, and filet of beef with hazelnut butter.

Desserts are also a special treat here—from chocolate rum mousse, to creme de menthe cheesecake, and flaming fruit with brandy. By day, pub-style lunches are served in the bar area or outside on the patio adjacent to the old abbey walls. Hot crab claws, quiches, club sandwiches, and ploughmen's platters are favorite mid-day choices. *Moderate.*

For additional dining suggestions near Ennis, see also Corofin.

Pubs

★★ BROGAN'S
24 O'Connell Street. Tel. (065) 29859. An old-timer in the center of town, this pub is known for its hearty meals throughout the day, and ballad music on Tuesday and Thursday nights.

★★ CONSIDINE'S
26 Abbey Street. Tel. (065) 29054. A traditional meeting place on marketing day, there's nothing fancy here, but it's a favorite with the locals who come for the lunchtime Irish stew and shepherd's pie.

Entertainment

COIS na hABHNA (Pronounced "Cush-na howna")
Gort Road. Tel. (065) 29345. This modern building on the main road north of Ennis is the Irish Traditional Cultural Center for the area. On summer evenings, music concerts are held, followed by ceili dancing with audience participation. The schedule varies, but Monday, Thursday, and Saturday are usually the best nights for visitors. Starting time to 9 P.M. and admission is less than $5 which includes a snack of tea and brown bread.

Shopping

BELLEEK SHOP
36 Abbey Street. Tel. (065) 22607. Located on a corner in the center of Ennis, with a public parking lot behind it, this shop dates back over 50 years and was the first Belleek China outlet in southern Ireland. In the hands of Liam and Angela Cahir for the last 10 years, it has expanded to include other Irish products such as handmade character dolls and turf crafts as well as crystal, pottery, pewter, and fashionable tweeds.

Festival

May 27-29: Fleadh Nua. Singers, instrumentalists, and dancers from all over Ireland come to this annual cultural feast of Irish music.

LAHINCH, Co. Clare

Hotel

★★ **VAUGHANS' ABERDEEN ARMS** (For Location)
Main Street. Tel. (065) 81100. 48 rooms. This homey family-run
hotel is an ideal base, if you want to be within swinging distance
of the famous Lahinch golf course down the road. The bedrooms
are modern and functional with tweedy furnishings, and the
public rooms have a country inn atmosphere. Facilities include a
restaurant and a lounge bar where the chat is usually centered on
golf, golf, and more golf. Open mid-April through early-October.
Moderate.

Sports

Golf

LAHINCH GOLF CLUB
Tel. (065) 81003. Located 35 miles from Shannon Airport along the
Atlantic coast, this course has been variously praised as the "St.
Andrews of Ireland" and the paradigm of Irish links golf. There are
actually two 18-hole courses here, but the longer championship course
is the one which has given Lahinch its far-reaching reputation. This
course's elevations, such as the 9th and 13th holes, reveal open vistas
of sky, land, and sea; they also make the winds an integral part of the
scoring.
    Watch out for the goats—they are Lahinch's legendary weather
forecasters; if they huddle by the clubhouse, it means a storm is
approaching. Visitors are welcome to play any day, especially on
weekdays; greens fees range from $18 to $22 on the championship
course, and are about $13 on the alternate family-oriented course.
Clubs can be hired for about $5 and caddie pull-carts are $1 per
round. The manager is Michael Murphy.

NEWMARKET-ON-FERGUS, Co. Clare

Hotels

★★★★★ **DROMOLAND CASTLE**
Limerick/Ennis Road (N 18). Tel. (061) 71144. 77 rooms. Live like a
king or queen in a fairytale setting of turrets and towers, but with every

20th century luxury. Situated just eight miles from Shannon Airport, this is Ireland's most impressive castle hotel, situated on 400 acres of parklands and gardens, beside the River Rine, and home to varied species of wildlife including a deer herd.

Dating back to 1686, it was originally built by the O'Briens, the High Kings of Ireland, and was restored and refurbished 20 years ago as a hotel. As befits its regal exterior, the green-carpeted drawing rooms and stately halls are full of splendid wood and stone carvings, medieval suits of armor, rich oak paneling, and original oil paintings. The guest rooms are individually decorated with designer fabrics and reproduction furniture; and many rooms look out onto the water or the romantic walled gardens. Amenities include a candlelight dining room, piano bar, an 18-hole golf course, tennis courts, and walking/jogging trails, plus facilities for fishing, boating, and biking. Horseback riding can also be arranged. Among its various credits, Dromoland is a member of the prestigious Relais and Chateaux group. *Very expensive.*

★★★★ CLARE INN
Limerick/Ennis Road (N 18). Tel. (061) 71161. 121 rooms. Panoramic views of the River Shannon and the Clare hills are part of the scene at this contemporary Tudor-style hotel, situated within eight miles of Shannon Airport. It's a perfect location for the starting days or finale of your Irish trip. Owner/managed by one of Ireland's most respected hoteliers, Patricia Barry, the inn exudes a warm and friendly ambience—looking out for guest comfort and enjoyment are second-nature to the Clare Inn team.

The immaculately maintained bedrooms are furnished in cheery colors and floral prints, with spacious American-style bathrooms. Facilities include a full-service restaurant, lounge bar with evening entertainment, and airy public rooms, all with large picture windows framing the countryside vistas. There is also an on-premises shop stocked with unusual local crafts. In addition, Clare Inn guests enjoy the use of the 18-hole golf course and other sporting amenities of the neighboring Dromoland Castle. *Moderate.*

Restaurants

★★★ CRONIN'S
Main Street. Tel. (061) 71157. By day, this is a homey village pub, which serves pastas, soups, and stews for lunch. In the evening, an adjacent candlelit dining room opens to offer a haute cuisine menu ranging from paupiettes of trout with blue cheese sauce, and prawns in asparagus cream sauce, to filet of beef en croute, loin of veal stuffed with smoked salmon, or breast of turkey in whiskey and mustard sauce. It's a surprising little culinary oasis, just off the main road between Shannon and Ennis. *Moderate.*

QUIN, Co. Clare

Hotel

★★★ BALLYKILTY MANOR
Tel. (065) 25627. 11 rooms. Nestled in an historic inland setting beside 15th century Quin Abbey, Ballykilty was originally built by the McNamaras in 1614 and is within three miles of the McNamara castle stronghold of Knappogue (currently known for its nightly medieval banquets; see "Evening Entertainment" below). Over the years, this Georgian-style residence was also home to the Blood family, distinguished for a different reason (one of them stole the British crown jewels).

Recently renovated, extended, and refurbished by Tom and Maura Conroy, it is set on 50 acres of rolling hills, verdant woodlands, and flowering nature trails, less than nine miles from the jetways of Shannon Airport. Guest rooms are country-style and functional, with a mixture of heirlooms and modern comforts. Amenities include a full-service restaurant, old-world lounge bar, nine-hole golf course, and trout/salmon fishing privileges on the River Rine which runs through the hotel property. *Moderate.*

Entertainment

KNAPPOGUE CASTLE
Tel. (061) 71103 or 61788. Built in 1467, this castle was once the stronghold of the McNamara clan. Now fully restored, it is the setting for authentic medieval banquets during the summer season. It is a smaller and more intimate castle than Bunratty, but you will still feast on a medieval meal, followed by a colorful pageant of Irish history, complete with rhyme and mime, song and dance. Nightly at 6 P.M. and 9 P.M., May through October; the cost for the complete evening is approximately $35. For full details on other medieval banquets in the area, see also Bunratty, Co. Clare, and Kinvara, Co. Galway.

SHANNON, Co. Clare

Hotel

★★★ SHANNON INTERNATIONAL—QUALITY INN
Airport Road (N19). Tel. (061) 61122. 126 rooms. This has to be among the most convenient airport hotels in the world, situated right across the street from the main Shannon departure area. You can not only walk to/from your flights, but you can also enjoy fine views of the Irish countryside including glimpses of the adjacent River Shannon.

Administered by the Irish Airports Authority, Aer Rianta, this modern two-story hotel has every up-to-date convenience and makes a good touring base if you are only remaining in Ireland for a day or two. The Shannon Airport complex also includes an 18-hole golf course, just a half-mile from the hotel (See "Sports" below). *Moderate.*

For other accommodations suggestions and dining tips for the Shannon area, see also Bunratty, Newmarket-on-Fergus, Ennis, Quin, and Limerick.

Shopping

SHANNON DUTY FREE SHOPS
Shannon Airport. Tel. (061) 61444. Founded in 1947, the Shannon shops are known throughout the world. Open every day, from early morning till late at night, this complex offers tax-free bargains to shoppers in transit or departing from the airport. A good portion of the products are Irish (65%), such as Waterford Crystal, Belleek China, Donegal tweeds, Aran knitwear, Connemara marble, ceramic leprechauns, shillelaghs, and smoked salmon, but you'll also find names like Wedgwood, Bing and Grondahl, Lladro, Anri, Limoges, Orrefors, and Pringle.

BALLEYCASEY CRAFT CENTER
Off the Airport Road (N 19). Tel. (061) 62105. You'll find this craft cluster within the airport complex, just three miles from the main terminal. Housed in the courtyard of a restored Georgian manor house, these workshops feature an array of hand-fashioned items, ranging from basketry, leatherwork, pottery, and jewelry, to knitwear, embroidery, and patchwork. Whether pondering a purchase or just browsing, you can chat with the artisans as they work and learn more about their trades. The main house also includes an art gallery.

Sports

Golf

SHANNON GOLF CLUB
Shannon Airport, Airport Road (N 19). Tel. (061) 61020. This 18-hole championship course welcomes visitors any day of the week. Located within a half-mile of the main terminal, it is surrounded by scenic vistas of Co. Clare and the Shannon River as well as the busy jetways. Greens fees are approximately $14; golf clubs can be hired for $7.50 per round, and caddie pull-carts for about $1.50. To book a starting time, phone the manager, Mr. M. Sheehy (direct line: 61849).

Getting Around

Airport Transfers

Bus Eireann operates a daily service between Shannon International Airport to/from Limerick Railway Station, in conjunction with scheduled flight departures and arrivals (normally every 30 minutes). The one-way fare is approximately $4.

In addition, some hotels, such as Fitzpatrick's Shannon Shamrock, operate a courtesy minibus service to/from the airport for overnight guests. To arrange for a minibus to meet you when you land at Shannon, it is necessary to advise the hotel in advance of your flight number and expected arrival time.

Taxis are readily available at Shannon Airport for transport to hotels in nearby Co. Clare towns or into Limerick City. Approximate fares to most hotels range from $8 to $15.

Car Rentals

More than a dozen car rental firms maintain desks in the arrivals hall of Shannon Airport. Among the companies with international affiliations are:

Avis, tel. (061) 61643.
Budget/Flynn Bros., tel. (061) 61366.
Hertz, tel. (061) 61369.
Inter-Rent/Bolands, tel. (061) 61877.
National/Murrays Europcar, tel. (061) 61618.

If you have no particular international favorite, you may wish to consider a local Irish-based agency which has a good reputation for competitive prices and reliability:

Dan Dooley Rent-A-Car, tel. (061) 61098. In addition to a fleet of up-to-date model cars, this company also offers minibuses, on a self-drive or chauffeur-driven basis.

Directory

Shannon Airport Tourist Office, Arrivals Concourse. Tel. (061) 61664.

Airlines with operations/ticket desks at Shannon:

Aer Lingus, Tel. (061) 61666.
British Airways, Tel. (061) 61477.
Delta Airlines, Tel. (061) 61200.
Northwest Airlines, Tel. (061) 62555.
Pan American, Tel. (061) 62093.
Shannon Executive Aviation, Tel. (061) 61211

ADARE, Co. Limerick

Hotel

★★★ DUNRAVEN ARMS

Main Street (N 21). Tel. (064) 86209. 24 rooms. Nestled on the banks of the River Maigue in one of Ireland's prettiest thatched-roof villages, this small 19th century inn is a charming country retreat just ten miles south of Limerick City. It is owner-managed by Bryan Murphy, a keen horse enthusiast who will assist guests in making riding arrangements; in the winter months, the Fox Hunting Centre of Ireland is also headquartered here. The hotel's gardens supply fruit and vegetables for its award-winning restaurant. *Moderate.*

Restaurant

★★★ THE MUSTARD SEED

Main Street (N 21). Tel. (061) 86451. Innovative Irish and international dishes are featured at this 26-seat restaurant in a renovated thatched cottage. The menu of chef-owner Daniel Mullane includes seafood and vegetable stir-frys, rack of lamb, beef Wellington, and poached pears in beaujolais sauce. Open for dinner year-round, except Sunday from May through September, and Sunday/Monday at other times. *Moderate.*

DRUMCOLLOGHER, Co. Limerick

Castle-for-Rent

SPRINGFIELD CASTLE

Tel. (063) 83162. Set on 240 acres of gardens and farmland with dozens of grazing cows, sheep, and lambs, Springfield was first built as a 16th century tower house of the Fitz-Geralds, then owned by the Fitzmaurice and Deane-Morgan families. Today it consists of the original four-story tower, a 19th-century Gothic manor house with pinnacled buttresses, and a courtyard, complete with an old carriage. To complete the tableau, red and fallow deer graze near the castle walls.

The estate also has a tennis court, croquet lawn, and patio with barbecue. Most of the furniture and other decoration is from the 18th century, including a family portrait gallery, a wall of miniatures, silver, animal-skin rugs, and a fan collection; the modern kitchen has every 20th century convenience with a country-cupboard motif. There are seven heirloom-filled bedrooms, with three bathrooms, which can accommodate up to 12 people comfortably.

This castle is available for rent on a self-catering basis throughout the year, from $500 to $850 per week. (Note: If you'd like some of your meals cooked and served for you, the castle owners will oblige, as requested, at about $15 extra per person for a four-course dinner). For further information and reservations, contact Jonathan and Betty Sykes, Springfield Castle, Drumcollogher, Co. Limerick.

Shopping

IRISH DRESDEN

Tel. (063) 83192. A blend of Irish craftsmanship and German tradition, this plant produces a selection of delicate figurines and decorative souvenirs. Originally founded in Volkstedt, Germany, the business was brought to Ireland 25 years ago by the Saar family. Using 400-year-old German master molds and new patterns inspired by aspects of rural life in Ireland, a team of 50 Irish potters, artists, and designers can be seen working together to transform a mixture of clay and lace into intricate works of art, ranging from collector's thimbles and bride/ groom pairs to castles, cottages, and leprechauns. Free guided tours are available Monday through Friday at 3 P.M. and by appointment. In addition, you can browse during normal weekday shopping hours in the adjacent showroom; Irish Dresden pieces are also on sale in stores throughout Ireland.

GLIN, Co. Limerick

Castle-for-Rent

GLIN CASTLE

Limerick/Tarbert Road (N 69). Tel. (068) 34173. Lilies of the valley and ivy-covered ash, oak, and beech trees line the driveway leading to this gleaming white castle, home to the Knights of Glin for the last 700 years.

The current (and 29th) Knight welcomes guest rentals for periods of two weeks or more, with all services including chef, housemaids, and gardeners. The castle is a showcase of elaborate plasterwork, fanciful fanlights, Corinthian columns, a unique double-ramp flying staircase, and colorful bedrooms, filled with 18th century Irish furniture. Nestled along the Shannon estuary, Glin is a walker's paradise, with 400 acres of farmland, forests, paths, and gardens, all within an hour's drive of Limerick, Killarney, or Tralee. Glin can accommodate 8 to 10 people in four deluxe suites, with five bathrooms; the rental charge per week including staff is approximately $5,500. All inquiries in the U.S. are handled by At Home Abroad, 405 E. 56th St., #611, New York, NY 10022. Tel. (212) 421-9165.

If you are not lucky enough to rent, during mid-May/mid-June you can also stop by for a visit; tours are given between 2 P.M. and 4 P.M. and at other times by appointment. From April through October, you can also visit the castle's Gate Shop, a delightful source of Irish crafts and curios; plus a cafe.

Pub

★★★ O'SHAUGHNESSY'S

Ivy House, Main Street. Tel. (068) 34115. A canary's song welcomes visitors to this old farmer's house near Glin Castle on the main street of a neat village along the Shannon estuary. The main bar room, where the bird cage hangs amid fish nets, barrels, and saddles, is full of farm memorabilia, books, and pictures. The adjacent lounge, formerly a kitchen and now a haunt for local musicians, has walls bedecked with guitars, accordians, and bodhrans, used many afternoons or evenings for a spontaneous foot-tapping session or two.

LIMERICK, Co. Limerick

Hotels

★★★★ JURYS

Ennis Road (N 18). Tel. (061) 55266. 96 rooms. The best place to stay in Limerick is not in the downtown business section, but at Jurys which is across the Sarsfield Bridge in a residential section adjacent to the banks of the Shannon River. Just a three-minute walk from the main city thoroughfare of O'Connell Street, this recently renovated hotel is laid out in a bright and airy contemporary style, with a skylit mini-atrium foyer, open-plan coffee shop, and an award-winning copper-motif restaurant.

To get you in the mood for a stroll around the city, there is also a new pub, "Limericks Bar," with walls full of quotable and lyrical limericks. The up-to-date bedrooms are spacious and practical, with views of the gardens and river; the tree-shaded grounds also include ample parking for all guests. *Moderate.*

★★★ LIMERICK INN

Ennis Road (N 18). Tel. (061) 51544. 153 rooms. A country club atmosphere permeates this rambling and modern hotel, located in a pastoral setting three miles west of the city. It is handsomely decorated with bright-toned designer furnishings and fabric-textured wall coverings. Guest facilities include a new health and leisure center with swimming pool, fitness equipment, hairdressing salons, and a billiards room. There is also a full-service restaurant, "The Burgundy Room," a coffee shop, piano lounge, spacious drawing rooms with views of the nearby grassy hills, and a large car park. *Moderate.*

★★★ CASTLE OAKS HOUSE
Off the Dublin Road (N 7), Castleconnell. Tel. (061) 377666. 11 rooms. For those who prefer an old-world setting, this hotel is unique in the Limerick area. Set on 25 acres of mature woodlands along the Shannon River, it is a two-story Georgian manor, dating back over 150 years.

Among the fittings which the original owners installed were classic bow windows, a decorative staircase, and a skylit central dome. Later used as a convent, it has also been left with such unique features as stained glass windows and a chapel which is now used as a reception room. It was re-styled, expanded, and opened as a hotel in early 1987 by the Hanrahan family. The luxurious bedrooms are furnished with crown-canopy beds, soft pastel fabrics, and choice antiques from the area; the suites also have jacuzzis. Guest facilities include a gourmet restaurant specializing in seafood, lounge bar, and ample parking. It is located six miles east of Limerick at the edge of a country village. *Moderate to expensive.*

For accommodations near Limerick, see also Adare, Bunratty, Ennis, Newmarket-on-Fergus, Nenagh, Quin, and Shannon Airport.

Restaurants

★★★★ THE SILVER PLATE
74 O'Connell Street. Tel. (061) 316311. Situated in the heart of Limerick City, this chic 40-seat French restaurant is in the basement of a re-fashioned Georgian townhouse, near the Crescent and Pery Square. Rich in dark woods and silver accessories, the decor is dominated by a blend of pastel pink tones. The menu leans toward seafood, with such specialties as lobsters from the tank, Kenmare Bay prawns thermidor, sole stuffed with shellfish, and salmon baked in a paper bag. Open for dinner only. *Moderate to expensive.*

★★★ PICCOLA ITALIA
55 O'Connell Street. Tel. (061) 315844. With a name that means "Little Italy," this "ristorante" adds a touch of the Mediterranean to the heart of Limerick. The decor is more typical of a Roman palazzo than a Limerick town house, with red and white check tablecloths and chianti baskets hanging from the ceiling. The menu is also delightfully Italian: from zuppe de funghi, canneloni, lasagne, and fettucine, to scampi, salmon alla griglia, and steak pizzaiola. Open seven nights a week for dinner. *Inexpensive to moderate.*

For more restaurants in the Limerick region, see also Adare, Bunratty, Ennis, and Newmarket-on-Fergus.

Pubs

★★★★ HOGAN'S
Thomond House, 72 Catherine Street. Tel. (061) 44138. Run by the same family for three generations, this small mid-city pub looks much the same way it did when it started in 1913. Step in and sit by the turf fire, listen to the old chiming clock, or explore the small snugs. It's a classic experience of yesteryear.

★★★ M.J. RIDDLER'S—THE CLOISTER
9 Sarsfield Street. Tel. (061) 44149. You'll find this cozy old pub just beside the Shannon River by the Sarsfield Bridge. The walls are wood-paneled, with shelves that are lined with brassy fixtures, old tinted bottles, and vintage clocks.

★★★ THE GRANARY TAVERN
Michael Street, Charlotte Quay. Tel. (061) 47266. Housed in a restored grain store near the Shannon River, this pub is full of vaulted ceilings, double arches, and original brickwork, all reflecting a dockside 19th century maritime aura. There is music most evenings and the "Viking Steak Bar" offers hearty meals at moderate prices.

★★★ LUCKY LAMP
9 Ellen Street. Tel. (061) 40694. Located in one of Limerick's older sections near the quays, this pub used to be a wine cellar and the decor reflects it— barrel seats and tables, oak casks, and dark paneled-walls. Today it is known as a meeting place for a young single clientele, drawn by evening sessions of traditional music. Pub snacks include salads, soups, and sandwiches.

★★★ THE JAMES JOYCE
4 Ellen Street. Tel. (061) 46711. As its name indicates, this pub has as literary ambience. With a bust of author James Joyce clearly on view, the walls also display Joycean photos, sketches, and quotes. Unique touches include thatching over the bar, fully carpeted floors, and cushioned benches.

★★★ OLDE TOM'S
19 Thomas Street. Tel. (061) 45961. A family-run pub in the heart of the city, this spot is known for its evening sessions of Irish music, ballads, dancing, and poetry readings. There is also a fine selection of pub meals and fresh salads throughout the day and evening.

★★★ M.J. FINNEGANS
Dublin Road (N 7), Annacotty. Tel. (061) 337338. Dating back to 1820, this restored alehouse takes its name from James Joyce's "Finne-

gans Wake" and the decor reflects a Joycean theme, with appropriate Limerick overtones. Special features include Irish ceili music on weekends, and picnic tables for sitting by the rose garden on warm summer days. The pub grub ranges from homemade soups and sandwiches to popcorn. It's located on the main road about 5 miles east of Limerick City.

★★★ MATT THE THRESHER
Dublin Road (N 7), Birdhill, Co. Tipperary. Tel. (061) 379337. Situated about 15 miles northeast of Limerick, this roadside tavern is a replica of a 19th century farmers' pub. A rustic, cottage-like atmosphere prevails inside, with antique furnishings, agricultural memorabilia, traditional snugs, and lots of cozy alcoves. There is music on many evenings, and the pub grub is very good—from onion and ham quiche, to traditional bacon and cabbage, fishermen's pie, and crab claw platters.

Entertainment

THE BELLTABLE ARTS CENTRE
69 O'Connell Street. Tel. (061) 319866. Dramas, musicals, and concerts are staged year-round at this mid-city theatre and entertainment center. The summer program also includes presentations of Irish traditional song, dance, and poetry on Wednesday, Thursday, and Friday evenings. Curtain time for most productions is usually 8 P.M. and tickets range from $5 to $7. By day, the building is also open for gallery exhibits showing the works of modern Irish artists and local crafts, such as the world-famous Limerick lace.

SON ET LUMIERE
St. Mary's Cathedral, Merchant's Quay. Scheduled from mid-June through mid-September, this is an impressive sound and light show, portraying the story of ancient Limerick. It is presented nightly at 9:15 P.M. inside 800-year-old St. Mary's Cathedral. Admission is approximately $4. Reservations are not necessary, but further details can be obtained from Shannonside Tourism, The Granary, Michael Street. Tel. (061) 317522.

See also Bunratty for descriptions of the medieval banquets and ceili evenings at nearby Bunratty Folk Park and vicinity.

Shopping

THE SPINNING WHEEL
8 Rutland Street. Tel. (061) 40289. Handmade crafts produced by people from the Limerick area are featured here, as well as a fine selection of woolens, pottery, blackthorn sticks, tin whistles, heraldic crests, leprechaun dolls, and Irish coffee glasses.

WHITE AND GOLD

34 O'Connell Street at Roches Street. Tel. (061) 49977. Irish Dresden figurines, the delicate porcelain pieces made at nearby Drumcollogher, are the special attraction of this chic gift shop. Other wares include fanciful European Christmas ornaments, intricate wind chimes, and Hummels.

TODD'S

O'Connell Street. Tel. (061) 47222. For more than 100 years, this has been Limerick's leading department store. Affiliated with the Switzer group of stores, the wares include Waterford crystal, Aran knitwear, Donegal tweeds, and ready-to-wear clothing of all types.

For additional shopping suggestions, see also Bunratty, Ennis, and Shannon Airport.

Sightseeing Tours

LIMERICK WALKING TOURS

Shannonside Tourism, The Granary, Michael Street. Tel. (061) 317522. During June through August, you can get to know the city by participating in a walking tour of Old Limerick. Accompanied by specially trained local guides, these tours are conducted daily, except Sunday, at 11 A.M.. 1:30 P.M., and 3:30 P.M. The cost is approximately $3 and no reservations are necessary, just show up at the tourist office.

Sports

Golf

For descriptions of golf courses in the area, see Lahinch and Shannon Airport.

Getting Around

Bus Eireann operates local bus service around Limerick and its environs; the flat fare is approximately 80 cents. Bus service to Shannon Airport costs about $4 one-way. Taxis line up outside of the railroad station, at all major hotels, and along Thomas Street and Cecil Street.

Festivals

March 18-20: Church Music International Choral Festival. Choirs from around the world gather to sing in the 800-year-old setting of St. Mary's Cathedral.

Mid-May: Limerick Game and Country Fair, an old-fashioned gathering which focuses on great food, crafts, and music.

Directory

The Shannonside Tourist Office, The Granary, Michael Street. Tel. (061) 317522.
CIE, Colbert Railway Station, off Parnell Street. Tel. (061) 42433. For buses, trains, and sightseeing tours.

RATHKEALE, Co. Limerick

Castle Bed-and-Breakfast

★★★ CASTLE MATRIX
Off the Limerick/Tralee Road (N 21). Tel. (069) 64284. 6 rooms. This is the restored 15th century stone fortress of the Earl of Desmond, now the residence of Col. Sean O'Driscoll (a former U.S. Air Force officer with Irish roots) and his Irish-born wife, Elizabeth. Nestled on the River Deel, it is a fairytale castle with suits of armor, antique musical instruments, 400-year-old furniture, ancient tapestries, rooftop battlements, an 83-step winding staircase, chapel, and authentic dungeon, complete with shackles. Avoid the latter, and book one of the modernized bedrooms, all with private facilities, and three with individual saunas.

If you're ancestor-hunting, take a browse through the library, the most complete private genealogy collection in Ireland. Open as a B & B only during mid-June through mid-August; the castle can also be rented outright by negotiation. It is handily located less than 20 miles southeast of Limerick City and 35 miles from Shannon Airport. *Moderate.*

BALLYPOREEN, Co. Tipperary

Pub

★★ THE RONALD REAGAN
Main Street. Tel. (052) 67133. Yes, there really is a pub named after the U.S. President, right in the middle of the town which was home to his great-grandfather Michael Regan. Filled with pictures and mementos of the President's June 3, 1984, visit to Ballyporeen, this bar is part of the pub-cum-gift shop complex of local entrepreneur John O'Farrell. Even the back wall features a mural of the original Reagan homestead cottage. Worth a stop for a toast or at least a picture.

CAHIR, Co. Tipperary

Hotel

★★★ KILCORAN LODGE

Mallow/Cashel Road (N 8). Tel. (052) 41288. 22 rooms. A former hunting lodge, nestled on 20 acres of wooded grounds on a hillside set back from the main road, this old Victorian treasure was completely renovated in 1986, updating the guest rooms (all now have private bath), but retaining the old world decor in the public areas. Step inside and relax amid open fireplaces, grandfather clocks, antique tables and chairs, brass fixtures, and tall windows which frame expansive views of the Suir Valley and Knockmealdown Mountains. This small hotel is your best bet if you want to overnight near the Reagan ancestral home in Ballyporeen. Even if you're just passing through, it's also an ideal place to stop for bar food, from Irish stew to traditional boiled bacon and cabbage, homemade soups, hot scones. *Inexpensive.*

Shopping

CROCK OF GOLD

Castle Street. Tel. (052) 41951. If you stop to explore Cahir Castle, this handy shop is nearby. It's a good oasis to know if you are in transit, because it stays open from 9 A.M. to 9 P.M., every day, not only selling a wide array of handmade quality souvenirs, but also serving light food, coffee, tea, and snacks.

CASHEL, Co. Tipperary

Hotels

★★★★ CASHEL PALACE

Main Street. Tel. (062) 61411. 20 rooms. If you stay here, it's not such a long way to Tipperary town; in fact, it's only 12 miles. Originally built in 1730 as a residence for Church of Ireland archbishops, this stately red brick Palladian mansion has been a hotel for the last 20 years. The current owner, Ray Carroll, has thoroughly up-dated the property and filled it with antiques and designer-coordinated fabrics. It has an ideal location—right in the middle of Cashel town, yet within its own walled grounds, with a well-tended back garden that includes mulberry bushes planted in 1702 to commemorate the coronation of Queen Anne, and a private pathway up a hill to the Rock of Cashel.

The house itself is a proud display of Corinthian pillars, mantelpieces of Kilkenny marble, and a paneled early Georgian staircase of red pine. Many of the high-ceilinged rooms, including the main restaurant, "The Four Seasons," offer splendid views of the revered Rock, especially at night when it is floodlit. If you are just in transit, you might also want to try the lower-level all-day coffee shop/pub called "The Buttery," for a snack, soup, sandwich, or cheese and fruit platter. *Expensive to very expensive.*

★★★★ DUNDRUM HOUSE
Dundrum. Tel. (062) 71116. 40 rooms. You'll find this impressive Georgian country manor six miles northwest of Cashel town, in the fertile Tipperary countryside, surrounded by 100 acres of grounds and gardens, with the River Suir running right through the property.

Originally built as a residence in 1730 by the Earl of Montalt, then used as a convent school, it was renovated, up-dated, and turned into a hotel ten years ago by local residents Austin and Mary Crowe. It is furnished with assorted heirlooms, vintage curios, Victorian pieces, and reproductions. Facilities include a fine restaurant, a unique pub with stained glass windows (formerly the chapel), tennis courts, riding stables, trout fishing privileges, and a ceramic studio/craft shop. It's a perfect spot to settle down for a few days or to use as a base when touring the Tipperary/Waterford/Limerick and Kilkenny areas. *Moderate.*

★★★ RECTORY HOUSE
Dundrum. Tel. (062) 71266. 11 rooms. About a half-mile from Dundrum House is this little inn, run by Stephanie and Paul Deegan. Like its neighbor, it also has a multi-purpose past, having been built in the mid-19th century by Viscount Hawarden, and then used as a Church of Ireland pastor's house until a few years ago.

Now a member of the Best Western group and outfitted with all the modern conveniences, Rectory House is surrounded by ancient trees and lovely gardens and is a very homey place to stay. The candlelit dining room has earned a reputation for fine French/Italian cuisine, and the bar is full of old world atmosphere, a favorite gathering spot for the locals. *Inexpensive.*

Restaurants

★★★★ CHEZ HANS
Rockside. Tel. (062) 61177. It is not surprising that the Rock of Cashel, a pivotal landmark in the course of Irish royal and ecclesiastical history, would inspire a great restaurant within its shadow. As befits the aura of this award-winning eatery, it is housed in a former Gothic chapel at the foot of the path that leads to the mighty Rock. The cathedral-style ceiling, original stone walls, lyrical background music, and candlelight atmosphere provide the perfect setting for the cooking of chef-owner Hans Pieter Mataier. Dishes range from quenelles of sea

bass and sole meuniere to a succulent herb-encrusted roast lamb. Open for dinner only, except Sunday and Monday. No credit cards.

For tips on nearby accommodations and shopping, also see Cahir.

NENAGH, Co. Tipperary

Hotel

★★★ THE WATERSIDE
Dromineer Bay. Tel. (067) 24114. 12 rooms. Located about 25 miles northeast of Limerick, off the main Dublin/Limerick (N 7), this hotel is tucked along the shores of the Shannon's Lough Derg. It's an ideal place to stay if you want an informal riverside retreat, while still being within touring distance of Limerick or Shannon. The rooms are small and simply furnished, although some have four-poster beds, and most have private baths.

If you are fond of fishing, sailing, windsurfing, or waterskiing, this is the right territory, and the hotel staff will obligingly make the necessary arrangements for you. The greatest attraction here, however, whether you are overnighting or just passing through, is the dining room. The menu includes such diverse items as Portuguese oysters, terrine of wild salmon and turbot, smoked pike, seafood en papilotte, noisettes of lamb, and steaks. Both the restaurant and the sporty sing-along pub with outdoor deck upstairs offer fine views of the water. *Moderate.*

The West

COUNTIES GALWAY AND MAYO

Situated along the rocky western coast, Galway and Mayo are Ireland's second and third largest counties, and together form the heart of the province of Connacht. "To hell or Connacht!" was the dubious choice which Oliver Cromwell offered to the Irish in the 17th century. Ravaging the land and chopping down choice trees, he attempted to push the native population westward, far from the more valuable midland farms.

The Irish chose to till the west's poor soil and eke out a living from the rocky land. Just as they were managing to raise a decent potato crop, the blight struck, and the famine years of 1845-49 took a further toll. Galway and Mayo were the most devastated regions in Ireland, thousands, either starving or sailing westward, never to return.

It is somewhat of a miracle to look around Galway and Mayo and see the recovery that has been made. But, most important, it is good to know that the progress has not interfered with the cherished ways of the people. You'll find some of the country's greatest hotels, restaurants, sports and shopping opportunities here, but they are all a part of a setting where Ireland's traditional customs, crafts, music, and lifestyle still thrive.

COUNTY GALWAY

Galway City (pronounced "Gawl-way") is the focal point of Co. Galway and of the west of Ireland. Situated at the mouth of Galway

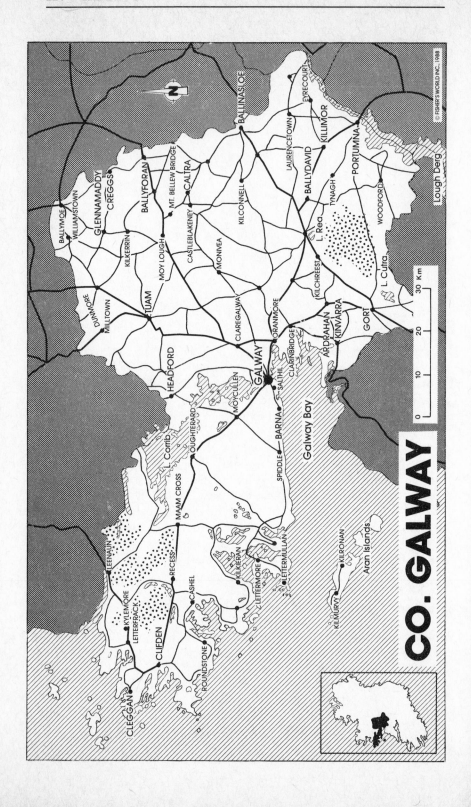

CO. GALWAY

Bay off the Atlantic, it is just a little over an hour's drive from Shannon Airport. With a population of 37,000, it is the principal city of Connacht and among the top five Irish cities.

The origin of the placename Galway is uncertain, but the most popular notion holds that it was named after some foreigners, or "Galls," who settled in the region. The earliest historic references to Galway date back to 1124 and describe the area as a Gaelic hinterland.

Because of its position on the Atlantic, Galway emerged as a thriving seaport and developed a brisk trade with Spain in particular. A group of fourteen wealthy merchant families, mostly of Welsh and Norman origin, dominated the town for many years and ruled it as an oligarchy. In time, these families (Athys, Blakes, Bodkins, Brownes, Darcys, Deanes, Fonts, Frenchs, Joyces, Kirwans, Lynchs, Martins, Morrises, and Skerrets) became known as the "Tribes of Galway." By far the most important were the Lynches, who not only gave the city its first mayor in 1484, but eighty-three others during the next 169 years.

In more recent times, two developments in the city have earned it a place of prominence in the west—the founding of the Queen's College (now University College-Galway) in 1848, and the establishment of a permanent rail link with Dublin in 1854.

Today's Galway revolves around a pedestrian park at Eyre Square (pronounced "Air"), originally a market area known as the Fair Green. It is officially called the John F. Kennedy Park, in commemoration of the U.S. president's visit here in June of 1963.

To the west of the park, Galway's main thoroughfare begins—a street which changes its name four times (from William to Shop, Main Guard, and Bridge), before it crosses the River Corrib and changes again. If that sounds confusing, don't worry. The streets are all very short, well-marked, and, with a map in hand, easy to follow. (Do stop at the tourist office just off Eyre Square for all kinds of maps and walking tour guides—see "Inside Information").

A town of medieval arches, alleyways, and cobblestone lanes, Galway is at its best when explored on foot. One of the first buildings ★ you will encounter (on Shop Street) is Lynch's Castle, dating from 1490 and renovated in the 19th century. It is the oldest Irish medieval town house used daily for commercial purposes (now the Allied Irish Bank). The exterior is full of carved gargoyles, impressive coats of arms, and other decorative stoneworks.

Venture next to St. Nicholas Collegiate Church, also off Shop ★ Street, originally erected in 1320, but enlarged, rebuilt, and embellished over the years. It has also changed denominations (from Roman Catholic to Church of Ireland) at least four times, but its main claim to fame rests in the local tradition that Christopher Columbus attended Mass here before setting sail for the New World in 1492. (One of his crew was a native of Galway.)

As you walk nearer to the city docks, you can also see the area where Spanish merchants regularly unloaded their galleons. The ★ Spanish Arch was one of four built in 1594, and the Spanish Parade is a small open square where the visitors used to stroll in the evening.

On the opposite or western side of the river is the Claddagh, a section of Galway remembered for totally different reasons. This was an old fishing village, thought by many to pre-date Galway itself. Taking its name from the Irish "An Cladach" which means "a flat stony shore," the Claddagh and its inhabitants differed in many ways from the people in the adjacent city. The Claddagh people were descendants of early Gaelic families and spoke only the Irish language. Their stone streets were haphazardly arranged, with small squares rimmed by thatched mud-walled houses. But don't go looking for this quaint scene today—it all came to an end in 1934 with the building of a modern housing development.

One Claddagh tradition, however, still survives, and that is the Claddagh ring, a simple piece of jewelry cast in the form of two hands clasping a heart, with a crown at the top. For the people of the Claddagh, the ring symbolized trust or plighted troth. Although many Galwegians and people throughout Ireland still choose a Claddagh ring as a wedding band, these rings have gained great popularity, particularly with tourists, as a friendship token or just as an unusual souvenir.

★   One of Galway's most modern and massive sights is the Cathedral of Our Lady, situated on the west bank of the River Corrib. Opened in 1965, it took eight years to build and is mostly in the Renaissance style, with fine-cut stone from local quarries, and statues, stained glass, and mosaics all designed by contemporary Irish artisans.

The next phase of your touring should be done by car. Head west of town via the Coast road (follow the signs for "Salthill"). Within two miles, you will be in Salthill, a modern Irish beach resort, somewhat similar to the American New Jersey shore, with a boardwalk and fine beach, plus lots of bars, fast food, amusement rides, and arcades of games. It is a mecca for Irish families in the summer, but we prefer to continue on this scenic road to the little towns like Barna or Spiddal, both of which have fine restaurants. Spiddal is also an ideal spot to shop for locally-made Aran knit sweaters and other handcrafts. (See "Inside Information.")

You'll get some of your best views of the water along this stretch of coastline; try to time part of your drive so that you can "watch the sun ★★★ go down on Galway Bay" from a good vantage point. All of this activity—walking around the city plus a coastal drive—will easily take a whole day, so it is best to save a new day for Connemara.

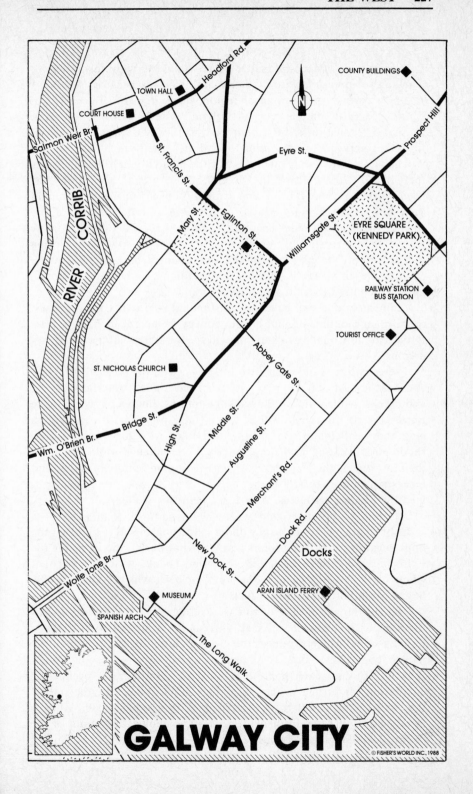

GALWAY CITY

© FISHER'S WORLD INC., 1988

CONNEMARA

If you look at an average map or road sign, you won't always see a marking or directional for "Connemara." That is because it is not a city or a town—it is an area or region, much like the "Burren" is in County Clare or the "Garden of Ireland" is in Wicklow. In general, Connemara constitutes the section west of Galway City, or starting out from Oughterard and continuing toward the Atlantic.

The largest town in Connemara is Clifden, so if you follow the signs for Clifden (from Galway or Oughterard), you can't go wrong. The road marked N 59 will bring you around the heart of Connemara and then onward to County Mayo. You can also follow many of the smaller roads and wander around Connemara for days. In fact, many people choose to stay in this region for a week or so, usually basing themselves in one or more of the fine country inns which dot the countryside, in places like Cashel, Ballynahinch, Letterfrack, Renvyle, and Clifden itself (See "Inside Information").

Connemara does not have any outstanding landmarks, great houses, or national monuments, but it does convey Ireland at its natural best. Drive around Connemara and you will see the Ireland of most people's dreams.

★★★★ The coastline is indented with little bays and inlets, small harbors, and beaches. At almost every turn, there are lakes, waterfalls, rivers, and creeks, while a dozen glorious mountains, known as the "Twelve Bens," rise at the center. All of this is interspersed with rock-strewn land and flat fields of open bog, and rimmed with gorse and heather, rhododendrons, and wild flowers. You'll see thatched-roof cottages in the most out-of-the-way places, sheep grazing on remote hillsides, and fences which are literally made of piles of rock, one of Connemara's greatest natural resources. You can't help but wonder—if the rocks ever turn to diamonds or gold, what a rich land this would be!

Connemara's other natural wonder is the bogland. It is said that the bogs began forming 2,500 years ago, and that during the Iron Age the Celts preserved their butter in the bog. Today, with one third of Connemara classified as bog, the "turf" or peat, which is cut from the bog, is an important source of fuel.

The cutting and drying of turf is an integral part of the rhythm of the seasons in Connemara. Cutting requires a special tool, a spade called a slane, which produces the pieces in a uniform size of about 18 inches long. These "bricks" of turf are spread out to dry and stiffen slightly, so they can then be stacked in pyramids to permit air circulation for further drying. They are finally stacked by the side of the road for transport to each cottage. You can always tell when a family is burning turf in their fireplace—the smoke coming out of the chimney will be blue and sweetly scented.

Another thing you'll notice as you drive around Connemara is an absence of trees, except in the gardens of major country inns. This is primarily attributed to the aforementioned Cromwell, who carted off some of the country's best wood for furniture and buildings in England. In recent years, however, the Irish government has undertaken an aggressive reforestation program and vast areas of land have been set aside for the planting of new trees; you'll pass quite a few of these forestry nurseries.

Another trademark of this region is the donkey, still a worker on the farms. In some places, you'll also notice a sturdy little horse known as a Connemara pony, the only native Irish breed of horse, though it has had an infusion of Spanish blood over the centuries. Raised in tiny fields with limestone pastures, these animals have great stamina and are invaluable for farming and pulling equipment. Also noted for its gentle temperament, the Connemara pony is ideal for children's riding. A Connemara Pony Show takes place annually at Clifden in mid-August.

A major part of Connemara is also designated as a "Gaeltacht" or Irish-speaking area, so you may hear many of the people conversing in their native tongue. Traditional music thrives in this part of the countryside as do hand-craft work and cottage industries.

The much-imitated Aran knit sweaters are synonymous with this region of Ireland. Made of an oatmeal-colored wool from the native sheep, these semi-waterproof sweaters were first knit by the women of the nearby Aran Islands for their fishermen husbands and sons; each family would have a different stitch or pattern. Years ago the pretty patterns served a more sombre purpose—they were a means of identifying men drowned in the rough waters off the coast.

Today these sweaters are knit commercially in the homes of Connemara and the nearby Aran islands, then sold in the many craft shops throughout the region. Other items which are usually associated with Connemara are the colorful tweeds made at Millar's of Clifden, and the distinctive green-colored Connemara marble from the quarry at Moycullen (see "Inside Information").

If you have an extra day to spare, you really should try to visit the Aran Islands, the three chunks of rocky land between Galway Bay and the Atlantic. Immortalized by the writings of J.M. Synge, and Liam O'Flahery, these three islands, known as Inishmore, Inishmaan, and Inisheer, were also the subject of the classic Robert Flaherty film, "The Man of Aran."

You can go to these outposts by air or sea (see "Inside Information"); the trip will take only minutes by plane or one/two hours by boat, but you will travel back several centuries in time. The islands will show you an Ireland of long ago, with simple stone cottages and pony-drawn transport. Most of the 1,500 people who live here wear the hand-knit bainin sweaters discussed above, as well as rawhide shoes, ideal for the islands' rocky terrain, and a finger-braided "crios" or belt of colored wool. They fish in the turbulent waters in traditional boats known as "currachs," seaworthy little craft made of tarred canvas stretched over a timber frame.

In addition to the Aran Islands, County Galway has several other noteworthy attractions situated south of Galway city. These include ★★ Thoor Ballylee, a 16th-century tower house at Gort just off the main Shannon/Galway road (N 18). For twelve years, this was the summer home of the Nobel prize-winning poet William Butler Yeats, who described it as "a tower set by a stream's edge." Now open to the public in the summer months, it served as the inspiration for the poet's "The Winding Stair" and "The Tower Poems."

★   Nearby is Coole Park, the former home of Lady Augusta Gregory, one of the founders of the Abbey Theatre. Although little remains of the house, the grounds are now a national forest and wildlife park open to the public. The chief attraction is an autograph tree which bears various sets of initials personally carved by such famous visitors as George Bernard Shaw, Sean O'Casey, John Masefield, Augustus John, Oliver St. John Gogarty, and Douglas Hyde, the first president of Ireland.

★★   Ten miles northwest at Kinvara, you will find Dunguaire Castle, a 16th-century fortress on the south shore of Galway Bay, open to the public by day and at night a venue for medieval-style banquets. (See "Inside Information.")

COUNTY MAYO

Although it has many diverse attributes, County Mayo has been primarily identified as "The Quiet Man country," every since the classic movie was filmed here in 1951. The exact setting for the film was at Cong, a little village wedged between Lough Mask and Lough Corrib, and back-to-back with the Co. Galway border.

To add to the glory of Cong, it is also the home of one of the most celebrated of Ireland's luxury hotels, Ashford Castle (See "Inside Information"). Ashford Castle alone is probably enough to draw most visitors to this part of Ireland, but there are also many other reasons to come.

First of all, if you are fond of fishing, Co. Mayo is readily recognized as one of the premier sources for salmon and trout. The waters of the Corrib, the River Moy, and Lough Conn offer some of the best fishing in Europe. Several of the county's fine country inns, such as Newport House at Newport and Mt. Falcon Castle and Belleek Castle at Ballina, have made their reputations catering to

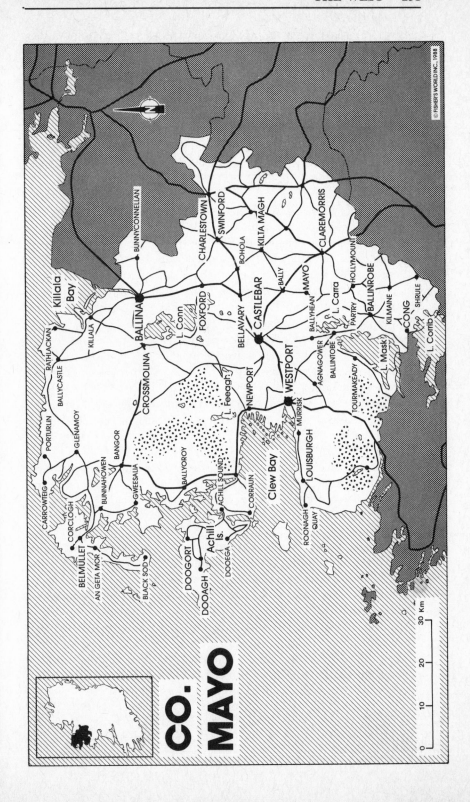

fishing enthusiasts (see "Inside Information"). Ballina (pronounced "Bal-in-ah"), Mayo's largest town, calls itself the "home of the Irish salmon." For those who prefer shark fishing or other off-shore recreation, the one-hundred-mile Mayo coastline, which reaches into the Atlantic between Killary Harbor and Killala Bay, is noted for deep sea sports.

★★★   Co. Mayo's loveliest town, Westport, is nestled on the shores of Clew Bay. Once a major port, it is one of the few planned towns of Ireland, designed by Richard Cassels with a splendid tree-lined mall, rows of Georgian buildings and an octagon-shaped central mall.

★★   At the edge of town you can visit Westport House, a late 18th-century residence, home of Lord Altamont, the Marquis of Sligo. The work of Richard Cassels and James Wyatt, the house's highlights include a staircase of ornate white Sicilian marble, unusual art nouveau glass and carvings, family heirlooms, and silver.

Southeast of Westport is Croagh Patrick, a 2,510-foot mountain which dominates the vistas of western Mayo for many miles. It was here in 441 A.D. that St. Patrick is said to have prayed and spent the forty days of Lent. To commemorate this, each year on the last Sunday of July thousands of Irish people make a pilgrimage to this site, which has since become known as "St. Patrick's Holy Mountain."

County Mayo is also the setting for several other major religious ★★★ attractions, including Knock Shrine. It was here in 1879 that local people claim to have seen an apparition of the Blessed Mother of Jesus. Now considered as the Lourdes or Fatima of Ireland, Knock achieved worldwide publicity in 1979 when visited by Pope John Paul II.

The centerpiece of Knock Shrine is a huge circular basilica which can accommodate 20,000 people. The architecture includes pieces or furnishings from every county in Ireland. Knock's success as a major place of pilgrimage has warranted the creation of its own airport, Msgr. Horan International Airport, named after the industrious cleric who helped to promote Knock to international status. Although several charters from the U.S. have landed at Knock, so far regularly scheduled services are operated only from Britain.

★★   About 20 miles west of Knock is Ballintubber Abbey, founded in 1216 by Cathal O'Connor, King of Connacht. Even though the forces of Cromwell took off the church's roof in 1653, among other repressive actions, the clerics persisted in discreetly conducting religious services through the centuries. Completely restored in 1966, Ballintubber is known as "the abbey that refused to die" because it is one of the few Irish churches in continuous use for nearly 800 years.

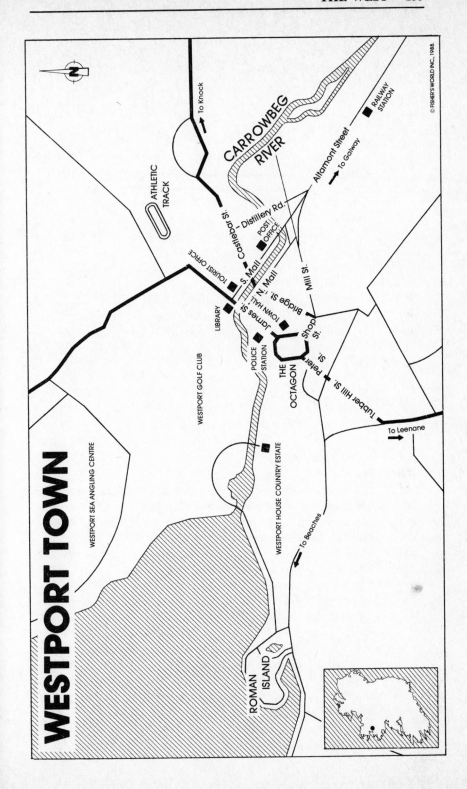

WESTPORT TOWN

WESTPORT SEA ANGLING CENTRE

WESTPORT GOLF CLUB

WESTPORT HOUSE COUNTRY ESTATE

ROMAN ISLAND

ATHLETIC TRACK

CARROWBEG RIVER

To Knock

Castlebar St.

Distillery Rd.

POST OFFICE

TOURIST OFFICE

S. Mall

N. Mall

LIBRARY

James St.

TOWN HALL

Bridge St.

Mill St.

Altamont Street

To Galway

RAILWAY STATION

POLICE STATION

THE OCTAGON

Peter St.

Shop St.

Tubber Hill St.

To Leenane

To Beaches

© FISHER'S WORLD INC., 1988.

BALLYNAHINCH, Co. Galway

Hotel

★★★★ BALLYNAHINCH CASTLE

Ballinafad. Tel. (095) 21269. 20 rooms, with 8 riverview suites currently
being added. Set on a 350-acre estate at the base of one of the Twelve
Ben Mountains, this turreted and gabled manor house overlooks the
Owenmore River, about 40 miles west of Galway City.

Dating back to the 16th century, over the years it served as a base
for such diverse owners as the O'Flaherty chieftains and the sea pirate
Grace O'Malley, and as the sporting residence of the Maharajah Jans
Sahib Newanagar, better known as Ranjitsinhgi, the famous cricketer.
The guestrooms are all individually named and decorated, many with
individual fireplaces, four-poster and canopy beds. The restaurant,
with its impressive Connemara marble fireplace, has been newly
extended and offers sweeping views of the countryside and the river.
Facilities include a tennis court and driving range, but the big draw
here is the access to top notch seatrout and salmon fishing. Open April
through October. *Expensive*.

CASHEL, Co. Galway

Hotels

★★★★★ CASHEL HOUSE

Cashel Bay. Tel. (095) 31001 or 21252. 18 rooms and 13 garden suites.
Set on 50 acres of exotic gardens and woodlands, this award-winning
100-year-old country inn of Dermot and Kay McEvilly is nestled deep
in the mountains and lakelands of Connemara, yet less than 40 miles
west of Galway City. A member of the Relais et Chateaux group, it
has attracted a wide range of discerning guests including General and
Madame deGaulle, who spent two weeks here in 1969.

Facilities include a private beach on the bay, tennis courts, fishing,
boating, and enchanting walking paths lined with rhododendrons,
azaleas, camellias, and magnolias, as well as flowers and plants from
as far away as Africa and Australia. With wide-windowed views of the
bay or the gardens from every room, the decor is a perfect blend of top
quality Irish fabrics, European antiques, sheepskin rugs, rattan pieces,
vintage paintings, and local heirlooms. The public rooms include an old
world lounge, TV room, skylit conservatory, well-stocked library, and a
restaurant which has been a benchmark for innovative Irish country
house cuisine. The menu features fresh seafoods, lobsters from the tank,
and local Connemara lamb, with vegetables from the garden; specialty

dishes include plaice stuffed with smoked salmon, poached turbot with lobster sauce, crab mornay, and a traditional chicken and ham with bread sauce. Open March through October. *Moderate to expensive.*

★★★ **ZETLAND HOUSE**
Cashel Bay. Tel. (095) 31011. 19 rooms. Built in 1850, this elegant manor house is less than two miles east of Cashel House and enjoys the same idyllic Connemara setting. Surrounded by lush gardens and ancient trees, the Zetland was completely up-dated and refurbished in 1985/6 under its current owner John Prendergast, a Paris-trained hotelier. The guest rooms, many of which look out onto the bay, have handsome reproduction or antique furnishings, and very modern bathrooms.

The dining room is known for its local seafood and lamb dishes; the vegetables and fruit come from the inn's own kitchen garden. If you enjoy fishing, take note that the Zetland owns one of the best private seatrout fisheries in Ireland, comprised of 14 lakes and four miles of river, and the staff eagerly caters to those who are fond of casting a rod on Irish waters. Open April through October. *Expensive.*

CLARENBRIDGE, Co. Galway

Pub/Restaurant

★★★★ **PADDY BURKE'S**
Ennis/Galway Road (N 18). Tel. (091) 96107. Besides the usual libations and snack food, platters of local oysters and mussels are served throughout the day at this homey thatched-roof tavern, situated on the main road ten miles south of Galway City. You can pick your favorite spot to relax amid a half-dozen rooms and alcoves, with a nautical decor of fish nets, original stone walls, open fireplaces, pot belly stoves, and traditional sugan chairs. In the evening, you can also order restaurant-quality meals in a moderate price bracket; choices range from scallops cordon rouge and grey sole on the bone to steaks, duck, or chicken. Every September, this pub is one of the focal points during the Galway Oyster Festival.

CLIFDEN, Co. Galway

Hotels

★★★ **ABBEYGLEN CASTLE HOTEL**
Sky Road. Tel. (095) 21070. 45 rooms. Although Abbeyglen has a history dating back to the 1820's, the present building was not known as a castle until the turreted facade was added a few years ago. Happily, the "new look" blends well with the Connemara countryside. The castle-like atmosphere is enhanced inside by such regal trappings

as brass candelabra chandeliers, arch-shaped windows, vintage settees, a Gothic-theme restaurant, and glamorous new bedrooms with crown-style canopies.

Located at the western edge of Clifden, on a hilltop overlooking the bay, it is undoubtedly the best place to stay in the immediate area of the town. Facilities include 12 acres of parkland, a heated outdoor swimming pool, nine-hole mini-golf, hard tennis court, table tennis, sauna, and sunbed. A resident pianist also enlivens the evening hours. In addition, personable proprietor Paul Hughes will also arrange fishing trips, packed lunches, and a host of other local activities. Open February through December. *Moderate.*

★★★ ROCK GLEN COUNTRY HOUSE
Ballyconneely Road. Tel. (095) 21035. 30 rooms. About a mile south of Clifden is this lovely country house, originally an 18th century shooting lodge. Expanded over the years and now in the hands of John and Evangeline Roche, Rock Glen is set back from the road, somewhat secluded amid flowering gardens, with views of Ardbear Bay and the Atlantic Ocean. It's a restful spot, with tastefully furnished bedrooms and homey public areas. Most rooms, including the restaurant, face the sea, and half of the bedrooms are on the ground floor. Open mid-March through October. *Moderate.*

★★★ HOTEL ARDAGH
Ballyconneely Road. Tel. (095) 21384. 17 rooms. In contrast to Rock Glen's 200-year-old charms are the sleek and modern appointments of the Ardagh, opened in 1982, and run by Dutch proprietors, Henk and Ria Berings. Also located on Ardbear Bay, about two miles south of Clifden, this two-story motor inn reflects a chalet-style atmosphere, with a decor of light woods and expansive windows. Many of the rooms, including the restaurant which is on the second floor, face the sea, and five guest rooms have individual balconies. The restaurant is known for its continental cooking including homemade goose liver pates, Dutch-style roasts, and shish kebabs. Open March through October. *Inexpensive.*

For other nearby lodging suggestions in the Clifden/Connemara area, see also Ballynahinch, Cashel (Co. Galway), Letterfrack, and Renvyle.

Shopping

MILLAR'S
Main Street. Tel. (095) 21038. This is the home of the colorful Connemara tweeds, an industry started in 1900 by Robert Millar as a small mill to process the wool from local mountain sheep. Although most people travel to Clifden just to buy Millar's skeins of wool or handwoven materials, plus ready-made ties, hats, caps, scarves, blan-

kets, and bedspreads, today's shop is more than just an outlet for tweeds. You'll also find Irish patchwork, rush baskets, Aran crios belts, embroidery work, handmade miniature currachs, tin whistles, and blackthorn pipes, plus an art gallery of regional paintings.

Sports

For information on the nearby Connemara Golf Club at Ballyconneely, see its listing under "Galway City—Sports."

GALWAY, Co. Galway

Hotels

★★★★ GREAT SOUTHERN HOTEL

Eyre Square. Tel. (091) 64041. 120 rooms. Dating back to 1845, this is truly the "grande dame" of the Galway area. Positioned right in the heart of the city overlooking the landmark Eyre Square pedestrian park, it is next to the bus and rail stations and within walking distance of all the major sights.

Recently refurbished, this handsome five-story hotel has an interior of high ceilings with elaborate plasterwork, spacious public rooms with original Connemara marble fireplaces, and bedrooms which are up-to-date and spacious. Guest facilities include a full-service restaurant, "The Oyster Room," an old-world lounge bar, a nightclub, and a rooftop health and leisure complex with heated swimming pool, sauna, sunbeds, and exercise room. In the summer months, there is also traditional Irish entertainment every Tuesday and Wednesday night. Parking is on a first-come basis around Eyre Square, but the hotel porter will usually help in finding a spot. *Expensive.*

★★★★ CONNEMARA COAST

Coast Road, Furbo. Tel. (091) 92108. 52 rooms and suites. If you want to see the sun go down on Galway Bay, this is the place to stay.

Located six miles west of the city, it is nestled right along the shores of the famous bay, with unobstructed views of the coast as well as the Aran Islands. Recently renovated and up-dated by enthusiastic owner Charles Sinnott, the guest rooms are decorated in a colorful tweedy style, each with a picture-window view of the water. The suites have turf-burning fireplaces and private verandas.

Amenities include a bi-level bayview restaurant, lounge bar with nightly traditional entertainment, an outdoor swimming pool, an enclosed sun porch, and plenty of parking space. Although modern in its structure and efficiency, this inn also has homey touches like shelves full of old books, country curios, and an indoor rock garden and waterfall. Open February through October. *Moderate.*

★★★ ARDILAUN HOUSE

Taylor's Hill. Tel. (091) 21433. 71 rooms. Named for the Irish phrase meaning "high island," this country inn was originally built in 1840 as a town house for a prominent Galway family, and was converted into a hotel in 1962. With ancient trees and elaborate gardens, it is located in a hilly residential section, only about a mile west of the downtown area. The Ardilaun has been expanded and up-dated in recent years; most of the guest rooms are in a modern three-story addition. Facilities include an old-world dining room, a hunting-theme lounge, an outdoor terrace, and ample parking. *Moderate.*

★★★ THE CORRIB GREAT SOUTHERN

Dublin Road (N 6). Tel. (091) 55281. 110 rooms. Situated on its own grounds two miles east of Galway City, this well-maintained five-story property is a favorite with touring motorists. The decor can best be described as modern Irish, with wide windows, many of which provide views of Galway Bay across the road. Facilities include a restaurant, lounge bar with evening entertainment, an indoor swimming pool, saunas, and lots of parking space. *Moderate.*

For other accommodations suggestions near to Galway City, see also Oughterard.

Restaurants

★★★★★ DRIMCONG HOUSE

Clifden Road (N 59), Moycullen. Tel. (091) 85115. Galway's best restaurant is not within the city at all, but in a tiny village nine miles northwest of downtown. A 300-year-old lakeside house is the setting for this award-winning 50-seat restaurant of Gerry and Marie Galvin (formerly of the "Vintage" in Kinsale).

With finesse and flair, the Drimcong staff deliver the quintessential Irish dining experience: as your order is taken, you relax in an elegant drawing room/cocktail lounge with an open fireplace; then you are escorted into one of two elegant dining rooms (the back room looks out onto the lake while the front windows have garden views). All the little touches await at your table—from fresh flowers, candlelight, fine Irish silver and glassware, to hot brown scones with butter twirls. The five-course dinners, to be sure, live up to the setting. Entrees range from a lasagne of wild salmon with oysters and avocado sauce, to confit of duck with pineapple and creme de cassis; other choices include wood pigeon, loin of veal, paupiettes of trout, stir-fried chicken, and rack of lamb. Open for dinner only, Tuesday through Saturday (except closed from mid-December through January). *Moderate to expensive.*

★★★★ THE MALT HOUSE
Olde Malte Arcade, High Street. Tel. (091) 67866. In decor and ambience, you'll appreciate the best of "old Galway" at this vintage restaurant, located within a cobblestone courtyard in the heart of the city. Chef/owner J.J. Coppinger offers a varied menu, ranging from prawn and shrimp thermidor to chicken stuffed with water chestnuts, ham, and mushrooms. Favorite desserts include homemade ice creams flavored with liqueurs. *Moderate.*

★★★★ TY AR MOR
Barna Pier, Barna. Tel. (091) 92223. Views of Galway Bay are in focus at this 35-seat stucco cottage at the edge of the water, five miles west of Galway City. The interior has a nautical atmosphere, to match the mostly seafood menu prepared by its chef-owner who hails originally from the Brittany coast. Entrees include giant prawn tails, ray wings, quenelles of brown trout, and lobster, as well as rack of lamb and pepper steak. Open for lunch and dinner daily during June through August, and dinner only the rest of the year except Tuesdays and the month of January. *Moderate.*

★★★★ CASEY'S WESTWOOD
Dangan, Upper Newcastle Road. Tel. (091) 21442. If you follow the Clifden Road (N 59) about a mile and a half from Eyre Square, you'll come to this elegant restaurant set back from the main road amid flowering gardens and tall trees. Owner Bernie Casey has converted an old brick house into a modern Georgian-style dining experience. The creative Irish menu includes turbot in chervil sauce; chicken stuffed with mangoes; brill with smoked salmon mousse in shrimp sauce; calf's kidneys in port wine sauce; and coquilles St. Jacques en croute. The complex also includes a trendy open-plan bar area called "The Elm"; light pub meals are available here at any time. With ample off-street parking, Casey's is open for lunch and dinner daily including Sunday. *Moderate.*

★★★ OLD GALWAY SEAFOOD RESTAURANT
2 High Street. Tel. (091) 61410. With a decor of pastel linens and nautical art, this cozy second-floor dining spot is a real find in the downtown area. As befits its name, the menu features such dishes as wild Aran salmon, Connemara scallops, Lough Corrib trout, and local lobster. It's currently open for normal lunch and dinner service, Monday through Saturday, but plans call for Sunday hours in 1988; check when you make a reservation. The entrance stairway is next to a pub called "A Bunch of Grapes." *Moderate.*

★★★ THE PARK HOUSE
Forster Street. Tel. (091) 64924. Located one block east of Eyre Square, this stylish basement restaurant is decorated with plush velour

fabrics, colored glass partitions, dark wood furnishings, and water-colors framed in brass. The cuisine is international, with such dishes as scampi thermidor, monkfish with strawberry sauce, steak au poivre, chicken stuffed with Stilton, and beef stroganoff. There is piano entertainment nightly. *Moderate.*

★★★ THE ABBEY
Sligo Road (N 17), Claregalway. Tel. (091) 98244. Located over the Summerfield Pub on the main street of this northeast Galway suburb, this homey restaurant seats 60 in a configuration of five small rooms and alcoves. It is a favorite with the local folk for its creative treatment of fresh Irish ingredients. The menu includes lettuce and almond soup; chicken stuffed with crab and oysters; a trio of beef, veal and lamb; and carpetbagger steaks. Open for dinner only. *Moderate.*

For an additional dining suggestion in the Galway area, see also Spiddal.

Pubs

★★★★ THE QUAYS
Quay Street and Chapel Lane. Tel. (091) 61771. This little treasure is in the heart of the city, a half-block from the Druid Theatre. The decor is decidedly nautical, with pictures of sailing ships and other seafaring memorabilia. The bar area is quite small, but there is also an enclosed skylit back courtyard which is a favorite for luncheon snacks. Evening music ranges from traditional Irish to Dixie.

★★★★ McSWIGGINS
3 Eyre Street. Tel. (091) 68917. Just west of Eyre Square, this grand old pub is really many pubs in one. There are at least eight different rooms, nooks, crannies, and alcoves where you can take a seat and sip a drink or coffee. The eclectic decor ranges from walls of brick, stone, tin, or wood paneling, to beamed ceilings, vintage ale posters, and an enclosed skylit veranda. A varied menu of substantial pub grub is also served in a large upstairs room.

★★★ RABBITT'S
23-25 Forster Street. Tel. (091) 62215. Dating back to 1872, this old-world pub is much the way it was a century ago. Old lanterns hang in the corner, skylights brighten the bar area, and the walls are lined with pictures of Galway in horse-and-carriage days. The only concession to the 20th century is the hefty bucket of ice on the counter. Run by the fourth generation of the Rabbitt family, it's located just a block east of the Great Southern Hotel.

★★★ CRANE BAR

2 Sea Road. Tel. (091) 67419. Situated in the southwestern part of the city at the corner of an open market area called the Small Crane, this rustic pub is known primarily for its nighttime music—Irish traditional tunes upstairs, and country and western downstairs.

★★★ MONROE'S TAVERN

Dominick Street. Tel. (091) 63397. This large three-story pub sits on a corner on the west side of the Wolfe Tone Bridge. It has a decor which reflects Galway's Spanish heritage, with white-washed rock walls, arches, and hangings of beaten copper and brass. Known for substantial seafood pub grub, it also has entertainment nightly and its own car park.

For additional pub/restaurant selections near Galway, see also Kilcolgan and Clarenbridge.

Entertainment

DRUID

Chapel Lane. Tel. (091) 68617. Modern international dramas and Anglo-Irish classics (such as "Playboy of the Western World") are the focus at this professional theatre in the heart of Galway. Started in 1975, it is housed in a converted grain warehouse which is configured with 65 to 115 seats, depending on the production. Offering an ever-changing program, it is open year-round, usually with an 8 P.M. curtain, Monday through Saturday, although lunchtime performances are often staged during the summer months. Tickets average $7 to $10; no credit cards.

TAIBHDHEARC

Middle Street. Tel. (091) 62024. Pronounced "Thive-yark" and officially known as An Taibhdhearc na Gaillimhe (the Theatre of Galway), this is Ireland's national stage of the Irish language. Founded in 1928, it is a 108-seat, year-round venue for both Irish plays and visiting troupes (such as ballet). In the summer months, the emphasis is on traditional music, song, and dance, and bi-lingual (English and Irish) folk productions. Tickets average $7 to $10, and performances are usually at 8:30 P.M. No credit cards.

For an entertainment/dinner suggestion not far from Galway City, see the reference to medieval banquets at Kinvara, Co. Galway.

Shopping

TREASURE CHEST

31 William Street, at Castle Street. Tel. (091) 63862. For over 20 years, this shop has been a veritable treasure-trove of top quality and hard-

to-find crafts, fashions, and gifts. You'll find everything from Waterford Crystal chandeliers and high fashion linen dresses to handmade leprechauns and Irish whiskey marmalade, as well as international products names like Hummel, Jaegar, and Aquascutum. If you prefer to order by mail after you return home, there is a 24-hour telephone ordering service.

PADRAIC O'MAILLE—THE HOMESPUN HOUSE
Dominick Street. Tel. (091) 62696. Established in 1938, this quality tweed and knitwear shop is celebrating its 50th anniversary in 1988. Over the years, regular customers have included John Wayne, Maureen O'Hara, and Peter Ustinov; many of the costumes for "The Quiet Man" were also produced here. Today you'll find a wide range of tweeds for men and women, including capes, shawls, suits, jackets, kilts, caps, hats, and ties. It's located on the west side of the city, next to O'Brien's Bridge, near the banks of the River Corrib.

KENNY'S BOOK SHOP AND GALLERY
Middle Street and High Street. Tel. (091) 62739. A Galway fixture for over 40 years, this shop is a sightseeing attraction unto itself. You'll find old maps, prints, engravings, and books of all topics and descriptions, many of Irish interest, wedged on shelves and window ledges, and piled in crates and turf baskets. The walls are lined with signed photos of more than 200 writers who have visited the shop over the years. In addition, Kenny's is famous for its antiquarian department, binding workshop, and an ever-changing gallery of watercolors, oils, and sculptures by local talent. No wonder there's enough to do here to keep eight members of the Kenny family busy!

DILLON
1 William Street. Tel. (091) 61317. If you are looking to buy a Claddagh ring, here is the best place. Founded in 1750, this jeweler's shop claims to be the original maker of the legendary clasped-heart ring.

HARTMANN'S
27-29 William Street. Tel. (091) 62063. The Hartmann family, who began in the jewelry business in the late 1800's in Germany, brought their skills and wares to Ireland in 1895, eventually opening this Galway shop in 1942. They still enjoy a far-reaching reputation as watchmakers, goldsmiths, and makers of Claddagh rings. This store also stocks Celtic crosses, writing instruments, crystal, silverware, and unusual clocks. It's in the heart of town, just off Eyre Square.

GALWAY CRYSTAL
Merlin Park. Tel. (091) 57311. Located east of the city on the main road (N 6), this is the home of one of Ireland's leading crystal manufacturers. Visitors are welcome to watch the craftsmen at work

blowing, shaping, and hand-cutting the glassware; demonstrations are given continually, Monday through Friday, from 9 A.M. to 5 P.M. In addition, the showrooms and shop are open seven days a week.

ROYAL TARA CHINA
Tara Hall, Mervue. Tel. (091) 51301. This is the production center for Ireland's premier fine bone china, both tableware and giftware. Well known for its delicate shamrock patterns, this distinctive china also features designs which reflect Irish history and culture such as the Book of Kells, Tara Brooch, and Claddagh ring. Guided tours are conducted daily at 11 A.M. and 3 P.M., and the showrooms/shop are open from 9 A.M. to 6 P.M., with evening hours until 9 P.M. in the summer months. Look for the sign, a mile east of Galway City, off the main Dublin Road.

CONNEMARA MARBLE INDUSTRIES
Galway/Clifden Road (N 59), Moycullen. Tel. (091) 85102. Connemara's unique green marble, diverse in color, marking, and veining, is quarried, cut, shaped, and polished here. On weekdays, you'll see craftsmen at work hand-fashioning marble jewelery, paperweights, ashtrays, Celtic crosses, and other giftware. The shop and showroom are also open during normal business hours on Saturdays.

For other nearby shopping suggestions, see also Spiddal.

Sports/Perks

Golf

GALWAY GOLF CLUB
Coast Road, Salthill. Tel. (091) 22169. Overlooking Galway Bay and less than two miles from the city, this 18-hole seaside course welcomes visitors any day of the week; greens fees are $18. Clubs can be hired for $5 and caddie pull-carts for about $2. The club manager is William Caulfield.

CONNEMARA GOLF CLUB
Ballyconneely, near Clifden. Tel. (095) 21153. It's worth the drive 50 miles west of Galway City to test your skills at this scenic 18-hole championship course, nestled in the heart of Connemara and looking out into the waters of the Atlantic. Visitor play is permitted every day; greens fees are $12; caddie carts can be hired for approximately $2, but no clubs are available. The manager is Hubert de Lappe.

Lake Cruising

CORRIB PRINCESS CRUISES
Waterside, Woodquay. Tel. (091) 68903. From May through October,

this modern enclosed cruiser offers daily one-and-a-half-hour trips along the waters of Lough Corrib, with departures at 11 A.M. and 3 P.M. You can just show up on the dock or book in advance at the Tourist Office on Eyre Square. The fare is approximately $6.

Trips to the Aran Islands

AER ARAN
Corrib Airport, Carnmore. Tel. (091) 55448. This airline offers flights to the Aran Islands, thirty miles out in the Atlantic. The service is via nine-seater, twin-engined aircraft, Monday through Saturday. You can arrange a trip at the Tourist Office; and a minibus will also take you from there to the airport. The round-trip fare is approximately $60.

M.V. NAOMH EANNA
Quayside, beside the Galway Docks. Tel. (091) 62141. If you'd like to take a boat trip across the 30 miles of water to the Aran Islands, CIE operates a regular service via this ship. The crossing takes approximately two-and-a-half hours and costs about $22 round trip. You can also fly out on Aer Aran and take the "Naomh Eanna" back (or vice versa) for a air/sea fare of approximately $45.

ARAN FERRIES
Eyre Square. Tel. (091) 68903. If you prefer a shorter sea route of ten miles (one hour in duration) to the Aran Islands, this company operates boats from Rossaveal, a coastal town 20 miles west of Galway City. The fare is approximately $18 round-trip, and a booking desk is located in the Tourist Office.

Festivals

May 27-29: Festival of the Tribes. An annual gathering with a genealogical slant, focusing on Galway's early days and the families who originated in this part of Ireland.

★★ *September 23-25:* Galway International Oyster Festival. First held in 1953, this event attracts people from all over the globe. Highlights include the World Oyster Opening Championships and a gala banquet.

Getting Around

Bus Eireann operates regular bus service within the city and its environs. The flat fare is approximately 80 cents. Most buses start or stop near Eyre Square. Taxis are also stationed at ranks around Eyre Square. Radio-dispatched 24-hour service is available from Galway Taxis, 7 Main Guard Street, tel. (091) 61111 or 61112.

Directory

Galway Tourist Office, Aras Failte, Eyre Square. Tel. (091) 63081.
C.I.E. Railway Station, off Eyre Square. Tel. (091) 62141. Here you
can arrange bus and rail transport to all parts of Ireland, sightseeing
excursions to Connemara, the Clare Coast, Knock Shrine and other
parts of Mayo, as well as boat trips to the Aran Islands.

HEADFORD, Co. Galway

Castle-for-Rent

CARRAIGIN CASTLE
Kilbeg Pier. Tel. (093) 35501. A winding rock-fenced road will bring
you to this white-washed castle on the shores of Lough Corrib,
midway between the busy city of Galway and the classic Ashford
Castle Hotel. Carraigin, which means "little rock" in Gaelic, is actually
a fortified house, with six-foot-thick walls, built on the remains of a
13th century ruin, and lovingly restored by owner Christopher Murphy.

The castle stands on a seven-acre estate, next to a wildlife sanctuary,
and is available for self-catering rentals, by the week, weekend, or negotiation. There are no family heirlooms here but it is furnished with
colorful tapestries, batik fabrics, sheepskin coverings on wicker chairs and
rockers, electric-candle wall fixtures, and knight-like figures hung above
the huge open fireplace/barbecue. The rental is $500 to $1,000 a week,
depending on the time of year (it can accommodate up to 12 persons
in six bedrooms, with two bathrooms). For further details, contact
Fiona Murphy, 14 E. 17th Street, Apt. 6, New York, N.Y. 10003, tel.
(212) 633–0849; or Christopher Murphy, 85 Rivermead Court, Ranelagh
Gardens, London SW6 3SA, England, tel. (01) 626–0566 or 736–9834.

KILCOLGAN, Co. Galway

Pub/Restaurant

★★★★ MORAN'S OYSTER COTTAGE
The Weir. Tel. (091) 96113. As presidents, prime ministers, and movie
stars can testify, it's worth the drive down a twisting lane, 12 miles
south of Galway to reach this 220-year-old thatched-roof pub. And it's
not just a thirst that draws visitors from all walks of life. Moran's is
known first and foremost for its nautical traditions and excellent seafood—succulent Galway Bay oysters plucked from the waters outside,
fresh salmon, prawns, and crab claws, all accompanied by heaping
platters of Kitty Moran's crusty brown bread, and the drink of your

choice. Amble into one of the cozy snugs, sit by the fireside, or take a place at one of the outdoor tables and watch the sun go down on Galway Bay. It's an experience worth planning your whole day around!

KINVARA, Co. Galway

Entertainment

DUN GUAIRE CASTLE
Ballyvaughan Road (N 67). Tel. (091) 37108 or (061) 61788. Set on the shores of Galway Bay, this restored 15th century fortress is about an hour's drive from the Shannon area, but only a half-hour from Galway. In the summer months, it is a romantic setting for authentic medieval banquets with a literary theme, using the works of Synge, Yeats, and Gogarty, and other Irish writers who knew and loved this area of western Ireland. Available nightly at 6 P.M. and 9 P.M., mid-May through September; the cost is approximately $35 for the complete dinner and show. For full details about other medieval banquets, see also Bunratty and Quin, Co. Clare.

LETTERFRACK, Co. Galway

Hotel

★★★ ROSLEAGUE MANOR
Clifden/Leenane Road (N 59). Tel. (095) 41101. 15 rooms. This is a lovely Georgian residence, situated seven miles north of Clifden and near the entrance to Connemara National Park. Surrounded by lush gardens and well-trimmed lawns, it occupies a sheltered spot with views of Ballinakill Harbor and the Twelve Bens mountains. Owners Paddy and Ann Foyle, a brother/sister team, have decorated the interior of the house with all sorts of antiques, polished heirloom silver, Waterford crystal chandeliers, and paintings of local scenes. The bedrooms have comfortable furnishings, with mostly floral patterns, and many enjoy views of the bay. Guest amenities include a fine restaurant, using produce from the garden, plus fishing privileges, boating, and beach swimming. Open April through October. *Moderate.*

Shopping

CONNEMARA HANDCRAFTS
Clifden/Leenane Road (N 59), Dooneen Haven. Tel. (095) 41058. Just north of Rosleague Manor is this unique craft shop. Situated right on

an inlet of the bay and surrounded by colorful flower gardens, it probably has the loveliest and most photographed location of any shop in Ireland. Best of all, the sublime surroundings are just a preview of the fine wares inside. Colorful Avoca tweeds are featured here, as are all sorts of local Connemara-made marble souvenirs, candles, copperwork, wood-carvings, pottery, and knits. There is also a snack shop on the premises. Open Monday through Saturday year-round, and on Sunday from June through August.

LOUGHREA, Co. Galway

Castle-for-Rent

CLOUGHAN CASTLE
Gort/Loughrea Road (N 66), Kilchreest. Tel. (091) 31457. Dating from the 13th century, this was a Norman outpost occupied by the McHugh-Burke family until it was abandoned toward the end of the 15th century and eventually fell into ruin. It was purchased in 1972 by local residents Michael and Mary Burke, who restored it into a 87-foot tall rectangular tower of granite, like its predecessor.

Sitting on one acre of pastureland, about 20 miles east of Galway, it is surrounded by a walled courtyard, with a small glass-roofed round tower on one side, for use as a sunroom and enclosed barbecue area. At night Cloughan is romantically floodlit, from its base to its battlements. Compared to other castles it is a narrow house, with only one room on each of five landings, all connected by a circular stone staircase. The three bedrooms have four-poster or brass-headboard beds and thatch-top curtained closets; there are also two bathrooms, a modern kitchen, and a sitting room. It is available for weekly rentals, on a self-catering basis, from $400 to $700 per week. For full details, contact Michael Burke, Chanelle, Main Street, Loughrea, Co. Galway. Tel. (091) 41788.

Sports

Horseback Riding

AILLE CROSS EQUITATION CENTRE
Aille Cross, Loughrea. Tel. (091) 41216. Run by personable Willy Leahy (who has appeared often on American television programs), this facility is one of the largest in Ireland, with 50 horses and 20 Connemara ponies. For about $10 an hour, you can arrange to ride through nearby farmlands, woodlands, forest trails, and mountain

lands. Week-long trail rides in the scenic Connemara region are also a specialty of this riding center, as is hunting with the Galway Blazers in the winter months.

OUGHTERARD, Co. Galway

Hotels

★★★★ CONNEMARA GATEWAY
Galway/Clifden Road (N 59). Tel. (091) 82328. 62 rooms and suites. You'll find this contemporary country inn on its own grounds, less than a mile from the village of Oughterard, and just 16 miles from Galway City. It is delightfully positioned near the upper shores of Lough Corrib, across the road from an 18-hole golf course, and on the gateway road to the scenic Connemara region.

Although it is basically a modern two-story property, enthusiastic proprietor Charles Sinnott (who also owns the Connemara Coast Hotel just west of Galway City), has achieved a hearthside ambience. The guest rooms are warmly furnished with local tweed fabrics and hangings, oak dressers and headboards, and scenes of Connemara; suites have sitting rooms with open turf fireplaces. Corridors are bedecked with leafy plants and homey bric-a-brac, and the public rooms are full of copper hangings, farming implements, and fishing memorabilia from the area. Facilities include a heated swimming pool, sun lounge, tennis court, putting green, croquet lawn, a lounge with a village pub atmosphere, and ten acres of gardens and walking trails. The restaurant, which is enhanced by a fine collection of original paintings by landscape artists John MacLeod and Kenneth Webb, features Irish specialty dishes with emphasis on seafood. Open from February through October. *Moderate.*

★★★ SWEENEY'S OUGHTERARD HOUSE
Galway/Clifden Road (N 59). Tel. (091) 82207. 20 rooms. A favorite with fishermen (and women), this ivy-colored 200-year-old early Georgian house has been run by the Sweeney-Higgins family since 1913. Situated across the road from the rushing and babbling waters of the Owenriff River, the inn is surrounded by flowering gardens and ancient trees, on the quiet western end of the village.

Basically two-stories, with modern extensions, the house has some attractive old-world features like multi-paneled bow windows and comfortable deep-cushioned original furnishings. The public rooms are rich with curios and paintings by Irish artists, while guest rooms vary in size and decor, from antique-filled to modern light-wood styles. It's a great spot for fishing, long countryside walks, or catching up on your reading. Amenities include a good dining room with an extensive wine cellar, sunroom, and a lawn tennis court. *Moderate.*

RENVYLE, Co. Galway

Hotel

★★★ RENVYLE HOUSE
Tel. (095) 43434. 40 rooms. Originally the residence of the Blake family, this grand old house on the Atlantic shoreline in the wilds of Connemara was purchased in 1917 by Oliver St. John Gogarty, a leading Irish poet, wit, surgeon, and politician. It has since been handsomely updated and refurbished while still preserving its turn-of-the-century ambience.

Facilities for guests include a 200-acre estate, private lake, horseback stables, par-3 golf course, outdoor heated pool, two all-weather tennis courts, fishing, boating, saunas, and sunbeds. There is also a fine restaurant, lounge bar, and chalet-style conservatory/sunroom. All of this is neatly packaged in a secluded seascape and mountain setting which Gogarty fondly called "the world's end." And that's putting it mildly; it really is off the beaten track, ideal not for a quick overnight, but for a few days' stay. The current owner, Hugh Coyle, is a congenial and clever host who often entertains guests at sing-along sessions around the piano after dinner each evening. Open mid-March through October. *Moderate.*

SPIDDAL, Co. Galway

Restaurant

★★★ BOLUISCE
Coast Road. Tel. (091) 83286. In the heart of a Gaelic-speaking area, this restaurant takes its name from an old phrase meaning "patch of grazing by the water." And, if you're fond of seafood, this is one patch where you'll want to graze. Boluisce is Connemara's original "seafood bar," allowing you to order as little as a cup of soup or as much as a four-course dinner, at any time of day.

Specialties include scallops, prawns, and lobster (it is said that more lobsters pass from pot to plate here than any other eatery in Ireland). Don't miss the house chowder—a meal in itself, brimming with salmon, prawns, monkfish, mussels, and more. Home-baked brown bread, made with wholemeal, bran, and buttermilk, accompanies every meal; it's rich and nut-like, and genial proprietor John Glanville will gladly share the recipe with you.

Located around 12 miles west of Galway City, this restaurant is on the main street of Spiddal, in an upstairs setting, with a cottage-like decor including an old spinning wheel, dark woods, and a copper fireplace. Open for lunch and dinner, daily except January and February, Good Friday, and Christmas. *Inexpensive to moderate.*

Shopping

MAIRTIN STANDUN
Coast Road. Tel. (091) 83102 or 83108. For over 30 years, knitters of traditional bainin sweaters from the nearby Aran Islands and the surrounding Connemara countryside have sent their handiwork to this family-run store for sale. Located in the heart of the Gaeltacht region, this large shop also features other colorful knits, tweeds, sheepskins, linens, glassware, and china. Open March through November.

SPIDDAL CRAFT CENTRE
Coast Road. Tel. (091) 83255. In a setting overlooking Galway Bay, this is a cluster of cottage shops where the craftsmen (and women) ply their trades each day. You can browse around and watch such crafts in-the-making as stone-carved heraldic crests, hand-thrown pottery, hand-woven tapestries, hand-screened printed fabrics, hand-knitted mohair sweaters, hand-built musical instruments, and gold jewelry hand-fashioned with ancient Celtic designs.

BALLINA, Co. Mayo

Hotels

★★★ THE DOWNHILL
Off the Sligo Road (N 59). Tel. (096) 21033. 54 rooms. Incorporating a gracious old manor house with a modern new wing, this busy hotel is situated amid 40 acres of wooded grounds on the banks of the River Moy, at the northern edge of town. The property includes a sport and recreation center with an indoor heated swimming pool, squash courts, sauna, jacuzzi, solarium, gym, hair salon, and game room.

Owned by the Moylett family, it has a good restaurant and a new conservatory-style piano bar called "Frogs," with all sorts of prints, statues, and bric-a-brac reflecting an amphibian motif, as well as lots of leafy plants and a trendy copper dance floor. The guest rooms have little extras like coffee-tea makers and hair dryers. *Expensive.*

★★★ BELLEEK CASTLE
Off Castle Road. Tel. (096) 22061. 16 rooms. This restored 17th century castle sits in its own secluded forest grounds about a mile north of Ballina town, near the banks of the River Moy. The decor is

very authentic with displays of knightly armor, antique coats of arms, huge wrought iron chandeliers, and impressive carved wood furniture and wall paneling. The bedrooms are furnished in the old style, many with four-poster beds. The front rooms are the best. The atmosphere of the medieval-style bar and candlelight restaurant will really take you back to days of old. Sporting activities on the grounds include a par-3 golf course, fishing, and clay pigeon shooting. *Moderate.*

★★★ MT. FALCON CASTLE

Foxford Road (N 57). Tel. (096) 21172. 10 rooms. Built in 1876 by the same man who did much of the exterior work at Ashford Castle in Cong, this multi-gabled structure has been owned and managed as a country house inn by the Aldridge family since 1932. The decor is an eclectic blend of comfortable old furniture with fluffy pillows, carved chests, and gilded mirrors. Mounted elk heads and local memorabilia line the entrance hall. If you are fond of fishing, this is a real find, because a stay here entitles you to salmon and trout fishing on Lough Conn, and preserved salmon fishing on the River Moy; and the management enthusiastically caters to all the needs of fishing folk. The house is set in a wooded park setting, four miles south of Ballina. Besides fishing, outdoor facilities include walking trails and tennis courts; open April to mid-December. *Moderate.*

CONG, Co. Mayo

Hotel

★★★★★ ASHFORD CASTLE

Tel. (092) 46003. 82 rooms. Chosen as the "West of Ireland White House," during President Reagan's 1984 visit, this castle sits on the northern shores of Lough Corrib amid 500 forested and flowering acres. It's in the heart of the scenic territory which provided the setting for the classic film "The Quiet Man," about 30 miles north of Galway City. Dating back to 1228, and once the country home of the Guinness family, it is now currently owned by a group of Americans who have outfitted the bedrooms in deluxe style.

From its turrets and towers to its drawbridge and battlements, Ashford is indeed a fairytale resort, with an interior of baronial furniture, medieval armor, carved oak paneling and stairways, objets d'art, and masterpiece oil paintings. Whether you dine in the lakeside restaurant, sip a cocktail in the vaulted dungeon bar, or stroll in the rose gardens, it won't be long till you feel like a king or queen. Sporting amenities include a nine-hole golf course, tennis, fishing, boating, and extensive hunting grounds. *Very expensive.*

NEWPORT, Co. Mayo

Hotels
★★★★ **NEWPORT HOUSE**
Tel. (098) 41222. 20 rooms. In western County Mayo, on the Clew Bay coast, nothing can quite compare with this ivy-covered Georgian mansion. Located at the edge of town along the Newport River, it was once part of the estate of the O'Donnell family, ancient Irish chieftains. An inn only in recent decades, it has maintained a noble aura by attracting presidents and prime ministers; even the late Princess Grace of Monaco frequently chose Newport House as her palace-away-from-home on her Irish visits. Most of all, it is a favorite with fishermen (and women) who are lured here to enjoy private salmon and seatrout fishing on the Newport River and Lough Beltra.

Recently re-furbished, the house has some splendid examples of ornate plasterwork and high ceilings; a skylit dome also crowns a curved central staircase. The public areas are filled with antique furnishings, oil paintings, and fish trophy cases. Guest rooms are spread among the main house and two smaller courtyard buildings. A member of the Relais and Chateaux group, the hotel maintains a highly ranked restaurant, not surprisingly distinguished for its fish dishes, including salmon which is smoked on the premises. If you catch a salmon, the chef will cook it for your dinner or smoke it for you to take home. Open from mid-March through September. *Expensive.*

WESTPORT, Co. Mayo

Hotel

★★ **RYANS** (Best in Town)
Louisburg Road. Tel. (098) 25811. 56 rooms. Nestled in a quiet woodland setting, this two-storey motor inn is Westport's best accommodations choice. It is conveniently situated mid-way between the historic downtown district and the quay area which overlooks Clew Bay. The public rooms are bright, woody, and airy, with contemporary furnishings and an informal ski-lodge type of layout. The bedrooms are well-maintained and offer standard comforts. Facilities include a full-service restaurant, spacious lounge with evening entertainment, tennis court, and ample parking. *Inexpensive to moderate.*

Pub/Restaurant

★★ **THE ASGARD TAVERN** (For Location)
The Quay. Tel. (098) 25319. Among the various pubs and eateries in a strip overlooking Clew Bay, this is one of the best. The ground-floor level houses a lively nautical-style pub where you'll find a folk/ballad sing-along taking place most nights. Upstairs there is an award-winning 50-seat dining room which features a straight-forward menu of steaks and local seafoods. The restaurant is open for dinner only, Tuesday through Sunday. *Moderate.*

Sports

Golf

WESTPORT GOLF CLUB
Carrowholly. Tel. (098) 25522. Just two miles from the center of Westport, this 18-hole championship course is set on the shores of Clew Bay, winding its way around the precipitous slopes of Croagh Patrick Mountain. It is one of the west of Ireland's most challenging and scenic courses. Visitors are welcome any day; just phone club manager Pat Murphy to make arrangements. Greens fees are $12, golf clubs can be rented for about $4 a round, and caddie carts for less than $1.

Directory

Westport Tourist Office, The Mall. Tel. (098) 25711. This is the only tourist office in Co. Mayo that is open all year round.

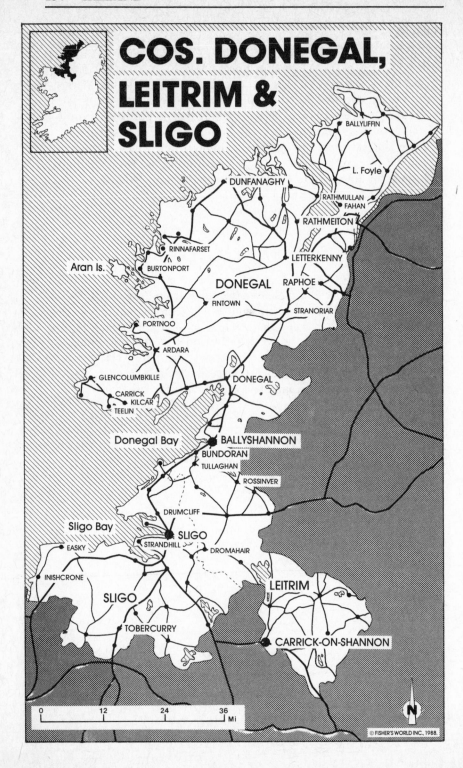

COS. DONEGAL, LEITRIM & SLIGO

BALLYLIFFIN

L. Foyle

DUNFANAGHY

RATHMULLAN
FAHAN

RATHMEITON

RINNAFARSET

LETTERKENNY

Aran Is.

BURTONPORT

DONEGAL

RAPHOE

FINTOWN

STRANORIAR

PORTNOO

ARDARA

GLENCOLUMBKILLE

DONEGAL

CARRICK
KILCAR
TEELIN

Donegal Bay

BALLYSHANNON

BUNDORAN

TULLAGHAN

ROSSINVER

DRUMCLIFF

Sligo Bay

SLIGO

EASKY

STRANDHILL

DROMAHAIR

INISHCRONE

LEITRIM

SLIGO

TOBERCURRY

CARRICK-ON-SHANNON

| 0 | 12 | 24 | 36 |
| | | | Mi |

© FISHER'S WORLD INC., 1988.

N

The Northwest

COUNTIES SLIGO, LEITRIM, AND DONEGAL

If you are traveling from Shannon or Dublin, it takes a day's driving to reach Ireland's northwest corner. Irish roads being what they are, you just can't zip up to Sligo, Leitrim, or Donegal, see the sights, and return southward a day or two later; in fact, you'll need almost a week to do justice to this off-the-beaten-track part of Ireland.

But, if you are planning on staying two or three weeks in the country, or if you've already seen the south, west, and east on previous trips, then you owe it to yourself to travel the extra few miles to this special corner of the Emerald Isle. In many ways, the northwest offers the best of Ireland in miniature—panoramas of seacoast and mountain scenery, sylvan lakes and rivers, hillsides full of grazing sheep, sheltered parklands, ancient forts, historic landmarks, clusters of craft centers, walkable cities, and picturesque villages.

COUNTY SLIGO

From ancient times, the northwest's gateway has always been Sligo town (pronounced "Sly-gó"), situated in the more narrow upper half of County Sligo. Not only is it the largest town in this part of Ireland (population: 18,000), but it is also the junction for major roads leading to this area—the N 4 from Dublin and the east, the N 17 from Galway and the south, and the N 16 from Northern Ireland.

Sligo town is situated in an idyllic location, in a valley between two mountains, Benbulben on the north and Knocknarea on the south, and at the mouth of the River Garavogue, with Sligo Bay and the Atlantic on its western shores, and Lough Gill to the east. The name Sligo is derived from the Irish or Gaelic word meaning "the shelly river." It is no wonder that the poet William Butler Yeats, who spent much of his time here, called Sligo "The Land of Heart's Desire." He also took inspiration from many places in the area and wrote glowingly of them (i.e., The Lake Isle of Innisfree, Dooney Rock, Lissadell, and Benbulben). This is why the Sligo region is usually referred to as "Yeats' Country."

★ The best place to start a tour of Yeats' Country is in the heart of Sligo town. Although it goes back at least to Viking times, not much remains from the early days except for the ruins of Sligo Abbey on Abbey Street. Founded as a Dominican house in 1252 by Maurice Fitzgerald, the Earl of Kildare, it was accidentally destroyed by fire in 1414 and rebuilt two years later. It flourished in medieval times and was the burial place of the kings and princes of Sligo. After many raids and sackings, the abbey was eventually closed in 1641. Much restoration work has taken place in recent years, however, and the cloisters are considered to be outstanding examples of stone carving; the 15th-century altar is one of the few medieval altars still intact in Ireland.

★★ The other notable building in town is the Sligo County Museum on Stephen Street, located in the Manse of the old Congregational Church, built about 1850. If you want to trace Yeats' footsteps, this is undoubtedly the best place to start. Here you will find a room completely devoted to items relating to William Butler Yeats, including first editions of his complete works, poems on broadsheets, letters, and his Nobel Prize (1923) for literature. There is also an art gallery containing a permanent collection of modern Irish art including oils, water colors, and drawings by the poet's brother, Jack B. Yeats.

★★★ The other highlights of "Yeats' Country" are in the surrounding countryside. Drive a couple of miles south of town and follow the signs for "Lough Gill." Within two miles, you'll be on the lower edge of the shoreline which encircles the beautiful lake that figured so prominently in Yeats' writings. Just five miles long and about a mile wide, Lough Gill easily rivals Killarney for its tree-shaded setting. Among the attractions are Dooney Rock, with its own nature trail and lakeside walk (the inspiration for the poem "Fiddler of Dooney"), and the isle of Innisfree.

The storied Lake Isle of Innisfree is only one of 22 islands in Lough Gill. You can drive the whole lakeside circuit in one sweep (in less than an hour), or you can stop at the east end and visit Dromahair. This delightful village on the River Bonet is technically part of County Leitrim, but close enough to Sligo to be discussed in this section. Dromahair is also the home of one of the area's best country inns,

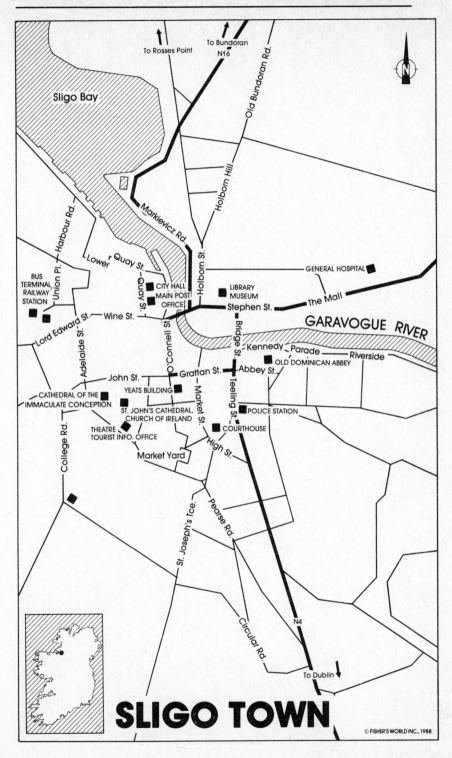

SLIGO TOWN

© FISHER'S WORLD INC., 1988

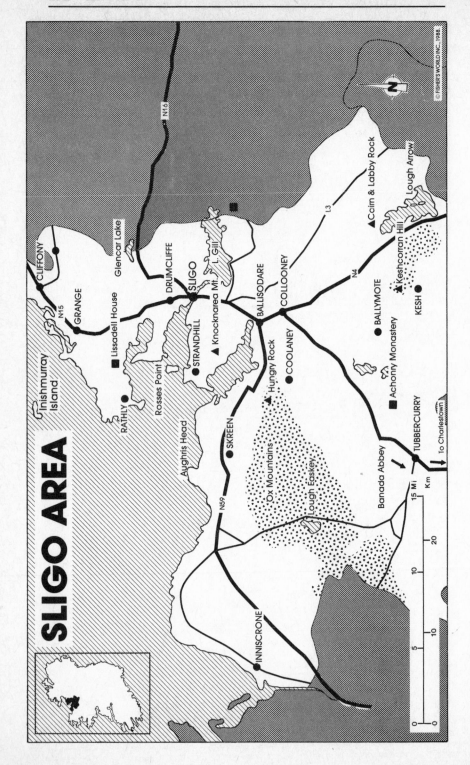

SLIGO AREA

Drumlease Glebe House, and an atmospheric pub, the Stanford Inn
(See "Inside Information").

The road along Lough Gill's upper shore brings you back to the
northern end of Sligo town. If you turn right and continue in a
northerly direction on the main road (N 15), you can tour three more
Yeatsian sights.

First is the profile of graceful and green Benbulben (1,730 feet), part
of the Dartry Mountains, rising to the right. Five miles away, at
Drumcliffe, is the churchyard where William Butler Yeats chose to be ★★
buried. It's well sign-posted, so you will easily find the poet's grave, its
simple headstone bearing the dramatic epitaph he composed: "Cast a
cold eye on life, on death; Horseman, pass by." This Church of Ireland
cemetery also contains the remains of an early Christian monastery
founded by St. Columba in 745 A.D.

From Drumcliffe, it is less than five miles to Lissadell, another
favorite Yeats' haunt. Here you can visit Lissadell House, the home of ★★★
the Gore-Booth family and one of Ireland's stately homes open to the
public. A large Neo-Classical building on the shores of Sligo Bay, it
was erected in 1830-35 and is full of memorabilia from the last 150
years. Lissadell's greatest claims to fame, however, are two of its one-
time inhabitants, the poetess Eva Gore-Booth and her more famous
sister, Constance, who became the Countess Markievicz (by her marriage to a Polish count). One of the first truly liberated women,
Constance took part in the 1916 Irish Revolution and later became the
first woman to be elected to the British House of Commons. Both
women were immortalized in the writings of their good friend, William
Butler Yeats.

There are three other "must see" places in the Sligo area, perhaps
not immortalized by Yeats but no doubt also favorites of his. The first
is the mountain which rims the southwest edge of Sligo town, Knockarea (1,078 feet). On the summit is a gigantic cairn or grave site,
known as "Miscaun Meadhbh" (Maeve's Mound). It has traditionally
been considered the resting place of Queen Maeve, who reigned in the
first century of the Christian era. Six-hundred and thirty feet around
the base, 80 feet high, and 100 feet in diameter, this rocky structure
can be seen for miles around.

At the foot of Knockarea is Strandhill, five miles from Sligo town.
A delightful resort area stretching out into Sligo Bay, it offers a sand-
duned beach and a patch of land nearby called "Coney Island" which
is usually credited with lending its name to the New York beach
amusement area.

Across the bay, about four miles north of Sligo town, is another
beach resort known as Rosses Point. Some of the best places to stay or
eat in the Sligo area are in or near Rosses Point, which also has an
outstanding golf course (see "Inside Information").

COUNTY LEITRIM

Although classified as part of the northwest, County Leitrim has more characteristics in common with the lakeland counties than with its neighbors, Sligo and Donegal. Dominated by inland lakes, Leitrim extends for over 50 miles from the County Longford border to Donegal Bay. Unlike the other lakeland counties, however, it cannot be considered land-locked because it has a coastline, though minuscule by Irish standards (a two-and-a-half-mile stretch at Tullaghan, wedged in between Sligo and Donegal).

Shaped somewhat like two equal diamonds, this county is divided into two parts almost wholly separated from one another by an expansion of the River Shannon, Lough Allen, a body of water that is seven miles long and three miles wide. North of the lake is mountainous, while the southern portion is an area of little hills interspersed with many lakes. All of this makes for extremely good fishing, especially for trout and for pike, perch, and bream. With few exceptions, the fishing is free or easily arranged through your hotel for a nominal fee.

The town of Carrick-on-Shannon, situated on one of the great ancient crossing places of the River Shannon, is particularly well known as a center for boating as well. There is a vast marina in the middle of the town and many local companies rent cabin cruisers by the week. (The Irish Tourist Board can supply you with a full list and details in advance of your visit.)

★★ Like County Sligo, Leitrim's major sightseeing attraction is associated with William Butler Yeats. The poet's work, "The Stolen Child," speaks wonderously of Glencar Lake. Situated almost at the Sligo/Leitrim border (on N 16), Glencar stretches eastward for two miles along a verdant valley. It is highlighted by two waterfalls, one of which rushes downward for 50 feet.

COUNTY DONEGAL

Like so many parts of Ireland, County Donegal (pronounced "Donnygawl") can trace its roots back thousands of years. The Vikings were among the first foreign visitors to discover the joys of Donegal, establishing a fort here. The native Irish soon described the fort as "Dun na nGall," meaning "The Fort of the Foreigner" and that's how the name "Donegal" is said to have originated.

As Ireland's northernmost county and a part of the province of Ulster, Donegal is sometimes thought to be part of Northern Ireland, although it is, of course, one of the 26 counties of the Irish Republic. Because Donegal is so close to Northern Ireland, it is a favorite vacation destination for people from the other side of the border, so you will often hear a variety of accents (or brogues). Vacationing in Donegal will also give you an opportunity to cross over the border to pay a visit to the Belleek China factory and other attractions.

To reach County Donegal, just stay on the N 15 up the Atlantic coast, and, about 22 miles north of Sligo, you'll come to Bundoran, the southern tip of the county and a major beach resort. A favorite with Irish and Northern Irish visitors, Bundoran takes on an almost carnival-like atmosphere in the middle of summer. In addition to its busy beaches and amusement arcades, there is an 18-hole golf course on the north side of the town, overlooking Donegal Bay.

Continue up the coast and you'll pass Ballyshannon, one of the oldest inhabited towns in Ireland and the headquarters of the Donegal Irish Parian China works, a craft center well worth a stop for a craft tour or shopping spree (see "Inside Information").

At this point you may wish to leave the main road and head for the coastal resort of Rossnowlagh, on one of the loveliest stretches of beach in all of Ireland. This is also the home of Donegal's best hotel, the Sand House, where you may wish to base yourself for a few days while you tour the rest of the county (see "Inside Information").

From Rossnowlagh, it is less than ten miles to Donegal town. Situated on the estuary of the River Eske on Donegal Bay, this is a very walkable little metropolis (population: 2,000) and a pivotal gateway to the remainder of the county. Laid out around a central mall or market area called "The Diamond," Donegal town is the home of Magee tweeds and several other local craft centers (see "Inside Information" for full descriptions).

The Diamond is dominated by a 25-foot-high obelisk erected as a memorial to the four Irish clerics from the local abbey who wrote "The Annals of the Four Masters" in the early 17th century. At the time, it was the first recorded history of Gaelic Ireland. The remains of their friary, built in 1474 on the banks of the River Eske south of town, are still visible.

Also on a religious note, about five miles east of Donegal is Lough Derg, a lake with many islands where St. Patrick is said to have spent forty days and nights fasting in a cavern. Each summer, from June 1 to August 15, thousands of Irish people take turns coming to Lough Derg to do penance for three days at a time. It is considered one of the most rigorous pilgrimages in all of Christendom.

Before you leave Donegal town, take a look at the ruins of Donegal ★ Castle, completed about 1471, and once the chief stronghold for the O'Donnells, a powerful Donegal clan.

From Donegal, follow N 56 for a very scenic, but slow, drive along the southern coast of the county. You'll encounter narrow roads, sheer cliffs, craggy rocks, boglands, and panoramic mountain and sea views.

You'll also see the thatched roof cottages that are distinctively typical of this area—with rounded roofs, because the thatch is tied down by a network of ropes (sugans) and fastened to pins beneath the eaves to protect it from the prevailing winds off the sea. It's only thirty miles out to Glencolumbkille, but allow at least a couple of hours, especially if you want to stop in the craft centers along the way at Bruckless and Kilcar (see "Inside Information") or at the busy fishing port of Killybegs. Note: Just before you come to Killybegs, you'll actually leave the N 56 road which swings inland and northward; you'll continue on the coastal road westward.

Glencolumbkille is an Atlantic outpost dating back 5,000 years. It is said that St. Columba established a monastery here in the 6th century and gave his name to the glen forevermore. ("Glencolumbkille" literally means "The Glen of Columba's church"). You'll be hard pressed to see a more beautiful landscape anywhere and you certainly can't beat the peace and quiet. This is one spot where the sheep far outnumber the people!

★★★ And if that's not enough, then you may enjoy a visit to the Glencolumbkille Folk Village. Built in the format of a tiny village or "Clachan," this mini-theme park of Donegal thatched cottages is designed to reflect life in this part of the world over the years. Each house is an exact replica of a dwelling used by the local people in each of three consecutive centuries and is equipped with the furniture, artifacts, and utensils of its particular period.

Founded in 1967, the Folk Village was the brainchild of the local priest, Rev. James McDyer, who sought to create a "living history" attraction in the area and thus provide jobs and turn back the tide of emigration. It was entirely built and assembled by the people of Glencolumbkille, who maintain it now. The complex includes a craft shop, tea room, cultural center, old school, bakery, herb garden, and a nature walk.

★★ To continue touring from Glencolumbkille, follow the signs for Ardara over a mountainous inland road. Soon you will come to Glengesh Pass, a scenic but narrow roadway which rises to a height of 900 feet before plunging into the valley below. At Ardara, you may wish to visit one of the many tweed-weaving centers.

Working your way up the rest of the Donegal coast can take four hours or four days, depending on your time schedule and interests. The deeper you get into this countryside, however, the more you'll be immersing yourself in a section known as "the Gaeltacht" or Irish-speaking area. This really presents no problems, except that most of the road signs are only in Irish. If you keep to the route of the main (N 56) road, you should have no difficulties, but if you follow little roads off to the seashore or down country paths, you may have a problem figuring out where you are going (unless you can read Irish). In many cases, the Irish word for a place bears no resemblance to the English equivalent (i.e., "An Clochan Liath" in Irish = "Dungloe" in English); our advice is to buy a map which has placenames in both languages or stick to the main road.

Some of the highlights on this route include an area known as "The Rosses," extending from Gweebarra Bridge as far north as Crolly. This ★★ stretch presents a wealth of rock-strewn land with frequent mountains, rivers, lakes, and beaches. Here you can visit Burtonport (otherwise known as "Ailt an Chorrain"), one of the premier fishing ports of Ireland; it is said that more salmon and lobster are landed here than at any other port in Ireland or Britain.

North of the Rosses is an area known as the Bloody Foreland, between Derrybeg and Gortahork, a stretch of land which derives its name from the fact that the rock takes on a warm, ruddy color when lit by the setting sun. The sunsets should not be missed!

By now you'll be approaching the top rim of Donegal, which is dominated by a series of small peninsulas jutting out into the sea. Chief among these scenic areas are Horn Head and Ards; the latter ★★ contains a forest park with a wide diversity of terrain including woodlands, a salt marsh, sand dunes, seashore, freshwater lakes, and fenland.

The next spit of land to the east is Rosguil, which is home to the famed Rosapenna Golf Club. The ten-mile route around this peninsula is known as the Atlantic Drive and leads to yet another peninsula, the Fanad, with a 45-mile circuit between Mulroy Bay and Lough Swilly. The resort of Rathmullan, with its fine country inn and restaurant, makes a good overnight stop here (see "Inside Information"). If you have driven all of these peninsulas, you'll need a rest!

Whether you spend the night in Rathmullan, Donegal town, or another nearby village, you'll need a new day to take on the largest, most northerly, and the best of Donegal's peninsulas—the Inishowen. ★★★ Bounded by Lough Swilly on the left and Lough Foyle on the right, Inishowen (or "Inis Eoghain" meaning "the island of Owen") is a triangular peninsula stretching from Bridgend to Ireland's most northerly point, Malin Head.

Thanks to a new sign-posting system launched in 1985, this is among the best marked roads in Ireland, with all directionals clearly printed in English and Irish as well as in miles and kilometers. Among the many features of this 100-mile route are a string of beach resorts like Ballyliffin, Buncrana, and Fahan; the Gap of Mamore, a pass which rises to 800 feet and then slowly descends to sea level; Slieve Snacht, a 2,019-foot mountain; and Grianan of Aileach, one of Ireland's best examples of a ring fort, built originally as a temple to the sun around 1700 B.C. From the middle of the 5th century to the early 12th, it was the royal residence of the O'Neills, the kings of this area.

★★★ One of the newest attractions of the Inishowen circuit (opened in 1986) is Fort Dunree, a military/naval museum incorporating a Napoleonic Martello tower at the site of World War I defenses on Lough Swilly. It has a wide range of exhibitions, an audio-visual center, and a cafeteria housed in a restored forge (you can lunch in a former horse stall). Even if you have no interest in military history, it's worth a trip for the view. Dunree has one of the best vantage points in Donegal, or in all of Ireland, for picture taking or for just enjoying unencumbered seascapes and broad mountain vistas.

After you have toured the Inishowen, perhaps stayed a few days in this area, now head back in a southerly direction. Drive through Letterkenny, the largest town in the county (population: 5,000), situated on a hillside overlooking the River Swilly. Then proceed inland to ★★★ Kilmacrenan and follow the signs to Glenveagh National Park, Donegal's foremost attraction (about fourteen miles northwest of Letterkenny).

Designed as the home of Lord Leitrim in the 1870's, this 24,000-acre fairytale setting includes extensive woodlands, alpine gardens, a sylvan lake, baronial castle, and herds of rare red deer. The estate was purchased in 1937 by Henry McIlhenny, a distinguished Philadelphia art historian (of the Tabasco Sauce family), who restored the castle and planted the gardens with exotic species of flowers and shrubs. He subsequently gave Glenveagh to the Irish government, and it was opened as a park in 1986. Guided tours are given regularly of the house, and you are also free to roam the gardens on your own. The complex includes a visitor center with an audio-visual show and displays, plus a very good all-day restaurant, a self-guided nature trail, and nature walks. In addition, the parklands encompass the peak of the highest mountain in Donegal, Mt. Errigal.

Four miles southeast of Glenveagh, at Church Hill on the shores of Lough Gartan, you can view a first rate 20th-century art collection, a rather surprising attraction in this remote part of Donegal. It's called ★★★ the Glebe Gallery, and was formerly owned by Derek Hill, a leading English artist who presented both his gallery and his Regency-style house to the Irish government in 1981. The collection includes works by Hill plus Annigoni, Bratby, Landseer, Picasso, and Sutherland.

Heading back toward south Donegal, link up with N 56, the main road and drive to the junction of the twin towns, Ballybofey and Stranorlar, changing here to N 15. This will take you to yet another ★★ scenic Donegal drive, the Barnesmore Gap, a vast open stretch through the Blue Stack Mountains, which in turn will lead you into Donegal town and points south.

SLIGO, Co. Sligo

Hotels

★★★ BALLINCAR HOUSE

Rosses Point Road. Tel. (071) 5361. 20 rooms. Built originally as a
private residence in 1848, this country inn was extended and opened as
a hotel in 1969. It is located two miles northwest of the town center,
on six pastoral and tree-shaded acres overlooking Sligo Bay. The
public rooms preserve the house's old world charm, with period
furnishings and original oil paintings of the area. The guest rooms are
decorated in a contemporary-country style, with modern tiled bathrooms; most rooms look out onto the gardens or vistas of Sligo Bay.
Amenities include a full-service restaurant, two squash courts, a hard
tennis court, sauna, and sunbed; and the widely acclaimed County
Sligo Golf Club at Rosses Point is two miles away (See "Sports"
below). Open mid-January through mid-December. *Inexpensive to
moderate.*

★★★ YEATS COUNTRY RYAN

Rosses Point Road, Rosses Point. Tel. (071) 77211. 79 rooms. Of all
the modern glass-and-concrete motor inns in the Sligo area, this one
has the most to offer. It is not located in the busy downtown district,
but in a nearby coastal suburb, four miles away. With an 18-hole golf
course next door, this hilltop property overlooks several miles of
sandy beach and the waters of Sligo Bay. The interior is decorated in a
bright contemporary style, with lots of wide windows looking out onto
the neighboring attractions. The hotel's own amenities include a full-
service restaurant, lounge bar, two tennis courts, and a pitch-and-putt
area. *Moderate.*

For additional accommodations in the Sligo area, see also the
Knockmuldowney listing under "Restaurants" below, and Dromahair,
Co. Leitrim.

Restaurants

★★★★★ REVERIES

Rosses Point Road, Rosses Point. Tel. (071) 77371. If your timing is
right (and the weather is in your favor), a dinner at Reveries will be
accompanied by one of the most magnificent sunsets you'll ever see.
The proprietors, Damien Brennan and his wife Dr. Paula Gilvarry,
have done their best to provide the perfect setting—their intimate 32-
seat restaurant has been purpose-built, with a two-story window-wall
looking out onto Sligo Bay, Oyster Island, and Knockarea Mountain.

The dining tables are positioned on three tiers, so that no matter where you sit, the view is panoramic.

But gazing upon Sligo's vistas is only part of the allure at this award-winning dining spot. The food and enthusiastic service are primary. The creative menu includes such dishes as lasagne of seafoods, monkfish in red pepper sauce, filet of beef with shallots, brace of quail, or gourmet chicken fricassee with saffron rice. Only the freshest and most healthful ingredients are used, but what else could you expect with a doctor in the kitchen (chef Paula, a qualified physician, maintains a part-time medical practice). The ever-tempting dessert cart is surpassed only by the all-Irish cheeseboard, displaying more than thirty local creations. To top it off, the wine list offers vitanges of from more than a dozen countries. Reveries is a restaurant well named! Open for dinner only. *Moderate to expensive.*

★★★★ KNOCKMULDOWNEY

Coast Road, Culleenamore, near Strandhill. Tel. (071) 68122. Although Knockmuldowney's proprietors, Charles and Mary Cooper, have recently restored and updated six small rooms with bath upstairs for guest accommodations, this highly praised inn is primarily known as a restaurant.

To start with, the setting is lovely—a Georgian country house nestled amid four acres of trees, shrubs and lawns, just five miles west of Sligo, at the base of Knocknarea Mountain and on the shores of Ballisodare Bay. You'll sit in the drawing room, sipping an appertif as you place your order and then be escorted into one of two dining rooms, both overlooking the gardens and decorated in a country cupboard motif.

The eclectic menu features such specialties as muligatawney soup, cheese souffle, mushroom pate, veal in sour cream, chicken with sharp tomato sauce, and beef bourguignon. Salmon and seatrout, fresh from the local fishery, are also smoked on the premises. Desserts range from gooseberry flan to banana rum mousse and praline ice cream. A complimentary little after-dinner treat, like buttery homemade fudge, also comes with coffee. Open for dinner only, daily from March through October. *Moderate.*

Pubs

★★★★ HARGADON'S

4/5 O'Connell Street. More than a century old, this is the most atmospheric bar in the center of the downtown area. Although it is strictly a pub now, it also used to be a grocery shop, as you'll see if you glance at the shelves on the right. The decor is a melange of dark wood walls, mahogany counters, stone floors, colored glass, old barrels and bottles, genuine snugs, and alcoves lined with early prints of Sligo.

★ ★ ★ ★ THE THATCH

Dublin/Sligo Road (N 4), Ballisodare. Tel. (071) 67288. Established in 1638 and originally a coaching inn, this pub is about five miles south of Sligo on the main road. As its name suggests, it has a fully thatched roof and a white-washed exterior, with a country cottage motif inside. It's a good spot for picture-taking, as well as refreshments like soup and sandwiches. Irish traditional music is usually on tap Tuesday through Friday nights.

★ ★ ★ AUSTIE'S/THE ELSINORE

Rosses Point Road, Rosses Point. Tel. (071) 77111. Set on a hill within yards of the beach four miles northwest of Sligo, this pub has a suitably sea-faring decor, from nautical nick-nacks and fish nets, to periscopes, corks, and paintings of sailing ships. Substantial pub grub is also available here, ranging from open-face "sandbank" sandwiches of crab, salmon, or smoked mackerel, to crab claw and prawn salads.

★ ★ ★ YEATS' TAVERN

Ballyshannon Road (N 15), Drumcliffe. Tel. (071) 73117. Located four miles north of Sligo across the road from the famous churchyard where William Butler Yeats is buried, this pub honors the poet's memory with quotations from his works, as well as photos, prints, and murals. Basically a modern tavern, with a copper and wood decor, it is a good place to stop for a snack or refreshment when touring "Yeats' Country."

★ ★ ★ LAURA'S

Off the Ballyshannon Road (N 15), Carney. Tel. (071) 63056. Named for the present owner's octogenarian aunt, this century-year-old family pub is now in the hands of the third generation, personable Jill Barber. The building is full of local memorabilia, dating back to pre-pub days when it was a general store. Located in a small village off the main road, about five miles north of Sligo, Laura's is a good choice for interesting pub grub (ranging from seafood chowder and garlic bread to spare ribs or a platter or Lissadell mussels). There's music on Friday and Saturday nights.

Entertainment

HAWK'S WELL THEATRE

Temple Street. Tel. (071) 61526. The premier stage of Ireland's northwest region, this modern theatre presents a varied program of drama, concerts, modern and traditional music. A resident professional group performs throughout the year, augmented by visiting troupes and individual artists. In the summer, the schedule includes both lunchtime and evening events. Tickets range from $5 to $10. (The theatre is housed in the same complex as the tourist office.)

Shopping

SLIGO CRYSTAL GLASS

Ballyshannon Road (N 15), Grange. Tel. (071) 63251. Located six miles north of Sligo, this workshop is noted for its personalized engraving of such items as family crests on mirrors or glassware. Owner Michael Power and his staff also produce handcut crystal candlesticks, glasses, and curio items like crystal bells and scent bottles. If you visit on a weekday, you'll see the craftsmen at work, year-round, from 9 A.M. to 5 P.M.; during June through August, the shop and showrooms are also open on weekends.

INNISFREE CRYSTAL

The Bridge, Dublin Road (N 4), Collooney. Tel. (071) 67340. Taking its name from the Lough Gill island immortalized in William Butler Yeats' famous poem, "The Lake Isle of Innisfree," this crystal factory produces individually handcut glassware items such as punch bowls, decanters, vases, and bowls. Each piece is hand-signed by proprietor Jim Hughes or one of his craftsmen. You can watch them work or browse in the showroom, Monday through Friday, from 9 A.M. to 5:30 P.M., and on Saturdays (summer only) from 10 A.M. to 1 P.M.

Sports

Golf

COUNTY SLIGO GOLF CLUB

Rosses Point Road, Rosses Point. Tel. (071) 77186. Overlooking Sligo Bay and under the shadow of Ben Bulben mountain, the County Sligo Golf Club is more popularly known simply as "Rosses Point." Located five miles northwest of Sligo town, it is an 18-hole championship seaside links famed for its wild, natural terrain and constant winds. Visitors are always welcome; greens fees range from $12 on weekdays to $15 on weekends, golf clubs can be hired for $7.50 per round, and caddie pull-carts are available for $1.50. To arrange a game, contact the club manager, John McGonigle.

Horseback Riding

MONEYGOLD RIDING CENTRE
Off the Ballyshannon Road (N 15), Grange. Tel. (071) 63337. This equestrian center, located about seven miles north of Sligo, will arrange beach and mountain trail rides in the Sligo countryside. An hour's riding averages $10.

Sightseeing Tours

SLIGO WALKING TOURS
Guided walks around Sligo's historic district are available during July and August, departing on a regular basis from the Tourist Office, Temple Street. Tel. (071) 61201. The schedule depends on demand, so inquire in advance; the fee is approximately $1.50.

Festival

August 13-27: Yeats International Summer School. Now in its 29th year, this scholarly gathering focuses on the works of William Butler Yeats. Plays, recitals, poetry readings, and scenic tours to Yeatsian sites are all part of the agenda.

Directory

Sligo Tourist Office, Temple Street. Tel. (071) 61201.
CIE, Lord Edward Street. Tel. (071) 62051. From this depot, you can arrange rail or bus transport from Sligo, as well as bus sightseeing tours of the Yeats Country attractions, Donegal, and Northern Ireland.

DROMAHAIR, Co. Leitrim

Guesthouse

★★★★ DRUMLEASE GLEBE HOUSE
Tel. (071) 64141. 8 rooms. Andrew Greenstein, a lawyer from Rochester, and his wife Barbara, an actress/singer/harpist whose maiden name was Flanagan, are two Americans who are best described as "more Irish than the Irish." They have taken to the Emerald Isle in a big way, and, to prove it, they have lovingly turned Drumlease Glebe House into one of the country's finest inns.

Nestled beside the meandering River Bonet amid ten acres of gardens and woodlands, this beautifully restored Georgian residence is filled with exquisite antiques, one-of-a-kind curios, colorful quilts, and handmade wall hangings, with character dolls and little stuffed lambs and sheep adding a country charm in nooks and crannies. Best of all, the Greensteins extend the warmest of welcomes and personal attention, creating an on-going "house party" atmosphere. Each evening guests can enjoy superb candlelight dinners, enhanced by Waterford Crystal glassware, Irish silver, and Belleek china.

Amenities include a library stocked with books of Irish interest and music tapes; a tiled outdoor sundeck and swimming pool, plus private salmon fishing, picnic tables by the river, and three friendly Irish donkeys on the grounds. Although its address is Co. Leitrim, Drum-lease is actually an ideal place to stay when you are touring Yeats Country, as it is situated 12 miles east of Sligo town near the eastern shores of Lough Gill. Open from mid-April through October; no children under age 15. *Moderate.*

Pub

★★★ STANFORD VILLAGE INN
Main Street. Tel. (071) 64140. If you are driving around Lough Gill from Sligo, this 150-year-old pub is a great mid-way stop for a drink or a snack (sandwiches and salads). The decor is a delightful blend of old stone walls, vintage pictures and posters, oil lamps, and tweed-covered furnishings.

ARDARA, Co. Donegal

Shopping

JOHN MOLLOY
Killybegs/Glenties Road (N 56). Tel. (075) 41133. In the heart of wool and weaving country, this factory shop is well-stocked with handknits, homespun fashions, sports jackets, tweed scarves and rugs, and all types of caps, from kingfisher to ghillie styles.

BALLYLIFFIN, Co. Donegal

★★ THE STRAND (Best in Town)
Tel. (077) 76107. 12 rooms. If you plan to tour Donegal's beautiful Inishowen Peninsula on the northern tip of the Irish Republic, this hotel is an ideal base. It's located in the middle of town, yet set apart amidst its own palm tree-lined rose gardens, on a hillside overlooking Pollan Strand and with views of nearby Malin Head. The decor is modern Irish, with wide windows, and traditional touches; the guest rooms offer little extras like coffee-tea makers and hair dryers. Amenities include a good restaurant and a lounge bar which is known for its local entertainment, as well as golfing privileges at the 18-hole Ballyliffin course. *Inexpensive.*

BALLYSHANNON, Co. Donegal

Shopping

DONEGAL IRISH PARIAN CHINA
Bundoran Road (N 15). Tel. (072) 51826. If you are traveling between
Sligo and Donegal, don't miss a chance to visit this relatively new
(established in 1985) Irish industry. Delicate wafer-thin china gift items
and tableware are produced here in patterns of the shamrock, rose,
hawthorn, and Irish flora. Regular pottery tours, every half hour,
enable visitors to watch as vases, bells, spoons, thimbles, jugs, wall
plaques, lamps, and egg shell coffee and tea sets are shaped, decorated,
fired, and polished. This facility also includes a showroom and shop,
for on-the-spot purchases.

BARNESMORE GAP, Co. Donegal

Pub

★★★ BIDDY O'BARNES
Donegal/Lifford Road (N 15). Tel. (073) 21402. At the southern
gateway to the scenic Barnesmore Gap, this pub has been in the same
family for four generations. Step inside and it's just like entering a
country cottage, with blazing turf fires, stone floors, wooden stools
and benches, and old hutches full of plates and bric-a-brac. A picture
of "Biddy," who once owned this house, hangs over the main fireplace.
This is a great place to stop for a soup-and-sandwich lunch when
heading for the Glenveagh National Park or other points in northern
Donegal. If you are passing by in the evening, you'll usually find a
session of spontaneous music in progress.

BRUCKLESS, Co. Donegal

Shopping

TERESA'S COTTAGE
Donegal/Killybegs Road (N 56). Tel. (073) 37080. For more than a
dozen years, Teresa Gillespie and her team of local folk have been
producing delicately embroidered linens and lace, crochet-work, and
knitwear. If you stop into this busy shop, you can not only buy at the
source, but you can also see the craftspeople at work.

BUNDORAN, Co. Donegal

Hotel

★★★ GREAT NORTHERN

Sligo/Donegal Road (N 15). Tel. (072) 41204. 96 rooms. Originally part of the Great Southern chain, this hotel is situated right on Donegal Bay, looking out onto the rolling waters of the Atlantic. And, if that weren't enough, it is surrounded by 130 acres of sand dunes and a challenging 18-hole golf links.

The interior of the hotel has been recently refurbished with a bright modern Irish motif, and the guest rooms have also been stylishly redecorated; most rooms have views of the sea or the golf course. Facilities include a full-service restaurant, a grill room, nightly entertainment in the summer season, a heated outdoor swimming pool, and lawn tennis court, plus free golf to overnight guests. It is on the northern edge of Bundoran, a favorite beach resort of the Irish, with lots of busy pubs, amusement areas, and a carnival-like atmosphere in the summer months. Open March through December. *Moderate.*

Sports

Golf

BUNDORAN GOLF CLUB

Off the Sligo/Ballyshannon Road (N 15). Tel. (072) 41302. Designed by the great Harry Vardon, this popular 18-hole seaside links overlooks Donegal Bay and the Atlantic. Visitors are welcome any day; just contact club manager Joseph Roarty in advance (direct line: 41360). Greens fees are approximately $12 (and free to those registered at the Great Northern Hotel); golf clubs can be rented for $6, and caddie pull-carts for less than $1.

Horseback Riding

STRACOMER RIDING SCHOOL

Off the Sligo/Ballyshannon Road (N 15). Tel. (071) 77121. Situated north of Bundoran, this popular riding center supplies horses for trekking on the surrounding farmlands, beaches, sand dunes, and mountain trails. An hour's ride averages $10. In the winter months, hunting can also be arranged with the nearby Sligo Harriers Club.

DONEGAL, Co. Donegal

Hotels

★★★★ ERNAN PARK

St. Ernan's Island. Tel. (073) 21065. 10 rooms. This is one of Donegal's (and Ireland's) most unique lodgings—a country house dating back to 1826, which by itself occupies an entire small island in Donegal Bay. The island, named for a 7th century Irish monk, is planted with hawthorn and holly bushes which have been blooming for almost three centuries.

Originally the family seat of John Hamilton, a benevolent 19th century Irish landlord, this house is connected to the mainland by its own causeway. Most of the bedrooms, all recently refurbished by new owner Brian O'Dowd to include private baths and elegant furnishings, have views of the water. The public areas are magnificently restored, with delicate plasterwork, high ceilings, crystal chandeliers, gilt-framed oil paintings, heirloom silver, and antique treasures. It's a delightful spot, almost like a kingdom unto itself, yet less than two miles south of Donegal town. *Moderate.*

★★★ THE ABBEY

The Diamond. Tel. (073) 21014. 40 rooms. In the heart of town, this old hotel has undergone a lot of renovation in recent years. The public rooms are open and airy and about half of the bedrooms are located in a new wing. Many guest rooms overlook the River Eske, which runs behind the hotel, and the clubby restaurant downstairs also looks out onto the water. It's a lively hotel, with entertainment on tap in one of the two lounges most evenings. *Inexpensive.*

★★★ HYLAND CENTRAL

The Diamond. Tel. (073) 21027. 58 rooms. A member of the Best Western group, this vintage property is adjacent to the Abbey. The hotel entrance fronts Donegal's main thoroughfare, while the rear boasts a modern extension which overlooks Donegal Bay. Ask for one of the newer rooms; the furnishings are rather standard, but the views are lovely. Guest facilities include a full-service restaurant and an old world pub which is the most charming and atmospheric watering hole in town. *Inexpensive.*

For a superb lodging suggestion, about 10 miles southwest of Donegal town, see Rossnowlagh.

Shopping

MAGEE

The Diamond. Tel. (073) 21100. Established in 1866, this is the home of Donegal hand-woven tweeds. Weaving demonstrations are given through-out the day, with complete factory tours at 11 A.M. and 4 P.M., Monday through Thursday, and at 11 A.M. on Friday. Products on sale include tweed jackets, suits, overcoats, hats, caps, ties, and batches of material.

DONEGAL CRAFT VILLAGE

Ballyshannon Road. Tel. (073) 22053. You'll find this cluster of in-dividual craftworkers' shops about a mile south of town in a rural setting. Encouraged and financed by Ireland's Industrial Development Authority and the E.E.C., this project provides a creative environment for an ever-changing group of artisans to practice ancient and modern crafts, ranging from hand-weaving and ceramics to batik, woodwork, fibreworks, and metalwork. You can buy some one-of-a-kind treasures or just browse from shop to shop and watch the craftspeople at work.

For other shopping suggestions in the vicinity of Donegal, see also Ardara, Ballyshannon, Bruckless, and Kilcar.

DOWNINGS, Co. Donegal

Hotels

★★★ ROSAPENNA GOLF HOTEL
Atlantic Drive. Tel. (074) 55301. 40 rooms. A member of the Best Western group, this modern two-story hotel is surrounded by Sheephaven Bay and the hills of Donegal. It's a favorite with golfers who flock here to enjoy the hotel's 18-hole seaside golf course (free to overnight guests; see "Sports" below). Non-golfers come just for the scenery and seclusion, as well as the hotel's proximity to northern Donegal attractions like Glenveagh National Park and Ft. Dunree. Other amenities include an all-weather tennis court and wind-surfing. The bedrooms, dining area, and lounges are modern, with emphasis on panoramic views of land and sea. Open early April through October. *Inexpensive.*

Sports

Golf

ROSAPENNA GOLF CLUB
Atlantic Drive. Tel. (074) 55301. Under the auspices of the Rosapenna Golf Hotel, this 18-hole seaside links course dates back to 1893, originally laid out by Tom Morris of St. Andrews. Greens fees are free to overnight guests at the hotel, and approximately $9 to others. Golf clubs can be hired for $5 per round, and caddy pull-carts are $1.50. To arrange a game, phone Frank Casey at the above hotel number.

FAHAN, Co. Donegal

Restaurant

★★★★ RESTAURANT ST. JOHN'S
Inishowen 100 Road. Tel. (077) 60289. If you are exploring the scenic Inishowen Peninsula, this is a restaurant to plan your schedule around.

Set on its own grounds overlooking Lough Swilly, this lovely Georgian house is the award-winning culinary domain of Reg Ryan. There are two dining rooms, each with a cozy elegance. Open turf fireplaces, Waterford crystal, embroidered linens, and richly textured wall paper add to the ambience. Best of all, the food is very good—from rack of lamb and filet of beef to local seafoods such as brill, turbot, and salmon. Open for dinner only, nightly in July and August; Tuesday through Sunday in June and October; and Wednesday through Sunday during the rest of the year. *Moderate.*

GLENCOLUMBKILLE, Co. Donegal

Hotel

★★ THE GLENBAY (For Ambience)
Tel. (073) 30003. 20 rooms. If you want to get away from it all, travel 30 miles west of Donegal town to this country hotel, encircled by craggy mountains that are populated mostly by meandering wooly sheep. Edged by Malin Bay and the Atlantic Ocean, it's a lovely outpost, with warming turf fireplaces and a cottage atmosphere. There's a good dining room, with panoramic views of the countryside, and the guest rooms are standard and up-to-date. The village of Glencolumbkille is just down the road, as is a fascinating Folk Village. Staying here for a few days will put color in your cheeks and recharge your inner batteries.

KILCAR, Co. Donegal

Shopping

STUDIO DONEGAL
Tel. (073) 38002. Started in 1979, this handweaving enterprise is distinguished by its knobby tweed which is subtly colored in tones of beige, oat, and ash. You can walk around both the craft shop and the mill and see the chunky-weave stoles, caps, jackets, ponchos, shawls, and cloaks in-the-making. Other products fashioned of this unique tweed include tote bags, cushion covers, table mats, tapestries, and wall hangings. It is located between Killybegs and Glencolumbkille, about 20 miles west of Donegal town.

LETTERKENNY, Co. Donegal

Hotel

★★ MT. ERRIGAL (For Location)
Derry Road, Ballyraine. Tel. (074) 22700. 56 rooms. Located less than a mile southeast of town, this contemporary two-story motor inn is a handy place to stay if you are touring the north/central parts of Donegal. It is just south of Lough Swilly and within 15 miles of the Glenveagh National Park. The hotel is decorated in a practical Irish tweedy theme, with wide windows looking out into the neighboring countryside.. Amenities include a full-service restaurant, lounge bar, and nightclub. *Inexpensive.*

Pub

★★ HALF-WAY LINE
Ramelton Road. One of Donegal's newest pubs (it still has no phone), this is a modern sports-oriented bar, owned by a local rugby club. It is located a few miles north of Letterkenny, in a country setting overlooking Lough Swilly. The staff are very friendly and the pub grub has an international flair—from lasagne and quiche to chili, burgers, and meat pies.

Festival

August 12-16: International Folk Festival, featuring traditional music, song, and dance.

Directory

Letterkenny Tourist Office. Derry Road. Tel. (074) 21160. This modern and functional office is Donegal County's only year-round source of tourist information. It is located in a purpose-built bungalow, about a half mile south of town.

RATHMULLAN, Co. Donegal

Hotels

★★★★ RATHMULLAN HOUSE
Tel. (074) 58188. 19 rooms. If you are touring northern Donegal, this country house will win your heart. Located on the western shores of Lough Swilly about a half-mile outside of town, it is surrounded by glorious gardens and mature trees. The mostly Georgian interior,

which includes a traditional drawing room and well-stocked library, is sprinkled with antiques and heirlooms collected over the years by owners Bob and Robin Wheeler.

The guest rooms vary in size and style of furnishings, but most have a comfortable Irish motif and overlook the lake and gardens; a few self-catering chalets are also available. Amenities include a fine restaurant housed in a glass-enclosed pavilion, a cellar bar, a private beach, and equipment for boating and seatrout fishing. A member of the Relais and Chateaux group, this welcoming inn is a favorite with British and French visitors. Open April through mid-October. *Moderate.*

Restaurant

★★★ WATER'S EDGE

The Ballyboe. Tel. (074) 58182. As its name implies, this restaurant is situated right on the edge of picturesque Lough Swilly, on the south end of town. Although the glassy facade on three sides gives the 70-seat dining area a modern look, the interior is actually quite traditional, with beam ceilings, open fireplace, nautical bric-a-brac, and watercolors of Donegal landscapes. The menu blends Irish dishes with international favorites,   such as pan-fried chicken and bacon,   honey-spiced ham, boned duck a l'orange, sole on the bone, local salmon, and sirloin steaks. Open for dinner only, year round. *Moderate.*

ROSSNOWLAGH, Co. Donegal

Hotel

★★★★★ THE SAND HOUSE

On the Coast, off the Ballyshannon/Donegal Road (N 15). Tel. (072) 51777. 40 rooms. Set on a crescent of beach overlooking the Atlantic coast, this three-story hotel is a stand-out among all the County Donegal lodgings. Although there are subtle suggestions of turreting on the roof, it does not pretend to be a castle. In fact, the Sand House had its early beginnings as a fishing lodge in 1886, and was used as a thatched pub by 1906; it was not until 1949 that Vincent and Mary Britton moved in and began their quest for a top notch hotel. The transformation did not happen overnight, nor in twenty or thirty years. But now, after much expansion and almost 40 years later, it has all come together.

The furnishings, carefully chosen or commissioned by Mary, are impeccably well coordinated, blending antiques with designer fabrics. Many of the bedrooms have four-poster or canopy beds, hand-carved armoires and vanities, and artistically hand-tiled bathrooms. Of course, the wide picture windows, with their ever-changing vistas of the

Atlantic and unforgettable sunsets, add the crowning touch to each room's individual tableau.

With open log and turf fireplaces, the public rooms are also decorated with antiques and local artwork, exuding a country inn atmosphere. The dining room, which, surprisingly, does not overlook the sea, is presided over by a creative chef whose dishes include crab and cucumber mousse, coquilles St. Jacques, and Gaelic steak with whiskey sauce. Best of all, the Brittons, and particularly son Conor who now manages the hotel, believe in offering guests the best of the local harvest, and have added newly cultivated Donegal Bay oysters, scallops, and mussels to the menu. In addition to swimming or walking the wide sandy beach, guests can enjoy surfing, tennis, fishing, and golf at the nearby 18-hole Murvagh golf course. Open from mid-April to early October. *Moderate to expensive.*

Shopping

BARRY BRITTON
On the Coast, off the Ballyshannon/Donegal Road. Tel. (072) 51974. Located in a cottage opposite the Sand House Hotel, this workshop is a source of unusual artistic crafts, such as mirrors or glass hand-etched with heraldic crests, floral and wildlife designs; wall hangings; and prints of Donegal.

TEELIN, Co. Donegal

Pub

★★★ THE RUSTY MACKEREL
Tel. (073) 39101. If you are touring southwestern Donegal, you'll enjoy a stop at this interesting pub which is the only one in the tiny village of Teelin, reaching out into Donegal Bay and just a stone's throw from Slieve League mountain (1,972 feet high).

Named for a favorite local fish, it has a facade painted the rusty color of a cured mackerel and a front door with a lifesize mural of a local man enjoying a drink at the bar. The interior of the pub is also filled with paintings of other Donegal people and scenes, the work of pub-owner Florian Binsack, of French/Swedish background, but Irish by choice. You'll usually find his Donegal-born wife, Una, behind the bar, an expert at serving anything from pints of beer to dry martinis. Evening is the best time to visit, when the locals gather for some traditional music.

The Lakelands

COUNTIES CAVAN, MONAGHAN, WESTMEATH, LONGFORD, AND ROSCOMMON

Geographic surveys tell us that there are over 800 lakes and rivers throughout the Emerald Isle, making fresh inland waters a prime natural resource. And this isn't hard to believe when you travel around the counties of Cavan, Monaghan, Westmeath, Longford, and Roscommon—a major share of the nation's lakes, rivers, streams, and brooks are located in these five counties. No wonder this part of north/central Ireland has been christened "the lakelands."

Two of Ireland's greatest waterways, the River Shannon and Lough Erne, both begin in this region. The Shannon, which has its source on the southern slopes at Cuilcagh Mountain in Co. Cavan, flows southerly through ten counties, down as far as Counties Clare and Kerry. Lough Erne, which rises in Lough Gowna on the Cavan/Longford border, meanders in a northwesterly fashion into Northern Ireland.

As can be expected, the waters of these five "lakeland" counties are rich in fish, from trout, pike, perch, and bream, to lesser known species like rudd, tench, and roach. With the exception of catching trout, this sport is known as coarse fishing, and it is free throughout this area. Trout fishing, referred to as game fishing, sometimes requires a permit, but many hotels and inns extend trout fishing privileges to guests.

As you drive around this area, however, you'll soon see that the lakelands offer a lot more than just water and fish. Rich and fertile, ideal for dairy and cattle farming, this part of Ireland is a sharp contrast to the more rocky and barren western counties.

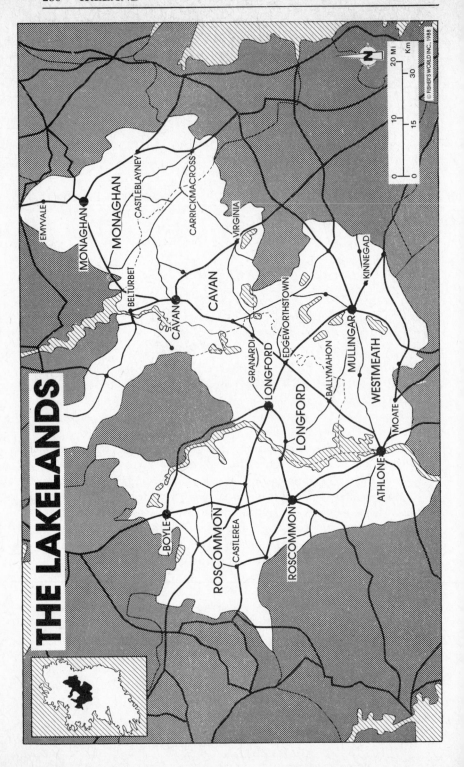

THE LAKELANDS

COUNTIES CAVAN AND MONAGHAN

If you are traveling from Dublin, the nearest of the lakeland counties is Cavan. Just follow the main road (N 3) and you will be in the midst of Cavan in less than fifty miles. The Cavan scenery is the epitome of this part of Ireland—myriad lakes, ancient trees, undulating land, and low round hills. You'll also see a goodly share of verdant parks and forests, walking trails, and valleys.

In fact, if you have ever heard the song, "Doonaree," this is the spot that inspired the romantic melody ("Oh, to be in Doonaree . . ."). The spelling is a little different, but Dun-A-Ri can be found at Kingscourt ★★ Forest, about fifteen miles off the main road as you enter the Cavan border. This park consists of a 560-acre estate beside the Cabra River, with both a commercial forest section and a recreational area. The latter includes nature trails, planned walks, picnic sites, waterfowl and deer enclosures, and a wishing well.

An unexpected placename in Cavan is Virginia, on the banks of Lough Ramor. Built in 1610 and named for Queen Elizabeth I, it claims no direct connections with the U.S. state, but it is the nearest village to Cuilcagh House, which Jonathan Swift often visited and where he is said to have begun writing "Gulliver's Travels" in 1726. Another interesting note about the area is that the famous songsmith, Percy French, who wrote "The Mountains of Mourne" and "Come Back, Paddy Reilly, to Ballyjamesduff," was born in Cavan town.

Immediately east and north of Cavan is Co. Monaghan. With a landscape characterized by great pasture lands, little hills, and endless lakes, this county also has literary associations. The 20th-century poet and novelist, Patrick Kavanagh, was born at Inniskeen on the eastern fringe of the county; a small village museum commemorates his work.

About five miles away is Carrickmacross, a town synonymous with the ancient art of lace-making. Here you can visit one of the chief sources for this delicate material at St. Louis Convent (see "Inside Information").

The county's principal attraction is the Monaghan Museum, a local ★★ history treasure-trove in the town of Monaghan. Established in 1974, it was awarded the Council of Europe Museum Prize in 1980. While the displays primarily cover the traditional life, costumes, coinage, and crafts of the area, there are also some rare exhibits of prehistoric pottery, 19th-century lace, and the 15th-century Cross of Clogher, an oak cross covered with bronze and semi-precious metals.

COUNTY WESTMEATH

Positioned in the center of the lakelands, County Westmeath is a mecca for fishing and for another popular water sport, boating.

Although many local people bring their own craft, visitors can rent cabin cruisers at many depots along the Shannon River.

Athlone, in particular, is a leading inland marina for mooring and hiring boats. This town's other claim to fame is that it produced Ireland's most famous operatic tenor, the late John McCormack, whose birthplace is marked by a plaque at the Bawn, off Mardyke Street.

About thirty miles to the northeast is Mullingar, another important Co. Westmeath town. Located on the shores of the Brosna River, midway between Lough Ennell and Lough Owel, Mullingar was once the seat of Irish high kings, and now it is the center of a prosperous cattle-raising area.

★★ County Westmeath's chief sightseeing attraction, Tullynally Castle and Gardens, is located thirteen miles north of Mullingar at Castlepollard. A turreted and towered Gothic-Revival manor, Tullynally has been the home of the Earls of Longford since the 17th century. The highlights include a great hall which rises through two storeys and has a ceiling of plaster Gothic vaulting, plus a collection of family portraits, china, and furniture. The thirty acres of grounds are an attraction in themselves, with various woodland walks, a linear water garden, a Victorian grotto, and an avenue of 200-year-old Irish yew trees. Tullynally is located a few miles east of Lough Derravaragh, an idyllic spot featured in the legendary Irish tale called "The Children of Lir."

COUNTIES LONGFORD AND ROSCOMMON

Sitting north of Westmeath is County Longford, bordered on the west by the Shannon River. An inland county of quiet farmlands, brown bogs, low hills, and lots of lakes and rivers, County Longford is primarily known for its literary associations. In fact, this area is usually referred to as "Goldsmith Country," because 18th-century dramatist, novelist, and poet Oliver Goldsmith was born here at Pallas, near Ballymahon. Although Goldsmith did much of his writing in London, it is said that he drew on many of his Irish experiences for such works as "She Stoops to Conquer."

The neat village of Edgeworthstown was likewise the home of Maria Edgeworth, the 18th-century novelist and essayist, while Longford town was the birthplace of Padraig Colum, the 20th-century playwright, biographer, folklorist, and writer of children's stories.

To the west of Longford, on the other side of the Shannon, is County Roscommon, the most westerly point of the lakelands. Roscommon is a mostly level plain with bogs, meadows, and sprawling lands, occasionally broken by low hills and dotted with many lakes. It is the setting for two major visitor attractions, conveniently situated within twenty miles of each other in the county's northern sector.

The first of these, Clonalis House, is at Castlerea, on the Longford/ ★★★
Castlebar Road (N 5). This 19th-century manor is one of the great
houses of Ireland which you really should try to see, especially if your
name is O'Connor or a variation of it, because it is the home of the
O'Conor Don, the direct descendant of the last high king of Ireland.
The house itself is a combination of Victorian, Italianate, and Queen
Anne architecture, with mostly Louis XV-style furnishings. Most of
all, it is a museum of the O'Conor family, with portraits, documents,
and genealogical tracts dating back 2,000 years. Displays also include
a rare ancient harp and the coronation stone of the kings of Connacht,
plus antique lace, and horse-drawn farm machinery, memorabilia, and
documents. Clonalis is surrounded by a well-maintained parkland,
with terraced and woodland gardens.

The other prized site of this county is the Lough Key Forest Park at ★★★
Boyle. Spanning 840 acres along the shores of Lough Key, it is one of
Ireland's foremost lakeside parks. The grounds include nature walks,
tree identity trails, ancient monuments, ring forts, a central viewing
tower, picnic grounds, a restaurant, and shop. In addition to cypress
groves and other diverse foliage, you'll find a unique display of bog
gardens, where a wide selection of peat-loving plants and shrubs
flourish. Fallow deer, otters, hedgehogs, birds, pheasants, and many
other forms of wildlife also roam the park.

CAVAN, Co. Cavan

Hotels

★★★ HOTEL KILMORE
Dublin Road (N 3). Tel. (049) 32288. 40 bedrooms. About two miles
south of Cavan town, this modern motor inn provides a pleasant
respite on one of the main roads between Dublin and Northern
Ireland. It's in the heart of the lakeland region, with dozens of good
fishing waters nearby. Built in the early 1980's, the hotel offers all the
modern conveniences including a full-service restaurant and a night
club which features top cabaret-style entertainment on weekends.
Inexpensive.

Pubs

★★★ DERRAGARRA INN
Butlersbridge. Tel. (049) 31003. This 200-year-old pub is four miles
north of Cavan town, in the valley of the River Annalee. The decor is
full of local farm implements and crafts as well as exotic souvenirs
collected by owner John Clancy during his travels around the world.

You can sip a drink by the old turf fireplace or on the garden patio. The food here ranges from salads and sandwiches to sole on the bone or smoked eel.

Shopping

CAVAN CRYSTAL

Dublin Road (N 3). Tel. (049) 31800. One of the top three crystal companies of Ireland, this establishment is known for its delicate glassware which is mouth-blown and hand-cut by skilled craftsmen. Tours are usually given, free of charge, at 10:30 A.M., 11:30 A.M., 2:30 P.M., and 3:30 P.M., Monday through Friday. In addition, the shop, which sells seconds, is open Monday through Saturday and Sunday afternoons.

VIRGINIA, Co. Cavan

Hotels

★★ THE PARK HOTEL

Cavan/Dublin Road (N 3). Tel. (049) 47235. 22 rooms. A Best Western affiliate, this hotel is set on 100 acres of woodlands and gardens beside Lough Ramor. On the northern edge of the town of Virginia and 50 miles from Dublin, it's in the heart of the Co. Cavan lakelands region, and a favorite with British visitors, especially fishermen.

The Park was originally a sporting lodge and summer residence of the Marquis of Headfort, and was converted into a hotel in the 1930's. It has since had a number of renovations and extensions, making for lots of connecting corridors and varying standards of bedrooms. Although they all have private baths, modern showers are hard to come by. The public rooms, however, retain a definite 18th century charm, with high ceilings, elaborate chandeliers, period furnishings, and impressive oil paintings. The amenities include a full-service restaurant, lounge bar, nine-hole golf course, hard tennis court, fishing privileges, boating equipment, and forest walking trails. For those traveling with families or planning to stay a while, there are also 11 mews-style cottages in a courtyard behind the hotel. Open February through December. *Inexpensive.*

CARRICKMACROSS, Co. Monaghan

Hotel

★★★ NUREMORE

Ashbourne/Slane/Ardee Road (N 2). Tel. (042) 61438. 39 rooms. In a town so famous for its lace, this modern hotel is equally well known for its hospitality and high standards. If you are touring the lakelands and intend to do some fishing, it makes an ideal base, just 50 miles from Dublin. The setting includes 100 acres of parkland and woods (including three lakes), plus a nine-hole golf course, hotel boat, heated indoor swimming pool, squash court, sauna, and whirlpool. The decor is airy and modern, with wide windows, and a mostly two-story facade. *Moderate.*

Shopping

ST. LOUIS LACE CENTRE
Tel. (042) 61247. In a convent, on a hill in the middle of town, you'll find this famous lace-making enterprise. The nuns sketch out designs, and then women in nearby cottages do much of the artful stitching. There is a display room where you can purchase items ranging from decorative collars to heirloom wedding veils. Hours are 10 A.M. to noon and 2 P.M. to 4 P.M. on weekdays only.

ATHLONE, Co. Westmeath

Hotel

★★ **PRINCE OF WALES** (Best in Town)
Church Street. Tel. (0902) 72626. 42 rooms. Dating back to 1848, and renovated in 1962, this fuctional three-story hotel is in the center of a town known as the birthplace of tenor John McCormack, and as a prime mooring site for Shannon River cruisers. It's a good place to break a cross-country journey or as a base for touring the lakelands. Facilities include a coffee shop, bar, and restaurant. *Inexpensive.*

Sports/Perks

SHANNON HOLIDAYS
Jolly Mariner Marina. Tel. (0902) 72892. If you'd like to rent a cabin cruiser to ply the waters of the Shannon for a week or weekend, this is the company to contact. The fleet ranges from three-to eight-berth craft, equipped with refrigerator, stove, toilet/shower, heater, electricity, life jackets, and other basics. Prices range from $250 to $1500 per week, and that includes preliminary instruction in operating the boat. Express bus transfers from Shannon or Dublin Airports can also be arranged. The season lasts from early April to October. No credit cards.

MULLINGAR, Co. Westmeath

Hotels

★★★ BLOOMFIELD HOUSE
Kilbeggan Road. Tel. (044) 80894. 33 rooms and suites. A Best Western affiliate, this two-story hotel is set on 20 acres of wooded land along the shores of Lough Ennell, deep in the heart of the Irish midlands and lakelands. A former country manor residence, it is furnished with period pieces typical of the local area. The atmosphere is pleasant and friendly and guests are encouraged to participate in boating, fishing, tennis, pitch-and-putt, or windsurfing on the lake. The hotel is also within walking distance of an 18-hole parkland golf course. Other facilities include a lounge bar and a full-service restaurant. *Inexpensive.*

Directory

Mullingar Tourist Office, Dublin Road. Tel. (044) 48761. Located in the heart of the lakeland district, this office remains open all year.

The Farmlands

COUNTIES KILDARE, CARLOW, OFFALY, AND LAOIS

Primarily located in the south/central section of Ireland, these four counties are sometimes referred to as part of the Irish "midlands." We feel that the term "farmlands" is a bit more descriptive, and it also distinguishes this quartet of counties from the cluster just above them (Cavan, Monaghan, Westmeath, Roscommon, and Longford, which we have identified, just to be different, as "the lakelands"). What all nine of these counties (the "farmlands" and the "lakelands") have in common, of course, is that they have no coastline at all—they are truly "in the middle" of the Emerald Isle.

In particular, Kildare, Carlow, Offaly, and Laois are four adjoining counties wedged in between two of Ireland's most popular sightseeing sections—the Dublin area and the Shannon region—and are consequently often overlooked. And that's a pity.

These four farmland counties have a lot to offer the visitor, and since they are off the usual tourist track, their roads (with the exception of N 7, the main Dublin/Limerick road) are also less crowded. Most of all, these rich and fertile farmlands played an important part in Irish history, and many great buildings, ancient ruins, and historic gardens remain—waiting to be explored by 20th-century visitors.

COUNTIES KILDARE AND CARLOW

Of all the farmland counties, Kildare, just west of Dublin, is probably

THE FARMLANDS

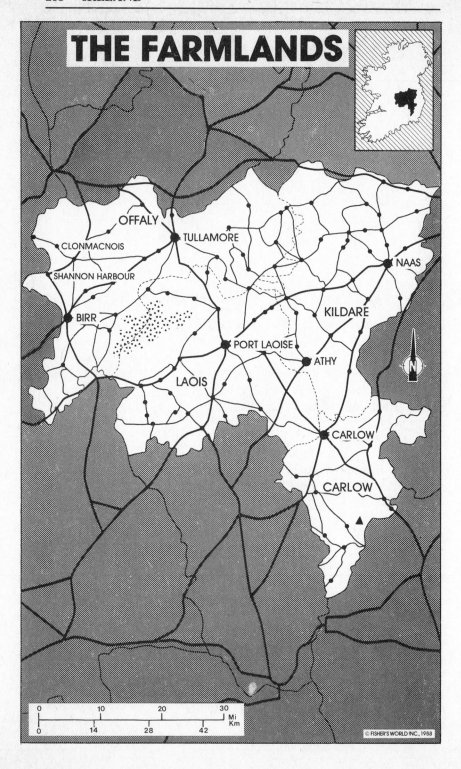

OFFALY

CLONMACNOIS

SHANNON HARBOUR

TULLAMORE

NAAS

BIRR

KILDARE

PORT LAOISE

ATHY

LAOIS

CARLOW

CARLOW

| 0 | 10 | 20 | 30 | Mi |
| 0 | 14 | 28 | 42 | Km |

© FISHER'S WORLD INC., 1988

the best known and the most popular. Just as Ireland and the horse are synonymous, Kildare and horse-racing go hand-in-hand, or, should we say neck-and-neck. Home of the Curragh racetrack, where the Irish Derby is held each June, County Kildare is also the heartland of Ireland's flourishing bloodstock industry. Many of the country's 300 stud farms are nestled in this panorama of open grasslands and fertile turf.

In fact, one of the chief visitor attractions of Co. Kildare is a government-sponsored stud farm, appropriately called The Irish
★★★ National Stud, a prototype for all others throughout the land. If you love horses, put this place on your "must see" list. Located at Tully, off the main Dublin/Limerick Road (N 7), the farm is a mile southeast of Kildare town and near the Curragh racetrack—all less than thirty miles from Dublin city. Some of Ireland's most famous horses have been bred and raised on these grounds; and visitors are welcome to walk around and watch the noble steeds being exercised and groomed.

In addition to the outdoor sights, there is an indoor museum which aims to bring to life the history of the horse in Ireland, with exhibits dating from the Bronze Age to the present. There are also displays on horses in transport, racing, steeplechasing, hunting, and showjumping, plus the skeleton of "Arkle," one of Ireland's most famous equine heroes, and an authentic jockey's weighing-in chair. For those only mildly interested in horses, there is an adjacent garden area which is designed to symbolize the life of man. An authentic Japanese garden, first laid out in 1906-10, it's considered to be among the oldest and
★★ finest Oriental gardens in Europe. This is one place where the bonsai trees outnumber the shamrocks.

If an urban setting is more to your liking, then you should spend a few hours in Co. Kildare's chief town, Naas (pronounced "Nay-se"). Taking its name from a Gaelic word which means "the assembly-place of the kings," Naas was once the seat of the kings of the province of Leinster, and was the site of an ancient royal palace where St. Patrick is said to have spent some time. Today's Naas, located within ten miles of the Curragh, is known primarily for its association with the sport of kings—this little town of 10,000 people also has its own grassy racetrack and is within three miles of yet a third County Kildare track at Punchestown, a steeplechase venue.

For a totally different look at Co. Kildare, you should also head about ten miles northeast of Naas to the little village of Celbridge.
★★★ Here you will find Castletown House, one of Ireland's architectural gems. A Palladian-style mansion built in 1722 for William Connolly, then Speaker of the Irish House of Commons, it was designed by Italian architect Alessandro Galilei and has been preserved and restored by the Irish Georgian Society. A showcase of 18th-century Irish furniture and paintings, Castletown's highlights include a long gallery

laid out in the Pompeian manner and hung with Venetian chandeliers, a main hall and staircase with elaborate Italian plasterwork, and an 18th-century print room.

In contrast, neighboring County Carlow is primarily a farming district, with gentle pasturelands and sturdy farmhouses. This little county is also traversed by two great rivers, the Barrow and the Slaney, so it is good salmon and trout fishing territory. The Blackstairs Mountains, to the east, complete the Carlow tableau.

COUNTIES LAOIS AND OFFALY

Laois and Offaly are often grouped together, and not just because they are situated side-by-side. Dating from the days of British rule, these two counties were respectively known as Queen's and Kings' Counties in deference to the monarchs on the throne in London.

County Laois (pronounced "Lee-sh"), with miles of lowlands and open bogs, forms part of Ireland's central plain, its sometimes stark landscape softened by the ridges of the Slieve Bloom Mountains to the west and northwest. The county's chief town, Portlaoise (pronounced "Portlee-sh"), is one place most tourists get to see, or at least drive around. It is an important junction on the roads to/from the south—both N 7 (the Dublin/Limerick road) and N 8 (the Dublin/Cork road) converge here. It's a pleasant town of 4,000 people, but really has no particularly notable sights other than a national prison on its outskirts.

The county's chief sightseeing attraction lies a few miles off the main road, northeast of Portlaoise, at Emo Park. Here you will find Emo Court and Gardens, where the focus is on a grand house built in 1895, according to designs of the celebrated architect James Gandon. It is surrounded by a wealth of flowering shrubs and magnificent trees for all seasons. The house is only open on Monday afternoons, but the gardens can be enjoyed daily.

After a stop at Emo Park, get back on the main road and head in a westerly direction to adjacent Offaly, the county that lies practically at the geographic center of Ireland. Although the terrain is an over-whelmingly flat mixture of farmlands and boglands, this area is also blessed with vistas of the heathery Slieve Bloom Mountains to the southeast and a shoreline along the Shannon River to the west.

If you turn off the main road at Roscrea and head north, you can now follow N 62 for about twelve miles to Birr, a neat little town with mostly Georgian architecture, situated at the juncture of the Little Brosna and the Camcor rivers.

Follow the signs to Birr Castle, and you'll be on the estate of the Parsons family, otherwise known as the Earl and Countess of Ross. Don't expect to be invited inside the house, however, as the 17th-century castle/residence is not open to the public. But this presents no problem, since the main attractions of Birr Castle are outdoors, and open to the public. The 100-acre garden, laid out around a lake and along the banks of the two adjacent rivers, contains over 1,000 different species of trees and shrubs, from magnolias and cherry trees to chestnut and weeping beech. The hornbeam alleys and box hedges are featured in the Guinness Book of Records as the tallest in the world.

As you proceed further along the path, you'll be able to combine a touch of star-gazing with the garden stroll because the grounds also contain an astronomical exhibit, thanks to the efforts of the 3rd Earl of Rosse, who, in 1845, built a giant 72-inch reflecting telescope. The largest in the world, it remained so for over 75 years. The display area also contains astronomical artifacts, drawings, photographs, and a scale model of the original telescope. As a bonus during the summer months, you can usually find additional rotating exhibits dealing with the history of Birr Castle and its residents.

★★★ From Birr, follow the road north to Cloghan and west to Shannon-bridge, and then it's only four miles along the Shannon River to Clonmacnois, one of Ireland's most significant ancient monuments. Founded as a monastery by St. Ciaran in 548, this site was one of Europe's great centers of learning for nearly 1,000 years, flourishing under the patronage of many Irish kings. The last High King, Rory O'Conor, was buried here in 1198.

In its later years, Clonmacnois was raided many times by native chiefs, Danes, and Anglo-Normans, until it was finally abandoned in 1552. Today's visitor can see the remains of a cathedral, a castle, eight churches, two round towers, three sculptured high crosses, and over 200 monumental slabs, all standing silently at the edge of the River Shannon.

You could easily spend a day at Clonmacnois, or at least the better part of an afternoon. If there is time, you may wish to drive about 20 miles eastward to Tullamore, and check out yet another of County Offaly's claims to fame—the distillery which produces the popular liqueur known as "Irish Mist."

Irish Cuisine

by
Brenda Weir

When I came to live in Dublin about 25 years ago, I found such natural products as eggs, butter, cream, and meat to be of splendid quality. I found marvelous home-baked delights such as rich tea cakes, soda breads, and scones, but overall, the diet was unimaginative. Breakfast generally consisted of eggs, bacon, fried bread, and black pudding. The midday and evening meals might include boiled cabbage, Crubbeens (pig's feet), and Irish stew (made of onions, potatoes, and breast of lamb). Part of the problem was lack of information. The Irish simply didn't know how to combine their resources into an appetizing meal.

Part of the problem, however, was supply. Twenty-five years ago, few Irish people had ever heard of an avocado pear; "tūna" was thought to be the way an Italian would say "tune." The supermarket did not exist. Staples such as flour and sugar were scooped from large sacks lined up along the back of a darkened grocery store. Biscuits came by the pound from a large tin, and everything was put into brown paper bags or wrapped in newspaper. Fresh fruits and vegetables were limited unless you grew your own. In town, you could buy a cabbage, a lettuce, or maybe a cauliflower. The fruit selection consisted of apples, pears, oranges, grapefruit, lemons, and bananas, plus the "soft fruits," strawberries and raspberries, but only in season. Out in the countryside, the variety was even more limited.

While freshwater fishes were readily available, fish was considered Friday-fare, a "fast-food," and was generally avoided on other days of the week. That situation, most fortunately, underwent a change when the Bord Iascaigh Mhara (Bord eeshkyworra: Sea Fisheries Board) ran competitions and put out free leaflets on fish recipes. A few years later, the Pope altered the requirements for Fasting-on-Fridays, and fish came into its own. Nowadays, it often costs more than meat. From penitential, fish has evolved into something of a status symbol.

There were a few good restaurants in those days, but they were confined almost entirely to the capital city and a couple of country hotels. *The Jammets Restaurant* was well-known, as much for its ambiance as for its menu. One dined under the limpid gaze of wall-mounted Rubensian nymphs in their swirling draperies, and was served in impeccable style by creaking waiters. *The Dolphin* offered massive masculine-style steaks amid a loud convivial atmosphere, and the elegant *Red Bank* had delicious fishy foods served in romantic style. Right up to the mid-fifties, an English friend used to remark that it was "hard to spend £5 on a night out in Dublin." That situation was shortly to change. Prices and costs rose in the sixties, so it was no longer possible for the average individual to patronize such restaurants. Sadly, they have all gone out of business.

In the early sixties, television exploded on the Irish country-side, bringing news and information about different places and cultures and, of course, food. New wage laws made domestic staff expensive and difficult to find, so the typical housewife was forced into taking more interest in cooking. Their demands made suppliers look to their stocks, and the Supermarket came. Trendier ethnic restaurants opened (primarily Indian and Chinese) and though not of a particularly high standard, were well-patronized. Next came the fast food chains. Fish and Chips gave way to the Burger and Coke which, in turn, made room for the Pizza Parlour.

Perhaps one of the most significant innovations of the sixties was the opening of the restaurant at Ballymaloe House in County Cork in 1964, where the Allen family, under the guidance of Myrtle Allen, began serving delicious and imaginative meals prepared entirely from their own farm produce, dairy products, and local meat and fish. Ballymaloe House marked the beginning of a revolution in public taste; people traveled from far and wide to dine there and still do. Awarded stars by nearly all the well-known food guides, this corner of the southwest of Ireland has become a center for excellent cuisine. A few years later, cookery classes were started here. Now there is a Cookery School, attended by students from all over the world as well as from Ireland. Other top-notch performers are *The Arbutus Lodge Hotel* in Cork, *Longueville House* nearby, and several restaurants in Cork City. The town of Kinsale runs a special Gourmet Festival each autumn in which its many fine restaurants participate. County Kerry, too, seems to be dotted with wonderful places to eat. They often need a bit of hunting out, but all bear the signature of fine cooking and use only locally produced ingredients. Fine dining is not limited to the Southwest of Ireland. Dublin and its environs have some excellent restaurants and hotels. The unique *Dunderry Lodge Restaurant* in Navan (just north of Dublin), has won nearly as many awards as Ballymaloe. Many of these establishments are members of a circle called *The Country House and Restaurants Association*. Membership of this exclusive circle virtually guarantees an owner-run establishment that offers good food and a friendly personal welcome. The Association issues a descriptive leaflet and it is well worthwhile if you plan a trip here. The leaflet is available from the Irish Tourist Board, or from me, for INSIDE IRELAND members.

The whole personna of food has changed over the years. In the 1950s, it was considered bad manners to compliment a hostess on the quality of the meal served in her house. It is interesting to note that, until quite recently, some of the worst meals I have ever eaten were served in the grandest homes. Presumably, the lady of the house was above concerning herself with such mundane matters. I still recall, with a shudder, a lunch of macaroni cheese, accompanied by crackers, and followed by rice pudding, served in an exquisitely maintained Irish castle by a lady of elegance and breeding. "How CAN she?" I moaned silently as I picked my way through mounds of colorless globules. Mercifully, this experience was counteracted later when dining at a shabby "Big House" where our Wellington-booted hostess, accompanied by an affable hound, greeted us heartily as she emerged from the garden bearing a pannier of vegetables, and announced that her son had just caught a salmon which would soon be on the table. The meal ended with garden-fresh strawberries topped with cream from the farm. Everything was ambrosial, and it was this sort of Country-House style that produced the late lamented *Snaffles* restaurant in Dublin City. It was here that game in season, kidneys, sweetbreads, and brains became a normal part of the menu and helped increase the public awareness of these delights.

In 1973 Ireland joined the European Economic Community (E.E.C.). This increased travel between Ireland and other European countries, bringing us even more information about food. Visitors delighted in our Country-House style while the Irish learned to appreciate paella, pasta, and quiche.

In the seventies, cookery courses became even more fashionable, so much so that Alix Gardner opened her "Cordon Bleu" school in Dublin. There was no loss in status in doing a cookery course now; lots of young girls (and some young men) were eager to master culinary skills, useful both at home and as a profession, since there seemed to be an endless demand for good cooks to work in the rapidly growing restaurant business. The level of knowledge continued to increase and, with it, demand, prompting the government to encourage food as an industry. Initially, this was limited to meat products: bacon in sealed packs, cooked meats, sausages, and black and white pudding. Soon fish joined in: smoked salmon and trout. Next came dairy products.

The removal of the tax concession on entertainment expenses in the seventies was a mortal blow to many of the newly-opened restaurants. The recession and high taxes of the eighties compounded the problem until come establishments were forced to close. Far from viewing this as regrettable, we Irish welcomed it, since many restaurants had begun over-charging for the quality of their menus. Realism has taken over. Prices are far more moderate in most places, and when you do pay a high price, you can count on matching quality.

Excellent restaurants can be found in most parts of the country but, unfortunately, not all. Many country hotels still cater to a clientele which likes a hearty three course mid-day meal of soup, roast and three vegetables, followed by apple pie and cream. This can be delicious, if plain, and it can also be frightful.

Nowadays, Irish supermarkets are fantastic! In response to the demands of our young for first class quality and service, the chains have given us huge, immaculate centers, stocked with the best fresh fruit and vegetables, well displayed fish and meat (tuna sandwiches are now commonplace), and a vast selection of canned and frozen foods. Though influenced by the American industry, our supermarkets still retain a uniquely Irish friendliness and shopping is a joy. Frankly, I find the typical Irish shopping center far more sophisticated than those in the U.K. These giant shops come to the cities first, of course, but they are gradually finding their way into the countryside. In return, the country areas are developing cottage industries which produce the foods stocked by markets. Cheeses are a noteworthy example. There are over sixty varieties of Irish cheese. Try Milleens (brie-type), Cashel Blue, Ring (hard), Burren Gold (gouda style), and Regatto (parmesan at a quarter the cost). Another country company is Lakeshore Foods, which produces wholegrain Irish mustards flavored with honey. For the drinker, there is Guinness Stout, Irish Whiskey, and Baileys Irish Cream Liqueur. For those with a sweet-tooth, try Irish chocolates.

Ireland could always delight the eye of the tourist with its startlingly beautiful countryside, but now it delights the palate as well.

Brenda Weir is the founder and editor of INSIDE IRELAND, a unique Information Service and Quarterly Review about Ireland and things Irish. It carries regular restaurant reviews.

Subscription is $30.00 p.a., and members receive (in addition to the Review itself) supplements on genealogy, plus a FREE initial genealogy advice service, a "Recommended Accommodation in Ireland" booklet, updated annually, a "Shopping and Touring" booklet, and a *Discount Voucher* which can be used for mail order shopping as well as shopping in person.

Full details are obtainable from: INSIDE IRELAND, P.O. Box 1886, Dublin 16, Ireland; Telephone: Dublin 931906.

Along the Historic River Boyne

COUNTIES MEATH AND LOUTH

Less than 30 miles northwest of Dublin is the River Boyne, surrounded by the rich and fertile countryside of Counties Meath and Louth. More than any other river in the country, this meandering body of water has been at the center of Irish history.

The banks of the Boyne are literally lined with reminders from almost every phase of Ireland's past—from the prehistoric passage tombs of Newgrange, dating back to 3,000 B.C., to the early Christian sights associated with the preachings of St. Patrick and the storied Hill of Tara, seat of medieval Irish high kings. This land was also the setting for the Battle of the Boyne in 1690, when King William of Orange crushed James II and so changed the course of English and Irish history that the effects are still felt today.

Although many of these places are nothing more than grassy mounds or ruins today, visitors flock to see the sites and walk the pathways of long ago. If you come this way, you'll also be rewarded by the pleasant seaside and mountain scenery of the two surrounding counties.

COUNTY MEATH

Along the southern edge of the Boyne is Meath, an area which consists almost entirely of a rich limestone plain, with verdant pasturelands and occasional low hills. Once a separate province which included

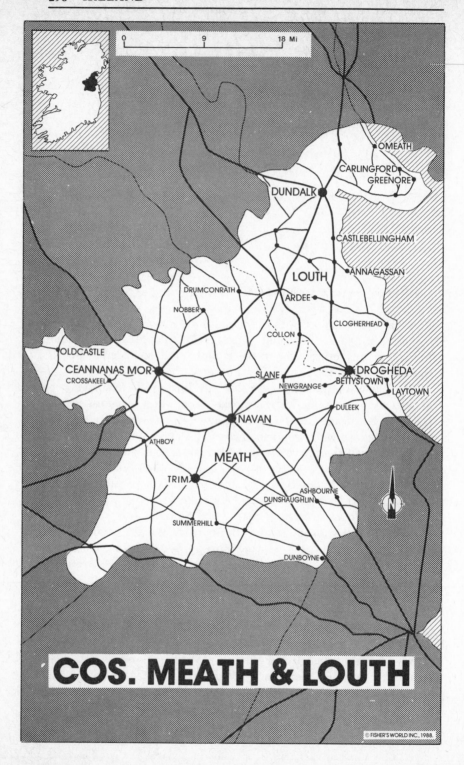

COS. MEATH & LOUTH

© FISHER'S WORLD INC., 1988.

neighboring Westmeath, it was usually referred to as "the Royal County Meath" since it was ruled by the kings of pagan and early-Christian Ireland.

While the chief town of County Meath is Navan, nearby Kells is better known to the average U.S. traveler. This is because of its association with the famous *Book of Kells*, the hand-illustrated gospel manuscript on display at Trinity College in Dublin. In 1977-78, the book was part of an exhibit which toured the U.S.

The town of Kells, known as "Ceanannus Mor" in Gaelic (meaning "Great Residence"), was originally the site of an important 6th-century monastic settlement founded by St. Colmcille and occupied for a time by monks driven from Iona by the Vikings. The *Book of Kells* was produced here, at least in part, in the 9th century. The monastery was dissolved in 1551, but remnants of buildings and high crosses can still be seen.

If you are heading in this direction, however, there is another site which even overshadows Kells, and that is the Hill of Tara. Located ★★ six miles south of Navan, Tara was the religious and cultural capital of Ireland in ancient times. It was here, every three years, that a great national assembly (feis) was held; laws were passed, tribal disputes were settled, and matters of peace and defense were decided. By the end of the 6th century, the Tara monarchy had become the most powerful of Ireland's five kingdoms. As the old song goes, "The harp that once through Tara's halls, the soul of music shed. . . . "

If you rally to Tara's halls today, however, you won't see any towers and turrets, or moats and crown jewels; in fact, you won't even see any halls. Be advised not to come at all, unless you wish to use your imagination and some good walking shoes. All that remains of Tara's former glories are grassy mounds and occasional ancient pillar stones. As you look around, however, you can see for miles, and surely the vistas are just as awesome as they were 1,500 years ago.

Note: In a way, Tara can take the credit for the shamrocks you see every March 17th. It all started in the 5th century when St. Patrick began to preach from Tara's heights. In an effort to convert High King Laoire to Christianity, Patrick plucked a three-leaf clover, or sham-rock, from the grass to illustrate the doctrine of the Trinity. The spell-binding saint made such an impression that the shamrock has since become synonymous with Ireland and the Irish all over the world.

Northeast of Tara is yet another lofty mound, the Hill of Slane, ★★ which overlooks one of the loveliest parts of the Boyne Valley. This hill knew its greatest moment in 433 A.D., when St. Patrick lit the paschal fire, proclaiming Christianity throughout all of Ireland. Al-though Patrick founded a church here and a monastic school, all that is left today are the remains of a subsequent 16th-century church which occupies the same site.

Like Tara, the 500-foot Slane offers an expansive vantage point for observing the countryside and for conjuring up visions of the past. The town of Slane, just a mile to the south, is also worth a visit, as is Slane
★★★ Castle (see "Inside Information").

If you prefer more ground (or underground) perspectives, then Newgrange offers a perfect contrast. Located two miles east of Slane, this is Ireland's best known prehistoric monument and one of the finest archeological wonders of western Europe. Dating back to 3,000 B.C., the Newgrange site is a huge mound 36 feet high and 280 feet in diameter, with a passage tomb in which Stone Age men buried the cremated remains of the dead nearly 5,000 years ago. You'll also see some fine specimens of geometrically carved stones. Members of the National Parks office provide guided tours on a regular basis, and in the summer months an information and interpretative display center is also open.

Even though Meath is primarily an inland county, it is also blessed with a short six-mile stretch of Irish coastline and two fine sandy beaches, Bettystown and Laytown. In County Meath, however, always be prepared to find an occasional piece of history even on the beach— it was at Bettystown in 1850 that the Tara Brooch was found. Often imitated in modern jewelry designs, this is one of Ireland's finest examples of early Christian goldsmithing artwork and is on view at the National Museum in Dublin.

COUNTY LOUTH

To the north and east of Meath is Louth, the smallest of Ireland's counties, but with a wide diversity of scenery as well as historic treasures. Rimmed on the east by more than 30 miles of coastline overlooking the Irish Sea, County Louth extends from the banks of
★★★ the Boyne to a hilly stretch of land known as Cooley Peninsula and the Northern Ireland border. With the Mountains of Mourne on its northern horizon, the Louth panorama includes the busy market town of Dundalk as well as little seacoast resorts and fishing villages such as Baltray, Blackrock, Gyles Quay, and Greenore.

The varied course of Louth's history is illustrated by the Celtic and early Christian sites in the southern part of the county, such as the
★★ ancient abbey at Monasterboice, just a couple of miles north of the Boyne off the main (N 1) road. The focus here is on Muiredeach's High Cross, seventeen feet tall and one of the most perfect specimens in Ireland. Dating back to 922 A.D., the cross is ornamented with sculptured panels of Biblical scenes from the Old and New Testaments. The monastery grounds also feature the remains of a round tower, two churches, two early grave-slabs, and a sundial.

Just two miles away, on the Collon Road, is Mellifont Abbey, ★
founded by St. Malachy of Armagh in 1142 and the first Cistercian
abbey in Ireland. With the exception of the chapter house, little more
than the foundations survive, but it's worth a visit just to pause a few
moments in this tranquil setting.

County Meath's history is also reflected in the ancient River Boyne
town of Drogheda (pronounced "Drah-ah-da"). A complex of medieval
walls, gates, and churches, Drogheda was established as a permanent
fortified settlement by the Danes in 911 and quickly ranked with
Dublin and Wexford as a trading center. By the 14th century, it was
one of the four principal towns in Ireland, and continued to prosper
until Oliver Cromwell took it by storm in 1649 and massacred its 2,000
inhabitants. Happily, the population has grown to ten times that
number today, and the town is a thriving port and industrial center.

Several miles west of Drogheda is the little village of Donore, and
the site of the Battle of the Boyne. From Donore Hill, the ground
slopes down to the river, and it was here, on July 1, 1690 (the 12th of
July by modern calendars), that William III defeated the exiled James
II for the crown of England. Where the clashing sounds of battle once
roared, there is now the stillness of a pastoral setting. If the River
Boyne could talk, what a story it would tell!

NAVAN, Co. Meath

Restaurant

★★★★★ DUNDERRY LODGE
Off the Athboy Road, Dunderry. Tel. (046) 31671. If you have a great
restaurant, people will come, no matter how out-of-the-way the location is—that must be the philosophy of Nicholas and Catherine Healy,
owners of this secluded country restaurant. And the fact that people
think nothing of driving 35 miles from Dublin proves the point.
Actually, if you ask for directions at the time you call for a reservation,
you should have no trouble, but do allow at least an hour from Dublin
and be prepared to travel down narrow country roads for the final leg
of the journey. It will all be worth it, however, when you pull up into
the farmyard car park of this converted barn and byre.

Step inside and you'll be greeted warmly and invited to relax in a
cozy white-washed drawing room, crowned with a burlap ceiling, and
furnished with such eclectic curios as a pot belly stove, rattan rugs, old
newspaper clips, and modern art sculptures. The red-carpeted 40-seat
dining room has a country cupboard look, enhanced by spotlights and
floral paintings, but the main attraction, of course, is the food. It can
best be described as "nouvelle Irish," artfully presented light portions,

using the freshest of local ingredients, including herbs and vegetables grown in the restaurant garden.

The menu changes daily, but often features such dishes as lamb sweetbreads, feuilletes of fresh crab, mussels with pasta, chicken with lemon balm, filet of turbot with nettles, and herby rack of lamb. All are accompanied by glorious brown bread, a salad of many leaves and edible flowers, and a selection of perfectly prepared and just-picked vegetables. The dessert trolley is pure ambrosia, and the cheese board is an impeccably presented array of at least a dozen Irish-made cheeses, all identified and described with zest and enthusiasm by host Nicholas. What more can we say; it is definitely worth the trip from any direction. Open for dinner Tuesday through Saturday, mid-February through mid-December; also open for lunch Tuesday through Friday from April through October. *Moderate to expensive.*

SLANE, Co. Meath

Restaurant

★ ★ ★ **SLANE CASTLE**
Off the Dublin/Ardee Road (N 2). Tel. (041) 24207. Dating from 1785, this is the family seat of the Earl of Mount Charles. Less than 30 miles northwest of Dublin, it is situated on a 1,000-acre estate, overlooking the River Boyne, and adjoining the historic Hill of Slane. Designed by James Gordon, James Wyatt, and the distinguished Irish architect, Francis Johnston, this castle is known for its diverse collection of pictures, furniture, and works of art.

The present Harvard-educated Earl has also put his home to use for such practical 20th century purposes as a conference center, movie location site, and an outdoor rock concert venue (for international stars including Bruce Springsteen, David Bowie, and Bob Dylan). On many weekends, the castle also houses a nightclub, and, above all, throughout the year it is a fully licensed restaurant. The ever-changing menu focuses on local seafood, produce, and game dishes. Open for dinner on Wednesday through Sunday and for lunch on Sunday only. *Moderate to expensive.*

DUNDALK, Co. Louth

Hotel

★ ★ ★ **BALLYMASCANLON HOUSE**
Off the Dublin/Belfast Road (N 1). Tel. (042) 71124. 36 rooms. Mention Ireland in the most remote corners of the globe and many

people will smile and say "Irene Quinn of Ballymascanlon." The charming Mrs. Quinn has made friends throughout the world and many guests return year after year to "Ballymac," just to see this personable lady.

An old country mansion dating back to the early 1800's, Bally-mascanlon was formerly the home of Baron Plunkett, converted into a hotel by the Quinns in 1947 and extended in 1958. Now a Best Western affiliate, it stands on 130 acres of award-winning gardens and grounds—a peaceful oasis just three miles from the Northern Ireland border. Mrs. Quinn's sons, Brian, Oliver, and Peter, help to keep the hotel in tip-top shape and they also oversee a sister operation, the Imperial, a modern 47-unit hotel in the main Dundalk business district.

An ideal base for touring the historic counties of Meath and Louth and for cross-border visits, Ballymac is the type of place that you'll want to stay for at least three or four days, as Irene Quinn will undoubtedly make you feel right at home. Guest facilities include a sports complex with an indoor heated swimming pool, tennis and squash courts, sauna, solarium, and gym. *Moderate.*

Festival

May 20-29: Dundalk International Maytime and Amateur Drama Festival. Theatrical groups from all over Ireland and abroad compete in this annual celebration of spring. Ancillary activities include craft shows and horse races.

Directory

Dundalk Tourist Office, Market Square. Tel. (042) 35484. Open all year.

The Hard Facts

The Hard
Facts

PLANNING AHEAD

Costs

Ireland can no longer be considered a bargain destination, but it is one
of the best "value for money" countries of Europe. This point is
underscored year after year by Irish Tourist Board surveys, which
indicate that more than 95% of North American visitors report a very
high satisfaction level with all the components of their Irish vacations.

Although the Irish pound has had its ups and downs, it has recently
hovered around the $1.40 to $1.60 level, which compares favorably to
a decade ago when it cost $2.50 U.S. to buy one Irish pound.

Inflation in Ireland, which reached over 20% annually just a few
years ago, has finally declined to a much more manageable level of
currently less than 3%. In many ways, the Irish economy has turned
the corner and is heading out of a long and damaging recession. Irish
hotels and other tourist components are re-investing in the tourism
plant by building new facilities and expanding or refurbishing others.

The current Irish government is making determined efforts to
stimulate tourism by keeping transatlantic airfares at the most competitive levels of any European country—as low as $399 round-trip in the
peak summer season. The government has also encouraged hotels and
other tourism segments not only to hold the line on prices, but also to
offer discounts and bonuses for overseas visitors.

In the past three years, VAT (value added tax) or sales tax has been
dramatically reduced on tourism-related services in Ireland. Tax rates
for car rental, coach tours, accommodations, and meals, which had

been as high as the 18% to 25% level, are now pegged at 10%. That is still a considerable tax, but it is a lot lower than many other European countries.

Some VAT rates are even less, such as those on live entertainment (now 5%). The tax on tourist purchases, such as knitwear, tweeds, and other clothing items, is 10%, but on other items, like crystal, pottery, and jewelry, is 25%. Fortunately the Irish government has instituted a system to refund taxes on purchases made by non-residents (see the "Shopping" section to learn how to get a refund of the VAT on *all* your purchases).

With regard to accommodations, you can easily spend over $150 a night in the top-rated hotels and castles, or less than $15-$25 a night by sampling some of the bed-and-breakfast homes or guesthouses. The vast majority of Irish lodgings fall into the inexpensive-to-moderate range, between $50 and $100 for a double room. And that includes a full multi-course Irish breakfast for two.

Your meal costs will also depend on your own preferences. You can spend $10-$20 for a four-course lunch at a hotel or restaurant or less than $5 for some sandwiches, soup, or salad in a pub or coffee shop. In this regard, the Irish Tourist Board has given a helping hand by encouraging hundreds of restaurants to offer fixed-price "tourist menu" options. (See the section on "Choosing a Restaurant" for full information.)

If you can travel in the March through May period, you can also take advantage of a special "Springtime in Ireland" promotion which extends considerable price breaks to visitors. Savings of up to 35% off normal summer prices are offered on self-drive and motorcoach vacations. Hundreds of restaurants, shops, and other tourists services also provide discounts or special incentives to "early bird" visitors. The Irish Tourist Board publishes a booklet outlining all the springtime sales.

A DAY IN DUBLIN

★★★★★ 5-Star Hotel Room		★★★ 3-Star Hotel Room	
Room, per person in twin	£50	Room, per person in twin	£30
Breakfast, full Irish	7	Breakfast, full Irish	5
Lunch (restaurant or hotel, expensive)	15	Light Lunch in pub or coffee shop	3
Dinner (restaurant or hotel, very expensive)	25	Dinner (moderate restaurant)	15
Total	£97		£53
	(approx. $145)		(approx. $80)

A DAY IN THE SHANNON REGION

★★★★ 4-Star Hotel Room		★★★ 3-Star Hotel Room	
Room, per person in twin £40 (Includes full Irish breakfast)		Room, per person in twin £30 (Includes full Irish breakfast)	
Lunch (restaurant or hotel, expensive)	8	Pub Lunch	3
Dinner (restaurant or hotel, very expensive)	20	Dinner (moderate restaurant)	14
Total	£68		£47
	(approx. $100)		(approx. $70)

The following list will give you an idea of some average prices:

	£	$
Picture postcard	.15	.22
Theater ticket	5.00	7.50
Man's haircut	3.50	5.25
Woman's shampoo and set	6.00	9.00
Gallon of gasoline	2.80	4.20
Glass of wine in pub	1.25	1.90
Carafe of house wine in a restaurant	8.00	12.00
Beer/ale/stout in large "pint"-size glass	1.42	2.13
Beer/ale/stout by the glass or bottle	1.00	1.50
Shot or measure of Irish whiskey	1.20	1.80
A measure of brandy	1.55	2.30
Soft drink or sparkling water	.65	.95
Sparkling bottled water	.80	1.20
Cup of coffee	.60	.90
Irish coffee	2.50	3.75
Pack of 20 cigarettes	1.90	2.85

Climate

Contrary to the time-worn stereotype, Ireland does not have constant precipitation. The average annual rainfall is 30 inches in the east and 50 inches in the western mountainous areas. You are certainly apt to see some rain and occasional mist during your visit, but you are also likely to experience glorious sunshine, sweeping cloud formations, and beguiling rainbows. The weather can vary from town to town; it can also change from fair to showery and back again to fair in a matter of minutes.

The reasons for Ireland's erratic weather patterns are many. Being an island is certainly a contributing factor, as is the presence of mountains all along the Irish coast. In addition, Ireland lies in an area where mild southwesterly winds prevail. Most of the country also comes under the influence of the warm drifting waters of the Gulf Stream.

On the plus side, all of these factors combine to make a mild and equable climate year-round. A former U.S. ambassador to Ireland described the country as "the land of perpetual springtime." Even in January, the countryside is green, and palm trees and other forms of sub-tropical vegetation flourish side-by-side with the shamrocks. Snow is a rarity in the winter, and summertime temperatures that reach into the 70's are usually considered to be a "heat wave" by the locals.

Here are some of the average temperatures (in degrees Fahrenheit) you can expect:

	Jan. Feb.	April April	May June	July Aug.	Sept. Oct	Nov. Dec.
Day	47	51	61	66	59	49
Night	35	36	45	51	44	37

Because of her northerly situation, Ireland enjoys long daylight hours in the spring/summer months, with sunrise as early as 4:55 A.M. and sunset as late as 11 P.M. This gives a few "bonus hours" of daylight after dinner for extra sightseeing, a walk in the country, or a game of golf. May, June, and July have the longest days, with August, April, and September the next best months.

The sunniest months are May and June, with an average sunshine duration of between six and seven hours per day over most of the country. The extreme southeast is the sunniest area, with an average daily duration of about eight hours in May and June and over six hours in July and August. This doesn't mean you can't have sunshine in October/November or even in February/March. We've often gone coatless in Ireland during October or early November.

People frequently ask "What will the weather be like in Ireland in the month of 'X'?" The answer most often heard on Irish radio weather reports is that the weather will be "normal." And in Ireland that means unpredictable! Come expecting the worst; bring a raincoat, umbrella, and waterproof footwear. Then count your blessings if you never have to unpack them. And don't forget a pair of sunglasses. The Irish sun can be blindingly brilliant, especially if you are driving on a summer's evening.

Holidays and Special Events

The following are the public holidays on the Irish calendar for 1988. (Note: when Christmas falls on a Sunday, the official days off for most businesses will be December 26 and 27).

New Year's Day, January 1
St. Patrick's Day, March 17
Good Friday
Easter Sunday
Easter Monday
Start of Summer Holiday, First Monday in June
Mid-Summer Holiday, First Monday in August
Autumn Holiday, Last Monday in October
Christmas Day, December 25
St. Stephen's Day, December 26

In the past 20 years, a major annual festival has developed around St. Patrick's Day, March 17th, in honor of Ireland's patron saint. The entire country celebrates for a full week, from March 13 to 20, with parades in dozens of cities and towns, competitions for bands and choral groups, civic ceremonies, concerts, and sporting events. Visitors from many lands, including thousands from the U.S. and Canada, join with the Irish in this nationwide party. St. Patrick's Week also signals the official start of the spring tourist season, and many hotels, restaurants, and attractions open their doors after the winter hiatus.

For information on local festivals and events, see "Inside Information."

Travel Agents, Tour Operators, and Suggested Tours

In planning a trip to Ireland, it is wise to consult an expert—your local travel agent. Your agent, in turn, will work directly with airlines, hotels, and tour operators or wholesalers to plan your trip.

All good travel agents are members of the American Society of Travel Agents, or, in Britain, of the Association of British Travel Agents. If you don't know an agent, you can write for recommendations to:

ASTA, American Society of Travel Agents, P.O. Box 23992, Washington, D.C. 20026; or

ASTA-Canada, 130 Albert Street, Suite 1207, Ottawa, Ontario; or

ABTA, Association of British Travel Agents, 53 Newman Street, London, W1P 4AH, England.

The leading tour operator to Ireland is CIE, a company which has been in the business of planning vacations to the Emerald Isle for over

55 years. The initials stand for the Gaelic words "Coras Iompair Eireann" which simply mean "Ireland's Travel Company."

A branch of the Irish government, CIE operates a series of escorted sightseeing tours of Ireland, from four to fourteen days, using a fleet of new wide-windowed luxury motorcoaches. CIE also offers self-drive and city-based vacations, in addition to running the Irish railroads and bus networks. Our first visit to Ireland 22 years ago was via a CIE tour—and so professional, comprehensive, and enjoyable was our trip that we have been returning to and writing about Ireland ever since. You can't go wrong with a CIE tour of the Emerald Isle.

Here are a few suggested tours from the CIE program:

14-Day "Irish Tradition" Tour. Operates April through October, departing Shannon on Sundays. This is a leisurely-paced two-week itinerary which provides a kaleidoscope of the Emerald Isle—from County Clare to Killarney, Blarney, Cork, Waterford, Wexford, Wicklow, Dublin, Donegal, Mayo, and Galway. It's priced from $989 to $1219 and includes deluxe and first class hotels, full Irish breakfasts, 12 dinners, theater tickets, sightseeing admissions, professional guides, and many extras.

7-Day "Irish Heritage" Tour. Operates March through November, departing Shannon on Sundays. This is Ireland's most popular one-week tour, highlighting the main attractions, such as Bunratty Castle, Killarney, Ring of Kerry, Blarney, Waterford, Kilkenny, and Dublin. The price, from $555 to $755, includes top hotels, all breakfasts and dinners, plus theater tickets, medieval banquet, escorted sightseeing, and many extras.

4-Day "Taste of Ireland" Tour. Operates May through November, departing Dublin on Mondays. If you only have a few days or a weekend, this will give you a mini-tour of the Emerald Isle including Dublin's Fair City, Kildare, Shannon, Killarney, the Ring of Kerry, and Cork. It's priced from $372 to $438 and includes first class hotels, all sightseeing, and most meals.

For 1988, CIE will also feature the Dublin Millennium celebrations on many of its departures; other tours include weekend shopping vacations, St. Patrick's week trips, and itineraries which combine Ireland with England, Scotland, and Wales. For complete information, ask your travel agent or contact CIE Tours International, 122 East 42nd Street, New York, NY 10168, tel. (212) 972-5604 or (800) 243-8687; or 19634 Ventura Blvd., Ste. 305, Tarzana, CA 91356, tel. (818) 345-0148, (800) 331-3824 (CA only), and (800) 423-8866.

Some other tour operators which have interesting programs include:

Abercrombie and Kent, 1420 Kensington Road, Ste. 111, Oak Brook, IL 60521, Tel. (800) 323-1012 (IL), (800) 323-3602, and (800) 323-7308; for "Elegant Ireland" individual tours of historic castles,

SCENIC TOUR ROUTE

© FISHER'S WORLD INC., 1988.

country mansions, and the private homes of Ireland's nobility, not normally open to visitors, as well as tours centered on archaeology, arts, architecture, gardens, genealogy, literature, mysticism, and theater.

Brian Moore International Tours, 149 Main Street, Medway, MA 02053, tel. (617) 533-6683 or (800) 343-6472 or (800) 982-2299 (MA only); for castle hotel tours, golf, and shopping weekends.

Brendan Tours, 15137 Califa Street, Van Nuys, CA 91411, tel. (818) 785-9696 and (800) 421-8446; for coach tours and pre-booked self-drive trips.

Fairways Tours Inc., 800 Second Ave., New York, NY 10017, tel. (212) 661-0550 and (800) 662-0550; for golf trips.

Lynott Tours, 350 Fifth Avenue, New York, NY 10118, tel. (212) 760-0101, (800) 221-2474 or (800) 537-7575 (NY); for castle hotel tours and craft tours.

Horses and Ireland, P.O. Box 10, Clinton Corners, NY 12514, tel. (914) 266-3171; for horse riding tours and hunting trips.

OwenOak International, P.O. Box 472, New Canaan, CT 06840-0472, tel. (203) 972-3777; for golf trips and garden tours.

Ideal Itineraries

To see all of Ireland, you'll need at least two weeks and possibly three. If you only have a week, however, you can certainly cover the main highlights.

Here are a few ideal itineraries, with the number of days suggested for each city or touring center. Each tour starts or finishes near Shannon or Dublin, the two main arrival/departure points. You can ask your travel agent to design a trip based on your interests or the amount of time you can devote to Ireland.

One Week—Southern Coast: Shannon area (1), Kerry (2), Cork (2), Wexford (1), Dublin (1).

One Week—Main Highlights: Shannon area (1), Kerry (1), Cork (1), Waterford (1), Dublin (2), Galway (1).

One Week—East Coast: Dublin (3), Dundalk (1), Kilkenny (1), Waterford (1), and Wexford (1).

One Week—West Coast: Kerry (2), Galway and Connemara (2), Sligo (2), and Shannon area (1).

One Week—The North West: Shannon area (1), Sligo (2), Donegal (3), Shannon (1).

Two Weeks—The Coastal Circuit: Shannon (1), Kerry (2), Cork (1), Wexford (1), Dublin (2), Sligo (1), Donegal (2), Mayo (1), Galway and Connemara (2), Shannon (1).

Three Weeks—The Complete Tour: Shannon (1), Kerry (3), Cork (2), Kilkenny (1), Waterford or Wexford (1), Dublin (3), Dundalk (1), Sligo (2), Donegal (3), Mayo (1), Galway and Connemara (2), Shannon (1).

Information Sources

As soon as you start to think about travel to Ireland, you should contact the Irish Tourist Board. A branch of the Irish government, the board has a number of useful publications that will help you plan your trip including a general information brochure, "Ireland—The Unexpected Pleasures," a map, and calendar of events, plus guides for hotels and guesthouses, bed-and-breakfast accommodations, restaurants, golf courses, and other sporting activities.

The Irish Tourist Board maintains two offices in North America as follows:

757 Third Avenue   and   10 King Street East
New York, NY 10017 USA   Toronto, Ont. M5C 1C3 CANADA
Tel. (212) 418-0800   Tel. (416) 364-1301

Irish Tourist Board Offices in other English-speaking countries include:

Great Britain: 150 New Bond Street, London W1Y 0AQ
                Tel. (01) 493-3201
Australia: M L C Centre, 37th Level, Martin Place, Sydney 2000.
                Tel. (02) 232-7117.
New Zealand: Dingwall Building, 2nd floor, 87 Queen Street,
                P.O. Box 279, Auckland 1. Tel. (09) 793 708.

The board also has offices throughout Ireland, with its world headquarters in Dublin (see "Inside Information").

In addition to its basic factual brochures, the board publishes a handsome color bi-monthly magazine, "Ireland of the Welcomes." It spotlights new attractions, special places, noteworthy events, and interesting personalities, with sections devoted to "Where to Stay" and "Shopping" in Ireland. The magazine is also a source for good tips in planning a trip, and, after you return home, each new issue helps you to relive the joys of your vacation again and again. An annual subscription costs $14 in the U.S. and Canada, £6 within Ireland and Great Britain, and A$16 to Australia/New Zealand. For further information contact "Ireland of the Welcomes," P.O. Box 84, Limerick, Ireland.

If you'd like the facts and some personal attention as well, then you can't beat a unique service called "Inside Ireland." For a once-yearly fee, you'll get 28-page quarterly newsletters, chock full of news on the latest trends and developments in Ireland, plus specific evaluations of accommodations, crafts, books, and restaurants. You will also get a variety of free publications including a genealogical supplement and questionnaire, a shopping and touring guide, a directory of recommended lodgings, and discount vouchers. The cost is $30 U.S., $38 Canadian, or £25 sterling.

Best of all, you can take advantage of an on-going information service available only to subscribers. You can ask for tips on your itinerary, shopping; a run-down on the Irish lifestyle; how to meet a person of your profession, rent a house, or find a certain recipe. If you have already been to Ireland, you can seek help in following-up on purchases you may have made when you were in Ireland, locating a particular expert on a certain topic, investing in property, or even finding a long-lost cousin. The editors of the newsletter, who constantly travel around Ireland, answer all letters personally and will do so time after time, not just once. "Inside Ireland" is like having your own on-the-spot correspondent, reporting back exclusively to you. For full details, write to Brenda Weir, "Inside Ireland," Rookwood, Stocking Lane, Ballyboden, Dublin 16, Ireland.

What to Pack

Comfortable and casual clothing is ideal for Ireland. Slacks, sports clothes, and good walking shoes are "de rigueur" for both men and women; always pack a sweater or two, which you can add to or subtract from your outfits as required. It is wise for men to include a jacket and a few ties for dinnertime, especially in Dublin restaurants. Women should likewise take a couple of dresses for special evenings.

Light rainwear or all-weather coats are advisable at any time of year, and don't forget a folding umbrella, just in case. Sunglasses can come in handy, too, especially if you'll be driving. Take a bathing suit, as many hotels have health centers with heated indoor pools.

Allow some extra room in your suitcase, so you can treat yourself to a hand-woven tweed jacket or some knitwear.

Don't panic if you forget your favorite toothpaste or hair spray. Ireland has just about everything you are used to, albeit sometimes with different brand names. Do remember to pack any prescription medicines you may have, and take along a copy of your prescription, just in case you need to get a refill. If you bring your hair dryer, don't forget to have a transformer and converter plugs.

Certain items, like camera film and cigarettes, are quite expensive in Ireland, so if you are a photographer or a smoker, do come well-stocked.

Documentation

In most instances, a valid passport is all that is required to enter Ireland for a stay of up to three months. Although visas are required in some cases, they are not necessary for citizens of the U.S., Canada, Great Britain, Australia, New Zealand, and many other European countries.

Travel for the Disabled

If you or any member of your traveling party is disabled, be sure to obtain a copy of the Irish Tourist Board's 72-page booklet entitled "Facilities and Accommodations Guide for the Disabled." It lists all accommodations which are geared to access for the disabled, plus particulars on medical services, insurance information, useful addresses, and participatory and spectator sports.

PERKS FOR THE EXPERIENCED TRAVELER

Meet the Irish

Well over twenty years ago, the Irish Tourist Board pioneered in setting up a "people to people" program which has since been imitated by governments and tourist offices around the world. As popular as ever, the "Meet the Irish" services will introduce you to Irish people of similar professions or interests. All you have to do is fill out a questionnaire (which requires the exact dates of your trip, where you'll be staying, and age group, plus occupation, and/or hobbies), and the Board does the rest. Thousands of "friends for life" have been introduced through the "Meet the Irish" network. The service is free; just ask for a "Meet the Irish" application from the Irish Tourist Board, 757 Third Avenue, New York, NY 10017, tel. (212) 418-0800. Allow at least a month prior to your departure for processing the form.

Emerald Holidays

A "sky's the limit" theme is the keystone of the "Emerald Holiday" vacations available year-round from Aer Lingus. Priced from $4,500 per person for one week, this "best of everything" travel experience includes round-trip first class transatlantic airfare, the use of a Mercedes car, accommodations in suites at Ireland's top hotels including Dromoland and Ashford Castles, the Park in Kenmare and the Westbury in Dublin, breakfasts and gourmet dinners.

Many VIP extras are also a part of the package, such as airport escorts on arrival and departure, 24-hour exclusive telephone advisory service, individually guided walking tours, shopping counselors, and arrangements for boating, salmon fishing, and golfing on championship courses.

The Emerald Holiday program is designed to provide unlimited options to please all whims, so no two itineraries are ever exactly the same. If you want to be pampered, this is the "ultimate" of first class vacations. Arrangements can be made through your travel agent or directly with Aer Lingus, tel. (800) 223-6537.

Rent-A-Castle

Ireland's legendary castle hotels—such as Ashford at Cong, Dromoland at Newmarket-on-Fergus, and Fitzpatrick's in Dublin—are favorite overnight stops for everyone who longs to live like a king or queen. If you'd prefer not to share your realm with other guests, however, you can also have a castle all to yourself.

Renting an entire castle on an exclusive basis is one of the newest lodging concepts to be developed in the Emerald Isle. These castles differ from hotels in that they are all privately owned and usually require at least a week's stay. This type of rental arrangement, which is ideal for families or several couples, gives you a choice of having your castle with a complete staff (butler, chef, housekeepers, etc.) or on a self-catering basis. The prices range from $500 to $9,500 per week, depending on the degree of service you require; the castles can normally accommodate from 6 to 10 people.

Most of these regal estates have fairytale settings, with gardens and rivers or lakes on the property; some also have fishing or golf privileges, tennis courts, or even a resident deer herd. You'll find each castle described individually in the "Inside Information" section under Glin Castle, Glin, Co. Limerick; Lismore Castle, Lismore, Co. Waterford, and Mallow Castle, Mallow, Co. Cork (all full-service castles); and Springfield Castle, Drumcollogher, Co. Limerick; Carraigin Castle, Headford, Co. Galway; and Cloughan Castle, Loughrea, Co. Galway (all self-catering castles). Look also under Castle Matrix, Rathkeale, Co. Limerick, for a castle which can be negotiated for rental and is also available in the summer months on a bed-and-breakfast basis.

Overnighting at a Lordly Manor

If you prefer reserving a room to renting an entire residence, you can also "live like a lord" for a few nights at "Thomond House"—the seat ★★ of Sir Conor Myles John O'Brien, otherwise known as the 18th Baron Inchiquin. Among other titles, he is head of the O'Brien clan, a direct descendant of Brian Boru, the last High King of Ireland. He is also the only man in Ireland to hold a British peerage and an Irish chieftaincy.

The Rt. Hon. Lord Inchiquin welcomes visitors as "private house guests" into his fully-staffed Georgian-style manor on the grounds of Dromoland Castle. There are five deluxe bedrooms, each with private bath and views of the 400-acre estate, plus elegant drawing rooms, and a library for guests to enjoy. As befits such a grand setting, dinner is served by candlelight each evening, presided over by the lord of the manor himself. Minimum stay is three nights and rates range from about $750 to $1,000 per couple. For further information, contact Lord Inchiquin at Thomond House, New Market-on-Fergus, Co. Clare. Tel. (061) 71304.

Floating Hotel

The "Shannon Princess" is a floating hotel or "floatel" which combines the adventure of cruising on the storied Shannon River with the comfort of hotel-style accommodations. Weekly cruises are operated on board this 105 foot-long luxury craft from April through mid-October. With space for twelve guests, the boat is fully carpeted and features wood-paneled decor in the cabins (all of which have private toilet, shower, and sink). In addition, there is a restaurant with panoramic views, sun deck, stereo system, and library.

Priced from $1,680 per person, plus airfare and based on double occupancy, these six-night cruises include all meals, prepared by a cordon bleu chef; table wines on board; and use of sporting equipment such as bicycles and fishing gear. On-shore excursions in the itinerary include Birr Castle, Limerick, Galway, a medieval banquet at Dun Guaire Castle, and visits to historic villages and riverside pubs.

Further information, brochures, and reservations can be obtained by contacting Horizon Cruises, 16000 Ventura Blvd., Encino, CA 91436. Tel. (818) 906-8086 or (800) 421-0454, and (800) 252-2103 (CA only).

Rent a Cottage

For more than twenty years, renting an Irish cottage has proved to be an enchanting and economical way to spend a week's vacation. Located in country and coastal villages near Shannon, these cottages are a unique blend of modern comforts with thatched-roof designs and traditional furnishings.

You'll shop in the local markets, cook your own meals, sit by the hearthside in the evenings, and take part in the local lifestyle. It's an ideal type of lodging for long stays or for families with children. These cottages are available from February through October, priced from $120 a week to $400, depending on size and season. For full particulars, contact the Shannon Development Company, 757 Third Avenue, New York, NY 10017. Tel. (212) 371-5550.

GETTING THERE

By Air from North America

Transatlantic access to Ireland is the best it has ever been. Scheduled flights are offered by the Irish national carrier, Aer Lingus (from New York and Boston to Shannon/Dublin), and three U.S. airlines: Northwest (from Chicago/Boston to Shannon); Pan American (from New York to Shannon) and Delta (from Atlanta to Shannon and Dublin).

Connecting flights from all parts of the U.S. and Canada feed into these east coast gateways.

The four carriers use either 747 or L-1011 wide-bodied aircraft, and all flights depart in the evening and land in Ireland early the following morning, Irish time. Estimated flight time between New York or Boston and Shannon is approximately six hours; from Atlanta to Shannon is seven hours. Some flights continue east to Dublin, another twenty-five minutes of flying time.

If you'd like your trip over the Atlantic to be more than just another airplane ride, however, we heartily recommend the jets with the green shamrock logo. You'll feel like you have arrived in Ireland from the minute you step on board—from the welcoming smiles of the cabin crew to the lilting Irish music and the hearty meals with such delicacies as Irish smoked salmon, Bewley's breads, and Golden Vale cheeses. Aer Lingus has flown the Atlantic for over thirty years and has an excellent record for safety and year-round reliability.

And when it comes to extra special customer comfort, you can't beat Aer Lingus' first class service, with fully reclinable sleeperette seats and gourmet dining, or its super executive class with two-abreast first-class-size reclining seats. So popular is the executive class section that Aer Lingus recently added more seats, converting its upper deck into a non-smoking 12-seat configuration. With that extra touch of upstairs exclusivity, the new cabin is just like traveling in a private plane, but at very affordable prices.

Speaking of prices, Aer Lingus also sets the trend for a variety of fares to Ireland. Although fares vary from season to season and are always subject to change, here is a summary of the type of fares you can expect to pay from New York to Shannon, adding $30 round-trip for Dublin. (Certain restrictions apply, especially for Apex or weekend fares.) Remember that fares change almost daily!

First Class (one-way)	$1456
Super Executive (one-way)	$764
Economy (one-way)	$495 to $564
Apex (round-trip)	$399, $499, or $599
Weekend (round-trip)	$375

Aer Lingus offers a wide variety of "Discover Ireland" self-drive and motorcoach trips in conjunction with its fares, including long-weekend shopping trips, priced from $499 including airfare, first class hotels, most meals, and sightseeing. For the same price, you can also sign up for a fully-escorted long-weekend "pub crawl," an innovative new tour which gives you a "taste" of Ireland in more ways than one.

By Air from Britain and Continental Europe

Ireland is just an hour away from London and two hours from Paris or Frankfurt. With routes from twenty cities directly to Shannon, Dublin, or Cork airports, Aer Lingus leads the way to Ireland from Britain and continental Europe.

In addition, another Irish-based airline, Ryanair, flies into the three main Irish airports plus Waterford and Knock from various points in Britain and continental Europe. Other airlines which fly trans-European routes into Ireland include Air France, Alitalia, British Airways, British Midland Airways, Dan Air, Iberia, Jersey European, KLM, Lufthansa, SAS, Sabena, and Swissair.

Fares from London start at approximately £100 ($150) round-trip.

By Ferry from Britain and Continental Europe

If you prefer to travel by sea, there are a least a dozen car/passenger ferry services between Ireland and Britain or continental Europe. Offering a mini-cruise atmosphere, these ferries are equipped with comfortable furnishings or cabin berths, good restaurants, duty-free shopping, and spacious lounges where you can relax in a friendly atmosphere.

Prices average $30 to $90 per person, depending on your route, time of travel, and other factors. It is best to check with your travel agent for up-to-date details.

One point worth noting: Since Irish Continental Line (ICL) is a member of the Eurail system, you can travel free on the ICL ferries between Rosslare or Cork on the Irish side, and LeHavre and Cherbourg on the French coast, if you are holding a valid Eurailpass.

Here is a chart to show you the ferry services at a glance:

Irish Port	To/From	Sea Carrier	Duration
Dublin	Holyhead, Wales	B + I Line	3–4 hours
	Liverpool, England	B + I Line	8–9 hours
Dun Laoghaire	Holyhead, Wales	Sealink	3–4 hours
Rosslare	Fishguard, Wales	B + I Line	3–4 hours
	Fishguard, Wales	Sealink	3–4 hours
	Le Havre, France	Irish Continental	19–21 hours
	Cherbourg, France	Irish Continental	17–18 hours
Cork	Swansea, Wales	Swansea Ferries	10 hours
	Roscoff, France	Brittany Ferries	14–16 hours
	Le Havre, France	Irish Continental	21–22 hours
Larne	Stranraer, Scotland	Sealink	2–3 hours
(No. Ireland)	Cairnryan, Scotland	Townsend Thoresen	2–3 hours

From Britain by Bus

Even though no bridges have yet been built across the Irish Sea, there is a bus service linking major points throughout Ireland with leading British cities, using short sea ferry routes as part of the bus ride.

Operated jointly by Ireland's Bus Eireann and Britain's National Express, these "Supabus" routes include London to Dublin, Edinburgh to Galway, London to Tralee/Cork, and Swansea to Limerick. One-way fares between Dublin and London start at £26, or approximately $39. Onward connections to continental Europe can also be arranged.

For full details on the Supabus routes, check with Bus Eireann when you reach Ireland or with National Express when in Britain.

FORMALITIES ON ARRIVAL

Customs

The Irish Customs system operates on a Red and Green Channel format. The Green Channel is for people with nothing to declare, and the Red Channel for those with goods to declare.

If you are like most visitors and bring in only your own clothes and personal effects, choose the Green Channel. There are occasional spot check luggage inspections, of course, but in most instances visitors with normal amounts of baggage are simply waved right through. On the other hand, if you are bringing in a large amount of gifts for friends or dutiable goods, head for the Red Channel for a full inspection.

In addition to your luggage, you can bring in sporting equipment such as golf clubs or tennis rackets for your own recreational use while in Ireland. U.S. and Canadian visitors are also allowed to take in the following items duty-free: gifts to the value of $43; 400 cigarettes, one liter of spirits, and two liters of wine. British citizens may bring in gifts to the value of £252 (Irish), 300 cigarettes, 1.5 liters of spirits or three liters of aperitifs, and five liters of other wine. There is no currency restriction.

Prohibited goods include arms, ammunition and explosives; birds, animals, and plants; CB radios capable of amplitude modulation and transmission on certain frequencies; fireworks; hay and straw; pornographic material; illegal drugs; and meat and animal products.

Currency and Credit

Ireland has its own independent currency system. The "punt" is the basic unit of currency, although most people refer to it as a "pound," like Britain. Do not, however, assume that all pounds are equal! The value of the Irish pound is about 10% less than the British pound. In dollar terms, the Irish pound has fluctuated throughout most of 1987 between $1.40 and $1.60, while the British pound has been between $1.50 and $1.80. So it will cost you less to buy an Irish pound than a British pound. Because of this difference, British money is not legal tender in Ireland and vice-versa.

The Irish pound is symbolized by a £ sign; each unit of paper currency is called a "note." The pound notes, which are printed in denominations of £1, £5, £10, £20, £50, and £100, come in different sizes and colors (the larger the size, the greater the value). Each pound is divided into 100 pennies (or "100p," for short); coins come in denominations of 50p, 20p, 10p, 5p, and 1p.

Note: The value of the Irish pound fluctuates daily, so it is best to check the exchange rate at the time of your visit. As we go to press, it is approximately £1 Irish = $1.60 U.S.

Traveler's checks (spelled "cheques" in Ireland) and leading international credit cards, such as American Express, Diners, Mastercard (sometimes called "Access"), and Visa, are readily acceptable throughout Ireland. Hotels, restaurants, shops, gas stations, and car rental firms usually honor credit cards. (Note: Gas stations do not usually accept oil company credit cards, as they do in the U.S.) Most establishments display the symbols or logos of the credit cards they accept on their windows or shopfronts.

Personal checks, or "cheques," even when presented with your passport, are not usually accepted by banks or places of business unless you have made prior arrangements.

The hours of business for banks are as follows: 10 A.M. to 12:30 P.M. and from 1:30 P.M. to 3 P.M., Monday through Friday. Dublin banks stay open until 5 P.M. on Thursdays. The only banks that are open seven days a week in Ireland are at Shannon and Dublin Airports; the Shannon branch maintains hours from 6:30 A.M. or 7:30 A.M. until 5:30 P.M. year-round; the Dublin branch is open from 7 A.M. to 9:30 P.M., with a "bureau de change" remaining open until 11:30 P.M. in the summer.

International banks with branches in Dublin include: Bank of America, Bank of Nova Scotia, Barclays Bank International, Chase Bank, Citibank, and First National Bank of Chicago. Chase also maintains a branch at Shannon.

Getting into Town

From Shannon Airport, there is regular bus service into Limerick, the nearest city, and taxi service to all major hotels in the area. More than a dozen car rental firms also maintain desks at Shannon, since many passengers prefer to rent a car on arrival. For full details of all of these services, see "Inside Information" for Shannon, Co. Clare.

Passengers arriving at Dublin Airport can avail themselves of regular bus service into mid-town Dublin, taxi services, or car rental desks. Full details are outlined in the Dublin City section of "Inside Information."

SETTLING DOWN

Choosing a Hotel

From chic castles and cozy country inns to modern motels and multi-story full-service hotels, Ireland offers a wide choice of lodgings to suit every taste and every budget. The latest count indicates a total of 650 hotels registered with the Irish Tourist Board. To be registered, hotels undergo regular inspections by tourist board representatives; when a hotel passes all tests, it is entitled to display the board's official sign of approval, a stylized green shamrock with a circle around it. This symbol is also granted to approved guesthouses and bed-and-breakfast homes; always look for it, no matter where you stay.

Each hotel is also graded by the Irish Tourist Board, using a system which awards an "A*" rating for the top (deluxe) establishments; "A" grade to the next category (comparable to first class); B* to the next level, with B and C ratings down the line. The hotels and inns featured in this book fall mainly into the Irish Tourist Board's "A*" and "A" categories, with a few "B*" or "B"'s when they merit consideration for special reasons. In addition, when we have found guesthouses or bed-and-breakfast homes to be outstanding in a particular city or region, we have also included them in our listings.

Note: In general, the hotels and inns listed in this book are open year-round; all rooms (or the vast majority) have a private bath/shower. Exceptions are listed.

Unless stated otherwise, the restaurants described are open year-round, Monday through Saturday, usually for lunch from noon or 12:30 P.M. to 2 P.M. or 2:30 P.M., and for dinner from 6:30 P.M. or 7 P.M. to 9:30 P.M. or 10:30 P.M.

Shopping establishments are generally open Monday through Saturday, from 9 or 9:30 A.M. to 5:30 P.M. or 6 P.M. Pubs follow normal daily hours, year-round.

Most major credit cards are accepted by hotels, restaurants, and shops, unless indicated to the contrary.

If any variations from the norm apply, they will be specified under each individual listing. Every effort has been made to obtain the correct information, but all data is subject to change. In the case of lodgings and restaurants, telephoning in advance for reservations is ALWAYS recommended.

Hotels

★★★★★   5 Stars. Super deluxe establishment. BEST of the best.

★★★★   4 Stars. Deluxe. As comfortable as your own home, and better service.

★★★   3 Stars. Superior. Has the facilities that make it stand out.

★★   2 Stars. Excellent. There is nothing to complain about at all. Listed for the reason cited.

★   1 Star. Good. One or two things may be missing, but an O.K. place. Listed for the reason cited.

Hotel Cost Chart — Based on a Double Room

Very Expensive	$150 and up
Expensive	$100 up
Moderate	$ 80 up
Inexpensive	$ 50 up
Bargain	under$ 50

Rates usually include full Irish breakfast and 10% VAT (local tax), but do not include service charges, normally 10–15%

International Chains

The better known worldwide hotel groups, like Hilton and Holiday Inn, Sheraton or Inter-Continental, are not represented in Ireland. In the past year, however, Quality Inns and Comfort Inns have come to the Emerald Isle. Unlike many U.S. locations, these inns are not new and not purpose-built as Quality or Comfort Inns—they are hotels that have previously existed independently and have now come together under the Quality-Comfort banner. Some of them, like the Aghadoe Heights/Quality Inn of Killarney, the Imperial/Quality Inn of Cork, or the Blooms/Quality Inn of Dublin, have well established reputations in their own right. Wherever we have mentioned a property that has now joined the Quality/Comfort chain, we have made note for you in the "Inside Information" section. By mid-1988, plans call for Quality/ Comfort Inns to be represented in all twenty-six counties of the Irish Republic and in the six counties of Northern Ireland as well.

If you are a Best Western fan, you'll be happy to know that twenty-two Irish hotels are affiliated with this international group. All of these are independent properties, usually owner-managed. Where possible, we have also indicated which hotels belong to this chain on the "Inside Information" pages.

In addition, eight Irish hotels are members of the prestigious international group known as "Relais et Chateaux." These include the Park Hotel, Kenmare; Ballylickey House in Bantry; Longueville House in Mallow; Dromoland Castle in Newmarket-on-Fergus; Cashel House in Cashel (Co. Galway); Newport House at Newport; Rathmullan House in Rathmullan; and Marlfield House at Gorey. We have noted the Relais affiliation where applicable.

The Trusthouse Forte Group also has several properties in Ireland including the Shelbourne in Dublin, Acton's in Kinsale, and the Old Ground in Ennis.

Irish Hotel Groups

What Ireland lacks in international hotel affiliations, it more than makes up for with national chains of great repute. When choosing an outstanding hotel, you can count on the following names:

Doyle's—an "all Dublin" group, consisting of the Berkeley Court, Westbury, Burlington, Montrose, Tara Tower, Skylon, and Green Isle (deluxe and first class).

Jurys—Dublin, Cork and Limerick (deluxe).

Great Southern—Killarney, Galway, Parknasilla, and Rosslare (deluxe and first class).

Ryans—Dublin, Dun Laoghaire, Killarney, Limerick, Galway, Westport, and Sligo (first class and budget).

Hotel Service Charges and Taxes

All hotel accommodations in Ireland are subject to a 10% value added tax. This is normally incorporated into the rates quoted to you. Service charges, or gratuities to staff, however, are not built into the rates, and constitute an extra charge.

Traditionally, Irish hotels automatically added a service charge of 10-15% to all bills; this was meant to be divided among the housekeeping staff, behind-the-scenes staff, porters, and other personnel providing services to guests. It also meant that you did not have to worry about tipping or leaving a gratuity in your room for the maid.

In the past five years, however, a number of establishments, ranging from the Clare Inn and Longueville House to Ashford Castle, have waived the automatic service charge and switched to a "tipping is at the discretion of the customer" policy. Unless it is plainly stated on your reservation form or in your room, always ask. If gratuities are not added to your bill, then tip as you feel it is merited, in amounts equivalent to U.S. norms.

Choosing a Restaurant

For many years, eating out in Ireland meant going to a hotel dining room and ordering a full four- or five-course meal. Independent restaurants were a rarity until about twenty years ago.

Now, however, Ireland is blessed with hundreds of innovative and award-winning restaurants housed in a variety of settings. You can dine in a converted railway station or on a floating barge, as well as in restored barns, schoolhouses, farmhouses, mews cottages, castles, churches, and country manors. Ireland also has its share of new purpose-built restaurants with picture windows overlooking seafront panoramas.

A majority of Ireland's fine restaurants are small (thirty to fifty seats) and owner-operated, allowing for a large measure of personal service and prepared-to-order items on the menu. You are free to choose four- or five-course feasts, or one or two items on an a la carte basis. Because most restaurants are modest in size and volume, many also have their own vegetable, herb, or fruit gardens, as well as direct suppliers of seafoods, meats, and free-range poultry.

The keynote of Irish restaurants today is freshness, making the best use of local seafoods and garden produce. You'll be hard pressed to find Irish stew and corned beef and cabbage on menus, except as specialty items. Instead you'll enjoy such creative dishes as chicken sauteed in honey and lemon, wild salmon poached with champagne, stir-fried fillet of beef in ginger, herbed baby rack of lamb, or veal steak with redcurrant and port sauce. Above all, Irish cuisine of the 1980s means great seafood—from oak-smoked salmon to succulent Dublin Bay prawns, Galway Bay oysters, Kinsale or Wexford mussels, Dingle Bay scallops, and Donegal lobster and crab.

The excellent raw materials and fresh ingredients available have also prompted culinary entrepreneurs from many other lands to open restaurants in Ireland, from Japanese, Chinese, and Indian fare, to French, Italian, Belgian, Breton, and Dutch.

To help you select a restaurant to your liking, the Irish Tourist Board publishes a very comprehensive "Dining in Ireland" booklet with descriptions of over 700 restaurants throughout Ireland, plus their locations, prices, and hours. Every establishment listed complies to a code of basic standards set by the board.

In addition, about 300 restaurants, hotels, and cafes offer budget-stretching "tourist menus" at certain times of the year and during specific hours. These are fixed-priced three-course meals, nationally set at two price levels, approximately $7.25 and $9.75. Restaurants belonging to this group display a distinctive "tourist menu" chef symbol and post a daily menu in a window or showcase. A list of these places is also readily available from any Irish Tourist Office.

About three dozen of Ireland's best countryside dining establishments are affiliated with an organization known as the "Irish Country Houses and Restaurants Association." The standards of this group are very high and the members have won many nationwide and international culinary awards. A directory of these premises is also available free from the Irish Tourist Board, or by directly contacting the Irish Country Houses and Restaurants Association, Ardbraccan Glebe, Navan, Co. Meath, Ireland, tel. (046) 23416.

In the "Inside Information" section of this book, we have selected a number of restaurants of different types, settings, and price ranges. We think you will find each to be special for a different reason. We have assigned star ratings, according to our own subjective opinions and experiences, and we have also indicated the price range you can expect to pay.

Restaurants

★★★★★	5 Stars.	Out of this world!
★★★★	4 Stars.	Fantastic!
★★★	3 Stars.	Superb!
★★	2 Stars.	Excellent. Listed for special reason cited.
★	1 Star.	Good. Listed for special reason cited.

Restaurant Cost Chart — Per Person

Very Expensive	$45 and up
Expensive	$35 up
Moderate	$25 up
Inexpensive	$15 up
Bargain	under $15

Cost is based on a complete three- or four-course dinner, with tax and service charge; drinks or wine are extra. Comparable lunch costs would be 30% to 50% less in each case.

Restaurant Liquor Laws

In choosing restaurants in Ireland, you should be aware of several local factors. The first is that the majority of independent restaurants have only wine licenses. If you prefer a cocktail or a beer with your meal, it is best to choose a restaurant in a hotel or a restaurant affiliated with a pub; if you are not sure of the status of a certain restaurant, be sure to inquire at the time you are making a reservation. This situation may change soon, however, as legislation is pending which would allow most restaurants to serve liquor and beer as well as wine.

Gratuities vs. Service Charge

Like hotels, restaurants in Ireland have traditionally followed the ancient rule of automatically adding a service charge to your bill. In the case of most restaurants, this sum is usually calculated at 10% to 12½% of your food and drink totals; some of the major city restaurants add as much as 15%. If you feel that the service has been exceptionally good, then the custom is to leave a few extra pounds or small change, particularly if only 10% has been added on. This old system often appealed to visitors, especially when they were not too familiar with the value of the local currency.

In the last five years, however, more and more restaurants are not adding any service charge onto your bill, but rather are leaving the tip totally to your discretion. It is imperative that you know whether a gratuity is added in part, in total, or not at all, so that you can tip accordingly. Restaurants usually print their policy right on the menu; if you forget to look or can't find it, be sure to ask. Never be afraid to inquire; with the system in a state of flux, restaurant staff and owners are used to explaining their own policy. A simple question on your part will avoid the embarrassment of not leaving an appropriate tip; better still, it will also prevent you from tipping twice.

A word on restaurant taxes: all restaurant meals are subject to a government tax of 10% (reduced from a previous high of 25%). You don't have to worry about this tax being added to your bill, however, as it is already built into the food prices on menus.

Lunches and Light Meals

Restaurant lunches can often mean full three- or four-course meals. If you prefer to eat more lightly in the middle of the day, then a good alternative is the pubs. As you will learn in the following section, pubs are a good source of soups, sandwiches, and salads. If you prefer to eat in a hotel or restaurant, however, don't be afraid to ask for something that is not on the menu, like a salad plate, cold seafood platter, or a selection of cold meats and cheeses—most restaurants will gladly oblige.

If you are visiting Ireland in the summer months, don't forget that picnicking can be a delightful experience. You can pick up cheese, meats, and bread at supermarkets or local delis; better still, most hotel personnel will gladly prepare a picnic lunch for you with a few hours' notice. What could be a better luncheon setting than a sheltered cove along the Atlantic or a look-out point above a verdant valley? In addition, many of Ireland's great houses and sightseeing attractions have on-premises cafes or tea rooms which serve sandwiches and light snacks throughout the day.

We should also warn you that an Irish breakfast is a major event— bountiful portions of hot cereal, home-baked breads and scones, farm-fresh eggs, country-cured bacon and tasty sausages, all served with unlimited pots of coffee or tea. After such an early-morning feast, you may find that little more than a light snack is needed until dinnertime.

For your handy reference, we have indicated restaurant opening hours at the beginning of the "Inside Information" section; when a premise varies from the norm, we have made note in each specific case.

The Pubs

In Ireland, the public houses (or "pubs," as they are usually called) are much more than just a place to go for a drink. An Irish pub is a focal point, a meeting place for locals and visitors alike. Harking back to the days when neighbors gathered in a country kitchen to sample some home brew, many pubs are hundreds of years old and have been in the same family for generations. Such vintage pubs often doubled as general stores, and to this day some publicans still sell groceries, leather goods, and household supplies; several also offer other services.

A few proprietors have added televisions, pool tables, and dart boards to their decor, but little else has changed. The typical pub is a microcosm of Irish lifestyle—a unique hybrid of open hearth, meeting room, showcase of local memorabilia, news depot, and, yes, a congenial setting for some liquid refreshment.

To paraphrase a famous advertising slogan, you don't have to be a drinker to love the Irish pubs. Any tour of the Emerald Isle should include a few pubs, if only for a cup of coffee, a soft drink, or to listen to the spontaneous music sessions.

In recent years, pubs have shown their versatility by introducing inexpensive food service, primarily at lunchtime. Christened "pub grub," the selection usually includes homemade soups, sandwiches, and stews. Many pubs are also producing more gourmet-style fare, ranging from seafood pies, crudite salads, and vegetable quiches, to smoked salmon or oyster platters.

The "piece de resistance" of many pubs is the "snug," a private closet-sized room. Snugs are a throwback to the times before women's lib when it was not considered proper for females to drink at bars.

In those days, ladies with a thirst were discreetly served through sliding wooden windows connecting the bar counter to the snugs.

Today's imbibers—both male and female—use snugs for tete-a-tete conversations, private meetings, or just for fun, gingerly ringing a bell to catch a bartender's attention.

Pub etiquette is based on the "round system" in Ireland. That means that each person in a group or conversation takes a turn buying a round of drinks; this can require great stamina if you happen to be in a large party. You also pay as you go, not running up a tab. It is not customary to tip in bars, except for table service. You'll have no trouble getting ice for your drinks, but "on the rocks" is not a familiar idiom in most country pubs, so just ask for the drink of your choice "with ice." Similarly, the expression "with a twist" could produce unusual results, so just ask for a slice of lemon or a lemon peel.

At last count, there were over 10,000 pubs in Ireland, each with its own special charm and ambience. We have selected our favorites and listed them in the "Inside Information" section, and we have also ranked them according to the star ratings given below. No doubt you will find a few other special favorites of your own.

Irish Pubs

★ ★ ★ ★ ★   5 Stars. A quintessential Irish pub — make it a top priority.

★ ★ ★ ★   4 Stars. A real gem — worth going out of your way to visit.

★ ★ ★   3 Stars. Unique in many ways — try not to miss it.

★ ★   2 Stars. A fine specimen — do drop in, if you are near.

★   1 Star. A good choice — one of the best in this neighborhood or area.

Pub hours are standard throughout the country, seven days a week. The current schedule is Monday to Saturday, from 10:30 A.M. to 11:30 P.M., from May through September, and until 11 P.M. during the rest of the year. The only exception is the pubs in Dublin city, which close from 2:30 P.M. to 3:30 P.M. for what is traditionally known as "the holy hour." On Sundays, the hours are the same year-round, from 12:30 P.M. to 2 P.M. and from 4 P.M. to 10 P.M. Pending legislation, if enacted by the time of your visit, may change the closing time to midnight on Monday through Saturday nights.

The only exceptions to these rules are special festivals or celebrations when bar-extension hours are granted; bar service at hotels is always available for registered guests, even after midnight.

Shopping

As a country known the world over for its handwoven tweeds and knits, crystal, lace, linens, pottery, and other crafts, Ireland is a shopper's paradise. Part of the fun in touring Ireland is stopping in country shops and craft centers, watching craftspeople at work, and making purchases right from the source. Throughout the "Inside Information" section of this book, we mention specific stores and craft centers that are worth a special visit.

Before you begin your shopping spree, however, you should know that your purchases will be subject to Irish sales tax, called VAT (value added tax). This tax ranges from 10% on adult clothing such as tweed jackets, suits or hats, wool sweaters, and linen dresses (it's zero for children's wear), to 25% on crystal, china, jewelry, pottery, heraldic crests, and most souvenirs. The VAT is normally built into the price of each item, so the amount you see on the price tag has been inflated by the applicable tax.

Fortunately, as a visitor, you can avoid paying this tax, if you follow a few simple procedures. The easiest way to make a VAT-free purchase is to arrange for a store to ship the goods directly abroad to your home; such a shipment is not liable for VAT. However, you do have to pay for shipping, so you may not save that much in the end. If you wish to take your goods with you, then you must pay the full amount for each item including all VAT charges. However, you can have that tax refunded to you through a system called "Cashback." More than 1,000 stores throughout Ireland participate in this system.

Here's how it works:

1. Each time you make a purchase, ask for a "Cashback" voucher from a participating store or shop.

2. Fill out each form with your name, address, passport number, and other required details.

3. If you are departing Ireland from either Shannon or Dublin Airports, allow enough time to go to the Customs and Excise office; show the goods you have purchased in Ireland, and have your "Cashback" vouchers stamped and validated by a customs official.

4. You can then go to the "Cashback" booth at Dublin Airport (in the Duty Free Area) or Shannon Airport (in the Arrivals Hall), turn in your stamped "Cashback" forms, and receive cash payments in U.S. or Canadian dollars, British pounds sterling, or Irish punts, whatever you prefer. (Note: There is an administration charge for the "Cashback" service, payable by the visitor. The charge is calculated on a sliding scale according to the total amount spent on taxable goods).

If you are departing from Ireland via a ferryport, or if you don't have time to get to the "Cashback" desk before you leave, you can also mail your stamped receipts in post-paid pre-addressed envelopes to the

"Cashback" headquarters. Your refund, issued as a check, will be mailed to your home within twenty-one days. You can also request to have your VAT refund applied to your credit card account.

Note: E.E.C. citizens must spend a minimum of £266 (Irish) in order to claim VAT refunds.

Visitor Assistance

If you ever need advice, information, or help when touring Ireland, just look for the large green "i" (for information) sign. In the summer months, more than seventy local and regional tourist information offices are open in convenient locations throughout the country. Operated under the auspices of the Irish Tourist Board, each office is equipped to give detailed information on its own region and on a national scale. They also provide an accommodations reservation service, for a small fee.

All tourist offices are open Monday through Saturday during July and August, and many are also open in May/June and September. In addition, the larger offices in major centers are open year-round, including Dublin and Shannon Airports, and the cities of Dublin, Dun Laoghaire, Wexford, Waterford, Cork, Killarney, Tralee, Limerick, Galway, Westport, Sligo, Letterkenny, Mullinger, and Dundalk. Hours are normally 9 A.M. to 6 P.M., but extended hours and Sunday service are also usually available during the peak summer months.

Walking Tours and "Tourist Trails"

We find that one of the best ways to get to know an Irish city or town is to walk the streets and to chat with the local folk. To assist visitors, guided walking tours are available in some of the leading Irish cities— such as Dublin, Cork, Limerick, Waterford, Wexford, Kilkenny, and Sligo. There is sometimes a small charge for these walking tours, ranging from $1.50 to about $5. Descriptions of these tours are given for each applicable city in the "Inside Information" section.

In addition, many towns and cities have devised sign-posted routes which visitors can follow independently. All you need to do is buy a "Tourist Trail" booklet (about $1) from the local tourist office and fol-low the suggested path. As we go to press, the following towns and cities have "Tourist Trails": Birr, Cork, Donegal, Drogheda, Dublin, Ennis, Galway, Kanturk, Kilkenny, Killarney, Kinsale, Limerick, Lismore, Monaghan, Naas, Nenagh, Rathmullan, Sligo, Waterford, and Youghal.

Museums, Galleries, and Historic Sites

A good way to learn about the lifestyle and folklore of Ireland is to stop into the many museums, galleries, and historic sites in every corner of the land. Museums and galleries, particularly in Dublin, are usually free; if there is an admission charge it will range from about 75¢ to $1.50. Unless otherwise noted, museums in Dublin are open daily year-round, with slightly abbreviated hours on Sunday.

Throughout the countryside, you'll find hundreds of historic sites, many of them in ruins. Access is normally free, although a token charge, generally between $1 and $2, may be requested to help with restoration, guide service, or other projects. Attractions outside Dublin are often seasonal, opening in March/April until October or November. Ireland really only has one genuine theme park, the Bunratty Folk Park in Co. Clare. It is open year-round, with an admission price of about $5, which includes a tour of Bunratty Castle.

Great Houses and Gardens

About fifty of Ireland's great houses, castles, and gardens are open to visitors. Admission is usually on a seasonal basis, April/May through September/October, with fees ranging from about $3 to $5. About a dozen properties do remain open all year—these include Malahide Castle and Newbridge House in Dublin; Castletown House at Celbridge, Co. Kildare; Blarney Castle, Fota Island, and Bantry House in Cork; Muckross House in Killarney; and the grounds of Birr Castle, Co. Offaly.

If you are planning on visiting several of these landmark attractions, you can save yourself some money by purchasing a discount booklet, called "The Passport to Ireland's Heritage and Culture," which contains coupons entitling you to one-third off normal admission prices at more than twenty of Ireland's leading great houses and gardens. Priced at $5, the "passport" is for sale at all of the Tourist Information Offices throughout Ireland or by writing in advance to Bill Morrison, Senior Marketing Executive, Bord Failte/Irish Tourist Board, Baggot St. Bridge, Dublin 2, Ireland.

Places of Special Interest

★★★★★   5 Stars. You should make a trip to Ireland if only to see this. (Example: The Lakes of Killarney)

★★★★   4 Stars. You should plan your trip to Ireland around this. (Example: the *Book of Kells* at Trinity College)

★★★   3 Stars. You should plan your day around this. (Example: the Waterford Crystal Factory)

★★   2 Stars. You should detour a mile in order to see this. (Example: Dun-A-Ri Forest Park)

★   1 Star. You should detour a couple of blocks to see this. (Example: Mellifont Abbey)

SPORTS

Ireland is a sports-loving land. From Dublin to Dingle and Cork Harbor to Cashel Bay, sporting events dominate the Irish national calendar and character. And if there's one thing that the Irish love more than participating, watching, wagering, and talking about their own athletic pursuits, it's sharing their sporting passion with visitors. Here are a few ways you can join in the fun.

Equestrian

In legend and lifestyle, Ireland has always been synonymous with the horse. Where else but in this horse-happy country would you find racing forecasts and results on the second and third pages of the major national newspapers, right after the main headlines?

Once considered the sport of kings, horse racing in the Emerald Isle is truly the sport of the people. With twenty-eight tracks spread throughout the country, races are scheduled 270 days of the year, with daily afternoon or evening sessions during the summer months. Admission to any track is about $4.50; in some cases, reserved enclosures require an added charge. There is standard betting at the windows, but the most fun is in watching the fast-fingered bookmakers chalking up the odds on their boards in the "betting ring."

Besides racing there are at least 500 other horsey events held in Ireland each year, from the open fields of the smallest villages to the grandstands of major cities. Ever since 1864, the benchmark of all these gatherings has been the Dublin Horse Show, a five-day early August program of show-jumping, exhibits, animal sales, and parties (see "Inside Information").

For horse lovers who prefer to ride in the saddle themselves, Ireland caters to both experienced and novice riders, with a choice of more than 100 riding stables which supply horses for rent by the hour, day, or week. Prices average about $10 an hour, with or without instruction. Many stables offer courses in show-jumping, dressage, prehunting, eventing, and cross-country riding, while others specialize in beginners. With a few hours' notice, most hotels can arrange for horses to be delivered to the front door for guests. For specific recommendations, see "Inside Information" listings under Bundoran, Dublin, Foulksmills, Loughrea, and Sligo, as a start, and then ask the Irish Tourist Board for a complete list.

During the months of November through March, the hunting season is in full swing. More than sixty recognized packs, with famous names like "The Galway Blazers," "Tara Harriers," "Clare Hounds," and the "Scarteen Black and Tans," all combine to make an exciting seven-day-a-week hunt schedule for eager participants. A full day's sport—including rental of a horse—can be arranged for approximately $150 a person at a venue such as the Dunraven Arms Hotel in Adare (see "Inside Information").

For a special insight on all equestrian activities in Ireland, be sure to read the article by one of America's leading television and radio broadcasters, Ray Brady, elsewhere in this book.

Golf

As a country known for its forty shades of green, Ireland's golfing greens are naturally plentiful—more than 180 courses are spread throughout cities and towns, and near the seaside, mountains and lakes. Except for city courses on weekends, Ireland's golf facilities are seldom crowded and waiting times are rare. Greens fees, which are based on a full day's play (not just a round), are a bargain—averaging about $12 to $20.

One of Ireland's most well known courses is Portmarnock, designed in the style of the Old Course at St. Andrews. Laid out like a figure-eight by the Irish Sea near Dublin, this course is often the site of "The Irish Open." Visiting golfers also flock to courses at Bundoran, Galway, Killarney, Lahinch, Tralee, Waterville, and even Shannon Airport itself. You'll find specific recommendations under "Golf" throughout the "Inside Information" section of this book; the Irish Tourist Board can also supply you with a complete listing of all courses in the country.

Fishing and Water Sports

Ireland is the ideal setting for those who enjoy fishing as part of their vacation activities. The opportunities to cast a line are endless—from 800 rivers and lakes to more than 3,000 miles of indented coastline.

With a season that starts early in the year, salmon fishing in Irish waters is at its peak from May through September. The Ballynahinch system in Connemara and the river valleys of the Blackwater, Barrow, Corrib, Moy, Nore, and Suir are particularly known for salmon fishing. Seatrout fishing (classified as salmon by Irish fishery officials) is at its best in the shorter coastal streams of the Waterville Fishery in Co. Kerry, as well as the myriad waters of Connemara, Mayo and Donegal. A day's outing can cost from $15 to $35 for various licenses and rod permits, although a certain amount of salmon fishing is free or available as part of hotel or guesthouse amenities.

Brown trout, the most common and widely distributed of Irish freshwater fish, is found in every river, stream, brook, and lake. No rod license is required, but a permit (about $5 a day) is usually necessary, although in some areas like Co. Mayo, brown trout fishing is generally free.

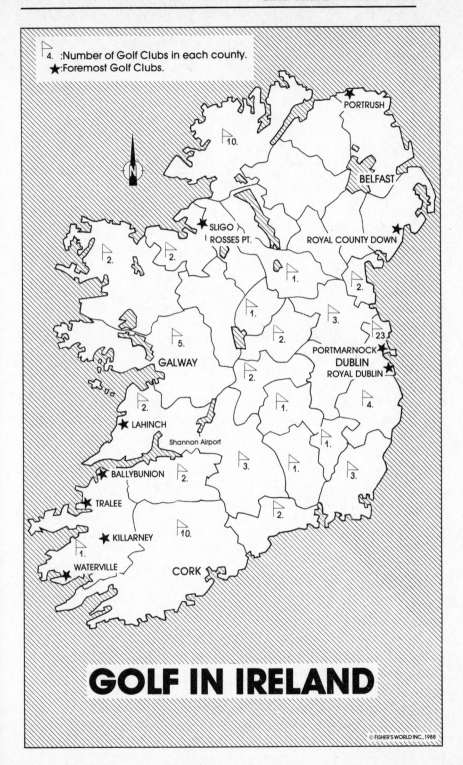

:Number of Golf Clubs in each county.
★:Foremost Golf Clubs.

PORTRUSH

BELFAST

SLIGO
ROSSES PT.

ROYAL COUNTY DOWN

GALWAY

PORTMARNOCK
DUBLIN
ROYAL DUBLIN

LAHINCH

Shannon Airport

BALLYBUNION

TRALEE

KILLARNEY

WATERVILLE

CORK

GOLF IN IRELAND

© FISHER'S WORLD INC., 1988

Ocean and sea fishing in Ireland is as varied as the coastline itself. Fishermen cast from the surf, piers, rocks, or boats, in pursuit of bass, turbot, cod, flounder, halibut, shark, or mackerel. More than 30 centers—from Kinsale in Co. Cork to Killybegs in Co. Donegal—offer deep-sea fishing day trips on 30- to 40-foot boats for about $25 a day.

Ireland also enjoys a long tradition of sailing, dating back to 1720 with the foundation of the Cork Water Club, now known as the Cork Yacht Club, and the oldest yacht club in the world. Throughout the summer, visitors are welcome to participate in or just watch the colorful festivities of weekend regattas and boat rallies.

Visitors can also rent cabin cruisers by the week or weekend for navigating the waters of the Shannon, the longest river (230 miles) in Ireland or Britain. One of the chief bases for cruiser rentals is at Athlone (see "Inside Information").

Other Sports

If you have the time, bicycling is a leisurely way to see the heart of rural Ireland along traffic-free (except for the cows and sheep!) roads and lanes. Almost 100 Raleigh Rent-a-Bike stations are scattered throughout the countryside, most of which stock 26 inch wheel models, as well as five-speed tourers, and some all-terrain vehicles. Rental charges are usually about $6 a day or $30 a week, and suggested bicycle tours are available free from bike shops, tourist offices, or hotels. For a complete list of dealers, contact the Raleigh Rent-a-Bike Division, TI-Irish Raleigh Ltd., Broomhill Road, Tallaght, Dublin 24, Ireland. Tel. (01) 521888.

If you happen to come to Ireland in the brisk outdoor winter months, November through March, you might like to try the Irish sport of "beagling." A tamer version of hunting, this is an on-foot sprint through the open fields of the countryside, with participants of all ages following packs of beagles in search of rabbits. Some clubs ask for a small fee, but beagling is basically a low-budget pastime, requiring only a warm outfit and stamina. It's a great way to meet the Irish, particularly on weekends.

Gaelic Games

No round-up of Irish sport would be complete without mentioning Ireland's traditional obsessions, the native games of hurling (one of the world's fastest field sports, played with wooden sticks and a small leather ball) and Gaelic football (a field game similar to rugby or soccer, except that the hands may be used).

With huge followings in each of Ireland's thirty-two counties (both north and south), these all-amateur sports are played every weekend throughout the summer, culminating in September with the All-Ireland Finals, an Irish version of the "Super Bowl." If you are interested in seeing a hurling or Gaelic football game, check at your hotel to see if one is scheduled during your stay; the hotel concierge should be able to arrange tickets for you.

LOCAL PRACTICES AND SERVICES

Business Hours

Most businesses in Ireland are open from 9 A.M. or 9:30 A.M. to 5:30 P.M. or 6 P.M., Monday through Friday.

Shops and stores normally adhere to the same hours, on a Monday through Saturday schedule. Many smaller cities and towns throughout Ireland also follow the practice of an "early closing day," which means that they are not open on one afternoon during the week, usually Wednesday or Thursday.

The early closing day for Dublin is Saturday, but the majority of shops remain open throughout the afternoon. Many shops in tourist-oriented towns, such as Killarney, often stay open as late as 9 P.M. or 10 P.M. and also maintain Sunday hours. In each case, it is wise to check in advance, particularly if you are heading to a certain area just to shop.

Gas stations are open seven days a week, from early morning until 9 P.M. or later, depending on the area.

Tipping

Although we have already discussed overall tipping for normal hotel, restaurant, and pub staffs, here are a few suggestions for other services. Tipping is not expected in shops, stores, and theaters. Taxi drivers are usually given a tip equal to 10-15% of the fare. Porters or bellmen at airports or train stations expect a tip of about $1 per bag. Doormen, if they perform some service like getting you a taxi, should get the equivalent of 50 cents to $1.

The hotel concierge, otherwise known as the head porter, should be tipped separately according to the assistance he provides, even when an overall gratuity is added to your hotel bill. Concierge services range from obtaining tickets for the theaters or sporting events to organizing a sightseeing tour or a rented car, as well as obtaining stamps, mailing your letters or packages, or arranging for a shoe shine. Generally, each time you ask for a favor, you should leave at least $1 on his desk, or $1 per day at the end of your stay, if he has performed many small favors.

Electricity

Ireland operates on a standard current of 220 V (50 cycles), a system that is common to most European countries and Japan, but is not used in the U.S. and Canada (110 V), Britain (240 V), Denmark, Sweden, Australia, New Zealand, or South Africa. Irish hotels usually have 220/110 volt sockets for shavers only.

To use the 110 V equipment that is standard in North America, you'll need both a travel transformer and adaptor plugs to fit Ireland's 3-pin (flat) or 2-pin (round) wall sockets. If none of the plugs you have bought fit, check with the hotel's front desk, as spare plugs are often kept for guest use. If you have a hairdryer that has a built-in transformer which can be set for 220 V or 110 V, you can do without buying a transformer, but you'll still need the adaptor plugs.

In hotels that are fairly new or newly renovated, you'll usually find hair dryers as standard equipment in the bathrooms, while many other hotels have a collection of hairdryers or other small appliances available on request.

Water and Drink

Irish water is not only plentiful, but pure and safe to drink. If you prefer carbonated bottled water, it is readily available throughout the country. You'll find international brands like "Perrier" as well as local bottled spring water such as "Ballygowan" or "Glenpatrick." All familiar soft drink brands, both regular and sugar-free, are on sale in Ireland.

Ireland also has a great reputation for "uisce beatha," translated as "the water of life," and Anglicized to "whiskey." There are lots of local brands worth trying, such as John Jameson, Paddy, Tullamore Dew, and Powers. Ireland is also famous for its unique dark brew, Guinness stout, as well as lighter beers and ales such as Harp and Smithwicks, and the alcohol-free beer, Kaliber.

Both Guinness stout and beer are sold on draft or by the bottle, but the locals think there is nothing like the freshly drafted drink. When stout or beer is drawn from a pump, it is put into a large glass and referred to as "a pint." A "half-pint" is an ordinary glassful. A drink or measure of whiskey is often called "a jar." So, if you are invited "to have a jar," you'll know what to order.

The word you'll hear most often, however, is "Slainte" (pronounced "slawn-che"), which is the traditional Irish toast. It means "To your health!"

Communications

Mailing postcards or letters from Ireland is as easy as going to the front desk of your hotel. Most hotels usually sell stamps and have postboxes on the premises. It costs 30p (about 45 cents) for an airmail postcard to North America, 46p (about 70 cents) per half ounce for an airmail letter.

If you are walking through a town or city, you can also look out for the sign "Oifig an Post," the local post office. The normal opening hours are from 9 A.M. to 5:30 P.M. or 6 P.M., Monday through Saturday, with an hour's closing at lunchtime in some cases. The General Post Office on O'Connell Street in Dublin is open from 8 A.M. to 8 P.M. daily, except Sunday when the hours are 10:30 A.M. to 6:30 P.M.

The Irish telephone system, Telecom Eireann, has improved dramatically in the past five years. Ninety-nine percent of all telephone numbers in Ireland can now be dialed automatically, without operator assistance. From your hotel you can also dial directly to most other countries including the U.S., Canada, all over Europe, Australia, and New Zealand. Reduced rates apply between 6 P.M. and 8 A.M. on weekdays, and all day on Saturday, Sunday, and public holidays.

Local calls from phone booths in Ireland cost 20p (about 30 cents); the coins required are 5p, 10p, or 20p coins, depending on the age of the phone booth. Be sure to read the instructions on the telephone, because you generally have to press a certain button to complete your connection, or another button to get your money back if there is no reply.

To obtain operator assistance, dial "10." If you need a telephone number, dial "190." You can make transatlantic calls from telephone booths by dialing "114" and then by reversing the charges or by using a U.S. telephone credit card. For the correct time, dial "1191," and for weather information, it's "1199."

The number to dial for emergencies of all kinds throughout Ireland is "999." Police are called "guards" in Ireland; that's short for "an garda siochana," meaning "guardians of peace."

Language

Although Irish (or Gaelic) is the official language of the country, everyone speaks and understands English. The use of Irish as a vernacular is limited to certain areas (known as Gaeltacht districts) along the south, west, and northwest coasts. However, many road signs and street signs throughout the country show placenames in both Irish and English. Public transportation destinations are also often shown in both languages. About the only two words that you will need to recognize are "Fir" (gentleman) and "Mna" (ladies), used on the doorways to public conveniences.

Time

From mid-March to the end of October, Ireland follows British Standard Time, which is the same as Central European Time. During the rest of the year, Irish clocks are set to Greenwich Mean Time, one hour earlier. With the exception of one or two weeks in the spring and fall, this means that Ireland is usually five hours ahead of North American Eastern time (i.e., when it is 5 P.M. in Ireland, it is noon in New York).

GETTING AROUND

By Air

Since Ireland is such a small country, it's unlikely that you'll be flying from place to place. If you do require an air transfer, however, Aer Lingus operates daily scheduled flights linking Dublin with Cork and Shannon. The equipment used is primarily Boeing 747 and 737 planes, and Shorts 360's.

From April through October, Aer Arann flies nine-seater planes on a regular schedule between Galway City and the Aran Islands. A number of local companies operate air taxi and charter services to other airfields within the country, using small airplanes and helicopters. It is best to inquire at Shannon or Dublin Airports for up-to-date information.

By Train

Irish Rail, a division of CIE (Ireland's National Transport Company), operates a network of swift and clean train services throughout Ireland. With the exception of flying, train travel is the fastest way to get around Ireland. Most lines radiate from Dublin to other principal cities and towns. Here are a few sample travel times for some of the most popular routes:

Route	Duration	One-way Fare	Round-Trip Fare
Dublin/Cork	2 hours, 30 minutes	$41	$50
Dublin/Galway	2 hours, 50 minutes	$31	$43
Dublin/Limerick	2 hours	$31	$43
Dublin/Waterford	2 hours, 35 minutes	$28	$38

Note: Round-trip journeys are based on one-week fares. Special reduced-rate weekend fares can also be purchased.

Rail Travel Passes

If your visit to the Emerald Isle is part of an overall European itinerary, you'll be happy to know that Ireland is a member of the Eurail network. This means that Eurailpasses are valid for unlimited inter-city travel throughout the Republic of Ireland.

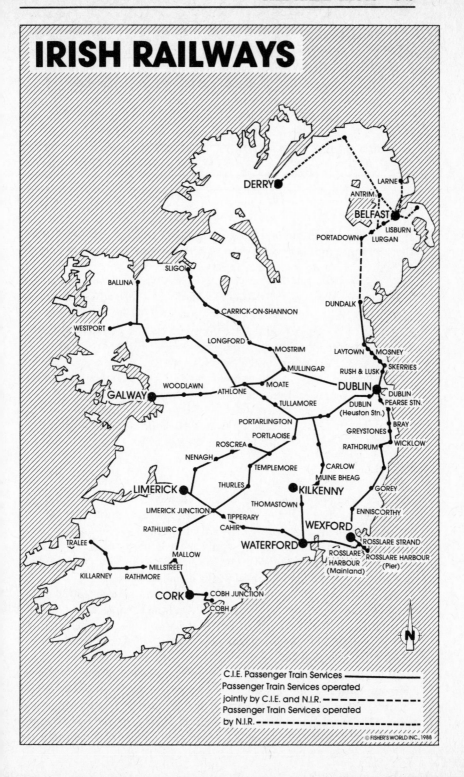

IRISH RAILWAYS

DERRY

LARNE
ANTRIM
BELFAST
LISBURN
PORTADOWN   LURGAN

SLIGO

BALLINA

DUNDALK

CARRICK-ON-SHANNON

WESTPORT

LONGFORD

MOSTRIM

LAYTOWN   MOSNEY

MULLINGAR

SKERRIES

RUSH & LUSK

WOODLAWN   MOATE

DUBLIN

GALWAY   ATHLONE

DUBLIN
PEARSE STN.

TULLAMORE

DUBLIN
(Heuston Stn.)

PORTARLINGTON

BRAY

PORTLAOISE

GREYSTONES

ROSCREA

RATHDRUM

WICKLOW

NENAGH

TEMPLEMORE

CARLOW

MUINE BHEAG

LIMERICK

THURLES

GOREY

LIMERICK JUNCTION

KILKENNY

TIPPERARY

THOMASTOWN

ENNISCORTHY

RATHLUIRC

CAHIR

WEXFORD

TRALEE

WATERFORD

ROSSLARE STRAND

MALLOW

ROSSLARE
HARBOUR
(Mainland)

ROSSLARE HARBOUR
(Pier)

KILLARNEY   RATHMORE   MILLSTREET

CORK   COBH JUNCTION

COBH

N

C.I.E. Passenger Train Services ——————
Passenger Train Services operated
jointly by C.I.E. and N.I.R. – – – – – – –
Passenger Train Services operated
by N.I.R. – – – – – – – – – – – – – – –

© FISHER'S WORLD INC., 1988

In addition, Irish Rail has its own travel pass, called "The Irish Rambler." Priced from £49 ($74), it entitles you to unlimited train travel for eight days throughout Ireland; the pass is valid for two weeks from the date of commencement of the ticket, so the eight days need not be in succession, but just within a two-week framework. A 15-day rambler (valid for a 30-day period) is also available, from £73 ($110). Tickets can be bought at any bus or train station in Ireland, or prior to departure through a travel agent or CIE Tours International, 122 E. 42nd Street, New York, NY 10168, tel. (800) CIE-TOUR or (212) 972-5600.

By Bus

If you want to use public transport to reach smaller cities and towns, then Bus Eireann, also a division of CIE, is your best bet. It operates an extensive system of "Expressway" buses on important non-rail routes such as Dublin to Donegal, Killarney to Shannon and Galway, Limerick to Galway, Shannon to Ballina, and Galway to Sligo. Individual cross-country fares range from £10 ($15) to £17 ($26), but, if you are planning to do a lot of bus travel, you can also avail of a special Rambler Bus Pass, priced at £49 ($74) for eight days and £73 ($110) for 15 days of unlimited travel.

In addition, there is a combination Rail/Bus Rambler Pass which will entitle you to unlimited travel on the trains and buses of Ireland for £62 ($93) for eight days and £90 ($135) for 15 days. This pass can also be purchased in Ireland or from CIE Tours International in New York (address above under "Rail Travel Passes").

By Car

Taking to the open road is one of the best ways to savor the delights of the Emerald Isle. Distances are short, roads are uncrowded, and visiting motorists can "meet the Irish" along the way. In many parts of the country, the only "traffic" you'll meet is herds of sheep or cows crossing the road. Ireland has the lowest traffic density of any E.E.C. country, and less than one-third of the density of U.S. roads.

It's true that the Irish drive on the left-hand side, but after a few hours of remembering to "think left," you'll be surprised how fast you can adjust. It is probably best not to drive too far after getting off a transatlantic flight, as jet-lag will slow your reflexes, but otherwise you should have no problem.

Ireland has very few highways; even the "main roads" can be narrow at times, and passing large trucks or turf wagons can be a challenge. Secondary roads, although fully paved, are no wider than country lanes. The national speed limit is 55 mph on the open country roads, but, in general, you will average about 35 or 40 miles an hour, and sometimes less. But that's what touring is all about.

IRISH BUS NETWORK

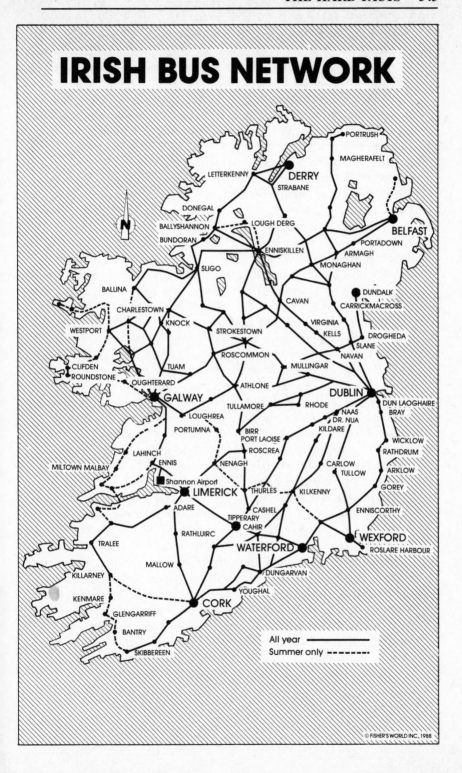

All year ————————
Summer only ---------

© FISHER'S WORLD INC., 1988

Here are some suggested driving times: four hours to drive between Dublin and Shannon (123 miles); four and a half hours between Dublin/Galway (136 miles); six hours between Dublin/Killarney (192 miles); and five hours between Dublin/Cork (160 miles).

You'll have no trouble following the road signs. Green and white signposts usually show distances in kilometers, while white and black signs indicate distances in miles. Many signs give placenames in both English and Irish. Major routes are designated with an "N" (for national road) and regional routes with an "R."

Unless you bring your vehicle, via Britain or Europe, you'll have to rent a car. As for documentation, all that is required is a valid U.S. or Canadian driver's license, or an international driver's license. To rent a self-drive car, as a general rule, you must be between 23 and 70 years of age, although some firms will rent to 21 year olds and others have no upper age limit.

Cars range from sub-compacts to full-sized sedans; stick-shift cars are the norm, but automatic transmissions are available at a higher cost. Rates, which are usually quoted on a weekly basis with unlimited mileage, vary according to car size, model, and time of year (prices also vary from company to company, so it pays to shop around).

The cost of a mid-sized stick-shift sedan will average from $200 to $300 a week, while a medium-sized automatic goes from $300 to $500 per week, and all rentals are subject to a 10% VAT or sales tax. The preferred method of payment is by major credit card; otherwise, you may be asked to leave a fully-refundable security deposit at the time of rental. Luxury Mercedes, station wagons, and mini-buses are also available at higher rates, as are the services of qualified chauffeurs, if you prefer to leave the driving to someone else. In every case, advance bookings are always recommended, particularly to get the best rate.

To reserve a car to await your arrival at Shannon or Dublin Airports, you can call your favorite international car rental company, such as Avis, (800) 331-2112; Budget, (800) 527-0700; Hertz, (800) 654-3131; InterRent, (800) 421-6868; or National, (800) 328-4300.

In addition, you should know that more than 20 Irish firms provide a year-round car rental service. Some of these companies are quite small by U.S. standards, but others are leaders in their field. One of the best—for good value and reliability—is Dan Dooley Rent-A-Car, with offices at Shannon and Dublin. This company also has a U.S. toll-free number: (800) 331-9301. Dan Dooley maintains a large range of new cars, with a wide selection of automatic models, at very competitive prices.

Here are some helpful general tips for driving in Ireland:

(1) Although all car rental companies are legally required to provide you with third party insurance as part of your rental charge, it is also very wise to pay a few pounds extra per day to take out collision damage waiver insurance as a protection against liability in the event of an accident.

(2) Wearing a seatbelt is the law for the driver and other front-seat passengers.

(3) Do not drink alcoholic beverages if you are driving; Irish laws are very strict and "breath-analyzer" tests are frequently given.

Compared to other aspects of an Irish vacation, the cost of filling the car tank with gas (or petrol) is very high. A gallon of gas is currently about $4. The only consolation is that cars are comparatively small and distances short; most tourists aim to drive about 100 to 150 miles a day, making a tank of gas last a lot longer than in the U.S. It might also cheer you up to know that a gallon in Ireland is an "imperial" measure, about twenty percent more than the U.S. gallon. Otherwise, be prepared to spend about $30 to fill a gas tank, an average touring cost of about $10 a day.

Gas stations are plentiful throughout Ireland, in cities, towns, and in remote regions. Most stations usually accept major credit cards, especially Mastercard (also called Access) and Visa; they do not, as a rule, honor U.S. gasoline company cards.

Some money-saving points: (1) The price of gas in Ireland can vary from brand to brand, station to station, and locality to locality. In other words, it pays to compare and shop around. (2) Irish car rental firms will give you a car with a tankful of gas, and they expect you to return it the same way. If you don't, they will add a re-fueling charge to your bill. Since the car rental firms usually charge the maximum rate per gallon for this convenience, it is wise to find a competitive rate at a local station and fill up the tank before you return the car. You'll save at least a few pounds.

Driving in Ireland has a terminology quite different from the usual American expressions—the most obvious difference is the word "petrol" (for gas). Other terms include "roundabout" (for traffic circle), "overtaking" (for passing), and "lay-by" (for scenic lookout point). Parts of a car also have different names, like "bonnet" (for hood), or "boot" (for trunk). A complete list of these terms and phrases is included in the "Useful Words and Expressions" section of this book.

By Ferry

Ireland has two passenger/car ferries, the Tarbert/Killimer ferry which connects Co. Clare to Co. Kerry, and the Passage East/Ballyhack ferry, linking Waterford with Wexford.

The two-mile Killimer/Tarbert route operates across the Shannon estuary and averages 20 minutes per trip; to make the journey between Clare and Kerry by road can require up to two hours and 85 miles of driving. The fare is $9 one-way and $13.50 round-trip. It operates on a drive-on/drive-off basis; fares are paid on board; no reservations are required. Here is the schedule:

SHANNON CAR FERRY	From KILLIMER Every Hour on the Hour	From TARBERT Every Hour on the Half-Hour
April/September	First Sailing	Last Sailing
Mon/Sat: 30 Sailings	7:00 A.M.	9:30 P.M.
Sundays: 26 Sailings	9:00 A.M.	9:30 P.M.
October/March	First Sailing	Last Sailing
Mon/Sat: 26 Sailings	7:00 A.M.	7:30 P.M.
Sundays: 20 Sailings	10:00 A.M.	7:30 P.M.

The passage East/Ballyhack ferry travels over the waters of Waterford Harbor and saves about an hour of driving time between the cities of Waterford and Wexford. The crossings, which operate continuously, are about ten minutes in duration. This ferry also runs on a drive-on/drive-off basis, with fares collected on board, and no reservations required. The one-way passage is $4.50; round-trip is $6.75. Here's the schedule:

PASSAGE EAST BALLYHACK FERRY	First Sailing	Last Sailing
April/September		
Mon/Sat	7:20 A.M.	10:00 P.M.
Sundays	9:30 A.M.	10:00 P.M.
October/March		
Mon/Sat	7:20 A.M.	8:00 P.M.
Sundays	9:30 A.M.	8:00 P.M.

Useful Words and Expressions

Although English is the everyday language of Ireland, the Irish have a special way of speaking that will enchant you. Often called "a brogue," this manner of speech adds a certain lilt to most words. As you travel

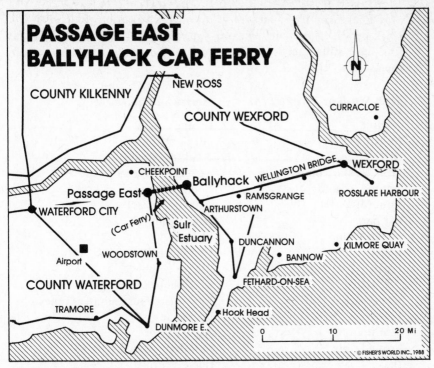

PASSAGE EAST
BALLYHACK CAR FERRY

COUNTY KILKENNY

NEW ROSS

COUNTY WEXFORD

CURRACLOE

CHEEKPOINT

Ballyhack   WELLINGTON BRIDGE   WEXFORD

Passage East

WATERFORD CITY

RAMSGRANGE

ARTHURSTOWN

ROSSLARE HARBOUR

(Car Ferry)

Sulr
Estuary

WOODSTOWN

Airport

DUNCANNON

BANNOW

KILMORE QUAY

COUNTY WATERFORD

FETHARD-ON-SEA

TRAMORE

DUNMORE E.

Hook Head

0   10   20 Mi

© FISHER'S WORLD INC., 1988

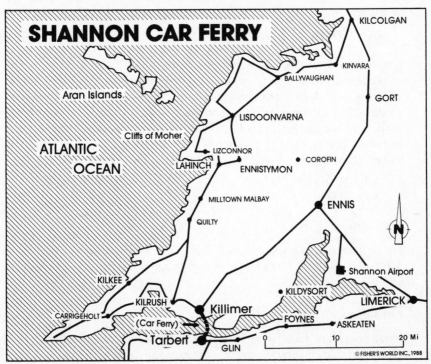

SHANNON CAR FERRY

KILCOLGAN

KINVARA

BALLYVAUGHAN

Aran Islands

GORT

LISDOONVARNA

Cliffs of Moher

ATLANTIC
OCEAN

LIZCONNOR

LAHINCH

COROFIN

ENNISTYMON

MILLTOWN MALBAY

ENNIS

QUILTY

Shannon Airport

KILKEE

KILDYSORT

LIMERICK

KILRUSH

CARRIGEHOLT

Killimer

(Car Ferry)

FOYNES

ASKEATEN

Tarbert

GLIN

0   10   20 Mi

© FISHER'S WORLD INC., 1988

around the country, you will also notice a variation in accents—the Cork people have their own sing-song pattern, the Donegal or Kerry folk have still other inflections, and the Dubliners are in a class by themselves.

Irish Word or Term	American Equivalent
angling	fishing
aubergine	eggplant
biro	a ball-point pen
(It is/was) a bomb	a great event or success
bonnet (of a car)	hood (of a car)
boot (of a car)	trunk (of a car)
car park	parking lot
chemist shop	pharmacy
chips	french-fried potatoes
crisps	potato chips
courgettes	zucchini or green squash
(the) crack is good	lots of laughter and good times
fairy	leprechaun
first floor	second floor
ground floor	first floor or main floor
(have a) jar	(have a) drink
head porter	concierge or bell captain at hotel

GOING HOME

One of the great things about returning home from Ireland is the opportunity to shop at Shannon's Duty Free Stores. All transatlantic flights either depart from Shannon or touch down at Shannon en route to North America. Shannon was the first duty-free shop in the world and continues to be a leader in the sale of Irish and international duty-free goods. (For complete information on the range of products in this duty-free zone, see "Inside Information" under Shannon, Co. Clare.) For Britain-bound travelers, Dublin Airport also maintains a well-stocked duty-free shop.

U.S. Citizens

On returning across the Atlantic, U.S. citizens are allowed to bring in $400 worth of duty-free goods, including 200 cigarettes and one liter of spirits or wine.

Canadian Citizens

Returning Canadians are allowed $300 (Canadian) worth of duty-free goods, plus 200 cigarettes, and 1.1 liters of spirits or wine.

British Citizens

As members of the E.E.C., British citizens may take home dutiable goods to the value of £252 Irish (but no one item may exceed £55 Irish in value); also 300 cigarettes, 1.5 liters of whiskey or three liters of aperitifs, and five liters of other wine.

"The Top Spots" — Ireland's ★★★★★ 5 Star Establishments
(In Alphabetical Order)

TOP TEN HOTELS

Ashford Castle, Cong, Co. Mayo
The Berkeley Court, Dublin City, Co. Dublin
Cashel House, Cashel, Co. Calway
Dromoland Castle, Newmarket-on-Fergus, Co. Clare
Fitzpatrick's Castle, Killiney, Co. Dublin
Jurys, Dublin City, Co. Dublin
The Park, Kenmare, Co. Kerry
The Sand House, Rossnowlagh, Co. Donegal
The Shelbourne, Dublin City, Co. Dublin
The Westbury, Dublin City, Co. Dublin

TOP TWELVE RESTAURANTS

Arbutus Lodge, Cork City, Co. Cork
Ballymaloe House, Shanagarry, Co. Cork
Doyle's Seafood, Dingle, Co. Kerry
Drimcong House, Moycullen, Co. Galway
Dunderry Lodge, Navan, Co. Meath
Ernie's, Dublin City, Co. Dublin
Le Coq Hardi, Dublin, Co. Dublin
Longueville House, Mallow, Co. Cork
MacCloskey's, Bunratty, Co. Clare
Patrick Guilbaud, Dublin City, Co. Dublin
Reveries, Rosses Point, Sligo, Co. Sligo
White's on the Green, Dublin City, Co. Dublin

TOP FOUR PUBS

The Brazen Head, Dublin City, Co. Dublin
Henchy's, Cork City, Co. Cork
Tynan's Bridge House Bar, Kilkenny, Co. Kilkenny
W. Ryan, Dublin City, Co. Dublin

INDEX

The letter **H** indicates Hotel listing, **R** a restaurant listing.

1989
Travel Planner

IRELAND

Patricia Tunison Preston
& John Preston

AUTHOR'S CHOICE

PROBABLE COSTS PER DAY FOR FOOD & HOTEL

Careful _$50_
Moderate _80_
Elegant _145_

PER PERSON

A WORLD OF TRAVEL PUBLICATION

The Travel Planner

This Travel Planner was created for the traveler who wants only the basic facts, with no embellishments, in a package small enough to fit into a purse or a back pocket. Perhaps we should have called it just that, "The Pocket Traveller" or "The Instant Guide". But, in any case, it is the perfect companion for anyone who wants information about places to go, how to make special arrangements, where to eat and a great deal more, with a minimum of fuss.

For the traveler who wants more, we suggest that you read the full guidebook from which this material has been extracted. When you need an indepth discussion of your travel destination, look to Fisher's World for the best in guidebooks, written for the curious, the careful, the committed traveler.

List of Maps

The World of Travel series is published by Fisher's World, Inc.
1988-89 Publications:

Australia & New Zealand	Hawaii	New York City
Bahamas	Italy	Pacific Northwest
Bermuda	Ireland	Paris/Northern France
Canada/East	London/England	San Francisco & North
Caribbean East	Los Angeles & South	Texas & Oklahoma
Europe/Major Cities	Mexico/Resorts	USA/Major Cities
Miami/Gold Coast	New England/Fall & Winter	

with more to come....

Map graphics by Marit Jaeger-Kanney
Cover design by Salie Clemente

© 1988 by Fisher's World, Inc.

ISSN 0894-2110
ISBN 1-55707-025-3

Inside Information

ADARE, Co. Limerick

Hotel

★ ★ ★ DUNRAVEN ARMS. Main Street (N 21). Tel. (064) 86209. *Moderate.*

Restaurant

★ ★ ★ THE MUSTARD SEED. Main Street (N 21). Tel. (061) 86451. *Moderate.*

AHAKISTA, Co. Cork

Restaurant

★ ★ ★ ★ SHIRO. Kilcrohane Road. Tel. (027) 67030. *Expensive.*

AVOCA, Co. Wicklow

Pub

★ ★ ★ THE MEETINGS. The Vale of Avoca. Tel. (0402) 5226 or 5291.

BALLINA, Co. Mayo

Hotels

★ ★ ★ THE DOWNHILL. Off the Sligo Road. Tel. (096) 21033. *Expensive.*
★ ★ ★ BELLEEK CASTLE. Off Castle Road. Tel. (096) 22061. *Moderate.*
★ ★ ★ MT. FALCON CASTLE. Foxford Road (N 57). Tel. (096) 21172. *Moderate.*

BALLYDEHOB, Co. Cork

Restaurant

★ ★ ANNIE'S. Main Street. Tel. (028) 37292. *Moderate.*

Pub

★ ★ V. COUGHLAN'S PUB. Main Street.

BALLYHACK, Co. Wexford

Restaurant

★ ★ ★ ★ THE NEPTUNE. Ballyhack Harbor. Tel. (051) 89284. *Moderate.*

BALLYLICKEY, Co. Cork

Hotels

★ ★ ★ ★ SEA VIEW. Bantry/Glengariff Road (N 71). Tel. (027) 50073. *Moderate.*

4

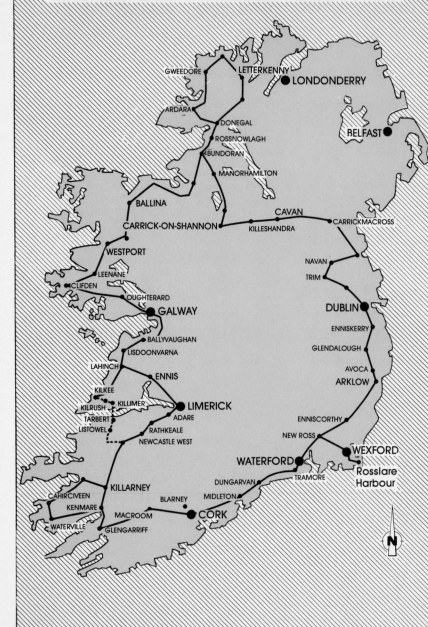

SCENIC TOUR ROUTE

GWEEDORE · LETTERKENNY · LONDONDERRY
ARDARA · BELFAST
DONEGAL
ROSSNOWLAGH
BUNDORAN
MANORHAMILTON
BALLINA · CAVAN · CARRICKMACROSS
CARRICK-ON-SHANNON · KILLESHANDRA
WESTPORT · NAVAN
LEENANE · TRIM
CLIFDEN
OUGHTERARD · DUBLIN
GALWAY · ENNISKERRY
BALLYVAUGHAN · GLENDALOUGH
LISDOONVARNA · AVOCA
LAHINCH · ARKLOW
KILKEE · ENNIS
KILRUSH · KILLIMER
TARBERT · LIMERICK
LISTOWEL · ADARE · ENNISCORTHY
RATHKEALE · NEW ROSS
NEWCASTLE WEST · WEXFORD
WATERFORD · Rosslare Harbour
DUNGARVAN · TRAMORE
KILLARNEY · MIDLETON
CAHIRCIVEEN · BLARNEY
KENMARE · MACROOM · CORK
WATERVILLE · GLENGARRIFF

© FISHER'S WORLD INC., 1988.

N

IRELAND

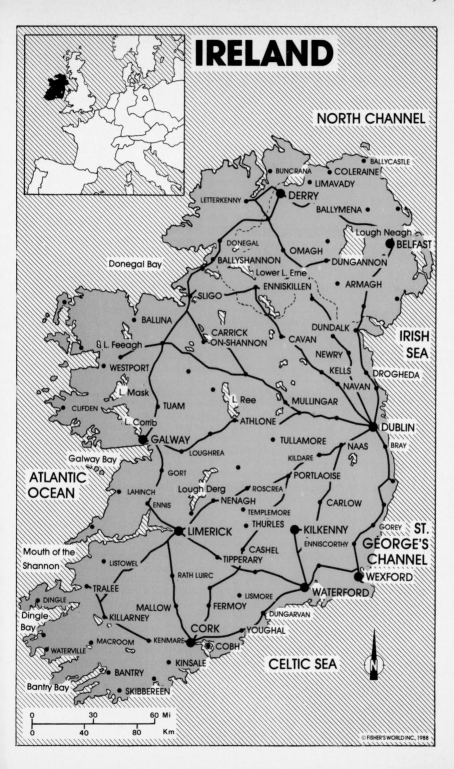

NORTH CHANNEL

BALLYCASTLE
BUNCRANA COLERAINE
LIMAVADY
LETTERKENNY DERRY
BALLYMENA

Lough Neagh BELFAST

DONEGAL OMAGH DUNGANNON
Donegal Bay BALLYSHANNON
Lower L. Erne
ENNISKILLEN ARMAGH
SLIGO

BALLINA DUNDALK
CARRICK CAVAN
ON-SHANNON
L. Feeagh NEWRY
WESTPORT KELLS
L. Mask NAVAN DROGHEDA
CLIFDEN TUAM L. Ree MULLINGAR
L. Corrib ATHLONE
GALWAY DUBLIN
LOUGHREA TULLAMORE BRAY
Galway Bay NAAS
GORT KILDARE
ATLANTIC PORTLAOISE
OCEAN LAHINCH Lough Derg ROSCREA
ENNIS NENAGH CARLOW
TEMPLEMORE
THURLES KILKENNY GOREY ST.
LIMERICK ENNISCORTHY GEORGE'S
Mouth of the CASHEL CHANNEL
Shannon LISTOWEL TIPPERARY WEXFORD
RATH LUIRC WATERFORD
TRALEE LISMORE
DINGLE MALLOW FERMOY DUNGARVAN
Dingle KILLARNEY YOUGHAL
Bay MACROOM CORK
WATERVILLE KENMARE COBH CELTIC SEA N
BANTRY KINSALE
Bantry Bay SKIBBEREEN

IRISH
SEA

0   30   60 Mi
0   40   80   Km

© FISHER'S WORLD INC., 1988

★★★★ BALLEYLICKEY MANOR. (N 71). Tel. (027) 50071. *Moderate to expensive.*

BALLYNAHINCH, Co. Galway

Hotel
★★★★ BALLYNAHINCH CASTLE. Ballinafad. Tel. (095) 21269. *Expensive.*

BALLYPOREEN, Co. Tipperary

Pub
★★ THE RONALD REAGAN. Main Street. Tel. (052) 67133.

BALLYVAUGHAN, Co. Clare

Hotel
★★★ GREGAN'S CASTLE. Foot of Corkscrew Hill. Tel. (065) 77005. *Moderate.*

Restaurant
★★★ CLAIRE'S. Main Street. Tel. (065) 77029. *Moderate.*

BANTRY, Co. Cork

Bed-and-Breakfast
★★★ SHANGRI-LA. Glengariff/Skibbereen Road (N 71). Tel. (027) 50244. *Bargain.*

BARNESMORE GAP, Co. Donegal

Pub
★★★ BIDDY O'BARNES. Donegal/Lifford Road (N 15). Tel. (073) 21402.

BUNDORAN, Co. Donegal

Hotel
★★★ GREAT NORTHERN. Sligo/Donegal Road (N 15). Tel. (072) 41204. *Moderate.*

BUNRATTY, Co. Clare

Hotel
★★★★ FITZPATRICK'S SHANNON SHAMROCK HOTEL. Limerick/Ennis Road (N 18). Tel. (061) 61177. *Moderate.*

Restaurants
★★★★★ MacCLOSKEY'S. Bunratty House, Bunratty Folk Park, Tel. (061) 74082. *Expensive.*
★★★ THISILLDOUS. 10 Firgrove, Hurlers Cross. Tel. (061) 74758. *Moderate to expensive.*

IRISH RAILWAYS

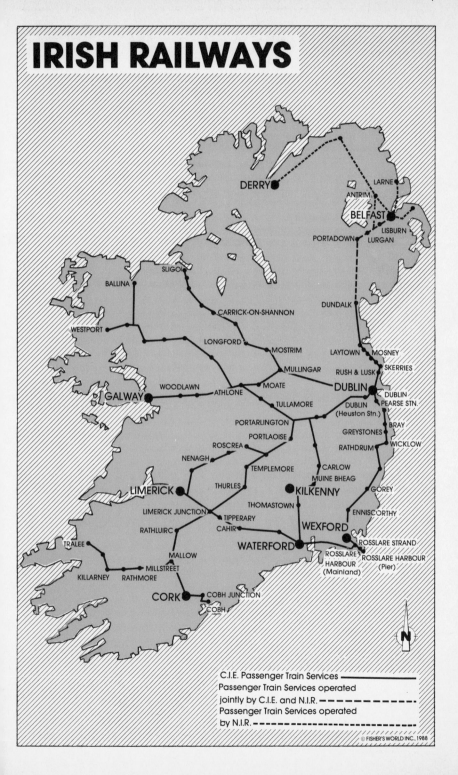

DERRY

LARNE

ANTRIM

BELFAST

LISBURN

PORTADOWN LURGAN

SLIGO

BALLINA

CARRICK-ON-SHANNON

DUNDALK

WESTPORT

LONGFORD

MOSTRIM

LAYTOWN MOSNEY

SKERRIES

MULLINGAR

RUSH & LUSK

WOODLAWN

MOATE

ATHLONE

DUBLIN

GALWAY

TULLAMORE

DUBLIN
PEARSE STN.

PORTARLINGTON

DUBLIN
(Heuston Stn.)

PORTLAOISE

GREYSTONES

BRAY

ROSCREA

RATHDRUM

WICKLOW

NENAGH

TEMPLEMORE

CARLOW

THURLES

MUINE BHEAG

LIMERICK

KILKENNY

GOREY

LIMERICK JUNCTION

TIPPERARY

THOMASTOWN

ENNISCORTHY

RATHLUIRC

CAHIR

WEXFORD

TRALEE

WATERFORD

ROSSLARE STRAND

MALLOW

ROSSLARE
HARBOUR
(Mainland)

ROSSLARE HARBOUR
(Pier)

KILLARNEY

MILLSTREET
RATHMORE

CORK

COBH JUNCTION

COBH

N

C.I.E. Passenger Train Services ——————————
Passenger Train Services operated
jointly by C.I.E. and N.I.R. — — — — — —
Passenger Train Services operated
by N.I.R. — • — • — • — • — • — • — • — • —

© FISHER'S WORLD INC., 1988

Pub
★★★★ DURTY NELLY'S. Limerick/Ennis Road (N 18). Tel. (061) 74861.

Evening Entertainment
BUNRATTY CASTLE. Limerick/Ennis Road (N 18). Tel. (061) 61788.
SHANNON CEILI. Banratty Folk Park, off the Limerick/Ennis Road (N 18). Tel. (061) 61788.

CAHIR, Co. Tipperary

Hotel
★★★ KILCORAN LODGE. Mallow/Cashel Road (N 8). Tel. (052) 41288. *Inexpensive.*

CARRICKMACROSS, Co. Monaghan

Hotel
★★★ NUREMORE. Ashbourne/Slane/Ardee Road (N 2). Tel. (042) 61438. *Moderate.*

CASHEL, Co. Galway

Hotels
★★★★★ CASHEL HOUSE. Cashel Bay. Tel. (095) 31001 or 21252. *Moderate to expensive.*
★★★★ ZETLAND HOUSE. Cashel Bay. Tel. (095) 31011. *Expensive.*

CASHEL, Co. Tipperary

Hotels
★★★★ CASHEL PALACE. Main Street. Tel. (062) 61411. *Expensive to very expensive.*
★★★★ DUNDRUM HOUSE. Dundrum. Tel. (062) 71116. *Moderate.*
★★★ RECTORY HOUSE. Dundrum. Tel. (062) 71266. *Inexpensive.*

Restaurants
★★★★ CHEZ HANS. Rockside. Tel. (062) 61177.

CAVAN, Co. Cavan

Hotels
★★★ HOTEL KILMORE. Dublin Road (N 3). Tel. (049) 32288. *Inexpensive.*

Pubs
★★★ DERRAGARRA INN. Butlersbridge, Tel. (049) 31003.

CLARENBRIDGE, Co. Galway

Pub/Restaurant
★★★★ PADDY BURKE'S. Ennis/Galway Road (N 18). Tel. (091) 96107.

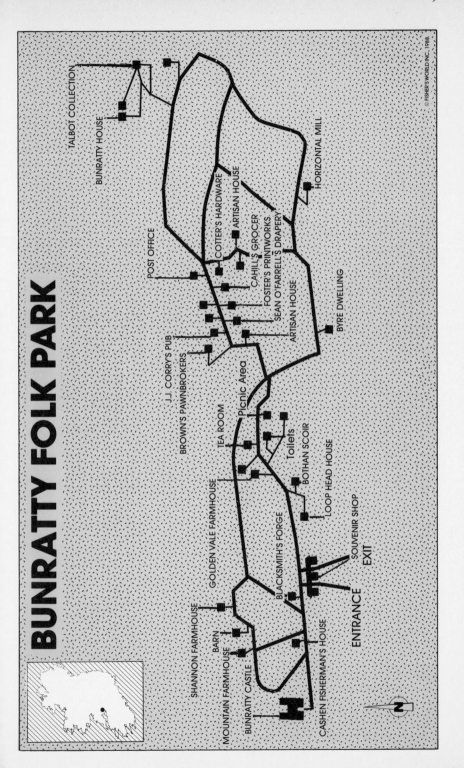

BUNRATTY FOLK PARK

TALBOT COLLECTION

BUNRATTY HOUSE

ARTISAN HOUSE

HORIZONTAL MILL

COTTER'S HARDWARE

POST OFFICE

CAHILL'S GROCER

FOSTER'S PRINTWORKS

SEAN O'FARRELL'S DRAPERY

ARTISAN HOUSE

BYRE DWELLING

J.J. CORRY'S PUB

BROWN'S PAWNBROKERS

TEA ROOM

Picnic Area

Toilets

BOTHAN SCOIR

GOLDEN VALE FARMHOUSE

LOOP HEAD HOUSE

BLACKSMITH'S FORGE

SHANNON FARMHOUSE

BARN

SOUVENIR SHOP

MOUNTAIN FARMHOUSE

EXIT

BUNRATTY CASTLE

ENTRANCE

CASHEN FISHERMAN'S HOUSE

N

CLIFDEN, Co. Galway

Hotels

★★★ ABBEYGLEN CASTLE HOTEL. Sky Road. Tel. (095) 21070. *Moderate.*
★★★ ROCK GLEN COUNTRY HOUSE. Ballyconneely Road. Tel. (095) 21035. *Moderate.*
★★★ HOTEL ARDAGH. Ballyconneely Road. Tel. (095) 21384. *Inexpensive.*

CONG, Co. Mayo

Hotel

★★★★★ ASHFORD CASTLE. Tel. (092) 46003. *Very Expensive.*

CORK CITY, Co. Cork

Hotels

★★★★ JURYS. Western Road. (N 22). Tel. (021) 966377. *Expensive.*
★★★ IMPERIAL HOTEL—QUALITY INN. South Mall. Tel. (021) 965333. *Expensive.*
★★★ ARBUTUS LODGE. Montenotte. Tel. (021) 501237. *Expensive, restaurant very expensive.*

Guesthouse

★★★ LOTAMORE HOUSE. Dublin/Waterford Road (N 8/25), Trivoli. Tel. (021) 822344. *Inexpensive.*

Restaurants

★★★★ LOVETTS. Churchyard Lane, off Well Road. Tel. (021) 294909. *Expensive.*
★★★ JACQUES. 9 Phoenix Street. Tel. (021) 502387. *Moderate.*
★★★ OYSTER TAVERN. Market Lane, off 56 Patrick Street. Tel. (021) 272716. *Moderate.*

Pubs

★★★★★ HENCHY'S. 40 St. Luke's. Tel. (021) 501115.
★★★★ MUTTON LANE INN. 3 Mutton Lane, off St. Patrick Street. Tel. (021) 273471.
★★★ THE OFFICE. 5 Sullivan's Quay. Tel. (021) 967652.
★★★ LeCHATEAU. 93 St. Patrick Street. Tel. (021) 203701.
★★★ MAGUIRE'S PENNYFARTHING INN. Daunt Square, Grand Parade. Tel. (021) 502825.
★★★ DeLACY HOUSE. 74 Oliver Plunkett Street. Tel. (021) 270074.

Theatres/Entertainment

CORK OPERA HOUSE. Emmet Place. Tel. (021) 276357 or 270022.
EVERYMAN PLAYHOUSE. Father Matthew Street, off South Mall. Tel. (021) 276287.
IVERNIA THEATRE. Grand Parade. Tel. (021) 272703 or 273156.

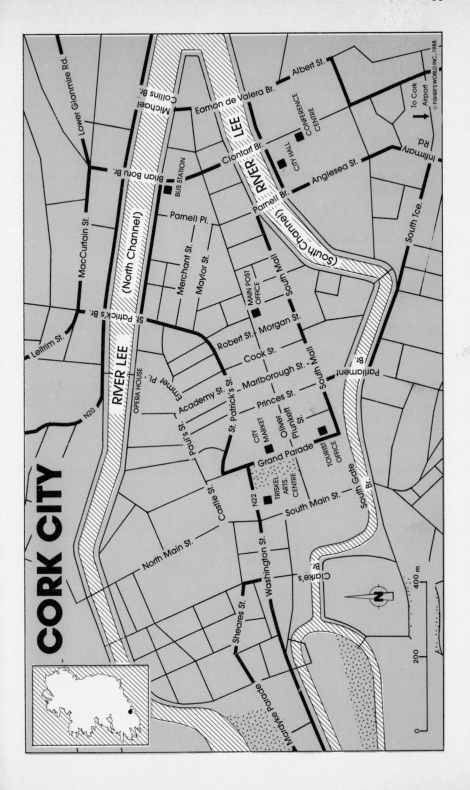

CORK CITY

© FISHER'S WORLD INC., 1988.

Lower Glanmire Rd.

Michael Collins Br.

Albert St.

Eamon de Valera Br.

To Cork Airport

Brian Boru Br.

Clontarf Br.

CONFERENCE CENTRE

RIVER LEE

Inniscarra Rd.

BUS STATION

CITY HALL

Anglesea St.

MacCurtain St.

Parnell Br.

Parnell Pl.

(North Channel)

(South Channel)

South Tce.

Merchant St.

Maylor St.

MAIN POST OFFICE

South Mall

Leitrim St.

St. Patrick's Br.

RIVER LEE

Robert St. Morgan St.

Cook St.

South Mall

Emmet Pl.

Marlborough St.

N20

OPERA HOUSE

Academy St.

St. Patrick's St.

Princes St.

Parliament Br.

Paul's St.

CITY MARKET

Oliver Plunkett St.

TOURIST OFFICE

Castle St.

Grand Parade

N22

TRISKEL ARTS CENTRE

South Gate Br.

North Main St.

South Main St.

Washington St.

Clarke's Br.

Sheares St.

N

Marlyke Parade

0   200   400 m

Getting Around

Bus Eireann provides regularly scheduled bus service throughout Cork City and its environs, from 7 A.M. to 11 P.M. on Monday through Saturday, and slightly shorter hours on Sunday. The flat fare is approximately 80 cents. Transfers to/from Cork Airport are available for about $2 each way. For further information, call Tel. (021) 503399.

Festivals

April 27-May 1: International Choral and Folk Dance Festival.
October 28-31: Guinness Jazz Festival.

Directory

The Cork Tourist Office, Grand Parade. Tel. (021) 273251.
Irish Rail, Kent Station, Lower Glanmire Road. Tel. (021) 504422.
Bus Eireann, Parnell Place, off St. Patrick Street. Tel. (021) 503339.

COROFIN, Co. Clare

Restaurants

★★★★ MARYSE AND GILBERT'S. Tel. (065) 27660. *Moderate.*
★★★ BOFFY QUINN'S VILLAGE INN. Main Street. Tel. (065) 27627. *Moderate.*

DINGLE, Co. Kerry

Hotel

★★ THE NEW SCEILIG—QUALITY INN. Annascaul Road. Tel (066) 51144. *Moderate.*

Restaurants

★★★★★ DOYLE'S SEAFOOD. John Street. Tel. (066) 51174. *Moderate.*
★★★★ THE HALF DOOR. John Street. Tel. (066) 51600. *Moderate.*
★★★ WHELAN'S. Main Street. Tel. (066) 51622. *Moderate.*

Pubs

★★★ O'FLAHERTY'S. Bridge Street. Tel. (066) 51461.
★★★ RICHARD MacDONNELL. Green Street.

DONEGAL, Co. Donegal

Hotels

★★★★ ERNAN PARK. St. Ernan's Islands. Tel. (073) 21065. *Moderate.*
★★★ THE ABBEY. The Diamond. Tel. (073) 21014. *Inexpensive.*
★★★ HYLAND CENTRAL. The Diamond. Tel. (073) 21027. *Inexpensive.*

DOOLIN, Co. Clare

Restaurants

★★★ KILLILAGH HOUSE. Roadford. Tel. (065) 74183.
★★★ THE IVY COTTAGE. Tel. (065) 74244.

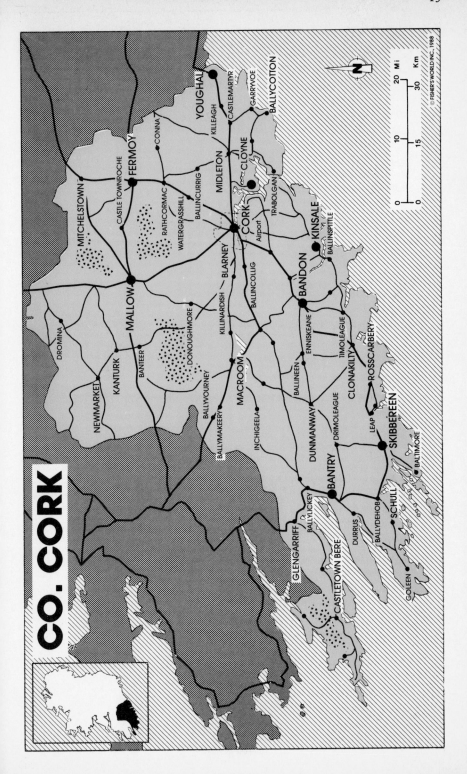

CO. CORK

Youghal
Castlemartyr
Garryvoe
Ballycotton
Killeagh
Conna
Castletownroche
Fermoy
Mitchelstown
Castle Townroche
Rathcormac
Ballincurrig
Midleton
Cloyne
Watergrasshill
Ballincollig
Cork
Airport
Trabolgan
Blarney
Mallow
Dromina
Banteer
Killinardish
Ballincollig
Bandon
Kinsale
Ballinspittle
Donoughmore
Kanturk
Newmarket
Ballyvourney
Macroom
Ballymakeery
Inchigeela
Ballineen
Enniskeane
Timoleague
Clonakilty
Rosscarbery
Dunmanway
Drimoleague
Leap
Skibbereen
Baltimore
Bantry
Ballydehob
Schull
Goleen
Glengarriff
Ballylickey
Castletown Bere
Durrus

20 Mi
30 Km
10
15
0
0

© FISHER'S WORLD INC. 1988

Pub
★★★ GUS O'CONNOR. Tel. (065) 74168.

DOWNINGS, Co. Donegal

Hotels
★★★ ROSAPENNA GOLF HOTEL. Atlantic Drive. Tel. (074) 55301. *Inexpensive.*

DROMAHAIR, Co. Leitrim

Guesthouse
★★★★ DRUMLEASE GLEBE HOUSE. Tel. (071) 64141. *Moderate.*

Pub
★★★ STANFORD VILLAGE INN. Main Street. Tel. (071) 64140.

DRUMCOLLOGHER, Co. Limerick

Castle-for-Rent
SPRINGFIELD CASTLE. Tel. (063) 83162.

DUBLIN CITY, Co. Dublin

Hotels
★★★★★ BERKELEY COURT. Landsdowne Road. Tel. (01) 601711. *Very Expensive.*
★★★★★ JURYS. Pembroke Road. Tel. (01) 605000. *Expensive.*
★★★★★ THE SHELBOURNE. 27 St. Stephen's Green. Tel. (01) 766471. *Very expensive.*
★★★★★ WESTBURY. Grafton Street. Tel. (01) 791122. *Very expensive.*
★★★★ THE BURLINGTON. Upper Leeson Street. Tel. (01) 605222. *Expensive.*
★★★★ THE GRESHAM. O'Connell Street. Tel. (01) 746881. *Moderate to expensive.*
★★★★ BLOOMS HOTEL—QUALITY INN. Anglesea Street. Tel. (01) 715622. *Moderate to expensive.*
★★★ BUSWELL'S. 25 Molesworth Street. Tel. (01) 764013. *Moderate.*
★★★ TARA TOWER. Merrion Road. Tel. (01) 694666. *Inexpensive.*
★★★ MONTROSE. Stillorgan Road. Tel. (01) 693311. *Inexpensive.*
★★★ SKYLON. Upper Drumcondra Road. Tel. (01) 379121. *Inexpensive.*

Guesthouses and Private Homes
★★★ ARIEL HOUSE. 52 Landsdowne Road. Tel. (01) 685512. *Inexpensive.*
★★★ MOUNT HERBERT. 7 Herbert Road. Tel. (01) 684321. *Inexpensive.*
★★★ GEORGIAN HOUSE. 20 Lower Baggot Street. Tel. (01) 604300. *Inexpensive.*
★★★ ANGLESEA TOWN HOUSE. 63 Anglesea Road. Tel. (01) 683877. *Inexpensive.*

Restaurants

★★★★★ ERNIE'S. Mulberry Gardens, Donnybrook. Tel. (01) 693300. *Very expensive.*

★★★★★ LE COQ HARDI. 35 Pembroke Road. Tel. (01) 684130. *Very expensive.*

★★★★★ PATRICK GUILBAUD. 46 James Place, off Lower Baggot Street. Tel. (01) 764192. *Very expensive.*

★★★★★ WHITE'S ON THE GREEN. 119 St. Stephen's Green. Tel. (01) 751975. *Very expensive.*

★★★★ CELTIC MEWS. 109-A Lower Baggot Street, at the corner of Lad Lane. Tel. (01) 760796. *Expensive.*

★★★★ DOBBINS. 15 Stephen's Lane, off Upper Mount Street. Tel. (01) 764679. *Moderate to expensive.*

★★★★ THE GREY DOOR. 23 Upper Pembroke Street. Tel. (01) 763286. *Expensive.*

★★★★ LOCKS. 1 Windsor Terrace, Portobello. Tel. (01) 752025. *Moderate to expensive.*

★★★★ RAJDOOT TANDOORI. 26/28 Clarendon Street. Tel. (01) 794274. *Expensive.*

★★★★ STOKERS. 16 Harcourt Street. Tel. (01) 782441. *Moderate to expensive.*

★★★ BENTLEY'S. 46 Upper Baggot Street. Tel. (01) 682760. *Moderate.*

★★★ GALLERY 22. 22 St. Stephen's Green. Tel. (01) 686169. *Moderate.*

★★★ LA GRENOUILLE. 64 South William Street. Tel. (01) 779157. *Moderate.*

★★★ THE LOBSTER POT. 9 Ballsbridge Terrace. Tel. (01) 680025. *Moderate to expensive.*

★★★ THE TAIN. 59 South William Street. Tel. (01) 791517. *Inexpensive to moderate.*

★★★ THE UNICORN. 12-B Merrion Court, off Merrion Row. Tel. (01) 688552 or 762182. *Inexpensive to moderate.*

Suggestions fo Light Lunches or Quick Meals

★★★★ BEWLEY'S CAFE. 78/79 Grafton Street. Tel. (01) 776761. *Bargain.*

★★★★ MITCHELL'S CELLARS. 21 Kildare Street. Tel. (01) 680367. *Bargain to inexpensive.*

★★★ SHRIMPS. 1 Anne's Lane, off South Anne Street. Tel. (01) 713143. *Inexpensive to moderate.*

★★★ TIMMERMAN'S. Powerscourt Townhouse Center, South William Street. Tel. (01) 794186. *Inexpensive.*

★★★ BEEFEATERS. 100 Lower Baggot Street. Tel. (01) 760784. *Inexpensive to moderate.*

★★★ FORTUNE COOKIE. 6 St. Stephen's Green. Tel. (01) 719371. *Bargain to inexpensive.*

★★★ THE GASWORKS. 21 Bachelor's Walk. Tel. (01) 731420. *Bargain.*

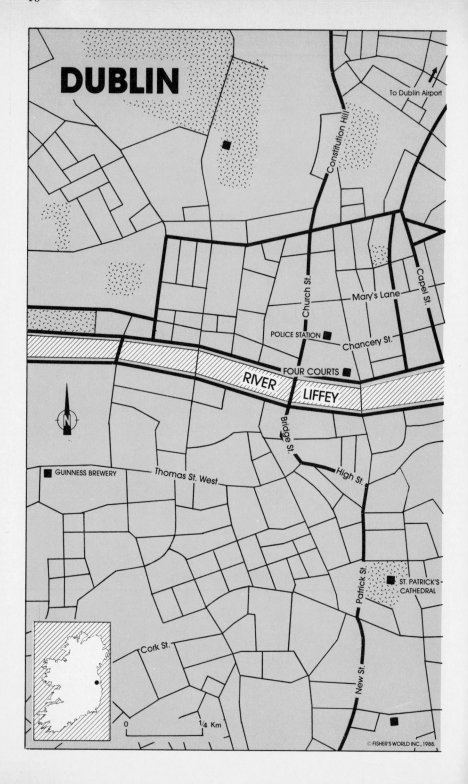

DUBLIN

To Dublin Airport

Constitution Hill

Church St.

Mary's Lane

Capel St.

POLICE STATION

Chancery St.

FOUR COURTS

RIVER LIFFEY

Bridge St.

High St.

GUINNESS BREWERY

Thomas St. West

Patrick St.

ST. PATRICK'S CATHEDRAL

Cork St.

New St.

0   1/4 Km

© FISHER'S WORLD INC., 1988.

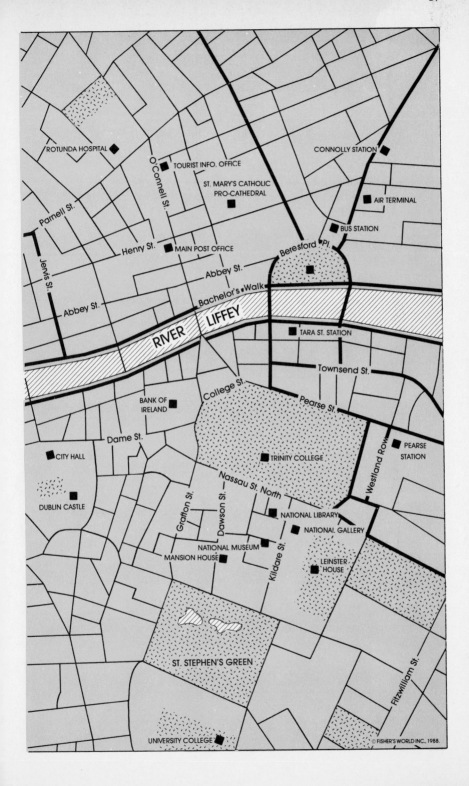

Pubs

★★★★★ **THE BRAZEN HEAD.** 20 Lower Bridge Street. Tel. (01) 779549.

★★★★★ **W. RYAN.** 28 Parkgate Street. Tel. (01) 776097.

★★★★ **KITTY OSHEA'S.** 23/25 Upper Grand Canal Street. Tel. (01) 609965.

★★★★ **THE STAG'S HEAD.** 1 Dame Court. Tel. (01) 779307.

★★★★ **DAVY BARNES.** 21 Duke Street. Tel. (01) 775217.

★★★★ **DOHENY AND NESBIT.** 5 Lower Baggot Street. Tel. (01) 762945.

★★★ **O'DONOGHUE'S.** 15 Merrion Row. Tel. (01) 607194.

★★★ **FOLEY'S.** 1 Merrion Row. Tel. (01) 606316.

★★★ **NEARY'S.** 1 Chatham Street. Tel. (01) 778596.

★★★ **THE OLD STAND.** 37 Exchequer Street. Tel. (01) 777220.

★★★ **THE BAILEY.** 2 Duke Street. Tel. (01) 773760.

★★★ **BRUXELLES.** 7 Harry Street, off Grafton Street. Tel. (01) 775362.

★★★ **THE PALACE.** Fleet Street. Tel. (01) 779290.

★★★ **MULLIGAN'S.** 8 Poolberg Street. Tel. (01) 775582.

Theaters

ABBEY THEATRE. Lower Abbey Street. Tel. (01) 787222.

PEACOCK THEATRE. Lower Abbey Street. Tel. (01) 787222.

GATE THEATRE. Cavendish Row, off Parnell Square. Tel. (01) 744045.

GAIETY THEATRE. South King Street. Tel. (01) 771717.

OLYMPIA THEATRE. Dame Street. Tel. (01) 788962.

PROJECT ARTS CENTRE. 39 East Essex Street. Tel. (01) 712321.

Concert Halls

NATIONAL CONCERT HALL. Earlsfort Terrace. Tel. (01) 711888.

THE ROYAL HOSPITAL. Military Road, Kilmainham, across from Houston Station. Tel. (01) 718666.

A NOTE ON DUBLIN THEATRE/CONCERT TICKETS:
In addition to visiting box offices, you can also obtain tickets at the theater desks at Brown-Thomas and Switzers Department Stores, both on Grafton Street, and from another single and centrally located source: **THE TICKET BUREAU**, 4 Westbury Mall, next to the Westbury Hotel, off Grafton Street. Tel. (01) 794455.

Cabarets/Shows

DOYLE'S IRISH CABARET. Burlington Hotel, Upper Leeson Street. Tel. (01) 605222, ext. 1162. Scheduled May to October, except Sundays.

JURY'S IRISH CABARET. Jurys Hotel, Pembroke Road, Tel. (01) 605000. Runs from May to October, except Mondays.

Discos/Nightclubs

ANNABEL'S. Burlington Hotel, Upper Leeson Street. Tel. (01) 605222. Open Tuesday through Saturday.

CLUB NASSAU. Nassau Street. Tel. (01) 605244. Wednesday through Sunday.

BOJANGLES. 26 Lower Leeson Street. Tel. (01) 789428.

BUCKS. 67 Lower Leeson Street. Tel. (01) 761755.

CLUB TROPICANA. 68 Lower Leeson Street. Tel. (01) 616154.

FANNY HILLS. 70 Lower Leeson Street. Tel. (01) 614943.

SAMANTHA'S, 33 Lower Leeson Street. Tel. (01) 765252.

STRINGS. 24 Lower Leeson Street. Tel. (01) 613664.

STYX. 65 Lower Leeson Street. Tel. (01) 682896

SUESEY STREET. 25 Lower Leeson Street. Tel. (01) 604928.

Museums and Libraries

★★★★ NATIONAL MUSEUM. Kildare Street. Tel. (01) 765521. Closed Mondays.

★★★ CHESTER BEATTY LIBRARY. 20 Shrewsbury Road. Tel. (01) 692386. Closed Sunday, Monday.

★★ NATIONAL GALLERY. Merrion Street. Tel. (01) 608533. Open daily.

★★ NATIONAL LIBRARY. Kildare Street. Tel. (01) 765521. Open weekdays and Saturday mornings.

★★ MARSH'S LIBRARY. St. Patrick's Close, Upper Kevin Street. Tel. (01) 753917. Open Monday afternoons, Saturday mornings, and Wednesday through Friday, from 10:30 A.M. to 12:30 P.M. and 2 P.M. to 4 P.M.

★ DUBLIN CIVIC MUSEUM. 58 South William Street. Tel. (01) 771642. Closed Monday.

★ NATIONAL WAX MUSEUM. Granby Row, off Parnell Square. Tel. (01) 746416. Open daily.

THE MUSEUM OF CHILDHOOD. The Palms, 20 Palmerstown Park, Rathmines. Tel. (01) 973223. Open Tuesday through Sunday in July and August, 2 P.M. to 5:30 P.M., and on Sunday afternoons only in September and from November through June.

IRISH THEATRE ARCHIVE. City Hall, Dame Street. Tel. (01) 776811, ext. 113. Open weekdays only.

IRISH JEWISH MUSEUM. 3/4 Walworth Road, off Victoria Street, South Circular Road. Tel. (01) 693873 or 534754. Open Sunday, Monday and Wednesday, from 11 A.M. 3:30 P.M. during the spring through fall months, and on Sunday only in the winter.

Tracing Your Roots

GENEALOGICAL OFFICE AND HERALDIC MUSEUM. 2 Kildare Street, Tel. (01) 608670. Open weekdays.

THE NATIONAL LIBRARY. Kildare Street. Tel. (01) 765521. Open weekdays and Saturday mornings.

THE PUBLIC RECORD OFFICE. Four Courts, Ormond Quay. Tel. (01) 733833. Open weekdays only.

REGISTRAR GENERAL. Joyce House 8/11 Lombard Street East. Tel. (01) 711000. Open weekdays only.

THE STATE PAPER OFFICE. Dublin Castle, Lord Edward Street. Tel. (01) 792777, ext 2518. Open weekdays only.

Public Transport

CIE—Main Office, 59 Upper O'Connell Street, Tel. (01) 731211; for telephone inquiries only: Tel. (01) 787777. Additional ticket/info office: 14 Upper O'Connell Street.

Bus service is daily throughout the city, starting at 7 A.M. (on Sundays, at 10 A.M.), with last bus runs of the night at 11:30 P.M. Minimum fare is about 70 cents.

Airport Bus daily between Dublin Airport and the city center every forty minutes, from 7:20 A.M. to 11:05 P.M. To the airport from downtown, it is every forty minutes, starting at 6:40 A.M. and finishing at 10:25 P.M. The one-way fare is approximately $4.

Taxis

You can phone and request a taxi from a specific rank nearby, such as Upper O'Connell Street, tel. (01) 744599; Lower O'Connell Street, tel. (01) 786150; College Green, tel. (01) 777440; St. Stephen's Green, tel. (01) 767381; Aston's Quay, tel. (01) 778053; and Eden Quay, tel. (01) 777054. 24-hour radio-call service. Includes: Ryan's Cabs, tel. (01) 772222; Blue Cabs, tel. (01) 761111; and Irish Taxi Co-op, tel. (01) 766666.

Car Rental

Avis, 1 Hanover Street East. Tel. (01) 776971.
Budget/Flynn Bros. 151 Lower Drumcondra Road, Tel. (01) 379611.
Hertz, Leeson Street Bridge. Tel. (01) 602255.
Inter-Rent/Bolland's, 38 Pearse Street. Tel. (01) 770704.
National/Murrays Europcar, Baggot Street Bridge. Tel. (01) 681777.
Dan Dooley Rent-a-Car, 5 Lyon House, Cathal Brugha Street. Tel. (01) 720777.

Festivals

January-December: All of Dublin will be one big festival in 1988, as the city celebrates its 1,000 birthday.
May 1-6: Spring Show and Industries Fair. Royal Dublin Society Showgrounds in Ballsbridge.
June 2-11: Festival of Music in Great Irish Houses.
June 16: Bloomsday. James Joyce Tower in Sandycove, Dublin.
June 25-27: Dublin Street Carneival.
June 25: The Irish Derby. Curragh racetrack in nearby Co. Kildare (30 miles away).
August 2-7: The Dublin Horse Show. Royal Dublin Society Showgrounds, Ballsbridge.
September 26-October 2: Dublin Theatre Festival.
October 31: Dublin Marathon.

Tourist Services

Bord Failte, Baggot Street Bridge. Tel. (01) 765871.

Dublin Tourism information centers are located at Dublin Airport Arrivals Hall, tel. (01) 376387/8; 14 Upper O'Connell Street, tel. (01) 747733;

and at St. Michael's Wharf, Dun Laoghaire, tel. (01) 806984.
American Express, 116 Grafton Street, Tel. (01) 772874.
Thomas Cook, 118 Grafton Street. Tel. (01) 771721.

Diplomatic and Consular Offices
U.S.A./American Embassy and American Consulate, 42 Elgin Road,
Ballsbridge. Tel. (01) 688777.
Canadian Embassy, 65/68 St. Stephen's Green. Tel. (01) 781988.
British Embassy, 33 Merrion Road. Tel. (01) 695211.
Australian Embassy, Fitzwilton House, Wilton Terrace. Tel. (01) 761517.

Doctors
Irish Medical Association, 10 Fitzwilliam Place. Tel. (01) 762550.

Dentists
Irish Dental Association, 29 Kenilworth Square. Tel. (01) 978435.

Late Night Pharmacy
O'Connell Pharmacy, 310 Harold's Cross Road. Tel. (01) 973977. Open
Daily until 10 P.M.

DUBLIN CITY SUBURBS—South

Hotels
★★★★★ FITZPATRICK CASTLE. Killiney Hill Road, Killiney. Tel. (01)
851533. *Expensive.*
★★★ THE COURT HOTEL. Killiney Bay Road, Killiney. Tel. (01) 851622.
Moderate.
★★★ ROYAL MARINE. Marine Road, Dun Laoghaire. Tel. (01) 801911.
Expensive.

Restaurants
★★★★ THE PARK. 26 Main Street, Blackrock. Tel. (01) 886177. *Expensive.*
★★★★ GUINEA PIG. 17 Railway Road, Dalkey. Tel. (01) 859055. *Moderate
to expensive.*
★★★★ DIGBY'S. 5 Windsor Terrace, Dun Laoghaire. Tel. (01) 804600.
Expensive.
★★★ MIRABEAU. Marine Parade, Sandycove. Tel. (01) 809873. *Expensive.*
★★★ RESTAURANT NA MARA. 1 Harbour Road, Dun Laoghaire. Tel. (01)
806767 or 800509. *Moderate to expensive.*
★★★ SOUTH BANK. 1 Martello Terrace, Sandycove. Tel. (01) 808788.
Moderate.
★★★ BEAUFIELD MEWS. Woodlands Avenue, Stillorgan. Tel. (01) 880375.
Moderate.
★★★ THE BRASSERIE. Monkstown Crescent, Monkstown. Tel. (01) 805174.
Inexpensive to moderate.

Pubs
★ ★ ★ ★ P. McCORMACK AND SONS. 67 Lower Mounttown, Dun Laoghaire. Tel. (01) 805519.

★ ★ ★ ★ THE QUEEN'S. 12/13 Castle Street, Dalkey. Tel. (01) 859450.

★ ★ ★ HEROES. 66A Upper George's Street, Dun Laoghaire. Tel. (01) 800875.

Entertainment
CULTERLANN NA hEIREANN. 32 Belgrave Square, Monkstown. Tel. (01) 800295.

DUBLIN CITY SUBURBS—North

Restaurants
★ ★ ★ ★ JOHNNY'S. 9 James Terrace, Malahide. Tel. (01) 450314. *Expensive.*

★ ★ ★ ★ KING SITRIC. East Pier, Howth. Tel. (01) 325235. *Expensive.*

Restaurant with Entertainment
★ ★ ★ ★ ABBEY TAVERN. Abbey Street, Howth. Tel. (01) 390307. *Expensive.*

DUNDALK, Co. Louth

Hotel
★ ★ ★ BALLYMASCANLON HOUSE. Off the Dublin/Belfast Road (N 1). Tel. (041) 71124. *Moderate.*

Festival
May 20-29: Dundalk International Maytime and Amateur Drama Festival.

Directory
Dundalk Tourist Office, Market Square. Tel. (042) 35484. Open all year.

DUNGARVAN, Co. Waterford

Pub
★ ★ ★ THE SEANACHIE. Waterford/Cork Road (N 25). Tel. (058) 46285. Open April through mid-November only.

DURRUS, Co. Cork

Restaurant
★ ★ ★ ★ BLAIR'S COVE. Barley Cove Road. Tel. (027) 61127.

ENNIS, Co. Clare

Hotels
★ ★ ★ ★ OLD GROUND. O'Connell Street. Tel. (065) 28127. *Moderate.*

★ ★ ★ WEST COUNTY INN. Clare Road (N 18). Tel. (065) 28421. *Inexpensive.*

Restaurant
★ ★ ★ ★ THE CLOISTER. Abbey Street. Tel. (065) 29521. *Moderate.*

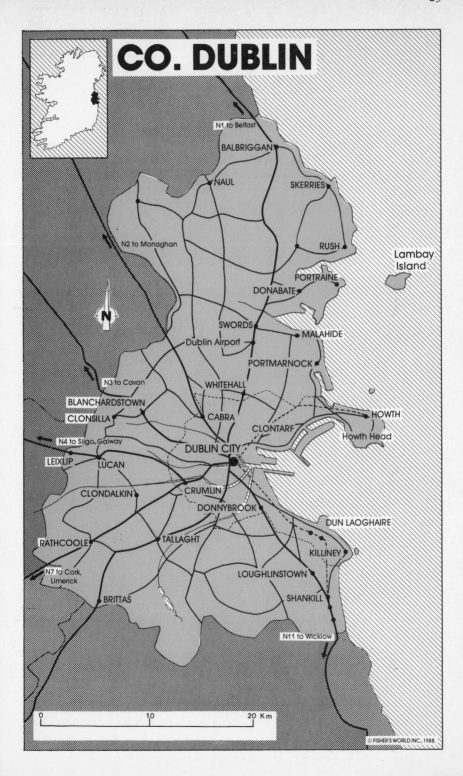

CO. DUBLIN

N1 to Belfast

BALBRIGGAN

NAUL

SKERRIES

N2 to Monaghan

RUSH

PORTRAINE

DONABATE

Lambay
Island

SWORDS

MALAHIDE

Dublin Airport

PORTMARNOCK

N3 to Cavan

WHITEHALL

BLANCHARDSTOWN

CABRA

CLONSILLA

CLONTARF

HOWTH

N4 to Sligo, Galway

Howth Head

DUBLIN CITY

LEIXLIP   LUCAN

CLONDALKIN

CRUMLIN

DONNYBROOK

DUN LAOGHAIRE

RATHCOOLE

TALLAGHT

KILLINEY

N7 to Cork,
Limerick

LOUGHLINSTOWN

BRITTAS

SHANKILL

N11 to Wicklow

0   10   20 Km

© FISHER'S WORLD INC., 1988.

24

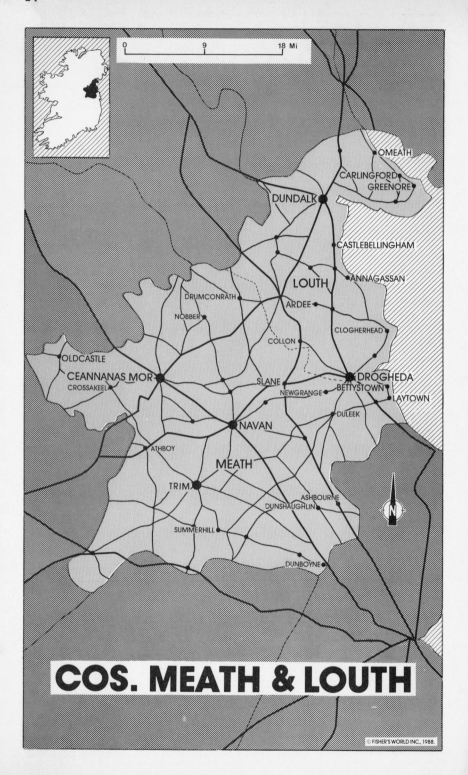

COS. MEATH & LOUTH

© FISHER'S WORLD INC., 1988.

Pubs
★★ BROGAN'S. 24 O'Connell Street. Tel. (065) 29859.
★★ CONSIDINE'S. 26 Abbey Street. Tel. (065) 29054.

Entertainment
COIS na hABHNA. Gort Road. Tel. (065) 29345.

Festival
May 27-29: Fleadh Nua. Irish music.

ENNISCORTHY, Co. Wexford

Pub
★★★★ ANTIQUE TAVERN. Dublin Road (N 11). Tel. (054) 33428.

Festival
Early July: Annual Strawberry Fair.

FAHAN, Co. Donegal

Restaurant
★★★★ RESTAURANT ST. JOHN'S. Inishowen 100 Road. Tel. (077) 60289.
Moderate.

FOULKSMILLS, Co. Wexford

Restaurant
★★★ THE CELLARS RESTAURANT. Horetown House. Tel. (051) 63706.
Moderate

GALWAY, Co. Galway

Hotels
★★★★ GREAT SOUTHERN HOTEL. Eyre Square. Tel. (091) 64041. *Expensive.*
★★★★ CONNEMARA COAST. Coast Road, Furbo. Tel. (091) 92108.
Moderate.
★★★ ARDILAUN HOUSE. Taylor's Hill. Tel. (091) 21433. *Moderate.*
★★★ THE CORRIB GREAT SOUTHERN. Dublin Road (N 6). Tel. (091) 55281.
Moderate.

Restaurants
★★★★★ DRIMCONG HOUSE. Clifden Road (N 59), Moycullen. Tel. (091)
85115. *Moderate to expensive.*
★★★★ THE MALT HOUSE. Olde Malte Arcade, High Street. Tel. (091)
67866. *Moderate.*
★★★★ TY AR MOR. Barna Pier, Barna. Tel. (091) 92223. *Moderate.*
★★★★ CASEY'S WESTWOOD. Dangan, Upper Newcastle Road. Tel. (091)
21442. *Moderate.*
★★★ OLD GALWAY SEAFOOD RESTAURANT. 2 High Street. Tel. (091) 61410.
Moderate.

★★★ **THE PARK HOUSE.** Forster Street. Tel. (091) 64924. *Moderate.*
★★★ **THE ABBEY.** Sligo Road (N 17), Claregalway. Tel. (091) 98244. *Moderate.*

Pubs

★★★★ **THE QUAYS.** Quay Street and Chapel Lane. Tel. (091) 61771.
★★★★ **McSWIGGINS.** 3 Eyre Street. Tel. (091) 68917.
★★★ **RABBITT'S.** 23-25 Forster Street. Tel. (091) 62215.
★★★ **CRANE BAR.** 2 Sea Road. Tel. (091) 67419.
★★★ **MONROE'S TAVERN.** Dominick Street. Tel. (091) 63397.

Entertainment

DRUID. Chapel Lane. Tel. (091) 68617. Professional theatre.
TAIBHDHEARC. Middle Street. Tel. (091) 62024. Ireland's national stage of the Irish language.

Festivals

May 27-29: Festival of the Tribes.
September 23-25: Galway International Oyster Festival.

Getting Around

Bus Eireann operates regular bus service within the city and its environs. The flat fare is approximately 80 cents. Radio-dispatched 24-hour service from Galway Taxis, 7 Main Guard Street, tel. (091) 61111 or 61112.

Directory

Galway Tourist Office, Aras Failte, Eyre Square. Tel. (091) 63081.
C.I.E. Railway Station, off Eyre Square. Tel. (091) 62141.

GLIN, Co. Limerick

Castle-for-Rent

GLIN CASTLE. Limerick/Tarbert Road (N 69). Tel. (068) 34173.

Pub

★★★ **O'SHAUGHNESSY'S.** Ivy House, Main Street. Tel. (068) 34115.

GOREY, Co. Wexford

Hotel

★★★★ **MARLFIELD HOUSE.** Courtown Road. Tel. (055) 21124. *Expensive.*

HEADFORD

Castle-for-Rent

CARRAIGIN CASTLE. Kilbeg Pier. Tel. (093) 35501.

KANTURK, Co. Cork

Guesthouse

★★★ **ASSOLAS HOUSE.** Tel. (029) 50015. *Moderate.*

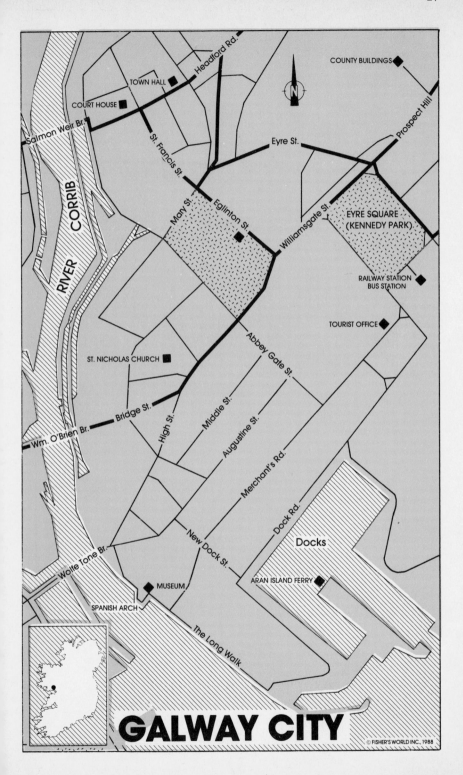

COUNTY BUILDINGS

TOWN HALL

COURT HOUSE

Headford Rd.

Salmon Weir Br.

St. Francis St.

RIVER CORRIB

Eyre St.

Prospect Hill

Mary St.

Eglinton St.

Williamsgate St.

EYRE SQUARE
(KENNEDY PARK)

RAILWAY STATION
BUS STATION

TOURIST OFFICE

Abbey Gate St.

ST. NICHOLAS CHURCH

Bridge St.

Wm. O'Brien Br.

High St.

Middle St.

Augustine St.

Merchant's Rd.

Dock Rd.

Docks

Wolfe Tone Br.

New Dock St.

MUSEUM

ARAN ISLAND FERRY

SPANISH ARCH

The Long Walk

GALWAY CITY

© FISHER'S WORLD INC., 1988

28

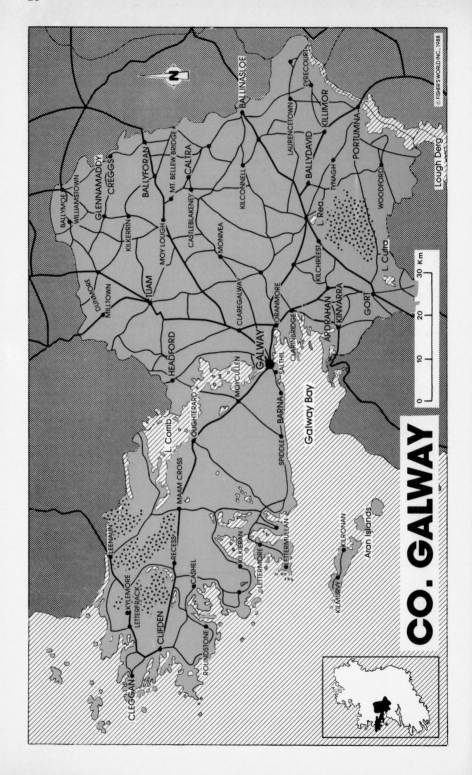

CO. GALWAY

KENMARE, Co. Kerry

Hotels
★★★★★ THE PARK. Tel. (064) 41200. *Very expensive.*
★★★ KENMARE BAY. Sneem Road. Tel. (064) 41300. *Inexpensive.*

Bed-and-Breakfast
★★ MUXNAW LODGE. Castletownbere Road. Tel. (064) 41252. *Bargain.*

Restaurants
★★★★ LIME TREE. Shelbourne Road. Tel. (064) 42225. *Moderate*
★★★ JUGS. Sneem Road, Gortamullen. Tel. (064) 41099.

Pub
★★ LANSDOWNE ARMS. Main Street. Tel. (064) 41368.

KILCOLGAN, Co. Galway

Pub/Restaurant
★★★★ MORAN'S OYSTER COTTAGE. The Weir. Tel. (091) 96113.

KILKENNY, Co. Kilkenny

Hotels
★★★★ THE NEWPARK. Castlecomer Road. Tel. (056) 22122. *Inexpensive to moderate.*
★★★ HOTEL KILKENNY. College Road. Tel. (056) 62000. *Inexpensive to moderate.*

Restaurants
★★★★ LACKEN HOUSE. Dublin/Carlow Road. Tel. (056) 65611. *Moderate.*
★★★ KYTELER'S INN. St. Kieran Street. Tel. (056) 21064. *Moderate.*

Pubs
★★★★★ TYNAN'S BRIDGE HOUSE. 2 Horseleap Slip. Tel. (056) 21291.
★★★★ EDWARD LANGTON. 69 John Street. Tel. (056) 21728.
★★★ MARBLE CITY BAR. 66 High Street. Tel. (056) 62091.

Festival
August 20-27: Kilkenny International Arts Week.

Directory
Kilkenny Tourist Office, Shee Alms House, Rose Inn Street. Tel. (056) 21755.
CIE, McDonagh Station, John Street. Tel. (056) 22024. For buses and trains.

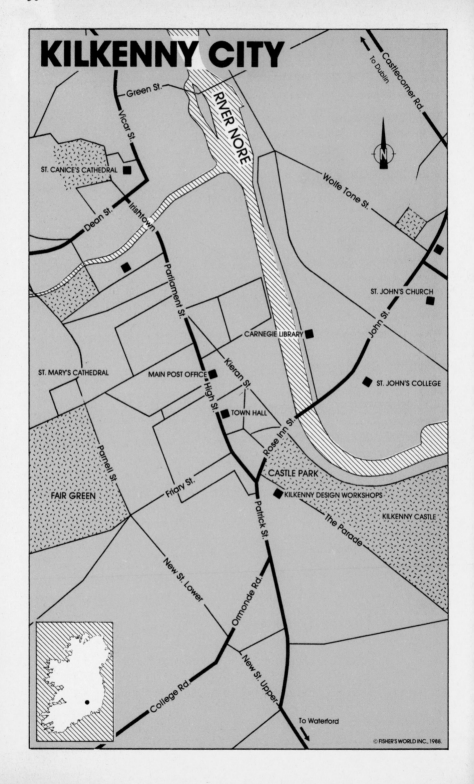

KILKENNY CITY

RIVER NORE

Green St.

Vicar St.

Castlecomer Rd.

To Dublin

N

Wolfe Tone St.

ST. CANICE'S CATHEDRAL

Dean St.

Irishtown

Parliament St.

ST. JOHN'S CHURCH

John St.

CARNEGIE LIBRARY

ST. MARY'S CATHEDRAL

MAIN POST OFFICE

Kieran St.

High St.

ST. JOHN'S COLLEGE

TOWN HALL

Rose Inn St.

Parnell St.

Friary St.

CASTLE PARK

KILKENNY DESIGN WORKSHOPS

FAIR GREEN

Patrick St.

The Parade

KILKENNY CASTLE

New St. Lower

Ormonde Rd.

College Rd.

New St. Upper

To Waterford

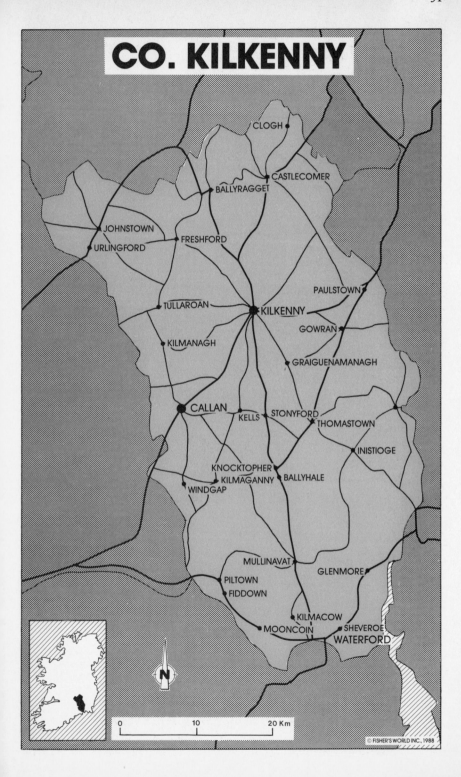

CO. KILKENNY

CLOGH

CASTLECOMER

BALLYRAGGET

JOHNSTOWN

URLINGFORD

FRESHFORD

PAULSTOWN

TULLAROAN

KILKENNY

GOWRAN

KILMANAGH

GRAIGUENAMANAGH

CALLAN

KELLS

STONYFORD

THOMASTOWN

INISTIOGE

KNOCKTOPHER

KILMAGANNY

BALLYHALE

WINDGAP

MULLINAVAT

GLENMORE

PILTOWN

FIDDOWN

KILMACOW

MOONCOIN

SHEVEROE

WATERFORD

0   10   20 Km

N

© FISHER'S WORLD INC., 1988

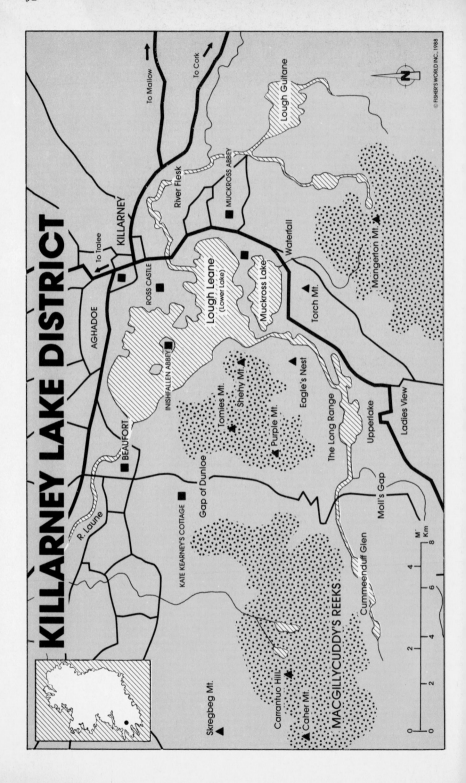

KILLARNEY LAKE DISTRICT

© FISHER'S WORLD INC. 1988

To Mallow

To Cork

Lough Guitane

River Flesk

MUCKROSS ABBEY

KILLARNEY

Waterfall

To Tralee

Mangerton Mt.

ROSS CASTLE

AGHADOE

Lough Leane
(Lower Lake)

Muckross Lake

Torch Mt.

INISHFALLEN ABBEY

Shehy Mt.

Eagle's Nest

Tomies Mt.

Purple Mt.

The Long Range

Upperlake

Ladies View

BEAUFORT

Gap of Dunloe

Moll's Gap

R. Laune

KATE KEARNEY'S COTTAGE

Cummeenduff Glen

MACGILLYCUDDY'S REEKS

Mi.
Km
8

4

6

Skregbeg Mt.

Carrantuo Hill

2

4

Caher Mt.

2

2

0

0

33

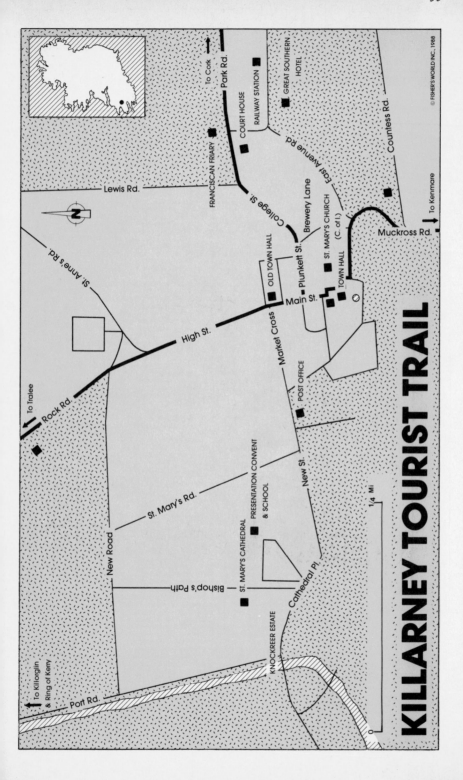

KILLARNEY TOURIST TRAIL

To Cork

Park Rd.

COURT HOUSE

RAILWAY STATION

GREAT SOUTHERN HOTEL

Countess Rd.

To Kenmare

FRANCISCAN FRIARY

Lewis Rd.

College St.

East Avenue Rd.

Brewery Lane

ST. MARY'S CHURCH (C. of I.)

Muckross Rd.

St. Anne's Rd.

OLD TOWN HALL

Plunkett St.

TOWN HALL

Main St.

Market Cross

High St.

To Tralee

Rock Rd.

POST OFFICE

New St.

PRESENTATION CONVENT & SCHOOL

St. Mary's Rd.

1/4 Mi

New Road

Cathedral Pl.

ST. MARY'S CATHEDRAL

Bishop's Path

KNOCKREER ESTATE

To Killorglin & Ring of Kerry

Port Rd.

KILLARNEY, Co. Kerry

Hotels

★ ★ ★ ★ THE GREAT SOUTHERN. Railway Road. Tel. (064) 31262. Open mid-March through December. *Expensive*.

★ ★ ★ ★ EUROPE. Fossa, off the Killorglin Road. Tel. (064) 31900. Open during March and from May through October. *Expensive*.

★ ★ ★ ★ DUNLOE CASTLE. Beaufort, off the Killorglin Road. Tel. (064) 44111. Open April through October. *Expensive*.

★ ★ ★ AGHADOE HEIGHTS—QUALITY INN. Aghadoe, off N 22. Tel. (064) 31766. Closed mid-December to mid-January. *Moderate*.

★ ★ ★ CAHERNANE. Muckross Road (N 71). Tel. (064) 31895. Closed November through March. *Expensive*.

★ ★ ★ THE TORC GREAT SOUTHERN. Cork Road. Tel. (064) 31611. Open mid-April through September. *Moderate*.

★ ★ ★ CASTLEROSSE. Killorglin Road. Tel. (064) 31114. Open from April through October. *Inexpensive to moderate*.

Guesthouse

★ ★ ★ KATHLEEN'S COUNTRY HOUSE. Madam's Height, Tralee Road (N 22). Tel. (064) 32810. Open from March through October. *Bargain to inexpensive*.

Restaurants

★ ★ ★ ★ GABY'S. 17 High Street. Tel. (064) 32519. Mid-March through November. *Expensive*.

★ ★ ★ DINGLES. 40 New Street. Tel. (064) 31079. Open daily for dinner only, except the end of December through February. *Moderate*.

★ ★ ★ FOLEY'S. 23 High Street. Tel. (064) 31217. *Moderate*.

Pubs

★ ★ ★ ★ BUCKLEY'S. 2 College Street. Tel. (064) 31037.

★ ★ ★ DUNLOE LODGE. Plunkett Street. Tel. (064) 32502.

★ ★ ★ THE LAURELS. Main Street. Tel. (064) 31149.

★ ★ ★ DANNY MANN. 97 New Street. (064) 31640.

★ ★ ★ KATE KEARNEY'S COTTAGE. Gap of Dunloe. Tel. (064) 44146.

Festivals

May 14-21: Pan Celtic Festival.
July 11-15: Killarney Racing Week.

Directory

Killarney Tourist Office, Town Hall, Main Street. Tel. (064) 31633.
CIE, Railway Station, next to the Great Southern Hotel. Tel. (064) 31067, for trains, buses, and local sightseeing tours.

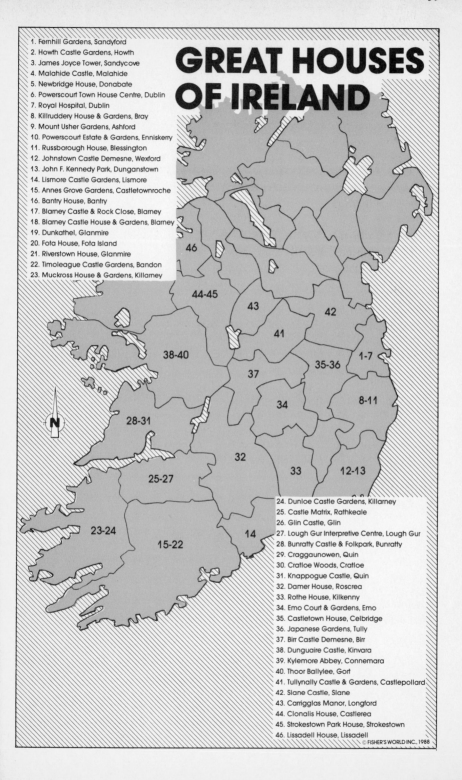

GREAT HOUSES OF IRELAND

1. Fernhill Gardens, Sandyford
2. Howth Castle Gardens, Howth
3. James Joyce Tower, Sandycove
4. Malahide Castle, Malahide
5. Newbridge House, Donabate
6. Powerscourt Town House Centre, Dublin
7. Royal Hospital, Dublin
8. Killruddery House & Gardens, Bray
9. Mount Usher Gardens, Ashford
10. Powerscourt Estate & Gardens, Enniskerry
11. Russborough House, Blessington
12. Johnstown Castle Demesne, Wexford
13. John F. Kennedy Park, Dunganstown
14. Lismore Castle Gardens, Lismore
15. Annes Grove Gardens, Castletownroche
16. Bantry House, Bantry
17. Blarney Castle & Rock Close, Blarney
18. Blarney Castle House & Gardens, Blarney
19. Dunkathel, Glanmire
20. Fota House, Fota Island
21. Riverstown House, Glanmire
22. Timoleague Castle Gardens, Bandon
23. Muckross House & Gardens, Killarney

24. Dunloe Castle Gardens, Killarney
25. Castle Matrix, Rathkeale
26. Glin Castle, Glin
27. Lough Gur Interpretive Centre, Lough Gur
28. Bunratty Castle & Folkpark, Bunratty
29. Craggaunowen, Quin
30. Cratloe Woods, Cratloe
31. Knappogue Castle, Quin
32. Damer House, Roscrea
33. Rothe House, Kilkenny
34. Emo Court & Gardens, Emo
35. Castletown House, Celbridge
36. Japanese Gardens, Tully
37. Birr Castle Demesne, Birr
38. Dunguaire Castle, Kinvara
39. Kylemore Abbey, Connemara
40. Thoor Ballylee, Gort
41. Tullynally Castle & Gardens, Castlepollard
42. Slane Castle, Slane
43. Carrigglas Manor, Longford
44. Clonalis House, Castlerea
45. Strokestown Park House, Strokestown
46. Lissadell House, Lissadell

© FISHER'S WORLD INC., 1988

KINSALE, Co. Cork

Hotels

★★★★ THE BLUE HAVEN. Pearse Street. Tel. (021) 772209. Open March through December. *Inexpensive* for the hotel and *Moderate* for the restaurant.

★★★ ACTON'S. The Waterfront. Tel. (021) 772135. *Moderate.*

Restaurants

★★★★ THE VINTAGE. Main Street. Tel. (021) 772502. Open for dinner nightly, March through December, except Sunday. *Moderate.*

★★★★ MAN FRIDAY. Scilly. Tel. (021) 772260. *Moderate.*

★★★★ COTTAGE LOFT. 6 Main Street. Tel. (021) 772803. *Moderate.*

★★★ LE BISTRO. Market Street. Tel. (021) 772470. *Moderate.*

★★★ MAX'S WINE BAR. Main Street. Tel. (021) 772443. March through September, except Tuesday. *Inexpensive to moderate.*

Pubs

★★★★ THE SPANIARD. Scilly. Tel. (021) 772436.

★★★ THE DOCK. Castlepark. Tel. (021) 772522.

★★★ JIM EDWARDS. Off Emmet Place. Tel. (021) 772541.

★★★ THE WHITE HOUSE. End of Pearse Street. Tel. (021) 772125.

★★★ THE GREYHOUND. Marian Terrace. Tel. (021) 772889.

★★★ LORD KINGSALE. Main Street. Tel. (021) 772371.

★★★ THE SHANAKEE. Market Street.

Festivals

August 6-7: Annual Regatta.
October 1-2: Kinsale Gourmet Festival.

KINVARA, Co. Galway

Entertainment

DON GUAIRE CASTLE. Ballyvaughan Road (N 67). Tel. (091) 37108 or (061) 61788. Mid-May through September.

LETTERFRACK, Co. Galway

Hotel

★★★ ROSLEAGUE MANOR. Clifden/Leenane Road (N 59). Tel. (095) 41101. Open April through October. *Moderate.*

LETTERKENNY, Co. Donegal

Hotel

★★ MT. ERRIGAL. Derry Road, Ballyraine. Tel. (074) 22700. *Inexpensive.*

Pub

★★ HALF-WAY LINE. Ramelton Road.

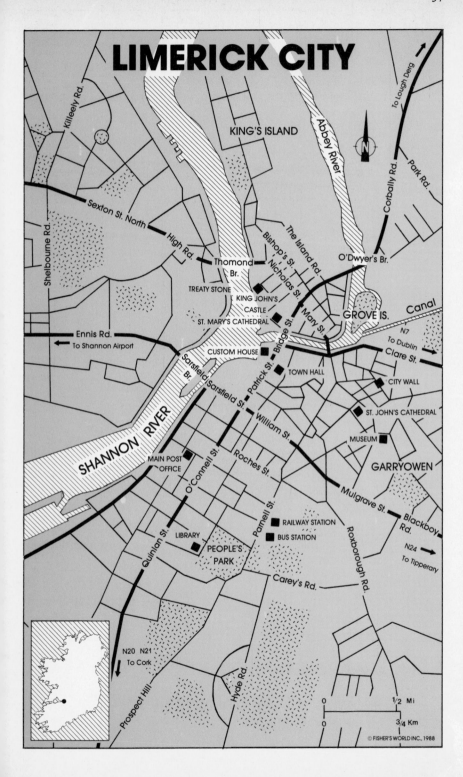

LIMERICK CITY

KING'S ISLAND

Abbey River

To Lough Derg

Corbally Rd.

Park Rd.

N

Sexton St. North

High Rd.

Shelbourne Rd.

Killeely Rd.

The Island Rd.

Bishop's St.

Nicholas St.

O'Dwyer's Br.

Thomond Br.

TREATY STONE

KING JOHN'S CASTLE

ST. MARY'S CATHEDRAL

Mary St.

GROVE IS.

Canal

N7

Ennis Rd.

To Shannon Airport

To Dublin

Clare St.

Sarsfield Br.

Sarsfield St.

CUSTOM HOUSE

Bridge St.

Patrick St.

TOWN HALL

CITY WALL

ST. JOHN'S CATHEDRAL

MUSEUM

SHANNON RIVER

William St.

Roches St.

MAIN POST OFFICE

O'Connell St.

GARRYOWEN

Mulgrave St.

Blackboy Rd.

Quinlan St.

LIBRARY

PEOPLE'S PARK

Parnell St.

RAILWAY STATION

BUS STATION

Roxborough Rd.

N24

To Tipperary

Carey's Rd.

N20 N21

To Cork

Prospect Hill

Hyde Rd.

0   1/2 Mi

0   3/4 Km

© FISHER'S WORLD INC., 1988

Festival

August 12-16: International Folk Festival.

Directory

Letterkenny Tourist Office. Derry Road. Tel. (074) 21160.

LIMERICK, Co. Limerick

Hotels

★ ★ ★ ★ JURYS. Ennis Road (N 18). Tel. (061) 55266. *Moderate.*

★ ★ ★ LIMERICK INN. Ennis Road (N 18). Tel. (061) 51544. *Moderate.*

★ ★ ★ CASTLE OAKS HOUSE. Off the Dublin Road (N 7), Castleconnell. Tel. (061) 377666. *Moderate to expensive.*

Restaurants

★ ★ ★ ★ THE SILVER PLATE. 74 O'Connell Street. Tel. (061) 316311. *Moderate to expensive.*

★ ★ ★ PICCOLA ITALIA. 55 O'Connell Street. Tel. (061) 315844. *Inexpensive to moderate.*

Pubs

★ ★ ★ ★ HOGAN'S. Thomond House, 72 Catherine Street. Tel. (061) 44138.

★ ★ ★ M.J. RIDDLER'S—THE CLOISTER. 9 Sarsfield Street. Tel. (061) 44149.

★ ★ ★ THE GRANARY TAVERN. Michael Street, Charlotte Quay. Tel. (061) 47266.

★ ★ ★ THE LUCKY LAMP. 9 Ellen Street. Tel. (061) 40694.

★ ★ ★ THE JAMES JOYCE. 4 Ellen Street. Tel. (061) 46711.

★ ★ ★ OLDE TOM'S. 19 Thomas Street. Tel. (061) 45961.

★ ★ ★ M.J. FINNEGANS. Dublin Road (N 7), Annacotty. Tel. (061) 337338.

★ ★ ★ MATT THE THRESHER. Dublin Road (N 7), Birdhill, Co. Tipperary. Tel. (061) 379337.

Entertainment

THE BELLTABLE ARTS CENTRE. 69 O'Connell Street. Tel. (061) 319866.

SON ET LUMIERE. St. Mary's Cathedral, Merchant's Quay. Mid-June through mid-September.

Festivals

March 18-20: Church Music International Choral Festival. St. Mary's Cathedral.

Mid-May: Limerick Game and Country Fair.

Directory

The Shannonside Tourist Office, The Granary, Michael Street. Tel. (061) 317522.

CIE, Colbert Railway Station, off Parnell Street. Tel. (061) 42433. For buses, trains, and sightseeing tours.

LISMORE, Co. Waterford

Castle-for-Rent
LISMORE CASTLE. Tel. (058) 54424.

LOUGHREA, Co. Galway

Castle-for-Rent
CLOUGHAN CASTLE. Gort/Loughrea Road (N 66), Kilchreest. Tel. (091) 31457.

MALLOW, Co. Cork

Hotel
★★★★ LONGUEVILLE HOUSE. Killarney Road (N 72). Tel. (022) 27156. *Expensive.*

Castle-for-Rent
MALLOW CASTLE. Tel. (022) 21469.

MULLINGAR, Co. Westmeath

Hotels
★★★ BLOOMFIELD HOUSE. Kilbeggan Road. Tel. (044) 80894. *Inexpensive.*

Directory
Mullingar Tourist Office, Dublin Road. Tel. (044) 48761.

NAVAN, Co. Meath

Restaurant
★★★★★ DUNDERRY LODGE. Off the Athboy Road, Dunderry. Tel. (046) 31671. *Moderate to expensive.*

NENAGH, Co. Tipperary

Hotel
★★★ THE WATERSIDE. Dromineer Bay. Tel. (067) 24114. *Moderate.*

NEWMARKET-ON-FERGUS, Co. Clare

Hotels
★★★★★ DROMOLAND CASTLE. Limerick/Ennis Road (N 18). Tel. (061) 71144. *Very expensive.*
★★★★ CLARE INN. Limerick/Ennis Road (N 18). Tel. (061) 71161. *Moderate.*

Restaurants
★★★ CRONIN'S. Main Street. Tel. (061) 71157. *Moderate.*

NEWPORT, Co Mayo

Hotels
★★★★ NEWPORT HOUSE. Tel. (098) 41222. Open from mid-March through September. *Expensive.*

OUGHTERARD, Co. Galway

Hotels
★★★★ CONNEMARA GATEWAY. Galway/Clifden Raod (N 59). Tel. (091) 82328. Open from February through October. *Moderate.*
★★★ SWEENEY'S OUGHTERARD HOUSE. Galway/Clifden Road (N 59). Tel. (091) 82207. *Moderate.*

PARKNASILLA, Co. Kerry

Hotels
★★★★ GREAT SOUTHERN. Ring of Kerry Road (N 70). Tel. (064) 45122. Open mid-April through October. *Expensive.*

QUIN, Co. Clare

Hotel
★★★ BALLYKILTY MANOR. Tel. (065) 25627. *Moderate.*

Entertainment
KNAPPOGUE CASTLE. Tel. (061) 71103 or 61788. May through October.

RATHKEALE, Co. Limerick

Castle Bed-and-Breakfast
★★★ CASTLE MATRIX. Off the Limerick/Tralee Road (N 21). Tel. (069) 64284. *Moderate.*

RATHMULLAN, Co. Donegal

Hotels
★★★★ RATHMULLAN HOUSE. Tel. (074) 58188. Open April through mid-October. *Moderate.*

Restaurant
★★★ WATER'S EDGE. The Ballyboe. Tel. (074) 58182. *Moderate.*

RATHNEW, Co. Wicklow

Hotels
★★★★ TINAKILLY HOUSE. Off the Dublin/Wexford Road, on R 750. Tel. (0404) 69274. Open February through mid-December. *Moderate.*

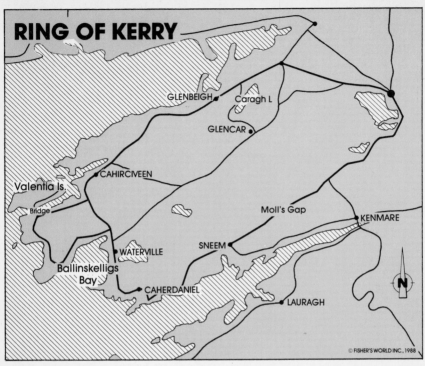

RING OF KERRY

GLENBEIGH

Caragh L

GLENCAR

CAHIRCIVEEN

Valentia Is.

Bridge

Moll's Gap

KENMARE

SNEEM

WATERVILLE

Ballinskelligs
Bay

CAHERDANIEL

LAURAGH

N

© FISHER'S WORLD INC., 1988

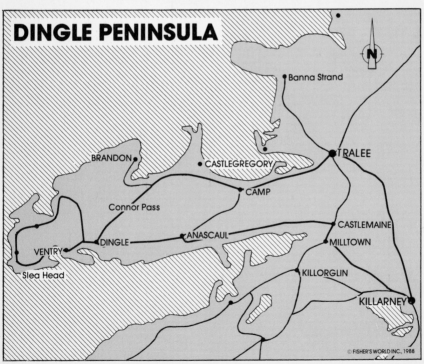

DINGLE PENINSULA

N

Banna Strand

TRALEE

BRANDON

CASTLEGREGORY

Connor Pass

CAMP

CASTLEMAINE

VENTRY

DINGLE

ANASCAUL

MILLTOWN

Slea Head

KILLORGLIN

KILLARNEY

© FISHER'S WORLD INC., 1988

42

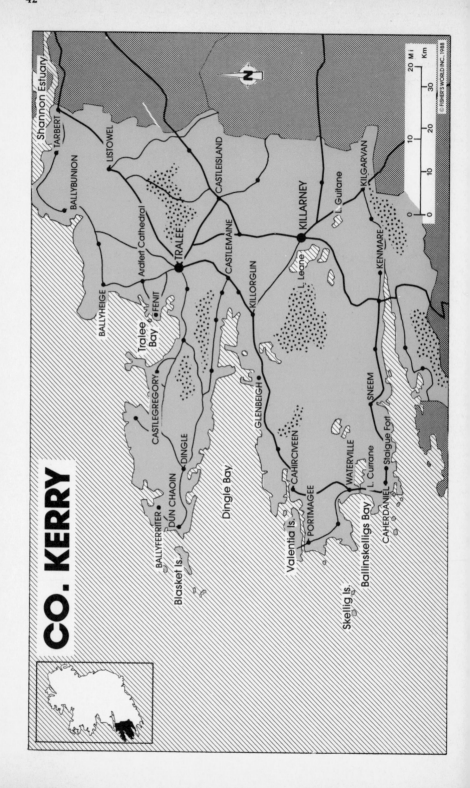

CO. KERRY

Shannon Estuary
TARBERT
BALLYBUNION
LISTOWEL
CASTLEISLAND
KILGARVAN
KILLARNEY
L. Guitane
Ardfert Cathedral
TRALEE
CASTLEMAINE
KENMARE
BALLYHEIGE
FENIT
Tralee Bay
KILLORGLIN
L. Leane
CASTLEGREGORY
GLENBEIGH
SNEEM
DINGLE
DÚN CHAOIN
BALLYFERRITER
Blasket Is.
Dingle Bay
CAHIRCIVEEN
WATERVILLE
Staigue Fort
PORTMAGEE
L. Currane
CAHERDANIEL
Valentia Is.
Ballinskelligs Bay
Skellig Is.

20 Mi
Km
30
20
10
10
0

© FISHER'S WORLD, INC. 1988

RENVYLE, Co. Galway

Hotel

★★★ RENVYLE HOUSE. Tel. (095) 43434. Open mid-March through October. *Moderate.*

ROSSLARE HARBOR, Co. Wexford

Hotel

★★★ GREAT SOUTHERN. Wexford/Rosslare Harbor Road (N 25). Tel. (053) 33233. Open from Easter through October. *Expensive.*

ROSSNOWLAGH, Co. Donegal

Hotel

★★★★★ THE SAND HOUSE. On the Coast, off the Ballyshannon/Donegal Road (N 15). Tel. (072) 51777. Open from mid-April to early October. *Moderate to expensive.*

ROUNDWOOD, Co. Wicklow

Pub

★★★ THE ROUNDWOOD INN. Glendalough Road. Tel. (01) 818107.

SCHULL, Co. Cork

Hotel

★★★ ARD NA GREINE. Goleen Road. Tel. (028) 28181. Open April to late October. *Moderate.*

Pub

★★★ BUNRATTY INN. Main Street.

SHANAGARRY, Co. Cork

Hotel

★★★★ BALLYMALOE HOUSE. Ballycotton Road. (L 35). Tel. (021) 652531. *Expensive.*

SHANNON, Co. Clare

Hotel

★★★ SHANNON INTERNATIONAL—QUALITY INN. Airport Road (N 19). Tel. (061) 61122. *Moderate.*

Airport Transfers

Bus Eireann operates a daily service between Shannon International Airport to/from Limerick Railway Station, in conjunction with scheduled flight departures and arrivals (normally every 30 minutes). The one-way fare is approximately $4.

44

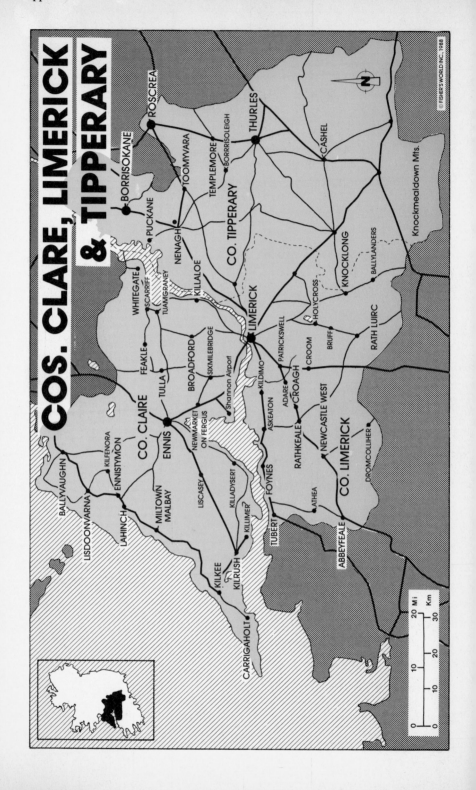

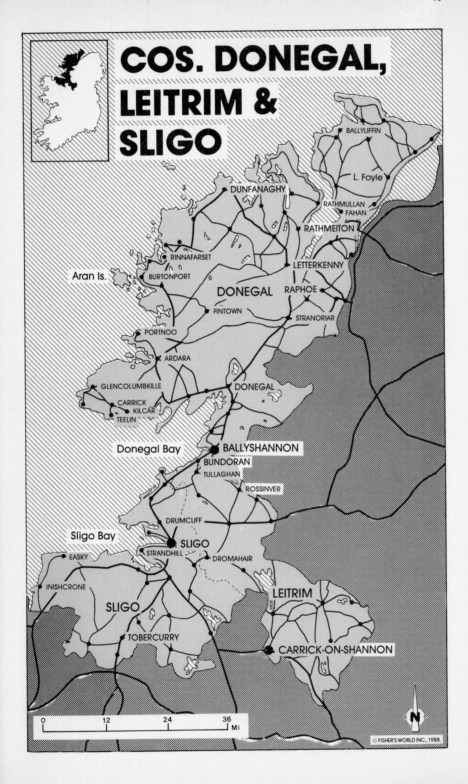

COS. DONEGAL, LEITRIM & SLIGO

BALLYLIFFIN

L. Foyle

DUNFANAGHY

RATHMULLAN
FAHAN

RATHMEITON

RINNAFARSET

LETTERKENNY

Aran Is.

BURTONPORT

DONEGAL

RAPHOE

FINTOWN

STRANORIAR

PORTNOO

ARDARA

GLENCOLUMBKILLE

DONEGAL

CARRICK
KILCAR
TEELIN

Donegal Bay

BALLYSHANNON

BUNDORAN

TULLAGHAN

ROSSINVER

DRUMCLIFF

Sligo Bay

SLIGO

EASKY

STRANDHILL

DROMAHAIR

INISHCRONE

LEITRIM

SLIGO

TOBERCURRY

CARRICK-ON-SHANNON

| 0 | 12 | 24 | 36 |
Mi

N

© FISHER'S WORLD INC., 1988.

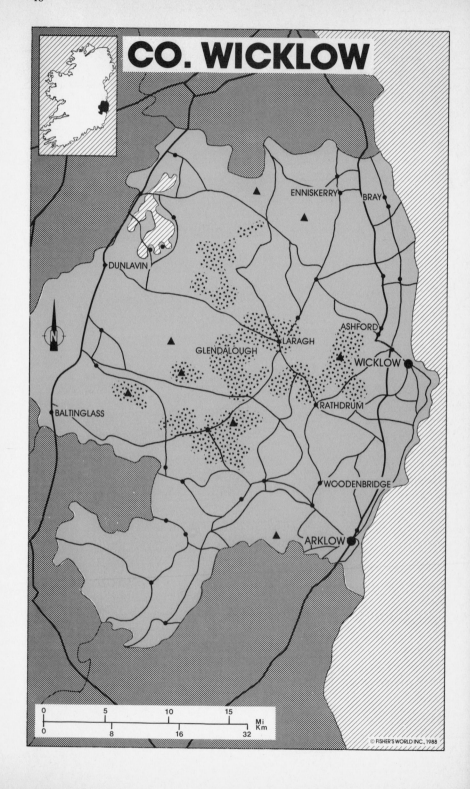

CO. WICKLOW

ENNISKERRY

BRAY

DUNLAVIN

ASHFORD

LARAGH

GLENDALOUGH

WICKLOW

RATHDRUM

BALTINGLASS

WOODENBRIDGE

ARKLOW

N

Mi				
0	5	10	15	
0	8		16	32

Km

© FISHER'S WORLD INC., 1988

Taxis are readily available at Shannon Airport for transport to hotels in nearby Co. Clare towns or into Limerick City. Approximate fares to most hotels range from $8 to $15.

Car Rentals
Avis, tel. (061) 61643.
Budget/Flynn Bros., tel. (061) 61366.
Hertz, tel. (061) 61369.
Inter-Rent/Bolands, tel. (061) 61877.
National/Murrays Europcar, tel. (061) 61618.
Dan Dooley Rent-A-Car, tel. (061) 61098.

Directory
Shannon Airport Tourist Office, Arrivals Concourse. Tel. (061) 61664.

SLANE, Co. Meath

Restaurant
★ ★ ★ SLANE CASTLE. Off the Dublin/Ardee Road (N 2). Tel. (041) 24207. Wednesday through Sunday. *Moderate to expensive.*

SLIGO, Co. Sligo

Hotels
★ ★ ★ BALLINCAR HOUSE. Rosses Point Road. Tel. (071) 5361. Open mid-January through mid-December. *Inexpensive to moderate.*
★ ★ ★ YEATS COUNTRY RYAN. Rosses Point Road, Rosses Point. Tel. (071) 77211. *Moderate.*

Restaurants
★ ★ ★ ★ ★ REVERIES. Rosses Point Road, Rosses Point. Tel. (071) 77371. *Moderate to expensive.*
★ ★ ★ ★ KNOCKMULDOWNEY. Coast Road, Culleenamore, near Strandhill. Tel. (071) 68122. March through October. *Moderate.*

Pubs
★ ★ ★ ★ HARGADON'S. 4/5 O'Connell Street.
★ ★ ★ ★ THE THATCH. Dublin/Sligo Road (N 4), Ballisodare. Tel. (071) 67288.
★ ★ ★ AUSTIE'S/THE ELSINORE. Rosses Point Road, Rosses Point. Tel. (071) 77111.
★ ★ ★ YEATS' TAVERN. Ballyshannon Road (N 15), Drumcliffe. Tel. (071) 73117.
★ ★ ★ LAURA'S. Off the Ballyshannon Road (N 15), Carney. Tel. (071) 63056.

Entertainment
HAWK'S WELL THEATRE. Temple Street. Tel. (071) 61526.

48

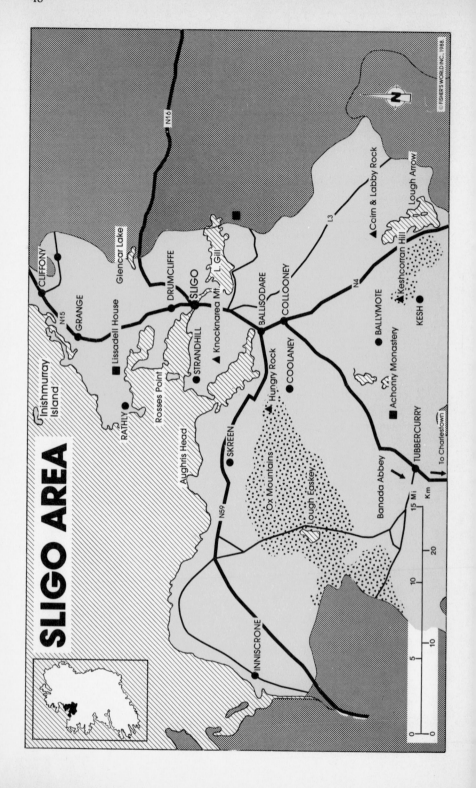

SLIGO AREA

© FISHER'S WORLD INC. 1988.

N16
N15
CLIFFONY
GRANGE
Glencar Lake
Lissadell House
DRUMCLIFFE
SLIGO
L. Gill
Knocknarea Mt.
STRANDHILL
Rosses Point
Inishmurray Island
Aughris Head
RATHLY
SKREEN
N59
Ox Mountains
Lough Easkey
Hungry Rock
COOLANEY
BALLISODARE
COLLOONEY
L3
N4
Colm & Labby Rock
Lough Arrow
Keshcorran Hill
BALLYMOTE
KESH
Achonry Monastery
TUBBERCURRY
Banada Abbey
To Charlestown
INNISCRONE

Mi
Km
0   5   10   15
0   10   20

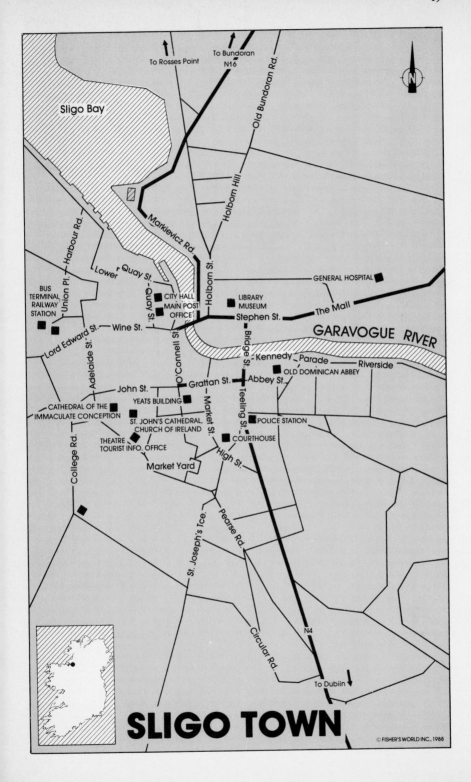

To Rosses Point

To Bundoran
N16

Old Bundoran Rd.

Sligo Bay

Holborn Hill

Markievicz Rd.

Holborn St.

GENERAL HOSPITAL

Lower

Quay St.

Harbour Rd.

Union Pl.

BUS
TERMINAL
RAILWAY
STATION

Quay St.

CITY HALL
MAIN POST
OFFICE

LIBRARY
MUSEUM

Stephen St.

The Mall

Wine St.

Lord Edward St.

Adelaide St.

O'Connell St.

Holborn St.

Bridge St.

GARAVOGUE RIVER

Kennedy   Parade   Riverside

John St.

Grattan St.

Abbey St.

OLD DOMINICAN ABBEY

YEATS BUILDING

CATHEDRAL OF THE
IMMACULATE CONCEPTION

St. JOHN'S CATHEDRAL,
CHURCH OF IRELAND

Market St.

Teeling St.

POLICE STATION

College Rd.

THEATRE
TOURIST INFO. OFFICE

COURTHOUSE

Market Yard

High St.

St. Joseph's Tce.

Pearse Rd.

Circular Rd.

N4

To Dublin

SLIGO TOWN

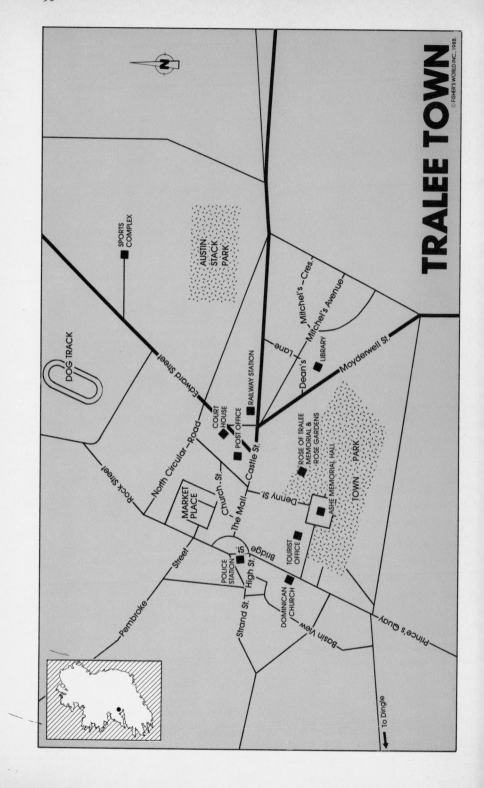

50

TRALEE TOWN

© FISHER'S WORLD INC., 1988.

Festival
August 13-27: Yeats International Summer School.

Directory
Sligo Tourist Office, Temple Street. Tel. (071) 61201.
CIE, Lord Edward Street. Tel. (071) 62051.

SPIDDAL, Co. Galway

Restaurant
★ ★ ★ BOLUISCE. Coast Road. Tel. (091) 83286. Daily except January and February, Good Friday, and Christmas. *Inexpensive to moderate.*

TEELIN, Co. Donegal

Pub
★ ★ ★ THE RUSTY MACKEREL. Tel. (073) 39101.

TRALEE, Co. Kerry

Hotels
★ ★ ★ BRANDON. Princess Street. Tel. (066) 21311. *Expensive.*
★ ★ ★ BALLYGARRY HOUSE. Tralee/Killarney Road, Leebrook. Tel. (066) 21233. *Moderate.*

Restaurants
★ ★ ★ BARRETT'S CORDON BLEU. The Square. Tel. (066) 21596. *Moderate.*
★ ★ ★ OCEAN BILLOW. 29 Lower Castle Street. Tel. (066) 21377. *Moderate.*
★ ★ ★ THE TANKARD. Kilfenora, Fenit. Tel. (066) 36164. *Moderate.*

Pubs
★ ★ KIRBY'S BROGUE INN. Rock Street. Tel. (066) 22126.
★ ★ SLATT'S BAR. 79 Boherbee. Tel. (066) 21161.
★ ★ OYSTER TAVERN. Spa. Tel. (066) 36102.

Entertainment
SIAMSA TIRE THEATRE. Godfrey Place. Tel. (066) 23055. The national folk theatre of Ireland. Scheduled on Monday and Thursday nights, June through September, with additional performances on Tuesday and Friday during July and August.

Festival
August 26-September 2: Rose of Tralee International Festival.

Directory
Tralee Tourist Office, Godfrey Place, on Princess Street. Tel. (066) 21288.

52

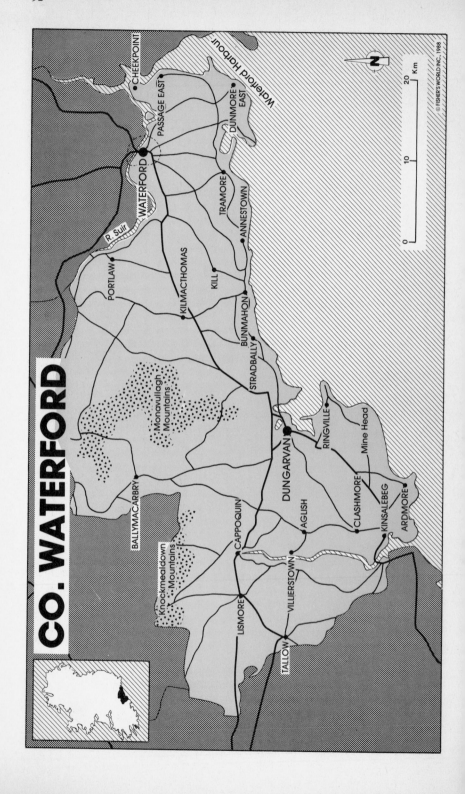

CO. WATERFORD

CHEEKPOINT

PASSAGE EAST

Waterford Harbour

DUNMORE EAST

WATERFORD

R. Suir

TRAMORE

ANNESTOWN

PORTLAW

KILMACTHOMAS

KILL

BUNMAHON

STRADBALLY

Monavullagh Mountains

RINGVILLE

Mine Head

BALLYMACARBRY

DUNGARVAN

CLASHMORE

KINSALEBEG

ARDMORE

Knockmealdown Mountains

CAPPOQUIN

AGLISH

VILLIERSTOWN

LISMORE

TALLOW

N

Km

0   10   20

© FISHER'S WORLD INC. 1988

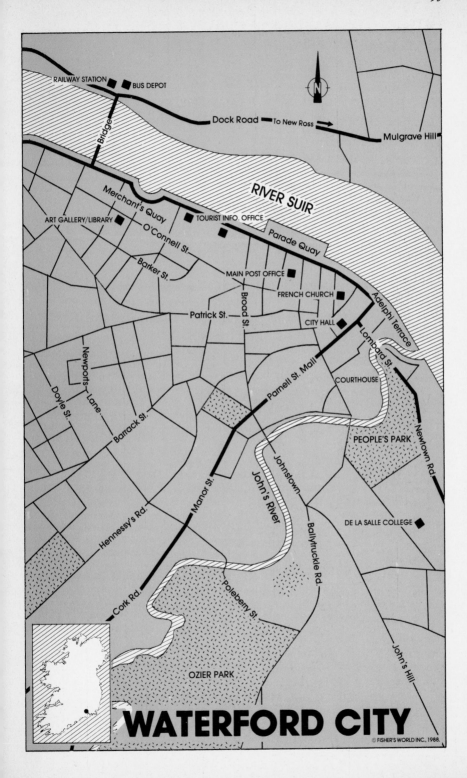

WATERFORD CITY

© FISHER'S WORLD INC., 1988.

WATERFORD, Co. Waterford

Hotels
★★★ ARDREE. Ferrybank. Tel. (051) 32111. *Moderate.*
★★★ GRANVILLE. Meagher Quay. Tel. (051) 55111. *Moderate.*
★★★ TOWER. The Mall. Tel. (051) 75801. *Moderate*

Bed-and-Breakfast
★★★ BLENHEIM HOUSE. Off the Passage East Road. Tel. (051) 74115.
Bargain.

Restaurants
★★★ JADE PALACE. 3 The Mall. Tel. (051) 55611. *Moderate.*
★★★ GALLEY CRUISING RESTAURANT. New Ross Quay, New Ross. Tel. (051)
21723. April through September. *Moderate.*

Pubs
★★★★ THE MUNSTER. Bailey's New Street. Tel. (051) 74656.
★★★★ T. & H. DOOLAN. 32 George's Street. Tel. (051) 72764.
★★★ EGAN'S. 36/37 Barronstrand Street. Tel. (051) 75619.
★★★ THE REGINALD. The Mall. Tel. (051) 55611.

Getting Around
Bus Eireann operates daily bus service within Waterford and its environs.
The flat fare is approximately 80 cents.

Festival
September 17-October 2: Waterford Festival of Light Opera.

Directory
Waterford Tourist Office, 41 The Quay. Tel. (051) 75788.
CIE, Plunkett Station, at Edmund Ignatius Rice Bridge on north side of
river. Tel. (051) 73401.

WATERVILLE, Co. Kerry

Hotels
★★★★ WATERVILLE LAKE. Off the Ring of Kerry Road (N 70). Tel. (0667)
4133. Open from April to mid-October. *Expensive.*
★★★ BUTLER ARMS. Tel. (0667) 4144. Open mid-April through mid-
October. *Expensive.*

Restaurants
★★★★ THE HUNTSMAN. Tel. (0667) 4124. Mid-March through October.
Moderate to expensive.
★★★ THE SMUGGLER'S INN. Cliff Road. Tel. (0667) 4330. March through
October. *Moderate.*

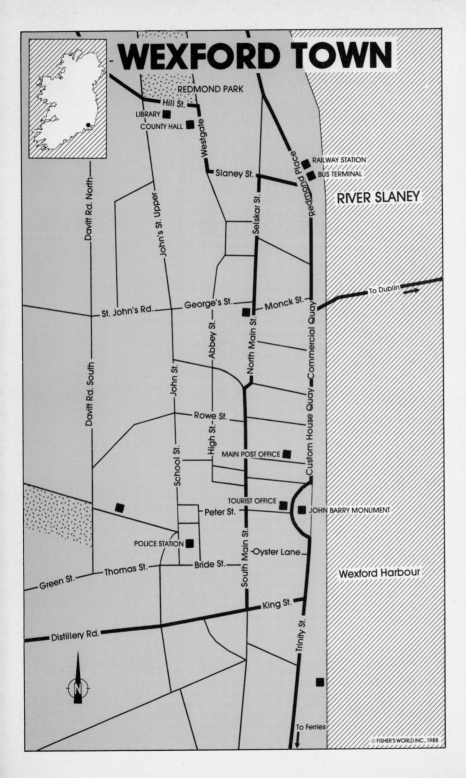

WEXFORD TOWN

REDMOND PARK

Hill St.

LIBRARY

COUNTY HALL

Westgate

Slaney St.

RAILWAY STATION

BUS TERMINAL

Redmond Place

Davitt Rd. North

John's St. Upper

Selskar St.

RIVER SLANEY

To Dublin

St. John's Rd.

George's St.

Monck St.

Abbey St.

North Main St.

Commercial Quay

Davitt Rd. South

John St.

Rowe St.

High St.

Custom House Quay

School St.

MAIN POST OFFICE

TOURIST OFFICE

JOHN BARRY MONUMENT

Peter St.

POLICE STATION

South Main St.

Oyster Lane

Wexford Harbour

Green St.

Thomas St.

Bride St.

King St.

Distillery Rd.

Trinity St.

N

To Ferries

© FISHER'S WORLD INC., 1988

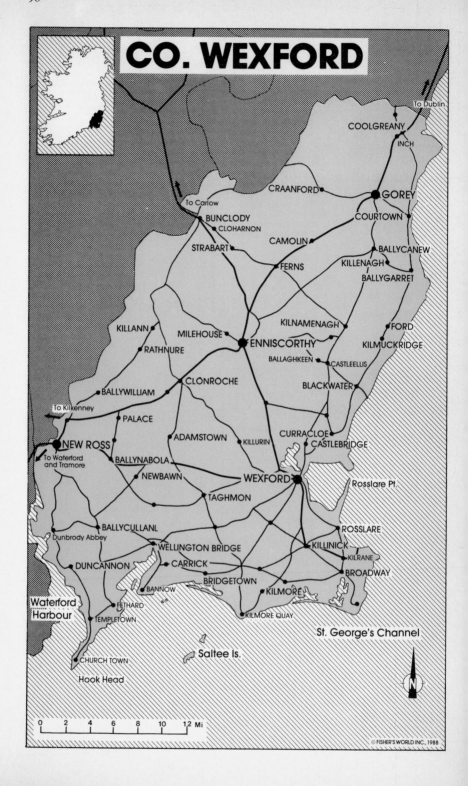

CO. WEXFORD

To Dublin

COOLGREANY

INCH

CRAANFORD

GOREY

To Carlow

BUNCLODY

COURTOWN

CLOHARNON

CAMOLIN

BALLYCANEW

STRABART

KILLENAGH

FERNS

BALLYGARRET

KILNAMENAGH

FORD

KILLANN

MILEHOUSE

ENNISCORTHY

KILMUCKRIDGE

RATHNURE

BALLAGHKEEN

CASTLEELLIS

CLONROCHE

BLACKWATER

BALLYWILLIAM

To Kilkenney

PALACE

CURRACLOE

ADAMSTOWN

KILLURIN

CASTLEBRIDGE

NEW ROSS

To Waterford
and Tramore

BALLYNABOLA

WEXFORD

Rosslare Pt.

NEWBAWN

TAGHMON

BALLYCULLANL

ROSSLARE

Dunbrody Abbey

WELLINGTON BRIDGE

KILLINICK

DUNCANNON

CARRICK

KILRANE

BRIDGETOWN

BROADWAY

BANNOW

KILMORE

Waterford
Harbour

FETHARD

TEMPLETOWN

KILMORE QUAY

St. George's Channel

CHURCH TOWN

Saltee Is.

Hook Head

N

0 2 4 6 8 10 12 Mi

© FISHER'S WORLD INC., 1988

WEXFORD, Co. Wexford

Hotels

★ ★ ★ ★ THE TALBOT. Trinity Street. Tel. (053) 22566. *Moderate.*

★ ★ ★ WHITE'S. George and Main Streets. Tel. (053) 22311. *Moderate.*

★ ★ ★ FERRYCARRIG. Wexford/Enniscorthy Road (N 11). Tel. (053) 22999. *Moderate.*

Restaurants

★ ★ ★ OLD GRANARY. Westgate. Tel. (053) 23935. *Moderate.*

★ ★ ★ OAK TAVERN. Wexford/Enniscorthy Road (N 11). Tel. (053) 22138. Closed Monday. *Moderate.*

Pubs

★ ★ ★ ★ THE CROWN. Monck Street.

★ ★ ★ CON MACKIN'S, THE CAPE OF GOOD HOPE. The Bull Ring, off North Main Street. Tel. (053) 22949.

★ ★ ★ BOHEMIAN GIRL. North Main and Monck Streets. Tel. (053) 23596.

★ ★ ★ THE WREN'S NEST. Custom House Quay. Tel. (053) 22359.

★ ★ ★ THE FARMER'S KITCHEN. Rosslare Road (N 25). Tel. (053) 23295.

Festival

October 19-30: Wexford Festival of Opera.

Directory

Wexford Tourist Office, Crescent Quay. Tel. (053) 23111.
CIE, Railway and Bus Station, Redmond Place. Tel. (053) 22522.

YOUGHAL, Co. Cork

Restaurant/Pub

★ ★ ★ ★ AHERNE'S. 162/163 N. Main Street. Tel. (024) 92424. Closed Monday. *Moderate to expensive.*

Pub

★ ★ ★ MOBY DICK. Market Square. Tel. (024) 92756.

Festival

June 24-July 2: The Gourmet Potato Festival.

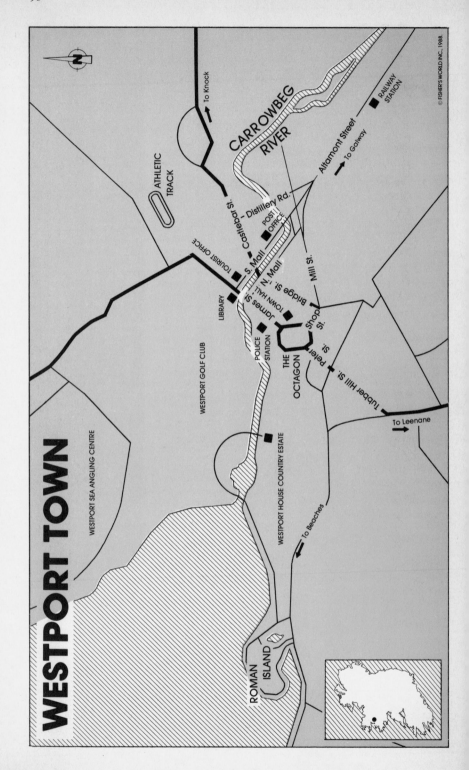

WESTPORT TOWN

CARROWBEG RIVER

To Knock

ATHLETIC TRACK

Castlebar St.

Distillery Rd.

POST OFFICE

S. Mall

N. Mall

TOURIST OFFICE

Altamont Street

To Galway

RAILWAY STATION

Mill St.

Bridge St.

TOWN HALL

James St.

LIBRARY

POLICE STATION

THE OCTAGON

Peter St.

Shop St.

Tubber Hill St.

To Leenane

WESTPORT GOLF CLUB

WESTPORT SEA ANGLING CENTRE

WESTPORT HOUSE COUNTRY ESTATE

To Beaches

ROMAN ISLAND

© FISHER'S WORLD INC., 1988.

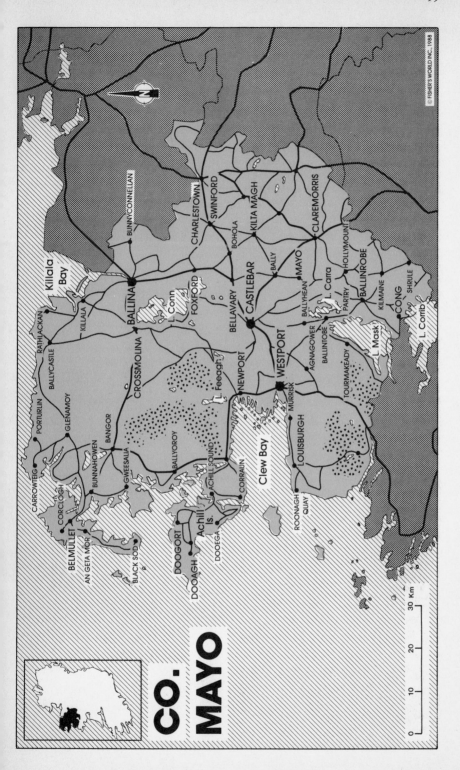

4. :Number of Golf Clubs in each county.
★:Foremost Golf Clubs.

PORTRUSH

BELFAST

10.

SLIGO
ROSSES PT.

ROYAL COUNTY DOWN

2.

2.

1.

2.

1.

3.

23

GALWAY

5.

2.

PORTMARNOCK
DUBLIN
ROYAL DUBLIN

2.

2.

1.

4.

LAHINCH

Shannon Airport

1.

BALLYBUNION

2.

3.

1.

1.

3.

TRALEE

2.

KILLARNEY

10.

1.

WATERVILLE

CORK

GOLF IN IRELAND

© FISHER'S WORLD INC., 1988

The Hard Facts

Documentation

In most instances, a valid passport is all that is required to enter Ireland for a stay of up to three months. Although visas are required in some cases, they are not necessary for citizens of the U.S., Canada, Great Britain, Australia, New Zealand, and many other European countries.

Customs

The Irish Customs system operates on a Red and Green Channel format. The Green Channel is for people with nothing to declare, and the Red Channel for those with goods to declare.

In addition to your luggage, you can bring in sporting equipment such as golf clubs or tennis rackets for your own recreational use while in Ireland. U.S. and Canadian visitors are also allowed to take in the following items duty-free: gifts to the value of $43; 400 cigarettes, one litre of spirits, and two litres of wine. British citizens may bring in gifts to the value of £252 (Irish), 300 cigarettes, 1.5 litres of spirits or three litres of aperitifs, and five litres of other wine. There is no currency restriction.

Currency and Credit

The "punt" is the basic unit of currency, although most people refer to it as a "pound," like Britain. Do not, however, assume that all pounds are equal! The value of the Irish pound is about 10% less than the British pound. In dollar terms, the Irish pound has fluctuated throughout most of 1987 between $1.40 and $1.50, while the British pound has been between $1.50 and $1.80. Because of this difference, British money is not legal tender in Ireland and vice-versa.

The Irish pound is symbolized by a £ sign; each unit of paper currency is called a "note." The pound notes, which are printed in denominations of £1, £5, £10, £20, £50, and £100, come in different sizes and colors (the larger the size, the greater the value). Each pound is divided into 100 pennies (or "100p," for short); coins come in denominaations of 50p, 20p, 10p, 5p, and 1p.

Note: The value of the Irish pound fluctuates daily. As we go to press, it is approximately £1 Irish = $1.45 U.S.

The hours of business for banks are as follows: 10 A.M. to 12:30 P.M. and from 1:30 P.M. to 3 P.M., Monday through Friday. Dublin banks stay open until 5 P.M. on Thursdays. The only banks that are open seven days a week in Ireland are at Shannon and Dublin Airports; the Shannon branch maintains hours from 6:30 A.M. or 7:30 A.M. until 5:30 P.M. year-round; the Dublin branch is open from 7 A.M. to 9:30 P.M., with a "bureau de change" remaining open until 11:30 P.M. in the summer.

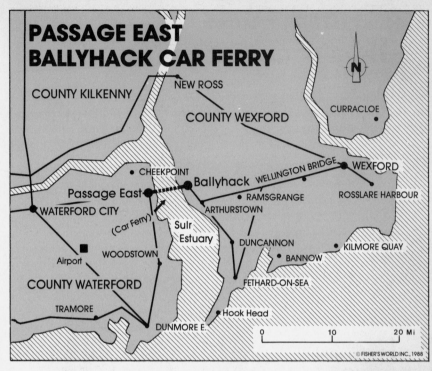

PASSAGE EAST BALLYHACK CAR FERRY

COUNTY KILKENNY

NEW ROSS

COUNTY WEXFORD

CURRACLOE

CHEEKPOINT

Ballyhack

WELLINGTON BRIDGE

WEXFORD

Passage East

RAMSGRANGE

ROSSLARE HARBOUR

WATERFORD CITY

ARTHURSTOWN

(Car Ferry)

Suir Estuary

DUNCANNON

KILMORE QUAY

Airport

WOODSTOWN

BANNOW

COUNTY WATERFORD

FETHARD-ON-SEA

TRAMORE

Hook Head

DUNMORE E.

0   10   20 Mi

© FISHER'S WORLD INC., 1988

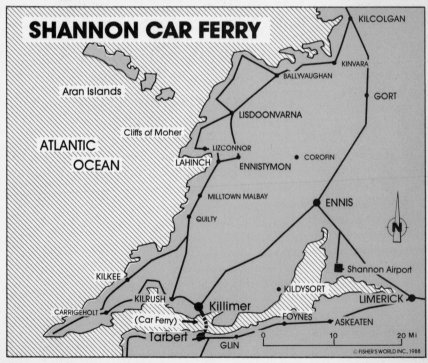

SHANNON CAR FERRY

KILCOLGAN

KINVARA

Aran Islands

BALLYVAUGHAN

GORT

LISDOONVARNA

Cliffs of Moher

ATLANTIC
OCEAN

LIZCONNOR

COROFIN

LAHINCH

ENNISTYMON

MILLTOWN MALBAY

ENNIS

QUILTY

Shannon Airport

KILKEE

KILDYSORT

LIMERICK

KILRUSH

CARRIGEHOLT

Killimer

(Car Ferry)

FOYNES

ASKEATEN

Tarbert

GLIN

0   10   20 Mi

© FISHER'S WORLD INC., 1988

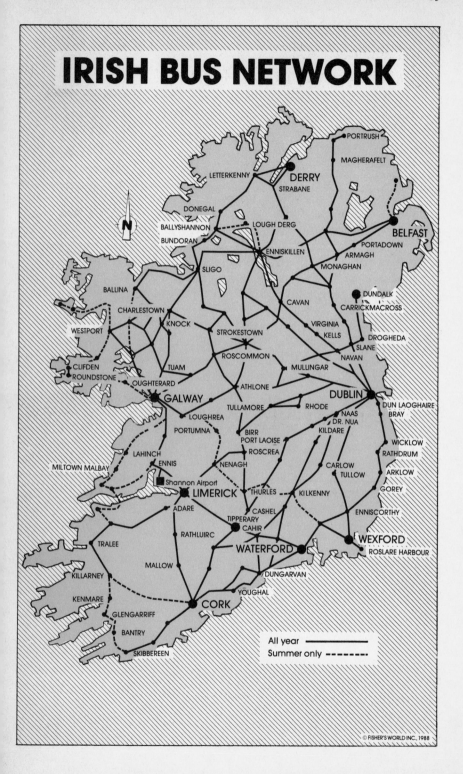

IRISH BUS NETWORK

All year ———————
Summer only - - - - - - -

© FISHER'S WORLD INC., 1988

Restaurant Liquor Laws

The majority of independent restaurants have only wine licenses. If you prefer a cocktail or a beer with your meal, it is best to choose a restaurant in a hotel or a restaurant affiliated with a pub.

Gratuities vs. Service Charge

Like hotels, restaurants in Ireland have traditionally followed the ancient rule of automatically adding a service charge to your bill. In the case of most restaurants, this sum is usually calculated at 10% to 12½% of your food and drink totals; some of the major city restaurants add as much as 15%. If you feel that the service has been exceptionally good, then the custom is to leave a few extra pounds or small change, particularly if only 10% has been added on.

In the last five years, however, more and more restaurants are not adding any service charge onto your bill, but rather are leaving the tip totally to your discretion. It is imperative that you know whether a gratuity is added in part, in total, or not at all, so that you can tip accordingly. Restaurants usually print their policy right on the menu; if you forget to look or can't find it, be sure to ask.

A word on restaurant taxes: all restaurant meals are subject to a government tax of 10% (reduced from a previous high of 25%). You don't have to worry about this tax being added to your bill, however, as it is already built into the food prices on menus.

The Pubs

Pub hours are standard throughout the country, seven days a week. The current schedule is Monday to Saturday, from 10:30 A.M. to 11:30 P.M., from May through September, and until 11 P.M. during the rest of the year. The only exception is the pubs in Dublin city, which close from 2:30 P.M. to 3:30 P.M. for what is traditionally known as "the holy hour." On Sundays, the hours are the same year-round, from 12:30 P.M. to 2 P.M. and from 4 P.M. to 10 P.M. Pending legislation, if enacted by the time of your visit, may change the closing time to midnight on Monday through Saturday nights.

Business Hours

Most businesses in Ireland are open from 9 A.M. or 9:30 A.M. to 5:30 P.M. or 6 P.M., Monday through Friday.

Tipping

Tipping is not expected in shops, stores, and theaters. Taxi drivers are usually given a tip equal to 10-15% of the fare. Porters or bellmen at airports or train stations expect a tip of about $1 per bag. Doormen, if they perform some service like getting you a taxi, should get the equivalent of 50 cents to $1.

Getting Around By Car

Unless you bring your vehicle, via Britain or Europe, you'll have to rent a car. As for documentation, all that is required is a valid U.S. or Canadian driver's license, or an international driver's license.